Jews and Muslims
in the Arab World

Jews and Muslims in the Arab World

Haunted by Pasts Real and Imagined

JACOB LASSNER AND S. ILAN TROEN

ROWMAN & LITTLEFIELD PUBLISHERS, INC.
Lanham • Boulder • New York • Toronto • Plymouth, UK

ROWMAN & LITTLEFIELD PUBLISHERS, INC.

Published in the United States of America
by Rowman & Littlefield Publishers, Inc.
A wholly owned subsidary of The Rowman & Littlefield Publishing Group, Inc.
4501 Forbes Boulevard, Suite 200, Lanham, Maryland 20706
www.rowmanlittlefield.com

Estover Road
Plymouth PL6 7PY
United Kingdom

British Library Cataloguing in Publication Information Available

Library of Congress Cataloging-in-Publication Data:
Lassner, Jacob.
  Jews and Muslims in the Arab world : haunted by pasts real and imagined /
Jacob Lassner and S. Ilan Troen.
     p. cm.
  Includes bibliographical references and index.
  ISBN-13: 978-0-7425-5841-0 (cloth : alk. paper)
  ISBN-10: 0-7425-5841-X (cloth : alk. paper)
  ISBN-13: 978-0-7425-5842-7 (pbk. : alk. paper)
  ISBN-10: 0-7425-5842-8 (pbk. : alk. paper)
  1. Arab-Israeli conflict. 2. Arab-Israeli conflict—(1993–)—Peace. 3. Jews—
Israel—Identity. 4. Jews—Israel—Politics and government. 5. Jews—Israel—
Attitudes. 6. Palestinian Arabs—Ethnic Identity. 7. Palestinian Arabs—Politics
and government. 8. Palestinian Arabs—Attitudes. 9. Jews—Israel—History. 10.
Collective memory. 11. Group identity. I. Troen, S. Ilan (Selwyn Ilan), 1940–
II. Title.
  DS119.7.L33 2007
  956.04—dc22   2007001031

Printed in the United States of America

∞™ The paper used in this publication meets the minimum requirements of
American National Standard for Information Sciences—Permanence of Paper for
Printed Library Materials, ANSI/NISO Z39.48-1992.

CONTENTS

LIST OF MAPS

PREFACE

This book highlights the effects of historical memory on the Arab-Israel conflict. We demonstrate that both Jews and Arabs employ narratives of distant pasts to construct identities and shape politics. Whether real or imagined, the past filtered through collective memory has had and will continue to have enormous influence on how Jews and Arabs perceive themselves and others. These perceptions are linked in turn to contemporary patterns of social and political behavior.

The conflict between Israel and the Arabs has deep roots in the past, and there is no apparent end in sight. To many bystanders, it seems to unfold like grim theater, an all-too-lengthy tragedy that exhausts actors and audiences alike. Many Western observers are impatient that the drama of Jews and Arabs contesting modern Palestine is still without a final act. Why isn't there a political solution to which all parties will give at least grudging approval? It cannot be for lack of attention. Surely, no other conflict has been scrutinized so closely and by so many observers for such a long period of time. Yet this surfeit of attention has not led to a profound understanding of the issues dividing Israelis and Arabs, particularly the Muslim Arabs who make up well over 90 percent of the Arab world.

Some analysts of the current scene often neglect or dismiss altogether the residual influences of memories derived from a Near Eastern past that reach back into distant centuries, and even millennia. Focused on the here and now, they move backward only through the Arab-Israel conflict and the Palestine problem that preceded it. The history of the Arab-Israel conflict, as they describe it, extends at most to the last decades of Ottoman rule in the nineteenth century. Viewed in that time frame, the conflict between Israel and its Arab neighbors and between the Jewish state and the as-yet stateless Palestinians is a dispute between modern political movements inspired by European trends in nation building and enflamed by the encroachment of Western imperialism. At one end of the political spectrum, they place the Zionists, returning to the ancient land of their ancestors, their purpose to reconstitute the Jewish people on familiar and revered terrain. At the other, they place Arab nationalism, a movement that began with a perceived need to lessen the oppressive yoke of Turkish rule in the Arabic-speaking provinces of the Ottoman Empire. When European powers replaced the Ottoman Turks following World War I, Arab nationalists demanded liberation from Western colonial influence, a concept and reality that included for them the encounter with Zionism. In these interpretations, history, relevant to illuminating the present, begins only at the end of the nineteenth century.

A contrary approach advances the view of a "Timeless Orient." Both the present conflict and the future Near East are the inevitable outcome of a history that repeats itself as it unfolds in successive eras. In this portrayal, Arab societies are intoxicated by memories of a glorious past and jarred by the trauma of foreigners and foreign culture penetrating their world in modern times. Reacting to unanticipated and unwanted incursions, the modern Islamic world, particularly the predominantly Muslim Arab portion, has become locked in conflict with the West and its invasive values. The result is a "clash of civilizations" that overrides virtually all other political sensibilities and robs Muslim Arabs of any tactile response to unfolding events.

From this perspective, the Zionist project is indistinguishable from a broadly based and now repudiated European colonialism that is locked in mortal struggle with the Arab nation. The alien Jewish state imbued with Western values and situated at the center of the Islamic heartland sticks in the throat of the Muslim faithful. There can be no compromise with the Jews allowing a permanent polity of their own within the traditional "abode of Islam." There is no precedent in all of Islamic law or tradition to allow for it. Those who are inclined to view contemporary events from this kaleidoscope of an Islamic past can point to the current outlook of Muslim militants, including Hamas, the Islamist movement that presently governs the Palestinian Authority and calls for the destruction of the Zionist state. The same can be said of the Hezbollah, the Islamist group based in Lebanon. For those who embrace the concept of Timeless Orient, the unyielding declarations of Hamas, Hezbollah, and other militant groups are ample proof that Islamic societies are changeless.

Yet this highly reductive, and hence seductive, notion of the Timeless Orient is itself a construct of Western origins and not always a fact of life when applied to Arab Muslims. From any vantage point, the civilization of Islam, particularly in the Middle Ages, reflects the capacity of Muslims to adapt to other civilizations while forging their own cultural and political institutions, often with considerable ingenuity. Islamic societies have never been unyieldingly static, if we mean by that a state of cultural and political equilibrium incapable of producing new forms of expression or developing new institutions. More to the point, they have not been inflexible in dealing with their non-Muslim enemies, not even in modern times. Muslims may be encumbered by their past, but they have been able to restructure debts to that past, however omnipresent in subsequent ages.

Rejecting the so-called clash of civilizations that they regard as a highly imaginative if not altogether fanciful approach devoid of analytic merit, some cultural theorists and social scientists have moved well beyond familiar historical narratives. They explain events as if these were generic phenomena inextricably linked to paradigms of a universal nature. Shorn of distracting details, the Arab-Israel problem becomes grist for these scholarly millers, working indiscriminately on various theoretical approaches to historical change in many venues. These approaches include the effects of modernization, the crippling legacy of dependency under colonial rule, the uses and misuses of intellectual capital in the postcolonial period, the effects of transnationalism, the proposed fallout from the new global economy on individual states and regions, and state formation, with particular reference to settler states (a way of linking Israel to apartheid South Africa and French Algeria). Mixing this yield with only a general knowledge of the immediate, let alone distant, past of Jews and Arabs makes for a concoction that tastes flat to a cultivated historical palate.

Such universal paradigms attempt to explain widely divergent historical developments as if differences in culture, time, and place had no vital bearing on historical outcomes. As a result, they do little to illuminate Arab-Israel relations. This vexing problem transcends narrow explanations rooted entirely in the circumstances of modern times just as it defies cosmic explanations that invoke the Timeless Orient or theoretical paradigms that reduce specific cultural entities to generic phenomena.

Our intention in writing this book is to move beyond such broad reductive explanations and to delineate in detail the ways in which the past is absorbed, internalized, and then processed for current use among Jews and Arabs. One should be wary of an analysis that explains too much too easily.

This book stresses the importance of historical imagination on evolving political cultures. We make no claim that cultural explanations drawn from an ancient or medieval past shed light on every aspect of contemporary events, and we acknowledge the delicate balance between the long-term effects of culture and the specific reactions generated by current realities.

Any satisfying explanation of current events is bound to be complex and contentious, especially when addressing ideologically freighted issues of Jewish-Muslim relations. Let no one misunderstand. In writing this book, we did not seek to displace the perspective of serious historians who treat the Arab-Israel dispute largely if not entirely as a phenomenon of modern history and politics. Our intention is to enrich their work by painting a vivid and detailed picture of Jews and Arab Muslims on a very large historical canvas. Our readers both inside the academy and beyond are invited to take in the canvas as a whole. At the same time, we encourage everyone to examine the individual elements, so what emerges is a painting that is greater than the sum of its many intricate and finely crafted representations, a montage that might be read as a tribute to the powerful effects of the past on the modern condition.

We do not believe that examining the Arab-Israeli conflict in isolation can lead to enlightenment any more than studying the Cold War without reference to the histories and cultures of the USSR and the United States can be of lasting value. Such a narrow focus distorts our understanding of these societies and simultaneously overlooks much that is germane to understanding that conflict. Similarly, it is important to delve deeply into the roots of Jewish and Muslim history and culture to understand the clash between contemporary Israeli and Arab society. We have examined texts that are essential and fundamental for understanding Muslim and Jewish history. These sources reveal the enduring salience of culture in the lives of the individuals and societies we have tried to understand.

This study obviously extends beyond the popular notion that modern states are "imagined communities." For more than a millennium in the case of Islam and several millennia in the case of Judaism, Muslims and Jews have nurtured understandings of themselves and of each other. Both sacred and secular texts have long been alive with meaning and continue to shape worldviews and behavior. Understanding the past has mattered for these peoples, and the past as they understand it still shapes their present and frames opportunities for their future.

This book was initially conceptualized by Jacob Lassner. He began writing at Yarnton Manor, the home of the Oxford Centre for Hebrew and Jewish Studies. As is often the case, Yarnton Manor proved a fertile setting for productive conversation. Over a number of years, beginning more than a decade ago, S. Ilan Troen, also a frequent visitor to Tarlton Manor, was invited into the conversation initiated by Lassner. Out of these conversations, this manuscript emerged. Humanists usually work alone. This project has been for the authors a wonderful intellectual and personal adventure. We hope readers will find value and enlightenment in what has been for us a stimulating learning experience.

At first glance, this joint venture represents a rather ambitious, if not risky, diversion from previous concerns. We began our academic careers with interests far removed from the volatile politics of the modern Near East. Trained in Semitic languages, Jacob Lassner first devoted himself to Islamic urban history and early Arabic historiography. Only decades later did he turn to Jewish-Muslim relations. Even then, he confined himself, by and large, to medieval times. S. Ilan Troen, despite extensive training in Jewish history, left graduate school a historian of the United States; his early publications were devoted to American social and urban history and transnational history. For reasons scholarly and personal, he then changed the focus of his research and gravitated to the modern Zionist project, mostly to Jewish settlement in Palestine and, following that, the State of Israel.

Given our preference for densely annotated publications, this book also represents a departure from previous practice. We have written this book without footnotes or extensive bibliography as is customary in a work for learned scholars. Rather, we seek a broader audience inside and outside the university. At the same time, the comments of the academic experts who have reviewed our manuscript reassure us that the substance of our text meets the rigorous demands of credibility and authority. For those who would like to go beyond this book, we provide a bibliography pertinent to this study and useful for pursuing the issues we raise. As the compass of this volume suggests, we plan to take the reader into a wide array of subjects, some of which may be familiar but are here recast on a large canvas, appropriate to the challenge of engaging the complexity of the topic.

Jacob Lassner, Evanston, Illinois
S. Ilan Troen, Omer, Israel

ACKNOWLEDGMENTS

Segments of this work were written while the authors were in residence at Yarnton Manor, the Oxford Centre for Hebrew and Jewish Studies. We would like to thank the staff of the Center for making our stay in Yarnton extremely pleasant, and, as always, extraordinarily fruitful. To single out any individuals who inspired our collaborative effort would do injustice to so many others who had a hand in guiding our research or in shaping our views. We would like to thank, however, Judah Troen, who shared with us his stimulating essay on the *nakbah*, the "catastrophe" that befell the Palestinians in 1948, and Abraham Troen, who despite an unexpected bout of surgery, managed to track down various biblical references that were integral to our work. Above all, professors Carol Troen and Phyllis Lassner offered constant encouragement and the kind of critical comments that forced us to reexamine our writing time and again. Our discussions with Carol and Phyllis brought the animated and intellectually invested discourse of Israeli and American café society to the venerable pubs of rural Oxfordshire.

Those who write books about the Near East are constantly plagued by problems of transliteration. When it comes to Arabic, scholars generally use one of several recognized systems. On the other hand, transliteration of Hebrew tends to be extremely chaotic. As this book was intended for a broad audience, we have transliterated familiar names and terms as readers would encounter them in the general literature. Hence, *Mahmoud Abbas* and not *Mahmud 'Abbas*. Where Arabic names and terms are not familiar, we have followed a standard system of transliteration, albeit without the determinants that would have complicated the typography. Readers well acquainted with Arabic need no more for understanding. We have tried to render Hebrew terms as they would sound to the average ear.

It often happens that new work comes to light after a book enters production and cannot be substantially altered. That was certainly the case here. After much deliberation we decided to go with the text as it was. For that we beg our readers' indulgence.

INTRODUCTION

The Uses and Misuses of the Past

The power of historical memory to justify political claims and shape
modern opinion and behavior should not surprise learned historians of
the Near East. In Jewish and Muslim societies, where the bonds of tradition are tightly wound, history has never been a subject whose importance
reflects mere antiquarian interest or whose lessons are confined to formal
instruction in classrooms or visits to shrines and museums. To the contrary,
the past has served and continues to serve as a model that reaffirms faith,
guides belief, and stirs individuals and more inclusive groups to action. Most
recently, Arabs and Jews have employed narratives of distant times to forge
modern concepts of nationhood and the nation-state.

Among Arab Muslims, the age of Muhammad and the Arab conquests
that followed, glorious and triumphal moments that took place more than
thirteen hundred years ago, remain deeply engraved on the consciousness of
the faithful. Muslims declare the emergence of the Prophet and the formation of the early Islamic community as nothing less than a watershed in the
history of humankind. A new era dawned when Muhammad, the last of a
series of prophets sent by God, brought a message representing the quin-
tessence of monotheist belief and practice. Although this latest expression
of monotheism was meant to supercede the traditions of Jews and Christians, there is much in the Prophet's message and in Muslim beliefs and rituals that was and is familiar to the older faiths. In defining themselves, the
Prophet and his followers embraced the spiritual outlook of the rightly
guided biblical peoples and looked to their experiences for instruction, not
only for Muslims of the time, but also for Muslims in all generations to
come. In such fashion, accounts of the ancient Israelites were woven into
the broad fabric of Islamic experience. Jews and also Christians became

1

integral elements of a rich and universal Islamic history that reached back into ages long before the birth of Islam.

As did their ancestors, today's Muslim faithful venerate the stories of the ancient Israelites, but rarely have Muslims, past or present, turned directly to Jewish or Christian sources. In embracing an earlier monotheist history, Muslims have always relied on "biblical" images refracted through the prism of the Qur'an and its extensive commentaries. There is also a popular literature and oral tradition based largely on refashioned Jewish and Christian tales disseminated by Muslim storytellers and street preachers. Collectively, the tales of the biblical prophets and their times are referred to in Arabic as *Isra'iliyat*, that is, Israelitica. From the outset of their religion, Muslims have focused on Islamized "Bible tales." The Prophet himself favored such stories. In any case, Muslim tradition has him promoting the study of his monotheist predecessors. There was much gain in that, or so Muslim authorities declared. The writings of Jews and Christians were said to contain references to the future coming of Muhammad. Once decoded, these references validated a sacred tenet of Muslim belief; namely, Muhammad was the last and most perfect link in a long line of messengers sent by God to humankind. In addition to predicting Muhammad's mission and the rise of Islam, the sacred writings of Jews and Christians were said to contain veiled references to persons and events of a later Islamic history. Citing a remote past thus allowed Muslims to legitimize the politics of the moment and anticipate events of the future.

Be assured, the tales of the Israelites were not a moral yardstick against which Muslims measured themselves alone. Nor were lessons gleaned from reading ancient monotheist history applicable only to Muslims interacting with one another. The biblical world, recast in Islamic garb, framed the polemical debate with Jews and Christians and shaped attitudes toward the older religious communities. Recalling that ancient past also set the tone for intercommunal relations wherever Jews, Christians, and Muslims lived in close proximity.

One might think, initially, that interrogating the early history of monotheists and monotheism should have led to sympathy for Jews and Christians. The Muslim embrace of the biblical past should have created true mutual understanding, particularly with the Jews who were equally zealous about the unicity of the one and only God. There was no belief in Jesus' divinity to compromise the strict monotheism Jews shared with the Muslims. Moreover, Jewish religious practice closely resembled that of the Muslims, especially regarding prayer, dietary restrictions, fasting, and laws of ritual purity. And yet, there was and continues to be discord between the oldest and youngest monotheists. With all that Judaism and Islam have in common, Muslims often found their most cherished traditions at odds with long-standing Jewish beliefs and practices. By holding firm to their own versions of the biblical past and to the rituals and observances that had guided their daily lives over countless generations, Jews, remaining loyal to Judaism, signaled their rejection of Muhammad's mission. How could Jews (and also Christians) reject Islam if it were indeed foretold in the Hebrew Bible and other sacred Jewish texts? Such cheeky Jewish intransigence spoke to the negation of the Jews' own authentic teachings and challenged the very legitimacy of the new faith. And so, a common affection for the biblical past that might have led to mutual understanding between Jews and Muslims became instead an arena in which to contest sacred history.

With Zionist settlement and the emergence of Arab nationalism, both phenomena of modern times, the traditional competition for sacred space was extended to the political sphere. Sacred space came to mean more than a contest over texts and their interpretation. At issue was the geographical region known to Arabs as Palestine and to Jews as the Land of Israel. For more than two thousand years, Jews, reading the Hebrew Bible, recalled that God promised Abraham and his Israelite descendants the land originally known as Canaan. It was there that the history of the Jewish people first unfolded; a checkered account of successes, the history also recounted political setbacks leading to a loss of sovereignty and exile. After two millennia of statelessness, Zionists rekindled hopes of returning to the land of their forefathers. No other land was worthy of Jewish dreams for redemption; none produced such longing during the lengthy and extensive dispersion of world Jewry. Were it not for powerful memories of the ancient Israelites and the Land of Israel, there would have been no modern Zionist movement and no Jewish claims to Palestine for Arabs to contest.

As for Muslims, however large the biblical past looms in Islamic memory, it is less central to Arab nationalist claims. Their feelings for Palestine are more firmly rooted in Islamic experience. When Arab nationalists first demanded sovereignty over the Holy Land, they rested their case on thirteen hundred years of continuous habitation, almost all of it under Muslim rule. They filled their brief with references to the Arab expansion of the seventh century and Muslim hegemony that resulted from that triumph of arms. Recalling that memorable moment thirteen hundred years ago, today's Arabs speak of the conquest of Palestine. The Arab conquerors of the time are considered the ancestors of today's Palestinian nation. Palestinian notables proudly trace their origins to famed warriors who crossed the Arabian frontier, a connection that bestows both honor and privilege to them and their extended families. But the Arab position did not remain so simply defined. The unfolding dispute with Zionism turned the debate between Jews and Arabs back to the biblical past. Sophisticated Arabs understood very well the potential appeal of Zionist arguments in the Western world. Peoples and governments in the Christian heartland might favor Zionist claims based on linkages to a land declared holy by Jews and Christians generations before the expansion of Islam. It was not enough that Muslims had long accorded Jerusalem a sacred status hitherto reserved only for Mecca and Medina. When the Western world thought of historic Palestine, it did not think of sacred geography connected in some manner to Arabia and the origins of Islam. References to the Holy Land in remote times conjured up exclusive memories of the Judeo-Christian biblical past. Arabs had no problem rejecting Zionist claims, but the more worldly Palestinians and their supporters understood the potential appeal of the Zionist position. Given Jewish and Christian memories, they had to weigh the powerful attraction of a modern Jewish state linked to a remote Jewish past revered by Christians and Jews alike. As a result, Arab nationalists have sought to root their sense of nationhood in a history that predates that of the Israelites in the ancient land originally known as Canaan. Leaping backward into still more remote times, they have taken to identifying modern Palestinians with the Canaanites, the indigenous peoples who were displaced by the ancestors of today's Jews. Even if one were to admit a link between ancient and modern Israel, Arabs could still maintain that the prior and binding claim on the land is that of its earlier inhabitants, the forerunners of the modern Palestinian nation.

Not surprisingly, the debates surrounding the Arab-Israel conflict are spiced with pungent references to the world of the Bible. Supporters of Zionism frequently juxtapose the ancient Israelites, their land, and their polity with current Israelis and the State of Israel. Various groups of Christians often join Jews in citing the Hebrew Bible/Old Testament to legitimize the Zionist enterprise, as an expression of religious faith and/or in keeping with a deep sense of historical destiny. Similarly, modern Palestinians and their Arab supporters draw on the same remote past to trumpet the legitimacy of a distinct Palestinian nation with even deeper roots in the land. In order to emphasize the manner in which Palestinians are connected to ancient Canaan, some advocates of Arab nationalism quote modern biblical scholarship, particularly the writings of a small group who undermine, if not deny altogether, any connection between the ancient Israelites (the forerunners of modern Jews) and the so-called Land of Israel. More than mere words are at issue in this acrimonious debate; there is a grim reality to the Arab-Israel conflict. For the first time since the Prophet Muhammad's sweeping victories some thirteen hundred years ago, Jews and Muslims have found themselves locked in territorial combat with all that that implies for the Near East and the world at large.

The emergence of the Prophet and his extended mission, events of the seventh century C.E., have had an even more profound effect on how Muslims understand history and are moved by it. Time and again, perceptions of early Islamic times have served traditional Muslims as touchstones for dealing with their present lives. Memories of Islamic history have influenced inter-Arab communal disputes as well as Arab relations with Muslims in the non-Arab world. For example, Shiites and Sunnites alike stress their links to the Prophet Muhammad, his family, and his community, as have dynasts and would-be dynasts seeking to command the allegiance of the faithful. Even Saddam Hussein, the so-called secular tyrant of Iraq, invented for himself a lineage that stemmed directly from the Prophet's closest kin. Similarly, non-Arab Muslims have invented specious genealogies to make them blood relations of the Prophet, thus establishing for themselves a most honored place within a larger Muslim society. References to the past have also become part of more wide-ranging rivalries: tribal versus sedentary society, local versus regional authority, regional versus centralized authority, the culture of the periphery versus the culture of the heartland, and the like.

Recalling events from the seventh century onward also affects Muslim views and behavior toward non-Muslims. As they have done with memories of the ancient Israelites, Muslims have invoked Islamic history to shape attitudes and behavior toward Christians and Jews in Arab lands. In particular, Muslim polemicists have focused on the Jewish tribes of Medina, those who took up arms against the Prophet and sought to betray him to his enemies as the latter besieged the city. There are even accusations that the Jews plotted against Muhammad's life, including a foiled attempt to poison the Prophet as he celebrated his victory over the Jews of Khaybar, oasis dwellers who gave comfort and support to their Medinese kin who had been exiled by the Muslims. This perfidious behavior, whether imagined or real, earned for Jews the reputation of being politically untrustworthy as well as deniers of what they knew to be true, namely the legitimacy of Muhammad's mission. Despite 1,200 years of subsequent Jewish passivity, these accusations and others like them helped define the conventional Muslim wisdom regarding Jews and Judaism. Time-honored, pejorative labels and negative images remain the stock and trade of Muslim polemicists in their ongoing condemnation of Jews, a people who had the audacity to think they had been chosen by God.

Muslims have also turned to the Islamic past when confronting a more-alien Other. At given moments in history, the faithful have been challenged by polities situated beyond the Abode of Islam (*dar al-Islam*), the juridical entity that signifies for Muslim legal scholars the geographical boundaries of Islamic authority. From time to time, the Islamic world has been shaken by foreigners invading the Muslim Arab heartland. Groups such as the Mongols, the Crusaders, and, more recently, the imperialist European powers have seriously disturbed the equilibrium of traditional Islamic societies. Arabs add to that list of intrusive forces Zionists settlers, at first mostly East European Jews who came to Palestine to claim that land as their divine birthright and, in having done so, usurped the legitimate rights of its native Arabs. To reassure the faithful and counter the most recent of these traumatic incursions, Muslims have turned, as always, to the comforting lessons of a happier past.

Unlike the modern world—in which believing Muslims are filled with apprehension toward their own failed governments, jealous of Western economic and military prowess, unnerved by the strength of a modern Israeli society, and, above all, fearful of a corrosive Western culture they regard as strange and morally compromising—the past is remembered by Muslims for seemingly endless triumphs. In the deplorable conditions of the moment, historical memories console an agitated and enraged Arab world. In addition, history provides the beleaguered Arabs with a plan of action to reverse their current misfortunes. To restore Arab dignity and self-confidence, Muslims have only to return to the ethos of a bygone era when Islamic lands were purportedly ruled with justice and Muslims dictated to foreign regimes and not the reverse. Were Muslims to comport themselves as they did in those halcyon days, the Western imperialists and the Zionist colonizers would surely suffer the fate of the previous invaders. That is, they would either become Muslims, as did the Mongols, or like the Crusaders they would be purged from the Abode of Islam by a reinvigorated Muslim polity. This vision of Islamic triumph may strike Westerners as phantasmagoria, but, as it resonates so strongly to a glorious Muslim past, it has the power to transcend the reality of the moment—at least for believing Muslims.

As does the Arab world, most Israelis and Zionist sympathizers reflect deeply about the meaning of history. In forging guidelines with which to shape the present and future course of the modern Jewish state, they too invoke memories of a distant past. Seeking proper models with which to reconstitute the Jewish people in their ancient homeland, the founding fathers of Israel disavowed a two-thousand-year Diaspora, the prolonged and bitter experience that often produced rootless and inward-looking Jewish communities. Creating a modern Jewish homeland that could take its place among legitimate nation-states required combining—or perhaps *reconciling* is more accurate—the outlook of newly enlightened European Jews with the experiences and cultural heritage of their most ancient forebears. And so the Zionists turned on the one hand to the world of contemporaneous Europe and on the other to that of the biblical kingdoms and the Second Hebrew Commonwealth, ancient Near Eastern polities that took shape in the Land of Israel, the historic home of the Jewish people. The boldness of the Zionist enterprise and the tenacity with which it was pursued by Jewish settlers and their allies have broken long-established precedents and changed completely Arab expectations of Jewish behavior in the Near East.

Following the Arab conquest of the seventh century C.E., what had been the Land of Israel became part a contiguous Arab-Muslim region stretching from the borders of modern Turkey and Iran to the distant reaches of North Africa and Spain. A small and politically impotent minority within an ever-so-proud and self-confident Muslim world, the Jews of Arab lands were, if nothing else, subservient following the Arab conquest. Having absorbed the lessons of their disastrous rebellions against the great ruling authorities of the past, Near Eastern Jewry soon accommodated itself to Muslim rule. Opting to preserve their communities, Jews recognized the authority of their Muslim sovereigns in exchange for the degrading status of protected minority.

That marriage of convenience between docile Jewish communities and a triumphalist Islamic state survived until the emergence of modern Zionism in the nineteenth century. The Zionist movement, born in the crucible of European nationalism and revolutionary politics, sought to create a new Jewish nation—proud, independent, and settled in its ancestral home. The demeaning experience of exile and Diaspora were rejected in favor of more inspiring memories: the stories of the biblical patriarchs and the promised land; Joshua's conquest and the settlement of Canaan; the emergence of powerful Israelite kingdoms under David and Solomon; the building of the holy temple and the sanctification of Jerusalem; the restoration of Jewish governance in the Land of Israel after the Babylonian exile; and the heroic, if futile, resistance in defense of national honor during the Roman wars.

Citing the past to privilege the present and future is commonplace in the long history of the Near East. Arab nationalists and Zionists have gone a step further in their quest to establish modern nations where none existed. When the claims made on the past are clumsy—that is, when the evidence drawn from history is not compelling, or, beyond that, totally inappropriate to contemporary pronouncements—modern ideologues have resorted to still another time-honored strategy. They have reinterpreted or even reinvented the past so that it would appear as a back projection of more recent events. As a result, critical moments of communal experience have been idealized by modern nations and recorded as distant echoes of one another. Complex realities have thus been endowed with a compelling but highly artificial sense of symmetry. If we may once again use a familiar metaphor of which we have grown fond, perhaps overly so, it is as though modern nation builders throw stones into the troubled waters of history and create with each toss perfectly concentric circles. In narrative after narrative, there are specific links, sometimes real but often contrived, between a distant history and the politics of the moment.

As often as not, that newly forged history, whether shaped or invented from whole cloth, transcends the meticulous studies of less-partisan writers. Scholars who interrogate the past for its own sake understand only too well that engaging history, even in the broadest sense, is a slippery enterprise. They tend to examine data, especially data that reflect times and places far removed from our own, with great caution. In publishing results, the more professional historians are apt to use circumspect language. That wariness to make unsupported claims enables their readers to understand how problematic it is when one seeks to recover the past.

It is often said that the truth is in the details. Broadly defined narratives, unsubstantiated by the particulars of historical evidence, become privileged tales, metatruths of distant eras intended to capture the imagination of present communities. Stories embellished or invented by nationalist ideologues and their supporters have thus become truer than history allows. These truths, so conceived, have a way of becoming binding wisdom for various peoples of the Near East and their supporters in other countries and climes. There seems to be no lack of individuals and groups who reflexively declare the absolute right of all peoples and would-be peoples to define their own identity and polity. At times, such declarations are made regardless of how schemes of national independence play out for the inhabitants of particular lands and neighboring states. It has often happened that behavior based on privileged readings of history has stimulated conflict both within and between the newly formed states in the region. We learn, too often the hard way, that the accumulated baggage of a real history can overwhelm an idealized present based on an imagined past. The history of the modern Near East is replete with examples of the sort, none more compelling than the clash between Zionism and various Arab nationalist movements. Jews and Arabs are indeed haunted by pasts, real and imagined.

Not all metatruths, however staunchly believed, are of equal weight. The critical issue is the kind of allegiances demanded by these so-called truths. More important is the kind of action generated by these allegiances. It is one thing to embrace the preferred narratives of a remote history, whether real or imagined. It is quite another matter for a society to mobilize all its available resources and actually create a viable present in the image of an idealized past. To quote an old Arab maxim: "The fingers of the hand are not of equal length." Zionist and Arab nationalist claims and the demands that these respective claims put on Jews and Arab Muslims are not two sides of the same coin, nor are they simply mirror images of one another. If we are to better understand the nature of the conflict between them, we will need a nuanced analysis that digs more deeply and more critically into history and the uses of the past. That is the modest aim of this book.

A word of caution is in order. However much we can recover of the past, and however much that accumulated knowledge informs the present, there is always the need to confront contemporary events on their own terms. Understanding the residual effects of ages long gone may indeed help us when we try to unravel the ideology and behavior of current Jews and Muslims, but fast-moving events, the outgrowth of specific incidents rooted in the present, have a dynamic all their own. For all intents and purposes, the first draft of this book was completed as Yasir Arafat lay on his deathbed. The last full draft was completed with Israel's premier Ariel Sharon in a coma and the nation electing a newly created party to office. The combination of events could well change the course of Israeli politics as we know it. The Palestinians, who recently concluded their own parliamentary election, rejected their current leaders and chose instead Hamas, an Islamist party dedicated to the destruction of the Jewish state, by force if necessary. The next months, perhaps only weeks, may well signal significant movement on the ground.

As historians about to go to press, fast-breaking events present us with a dilemma. With dramatic changes taking place, there is the temptation to integrate all the most recent developments into our narrative, even at this late hour. But by the time our book reaches the public, these added comments will likely to be seen as old hat, because at no point does history cease unfolding. And so we have decided not to update our narrative. We remain confident, nevertheless, that our analysis of the past will serve to clarify not only present but also future developments.

Part I

THE ARAB WORLD

*Imagining the Past, Defining
the Present, Anticipating the Future*

1

THE ARAB NATION-STATE

Marking Modern Identities by
Embracing Pasts Real and Imagined

At present, the Arab world comprises twenty-two nation-states, almost all of them situated in the Near East and North Africa. Many of these states took shape only in the twentieth century when, following World War I, European statesmen redrew the political map of the region. The rise of the modern Arab nation-state represents a marked departure in the experiences of Muslims. The very concept of citizens united in polity by virtue of living within well-defined national borders is alien to traditional Islamic theories of government. For true believers, there is only the *ummah*, the all-embracing religious community established by the Prophet Muhammad in the seventh century C.E.

In theory, the highly idealized ummah of Islam's founder drew no distinctions among Muslims, nor does it today. All Muslims were and are now part of a universal body of believers regardless of geographic, ethnic, or linguistic affiliation. For some thirteen hundred years the rulers of the ummah, whether Arab caliphs who succeeded the Prophet or Ottoman Turkish sultans who assumed the mantel of the caliphs, demanded a loyalty that transcended narrowly defined regional and ethnic allegiances. Even when provincial governors seized the opportunity and acted independently of the caliphate or the Ottoman Porte, they dutifully paid homage to their de jure if not de facto rulers, as required by custom and law. To reject the concept of a universal Islamic community and formally withdraw from the ummah invited cosmic disturbances, an end to the world as Muslims knew it. The modern Arab nation-state, with its separate communal identity and self-serving political agenda, is thus the very antithesis of a cherished and long-held Islamic ideal. In that sense, the Europeans did more than simply redraw the existing map of the Near East when they carved up the Arabic-speaking provinces of the Ottoman Empire; they presented the Muslims with alternative forms of governance that were bound to create tensions among more traditional believers.

THE MODERN ORIGINS OF THE ARAB NATION-STATE

Before the intrusion of an overbearing European imperialism, the peoples of the Arabic-speaking world had been subjected to four centuries of Ottoman Turkish rule. At the height of their power and influence, the Ottoman sultans presided over a geographical landscape that extended throughout almost the whole of Southwest Asia and the southern rim of the Mediterranean. Their far-flung empire, governed from Istanbul, also included vast regions of the Balkans and central Europe, stretches of land that had been overrun by seemingly invincible Ottoman armies. In the seventeenth century, a powerful Ottoman force advanced to the very gates of Vienna. Muslims brimmed with confidence as they had during the heyday of the great Arab caliphs when Muslim hegemony extended from the steppes of Central Asia to present-day Spain and Portugal. But the city did not fall, and Ottoman power gradually ebbed. One hundred and fifty years after the Turks stood poised to assault the remaining bastions of Western Christianity, Europeans not only beat back the Muslim advance, but also established themselves firmly in what had long been the Islamic heartland, first in North Africa and Egypt and then, following the Great War of 1914–1918, in the geographical arc extending from Palestine to the current borders of Turkey and Iran.

As the defeated Ottoman Empire entered its death throes, it left behind a political vacuum the major European powers were very willing to fill. Even before the war's end, the British and French set about dividing the anticipated spoils of conquest: the Arabic-speaking provinces of the Fertile Crescent, today the independent states of Israel, Syria, Lebanon, Iraq, and the Hashemite Kingdom of Jordan. After the Turks withdrew from the war, virtually the entire Arab world was subjected to colonial influence, if not direct European intervention. The encroachment of the Europeans, which began with Napoleon Bonaparte's invasion of Egypt (1798) and the French conquest of Algeria (1830), was sanctioned by the League of Nations in the 1920s when that international body issued mandates to Britain and France to administer the former Ottoman provinces of the Fertile Crescent. The French, who already controlled much of North Africa, extended their colonial influence into the Levant. At the behest of the league, they administered an area that became, in the 1940s, the independent states of

Syria and Lebanon. The British, who already exercised considerable influence over Egypt, received the league's authority to administer the Arab lands they conquered during the Great War. As a result, the British ruled a newly created Iraq until 1932 and Transjordan, later the Hashemite Kingdom of Jordan, until 1946.

Western Palestine (Cisjordan), with its large Jewish minority, proved the most difficult of all the British mandates. The Jewish and Arab communities clashed with one another and with the British authorities as well. In 1948, Great Britain was forced to relinquish control over Palestine in accordance with a much-debated United Nations resolution to partition the land into respective Jewish and Arab states. The Arabs of Palestine, having lost the political debate, preferred war to compromise and were defeated in the fighting that ensued. They have yet to establish a sovereign state of their own. The Jews who accepted the compromise partition plan established the State of Israel. The boundaries of the Jewish state were determined by the outcome of the military campaigns and fixed by armistice negotiations that ended the fighting in 1949. These were temporary lines pending a final peace settlement. More than fifty years and four wars later, there is as yet no final settlement and no permanent borders.

By the 1970s the British, in full recognition of their declining capacities, vastly reduced the size of their armed forces, redefined their geopolitical objectives, and gave up their last bases east of Suez. French concessions to changed political realities were decidedly more traumatic. The authorities in Paris, faced with an insurrection they could not completely subdue, grudgingly recognized the independence of Algeria in 1962. They thus relinquished control over a land they had populated with more than a million French settlers and, in defiance of history and geography, had declared part of metropolitan France.

The eclipse of the European powers did not occasion a purge or even a rejection of all things foreign. As is the case throughout the non-Western world, the legacy of Western imperialism, be it cultural or political, has had a powerful and lasting impact on local and regional environments. Many of today's Arab states still reflect exposure to Western ideas and institutions. The very concept of the Arab nation and nation-state was forged on the anvil of modern European nationalism. Arab forms of governance are often based on models of European parliamentary assembly. Similarly, Arab constitutions and ideological slogans pay lip service to democratic sentiments imported from the West, however much the style of local rule continues to resemble more traditional forms of autocratic state control, much to the chagrin of many Arabs, including Muslim revivalists suspicious of

European models of government and hostile to Western modes of thought and behavior.

The lingering influence of the West has created serious rifts in various Arab societies. While recognizing the powerful reality of the modern nation-state, many Muslims are leery and even contemptuous of a godless Western culture. Some, recognizing the efficacy of the modern nation-state, seek to influence the conduct of national politics with calls for traditional Islamic values. Others, more radical in outlook, reject the very concept of the nation-state and await the restoration of a transnational Arab caliphate, which conjures up for them memories of a triumphant Muslim ummah governed by the law of God. Even secular-minded Muslims are wont to revel in the celebrated history of their ancestors. Despite the enormous impact of the modern West, the Arab world continues to look to a more distant Near Eastern history and culture—a past often cited to define and legitimize the present, as well as plan for the future.

One should not devalue the significant links claimed by Arabs to that remote Near Eastern past, be it an authentic past, or, as is often the case, a history woven almost entirely from new cloth. Time and again, those who rule modern nation-states have invoked historical "memories" to define and legitimize the homeland and its artificial borders while trumpeting the new nation's destiny. There is much to consider about this tendentious use of the past, for what is perceived as historical precedent, even if there is no reality to that precedent, can exert a powerful influence on affairs of state, and more generally on social and political behavior. Above all, the past is used, or more properly misused, to establish markers of identity and demand loyalties for polities lacking legitimacy because the potpourri of Arab nation-states created by colonial mapmakers has neither geographic nor demographic coherence.

Markers of identity can be quite complicated for today's Arabs. Each individual Arab state demands unflagging loyalty from its citizens, but the latter are also subject to loyalties derived from more narrowly defined allegiances as well as a larger Arab identity that traverses the borders of modern states. That is to say, Iraqis, Syrians, Jordanians, Egyptians, Palestinians, and the like are not only citizens of their respective polities, but also consider themselves part of a more broadly constituted Arab nation and world, a nation whose origins are traced back by Arabs to the peninsula that bears their name. An even larger story has been scripted of late. The modern Arab world, which has always been beset by multiple loyalties, has recently branched out further and further in search of common roots. Having been exposed to Western scholarship, in most cases only indirectly, Arabs, regardless of their current national or local allegiances—if not, indeed, because of them—now seek to examine their Arab heritage in a wider Near Eastern context, a geographical expanse that includes the ancient lands beyond Arabia and histories that go back to a remote past.

To be sure, the expanded search for roots does not compromise the centrality of the Arabian past for those currently identifying themselves as Arabs, especially the Muslim Arabs, who represent virtually the entire Arab nation. Muslims, regardless of their origins, have always embraced the Arabian Peninsula and its history as being very special. Arabic chroniclers of the Middle Ages record extensive genealogies and detailed accounts of persons during the pre-Islamic era; anthologies preserving Arabic verse attributed to the great poets of that time have been recited with consummate delight for a millennium and more; and the holy sites, Mecca and Medina, are recognized by Muslims and non-Muslims alike as the spiritual epicenter of Islam. Arabic is the language of Muslim scripture, its classical and modern commentaries, and the most important religious writings. Mastery of the classical language and of Arabic literary and religious texts is the quintessential mark of an educated Muslim, regardless of his or her native tongue or ethnic background. Above all, the Arab conquering tribesmen who spread Muhammad's message in the Fertile Crescent and beyond were the vehicle for creating an Arab polity that rivaled all previous Near Eastern empires in size and splendor while establishing Islam as a universal faith. No small wonder those who call themselves Arabs in modern times have looked to the ancient and medieval past in defining their proudly proclaimed Arab identity. But what does it mean to be an Arab or the citizen of an Arab nation-state in today's world? What did it mean to be an Arab in a more remote Near Eastern past?

ARAB/'ARAB AS A MARKER OF IDENTITY

Among the many markers that establish identity in the Near East, perhaps none is more problematic than the ambiguous term *Arab*. There is, for one, understandable confusion differentiating Arab from Muslim, at least in the minds of the Western public. Although the Arabian Peninsula was the cradle of Islam, and Arab tribesmen brought the new faith to vast territories contiguous to and far beyond their homeland, the Arabs were and have remained at best a relatively small element of a continuously expanding Muslim community (ummah). Of the billion and more current Muslims, those who declare themselves Arabs number about 300 million. Arab Muslims may predominate in the Near East and North Africa, but the demographic centers of Islam are, and will remain, Southeast Asia and the subcontinent of India, areas that were brought under Muslim rule relatively late in the history of Islamic expansion.

Although today the Near East and North Africa are heavily populated by Muslim Arabs, the region is in fact a patchwork quilt of different groups bearing diverse and, at times, multiple identities. In the Arab world itself there are ethnic minorities professing the Muslim faith but retaining non-Arab affiliations. Their resistance to political and cultural assimilation has often pitted them against the Arab ruling authority. The Berbers of North Africa and the Kurds of Iraq are perhaps the most notable examples. There are also Near Eastern states whose societies are non-Arab at the core. Situated at the periphery of the Arab world, Turkey and Iran, the former a Muslim entity that redefined itself as a secular state, the latter a self-declared Islamic republic, both see themselves as fundamentally different from the Arab states with whom they share common borders and coexist warily. Even among those who declare themselves Arabs, there are striking divisions occasioned by lineage, local and religious loyalties, social grouping, and other conflicting, if not incompatible, associations. Despite the Arab conquest and the onset of Muslim rule, events that seemingly helped unify the region, the ethnic and cultural landscape of the Near East and North Africa has remained remarkably varied over fourteen Islamic centuries.

If all Muslims situated in the area are not Arabs, neither are all Arabs Muslims. The emergence of Islam as a world religion may have begun when Arab tribesmen crossed the frontiers of the Arabian Peninsula more than thirteen hundred years ago, but not all those invading tribesmen were of the new faith, nor are all those claiming to be Arabs today. With ethnic and cultural identities so intertwined and yet so separate in the Islamic Near East, the very idea of a discrete nation that embraces all Arabs, however we may wish to define *Arab*, is, to say the least, problematic. The same might be said of the individual nation-states that proudly declare themselves Arab today. What then defines the modern sense of Arab identity, how deeply rooted is that identity, and what has been the strength of its emotional appeal?

Like the nation-state, Arabism (*'urubah*), the concept of Arab unity based on a distinctive Arab civilization and identifiable Arab societies, does not have a long and honored place in Islamic culture. The Arab nation spoken of today, like the idea of individual Arab nation-states, is, in essence, a creation of the nineteenth century, stimulated in part by conceptions of race and society imported from the West to serve as an ideological prop against Ottoman Turkish rule and nascent European encroachment. Before the encroachment of the West there were narrowly based local and even regional affiliations that compelled allegiances, but there was no formal concept of patria other than the Islamic ummah, the idealized universal religious community that embraced all Muslims and governed their relations with nonbelievers both in and beyond the world of Islam.

Westerners, without special knowledge of the Near East, may instinctively link Arabism and today's Arabs to Islam. However arrived at, there is much to justify that perception. For among the more than twenty self-identified Arab polities, most of them nation-states created on the wreckage of the Ottoman, British, French, and Italian empires, all but one, Lebanon, declare themselves Islamic states. In fact, the Muslim inhabitants of these combined Islamic countries represent more than 95 percent of their populations. Current demographic surveys indicate that the overwhelming Muslim majority will be maintained, if not increase, throughout the region. To speak of Arab states now and in the future is to speak of political entities with a decidedly Muslim character. The same is true of the idealized Arab nation. *Arab* may not be synonymous with *Muslim*, but there can be no meaningful discussion of Arab identity without fully considering Islam. Put most succinctly: Those calling themselves Arabs, are, for the most part, Muslims; the Arab states that have emerged are in essence and, with the exception of Lebanon, by self-definition Islamic states.

This situation represents something of a paradox because Christians were the first to have a profound investment in Arabism. They envisioned that Arab nationalism would replace religious ties as the basic cement holding together the larger Arabic-speaking societies of the region. In theory, the creation of individual nation-states reflecting broadly defined Arab values, and concurrent with that a citizenry defined by geographical borders, would have put the Christian minorities on an equal footing with their Muslim neighbors. Hitherto, the Arabic-speaking Christians had lived as part of separate religious communities (*millah*) sharing the same homeland (*watan*) with a dominant Muslim majority, and their status, defined by Muslim religious law, designated them a "tolerated people" (*ahl al-dhimmah*), subject to various discriminatory regulations. Henceforth, Muslims and Christians alike would be citizens with equal rights and obligations, or so the Christians hoped. Given demographic realities and traditional Muslim opposition, the Christian dream of a Western-style citizenry and full equality, social as well as political, never materialized. Only in Lebanon, where diverse Christian communities were exceedingly numerous, were the indigenous Christians able to achieve parity with a fractious Muslim society.

The Lebanese model of governance was an unusual and ultimately un-
workable confessional system of representation based on a census taken in
1932 and never officially updated. The steady growth of the non-Christian
communities in Lebanon, coupled with factional violence, foreign intervention, and Christian migration to the West, has since led to a realignment
of political power and a decided weakening of the Christian position.

We might ask why Jews, the other monotheist community of the Islamic world, did not take up the cause of nascent Arab nationalism with
equal fervor. There is evidence that some individuals within the Jewish
communities appreciated the potential advantages of citizenship and with
that the expectations of liberalized governance. What then explains the hesitation of the larger Jewish community and its leadership to close ranks with
Arab nationalists—or, if you prefer, protonationalists? Near Eastern Jewry
was subjected to Islamic law in much the same fashion as their Christian
neighbors—they too were *dhimmis*. But they were far fewer in number than
the Christians and, for understandable reasons deeply rooted in past experience, they were extremely reluctant to establish a political profile of any
sort. With a long history of passivity to Islamic governance, the venerable
Jewish communities of the Arabic-speaking world showed little if any interest in challenging an Ottoman authority that could easily turn on them
if provoked by what was merely perceived to be Jewish disobedience. Nor
did the Jewish religious leadership wish to risk weakening its hold on the
community for fear of undermining the very institutions that allowed Jews
to cohere in the most trying of circumstances. Even after the emergence of
Arab nation-states, Jews preferred to retain their separate communal identity and, when possible, shun all forms of political activism, thus continuing a pattern of accommodating behavior that had existed for some thirteen hundred years. It seemed the safest course to follow.

The position of Near Eastern Jewry was complicated, however, by the
emerging strength of Zionism, the project to reconstitute the Jewish people
on the soil of their ancestors in Palestine. Modern Zionism, like Arab nationalism, was imported from Europe in the nineteenth century. But unlike
the latter, the Zionist effort relied on human and financial resources from
abroad. The relatively small Jewish population and the nascent Zionist movement that remained in Palestine throughout World War I was increasingly
augmented, first by idealistic pioneers mostly from Eastern Europe, and then
by skilled immigrants seeking refuge from Nazi Germany. These Jews of European origins, like their coreligionists who were long rooted in the Near
East, did not consider themselves an integral part of an imagined Arab nation. Even Jews of Arab lands who were not particularly sympathetic to the

Zionist cause and who were loyal subjects of their Muslim rulers or even citizens of Arab countries did not speak of themselves as Arabs.

The fulfillment of the Zionist project, the creation of the Jewish State of Israel in 1948, put the Jewish communities of the Arab world at risk, and led ultimately to a widespread Jewish exodus from their ancient homelands. Most of these Jews—some half million in all—settled in the State of Israel. At present, the Arab world has become, to all intents and purposes, a world without Jews. There are scattered Jews in environments that once bore witness to thriving Jewish societies, but only in Morocco has a truncated Jewish community managed to survive under the personal protection of its sovereign. Arab nationalism may have created Christian Arabs but it has never produced Arabs of the Jewish faith.

PAN-ARABISM

Because it was so unexpected, the Zionist triumph stimulated demands for a union of Arab polities that would transcend the more narrowly defined modern Arab nation-states. Various intellectuals, supported by elements of the Arab street, called for a single Arab polity or at the least a strengthened confederation of Arab states. The idea of a political entity that embraced all Arabs was not novel, nor was it merely a response to the emergence of an intrusive Jewish state in the Arab/Muslim heartland. The notion of a single Arab ruling authority had been in the air ever since Turkish Ottoman rule began to dissipate, and it became more pronounced as the Ottoman regime entered its final death throes during the Great War. But the collapse of the Ottoman state did not lead to a unified Arab nation in what had been the Arabic-speaking provinces of the empire. Nor is it likely that the leading Arab players, left to their own devices—that is, without European interference—could have created a single Arab polity, or even a confederation of Arab states to fill the political vacuum left by the Ottomans. The divisions and overlapping loyalties in the Arabic-speaking provinces of what had been the Ottoman realm were simply too profound to overcome. The sultan's rule in the former Arab provinces and subprovinces was replaced by a highly aggressive European colonialism. That being the case, the reality of a single Arab agenda and a unified Arab nation seemed remote.

Although by 1950, most of the Arabic-speaking regions had become independent of European stewardship, legally as well as in fact, the newly emergent Arab states could not completely free themselves of foreign political influence, nor did they demonstrate the political will and fighting courage to deal decisively with the new State of Israel, a "cancer in the heart of the Arab nation." There was a general perception that this latest and most deplorable state of affairs was the result of corruption, but also of disunity among recently minted and older national entities. Various segments of Arab society called for dramatic solutions, not only in the exercise of Arab governance, but also in the very structures of government. They insisted on a new and comprehensive pan-Arab agenda that transcended the parochial concerns of territorially based ruling elites. The immediate objective of a strengthened pan-Arabism would have been to modify the existing system of Arab nation-states, each of which was seen as acting in accordance with its own narrowly defined interests. While the Arab states paid lip service to notions of unity and formally rejected acceptance of the Jewish state in the aftermath of their defeat, they did not create any effective political mechanism to bind them for collective action against the Zionist interlopers. To the contrary, they have entered into bitter political rivalries among themselves. The ultimate aim of these anticipated changes was to establish the mutual cooperation necessary to combat external threats and to break the cycle of inter-Arab competition that works to the detriment of the idealized Arab nation.

Some fifty years later, the quest for Arab unity continues to remain elusive. Attempts to create a single polity out of individual Arab states have all been egregious failures. Policies arrived at in concert by blocs of independent Arab countries have tended to favor the more powerful, have ultimately led to dissension and divisiveness, and in the end have given rise to collective disaster. The events of 1967, in which a reckless Egypt involved several unprepared Arab states in a catastrophic war with Israel, is a case in point. As a result of only six days of fighting in June 1967, Arab regimes lost significant territory, their military and political leadership was humbled, and, more significantly, they were held up to ridicule throughout the non-Arab world. Reflective Arabs began to question the very nature of their political culture and wonder aloud why Arab politics evolved so badly after the initial promise of independence. Especially galling were the grandiloquent declarations of unity that always seemed to substitute for effective action. For a brief moment, a few openly questioned the efficacy of Islam, that is, before the authorities made the stakes in such open declarations more dangerous than the critics were willing to bear.

The most dramatic case for a break with tradition was made by Sadiq al-Azm, a young Syrian philosopher trained at an elite university in the United States. In publications that were widely and enthusiastically read in intellectual circles, al-Azm castigated the Arabs for their futile calls for unity, as if mere pronouncements could turn failure into success. Above all, he pointed to the debilitating effects of fantastical thinking on Arabs having to face reality in the modern world. When al-Azm went so far as to attack Islam, he quickly became persona non grata in his own country. Forced into a self-imposed exile for his own well-being, he eventually came to recognize the wisdom of a lower political profile.

Al-Azm's contention that the backwardness of the Arabs was bred into their culture may have been too much for the leaders of the Arab states to acknowledge, but they understood only too well that imposed attempts at Arab unity put them all at risk. Following the public mood, individual Arab nation-states absorbed the bitter lessons of the immediate past. Stung by an imposed unity gone awry, they increasingly came to privilege policies formed in their own best interests, even regarding their common enemy Israel. Observers following events in the Near East all recognize that the once compelling dream of pan-Arabism has been eviscerated. Many, if not most, actually declare it dead. That may well be true regarding the exaggerated expectations of the past but, when regarding a more general concept of Arab unity, the obituaries may be premature. Although there is little if any talk of a single Arab government—most discussion envisages a loose framework in which independent Arab states work cooperatively to solve common problems—individual Arabs, even the leaders of Arab states, still pay lip service to unity. The concept of an Arab nation has lost none of its appeal. Despite the continued absence of a unified Arab state or confederation of states, and despite the lingering resentment against false calls for political union, virtually all Arabs believe in the reality of an inclusive Arab nation or, if you wish, Arab people. But without deep roots in regional or religious culture, that broadly endorsed concept of a single Arab nation may never transcend past and present realities, much as the individual Arab states have been unable to unite effectively under a single umbrella.

It is not enough to declare the existence of the Arab nation just because those who proclaim themselves Arabs genuinely believe that it is now or once was in fact real. To create a truly viable Arab nation calls for forging a society with a coherent moral vision that gives it a real sense of unity as well as purpose. In order to achieve all that, those who broadly embrace 'urubah (and the few who still actively promote it in political terms) will have to diffuse, if not fully eradicate time-tested and immensely powerful markers of overlapping identities and allegiances. Given the resilience of the past and the familiar in Near Eastern societies and cultures, the goal of an Arab nation united in purpose, let alone polity, seems, at present, unrealizable.

Nevertheless, the emotional power of an Arab national identity, however contrived, has an actual life of its own. Precisely because there are so many who want to believe in it, it can be more real than reality itself. We are compelled to speak of an Arab world, an Arab nation, of Arab states, and of an Arab league that attempts to coordinate cultural and political affairs for its constituents. Western historians of sensibility continue to write weighty books like *A History of the Arab Peoples* by Albert Hourani (1991). Bernard Lewis's masterful and highly nuanced survey, *The Arabs in History*, first published more than fifty years ago, has been reprinted and/or revised many times and to great acclaim, most recently in 1998. Lebanese-born Fuad Ajami, by any yardstick the most perceptive and elegant analyst of contemporary Arab political culture, whether Arab or non-Arab, wrote *The Arab Predicament* (1981) and *The Dream Palace of the Arabs* (1999), both moving accounts of Arab disappointment in the course of their recent politics. In sum, we continue to speak of Arabs, their political and cultural institutions, their societies, and a time-honored Arab history and civilization, as if some thread actually unifies and gives precise meaning in all those cases to the descriptive label *Arab*. But what do we really mean by *Arab* and what is the affinity that causes those who declare themselves Arabs to embrace the concept of 'urubah as an ideal? Put somewhat differently, who are the Arabs of today, who were the Arabs of premodern times, and what does any distinction between premodern and modern Arabs portend for the future of the Arab world, particularly its relationship to Jews and to the Jewish State of Israel, a subject of our concern here?

With regard to today's Arabs, the safest course is to declare everyone who claims to be an Arab an Arab and leave it at that. But so general a statement does not make for a complex analysis of very complex political issues; more concrete markers of definition have to be considered. With race a scientifically discredited notion, the starting point for all discussions is the Arabic language and the culture to which it gives rise. Such as they are, contemporary affiliations with the idealized Arab nation seem to be based on discernible but not always discrete linguistic criteria. Those peoples of the Near East who use Arabic as the language of their cultural and religious traditions as well as the language of daily discourse generally consider themselves Arabs. The operative expression here is *the language of their cultural and religious traditions*. There are Near Eastern communities that do not consider themselves Arabs but who nevertheless speak Arabic flawlessly and use it constantly in their social relations. They may also read and write the language effortlessly. In any case, it is not knowledge or the daily use of Arabic that defines an Arab, but the use of that language for private and particularly religious/cultural purposes. Arabophones not considering themselves Arabs are the Jews and Armenians who reside or at one time resided in Arab lands: the Copts of Egypt; various Christian communities of Iraq who held fast to local Aramaic traditions before Arabic culture was imposed upon them by the Baathist regime; the Berbers of North Africa; and extremely marginal groups, such as the Abyssinians living in Jerusalem.

Speaking of Arabs, one includes as well various Christian denominations, both Protestant and Catholic, especially those whose church services are currently conducted in Arabic. To be sure, every rule of thumb in the Near East has its notable exceptions. The Greek Orthodox, with a supreme religious authority stationed outside the Arab world and a time-honored liturgical tradition in Greek, have emerged as vociferous champions of Arab unity and Arab nationalism. On the other hand, the Maronites of Lebanon ought to be considered Arabs, despite a Francophone background acquired in modern times and their claims of direct links to the ancient Phoenicians. When one adds for consideration the Kurds of Iraq, the Copts of Egypt, and the Berbers of North Africa (all non-Arabs but constituents of Arab states), it is clear that the Arab nation and Arab nation-state are ambiguous concepts that invite cautious analysis.

As a marker of identity, the Arabic language turns out to be a modern contrivance, much like the Arab states and the highly idealized Arab nation. If anything, the complex history that has shaped the Near East since the Arab conquest should make us wary of imposing modern sensibilities on the past. The claim that peoples sharing a rich linguistic background, namely Arabic, are in fact a distinct cultural or political entity with shared values and objectives would have struck earlier Muslims (and also non-Muslims) as rather bizarre. At one time or another, many groups from Iran to Andalusia used Arabic as their primary language but without any sense of common identity. To the contrary, many Arabophones, including those sharing the same geographical environment, competed for political and/or sacred space even as they valued the language and embraced its literary culture. For the premodern peoples of that vast cultural mosaic called the Islamic Near East, *Arab* (*'arab*) does not denote a speaker of Arabic but rather beduins or those related by blood or clientage to a particular Arab tribe or tribal configuration. This definition of *Arab* served as coin of the realm for well over two thousand years—even before the advent of Islam, and certainly well before the modern age gave the term *'arab* new meaning.

Mention of the Arabs as a distinct group first appears in a cuneiform inscription crafted in the reign of the Assyrian monarch Shalmaneser III. The text, composed after the Battle of Karkar (853/854 B.C.E.), relates how a coalition of forces led by Ahab, the king of Israel, stemmed the advance of an invading Assyrian army intent on subjugating vast tracts of territory on both sides of the Jordan River. In that coalition there was a force described as Arab cavalry. Thereafter, the Arabs appear with some frequency in Assyrian texts as well as in the Bible, where Arab (Hebrew *'arav*) begins to displace the specific names assigned to various beduin tribes, so that in the later traditions of the Hebrew scripture, *Arab* becomes the generic word for beduin. Arab, or some variation thereof, then appears in Persian, Greek, Southern Arabic, and finally classical Arabic, the language of early Islam, always with the meaning of tribesmen who move from place to place and never meaning a distinct linguistic or geographically rooted community.

It is clear that the people originally designated as Arabs live in the desert or on the periphery that divides desert from sown (Hebrew *'aravah* means desert). We are then obliged to ask what if any is the relationship between these tribesmen and the peninsula that came to be named after them, *Jazirat al-'Arab*, the Island of the Arabs. We have thousands of inscriptions from South Arabia, a land where rainfall allowed for large-scale agriculture, and hence sedentary populations and forms of centralized government. These inscriptions, which go back to the second millennium B.C.E., contain much information, but for a thousand years or so there are no references to Arabs, an indication that the inhabitants of the agricultural south did not consider themselves Arabs and that whatever contact they might have had with beduins was likely to have been marginal. When the Arabs finally appear in the inscriptions of the first century C.E., they are depicted as beduins who come into contact with the southern kingdoms, either as auxiliary troops—the role that they played in the Shalmaneser inscription— or as raiders who come to prey on settled areas, a description of the Arabs found in other Assyrian sources. In sum, the ancient Arabs, who are widely distributed in the less inhabitable areas of Arabia and in the desert that extends beyond the formal borders of that region, were a group apart from the sedentary inhabitants of the peninsula. Clearly, not all Arabians were referred to as, nor would they have considered themselves, Arabs.

When the southern kingdoms declined in the third and fourth centuries C.E., their lands became increasingly inhabited by beduins; conversely, many displaced southerners were themselves forced into new areas of settlement, perhaps even nomadism. Hence, the expression *Arab*, meaning nomadic tribesmen, began to designate, more generally, the inhabitants of the entire peninsula. Periodically, the Arabs of the desert would cross the northern frontiers that separated the peninsula from ancient Palestine-Syria and Iraq. Some tribesmen, having traversed the frontier, remained to settle on the periphery of the desert, occasioning the concern of local authorities who feared beduin raids. The prospect of instability along the border-lands called for protective measures. In the absence of large standing forces, the Byzantine and Sassanian authorities employed Arab tribes that had crossed their frontiers at an earlier time to prevent encroachment by other Arabs. There was, however, always a distinction between the indigenous population of the settled territories and the Arabs who protected them along the periphery. That distinction between the Arabs and the local population continued even after the massive Arab/Muslim conquest of the seventh century C.E. and the creation of permanent Arab settlements well beyond the border.

THE 'ARAB IN ISLAMIC HISTORY

Given the tendency of unruly tribesmen to encroach upon the lands of the sown, a pattern that continued well after the Arab conquest, it is not surprising that for premodern Muslims the term 'arab often conveyed negative connotations, indicating a certain kind of primitivism and uncontrolled anarchy. Resistant to any form of centralized authority the 'arab were generally seen as disruptive, if not menacing to public order. In various settings and times, beduin tribesmen actually controlled the countryside and threatened rural settlements. Even when held in check by the central authorities, their presence in populated areas was a potential source of concern. At the least, their entry into towns and cities could give rise to expectations of uncivilized behavior. Even the more settled tribes and their clients were regarded as difficult to control. Their compliance usually was bought by regular service pay, booty acquired from warfare, and the timely distribution of bonuses. But these measures were no guarantee that the tribes could be yoked to centralized authority. At the outset of Muslim rule, the caliphs and their representatives were forced to acknowledge the political autonomy demanded by large tribal associations, especially those tribal groups that had come to form major settlements within early Muslim military camps and garrison towns, the so-called *amsar*.

And so, we are faced with a nagging question. If linguistic affinity is a nonstarter for identifying Arabs in premodern times, and the term 'arab referred not to the vast indigenous population of what had been before the Islamic conquest parts of the Byzantine and Sassanian empires but to beduins and to tribal configurations settled in remote regions and in military enclaves and garrison towns, what is the residual history, if any, that connects some 300 million Arabs today?

Any claimed linkage through an Arab ethnicity forged over more than a thousand years is more than dubious. How many among those who now call themselves Arabs can trace their ancestry to the Arab conquerors of the seventh century C.E.? Indeed, the same question could have been posed for the vast majority of Muslim subjects during the formative period of the Islamic state when the non-Arab population of the region outnumbered its Arab conquerors many times over. The Arab armies that wrested Egypt, Palestine-Syria, and northern Syria from the Byzantines and Mesopotamia and Western Iran from the Sassanians, all within a decade or so, did not live among the local population, let alone meld with them. Instead they preferred to isolate themselves from the conquered peoples, even from the newly converted Muslims among them. Unfamiliar with the social terrain and lacking immunity to local diseases, which reportedly felled them in great numbers, the Arab conquerors established settlements of their own, usually adjacent to the kinds of wide expanses with which they were familiar and in which their light cavalry had a tactical advantage over slower-moving enemy armies.

Even among themselves, Arabs attempted to preserve tribal boundaries. The initial Arab settlements beyond Arabia were not integrated living units but rabbit warrens of separate tribal groups, each possessing its own carefully marked living quarters, cemeteries, and places of assembly. Some tribal groups of a more primitive nature could not even manage that, however. Instead, they lived outside the pale of settlement in the nearby camel grounds. In such fashion, they and their allies preserved their precious sense of autonomy and kept out of harm's way. Only on Fridays, when religious practice obliged Muslims to pray as a single assembly, were the different tribal configurations of any given settlement likely to commingle.

The aforementioned sense of separateness was actually encouraged by the central Muslim authorities who feared that excessive contact between proud and fiercely independent Arab tribal units would lead to blood feud and ultimately to anarchy. Worse yet, such contact might lead to occasional alliances among the tribesmen, thereby forming large fighting forces that could, in given circumstances, challenge the political authority of the caliphs and their governors. Any such rebellion was likely to be fueled by the riches of former imperial domains now in Muslim hands. The caliphs, situated in the Arabian Peninsula, recognized that they had limited means of controlling the unruly tribesmen despite the conversion of many, indeed most, tribesmen to Islam, an act that in theory subordinated their tribal identity to association in the ummah, or community, of the Muslims. In reality, these early conversions to Islam did not lead to privileging religious association over blood ties. Faced with potential insubordination, if not outward insurrection, the Commanders of the Faithful co-opted the tribal armies by adjusting to their anarchic sensibilities.

In the long run, the patterns of settlement and the sense of insularity to which they gave rise, as well as the lack of centralized control in the Arab garrison towns, proved counterproductive. Nominally independent tribal units resisted the imposition of any authority occasioning a constant danger to the state and its representatives. The ruling caliphs then attempted to break the tribal armies in a variety of ways or, at the least, mitigate the effects of Arab tribalism. Time and circumstances favored the central authorities. Over the course of centuries, many of the Arab tribesmen, who were but a tiny fraction of the total population of the Islamic Near East, became more and more assimilated to the local culture and lost their distinctive tribal ways, if not their ethnic identities. Arab tribesmen, at one time both cognizant and proud of their distinctiveness, eventually became part and parcel of that vast mosaic of peoples who had inhabited the settled areas of the Near East from more ancient times. Warriors initially numbering in the tens of thousands were literally swallowed up by a non-Arab population of tens of millions. They had ceased to be Arabs, as Arabs were then understood. Only in more remote areas, like the Arabian Peninsula where distances allowed for isolation, or along the periphery between the desert regions and the sown, did tribesmen, retaining their identities, remain apart and potentially troublesome as before. These remained true 'arab.

Arab tribalism never fully disappeared—it remains in evidence until this very day—but some two centuries after the initial Muslim conquest it had already lost much, if not most, of its force in the central lands of the caliphate. In 750 C.E., a more universal Islamic empire, that of the Abbasid caliphs, came to power. Although led by members of the most prestigious of all Arab clans, that of the Prophet Muhammad, the Abbasids looked beyond Arab tribalism when setting up the foundations of their state. Having overthrown the House of Umayyah, a polity dominated for some ninety years by Arabs whose political culture was derived from and catered to tribal sensibilities, the Abbasids transformed the very nature of Islamic ruling society. Arab Muslim rulers, whose forefathers were raised in the environment of the Arabian Peninsula, employed non-Arabs in critical government positions and within the security forces that protected their court and regime. More generally, they came to value the cultures of the conquered peoples, making the world of the non-Arabs part of their own developing intellectual and material world.

The emergent Islamic empire was in many ways the last great civilization of late antiquity, albeit a civilization inextricably linked to the Arabic language. The ultimate triumph of the Arabs was not that they successfully imposed a tribal culture and identity on their new subjects everywhere—they did not—but that their language, Arabic, achieved primacy beyond the Arabian Peninsula. Unequaled in status, Arabic, the language of Muslim scripture, and later Islamic religious scholarship, supplanted the various tongues of the conquered regions as the language of daily life and, more important yet, as the administrative language of a burgeoning Islamic state. A mere fifty years after the Arab conquest, the provincial bureaucracies, staffed largely by non-Muslim or converted Greek-, Aramaic-, and Iranian-speaking functionaries, formulated documents and conducted business in the language of their conquerors. Arabic thus became the common language for most of the peoples of the Near East and North Africa. The linguistic dominance of the language, spoken and written, remained even as the influence of the Arabs and the residual effects of tribal anarchy waned. But neither the Arabic language nor tribal affiliation served as the basis of a specific and widespread identity in the premodern Near East. Only the beduins and the tribes along the periphery of the desert could safely be described as Arabs, but that designation connoted no sense of unity even among them. Arab tribalism, anarchic by nature, resisted and continues to resist the formation of large, unified, and above all, enduring political entities.

As previously noted, the Arabs of today are a fairly recent invention; the ultimate shape of their association is yet to be determined. In all likelihood, the current system of Arab nation-states will continue; no other type of governance appears compatible with the current global environment. There is much talk of pan-Islam among Muslim revivalists, but not even the most radical among them seriously envisions that the caliphate or some similar imperial authority will be resurrected and take hold in the immediate future. The most optimistic of the Islamists regard the restoration of transnational Islamic government a long-range project. As one historian suggests: The Arab bloc will be a group of countries linked by common language and culture, a common religion, a common history, a common sense even of destiny, but not united in common polity.

This historian could have added to that list of commonalities various foundational myths, formulations that modern Arab writers had based on now-discarded theories of European scholarship.

Beginning in the 1930s, Arab intellectuals in search of deeply rooted, broadly based markers of identity linked contemporary Arabs to the inhabitants of the ancient Near East. The Semites, a so-called race widely distributed throughout the region in ancient times, were adopted by these authors as long-lost relatives from a remote past. The implications of such claims are far reaching. Accepting the proposed linkage between Arabs and Semites, one could argue the Islamic conquest of the seventh century C.E. was more than a geopolitical event nurtured by the religious fervor of the time. Seen from this perspective, Arab tribesmen flying the banners of Islam liberated a more ancient Arab/Semite population from oppressive foreign rule. In such fashion, we are being asked to believe, however indirectly, that the Byzantine Greek and the Sassanian Persian empires that ruled the Near East at the time of the Arab conquest are analogs of alien polities that have yoked the Arab nation more recently: namely, the Crusaders, the European colonialists of modern times, and the Zionists arriving from eastern and central Europe. The defeat of the Byzantines and Sassanians, and the later defeat of the Crusaders, portend a similar fate for the most recent foreigners to occupy Arab land.

THE SEMITES AS A MARKER OF IDENTITY FOR MODERN ARABS

The claim of a declared link between today's Arabs and the purported Semites of a remote past is not supported by what we now know of the ancient Near East. As with the term *Arab*, the well-known terms *Semite* and *Semitic* are problematic markers of identification. They too have no deep roots in Near Eastern culture, be it Muslim or Jewish. They, too, are Western constructs, resulting in this case from a modern fascination with typologies of peoples and languages. The identification of the Semites as a distinct racial or ethnic group, and of the Semitic languages as a related body of tongues, are the outgrowth of eighteenth- and nineteenth-century European views of anthropology and philology, in particular the differentiation of peoples, cultural traits, and language systems.

Admittedly, European scholars, especially those of the Enlightenment and its aftermath, were not the first to classify all of humankind into discrete units with identifiable characteristics and discernible patterns of behavior. Medieval Muslims, borrowing from the geography of the ancient Greeks, divided the world into seven inhabited climes and then proceeded to describe the peoples settled within them. As a rule, the most praiseworthy group is found in the Muslim author's own clime; others, particularly peoples outside the central provinces of the Islamic Near East, are often described in pejorative terms, whether they be Muslims or non-Muslims.

Peoples beyond the world ruled by Muslims were treated less kindly. Ironically enough, some of these negative comments bear resemblance to later European prejudices: the Chinese are vile, Greeks and Jews are unscrupulous, the Turks are crude and behave like course louts, the Blacks lazy and given to undisciplined merriment, and so forth. What marks Western scholarship as different from these Muslim expressions of cultural geography is not so much their respective attitudes toward the other, but the scientific claims advanced by supposedly enlightened Europeans when discussing perceived difference among the so-called races and other subgroups of humankind.

Nor were enlightened Europeans the first to appreciate that the specific languages they called Semitic languages are related to one another. Muslims recognized the intricate links between Arabic, Hebrew, and various forms of Western and Eastern Aramaic long before philology and linguistics attained scientific status in the West. In turn, learned Jews living in the orbit of Islam borrowed from Arabic grammatical theory to acquire better tools with which to tease meaning from the text of the Hebrew Bible. Nevertheless, it was left to the Europeans to examine in tandem the linguistic peculiarities of Arabic, Hebrew, various dialects of Aramaic, and also Ethiopic, languages classified as Semitic ever since August Schloezer coined that phrase in the 1781 volume of the *Repertorium fuer biblische und morganlaendische Literatur*, a scholarly journal edited by Johann Eichhorn, the leading Bible scholar of the time.

It is hardly surprising that the starting point for eighteenth-century European anthropology and philology was the Old Testament, in particular, the genealogies following the story of the Flood, when the Almighty, in his infinite wisdom, decided to reconstitute humankind through Noah's three sons: Shem, Ham, and Japheth (Gen. 10:21–9). European scholars understood the descendants of Noah, guided by the word of God, to be the progenitors of the races of humankind. Indeed, the genealogical lists of Genesis provide us with the names of eponymous ancestors that give rise to many groups later mentioned in the Hebrew Bible. But the picture obtained from Genesis is not always neat; some names appear there for the first and last time. The sons of Japheth, whom Western scholars declared the ancestors of the Indo-Europeans—that is, the so-called Aryan race—are represented by a curious amalgam of names, some not easily, if at all, identified with the ancient Near East or the lands contiguous to it. Perhaps that was not surprising since, for the learned Europeans, the sons of Japheth signified not only the progenitors of the Persians, the Medes, and of the peoples of Asia Minor and the Greek Isles—peoples generally familiar to them by way of ancient sources—but also nations strange to them, that is, population groups presumably inhabiting regions far removed from the Near East. In any case, all the descendants of Japheth were said to speak languages that scholars classified as Indo-European or Indo-Germanic.

Similar geographical and linguistic identities were attributed to the so-called Hamitic and Semitic peoples, the offspring of Ham and Shem, Noah's other sons. These descendants of Noah are represented by numerous names, all well known to us from the Bible and other ancient texts. Among them are Canaan and Mizraim (Egypt), the sons of Ham who become the eponymous ancestors of nations inhabiting lands named after them (Gen. 10:15–8). Still other descendants of Ham were linked by scholars to groups situated near ancient Egypt and within Mesopotamia and the Horn of Africa. All these groups descended from Ham were designated as speakers of Hamitic languages. And while none of the proposed Hamitic languages were known to Schloezer and his European contemporaries, it was no doubt assumed that, if and when discovered, they would represent a cluster of tongues sharing common linguistic characteristics, as all the peoples of the Hamitic race, and indeed all other peoples associated with a particular racial group, shared physical characteristics and cultural traits common to their own group.

It is the offspring of Shem, the so-called Semites invented by Schloezer and his European confreres, who titillate our interest here. Unaccustomed to pronouncing *sh*, the ancient compilers of the Septuagint and Vulgate, the Greek and Latin versions of Hebrew Scripture, transliterated *Shem* as *Sem*, hence Schloezer's designation "Semitic" languages. Initially, Hebrew and various forms of Aramaic were well known in the medieval West, as was Arabic. In the sixteenth century, Ethiopic, a language distantly related to the others, was added to the repertoire of learned European linguists. The study of these related languages in Europe, at one time closely linked to anti-Muslim and anti-Jewish diatribes, eventually took on a life of its own. Semitic philology, liberated from the crudest form of religious polemics, became an invaluable tool for understanding the literal meaning of the Old Testament. Dictionaries begot sophisticated lexicons, and teaching aids gave rise to grammar books that included comparative material acquired when archeological discoveries yielded the hitherto unknown languages of ancient Mesopotamia, beginning in the nineteenth century. Still other Semitic languages were discovered in the twentieth century: Ugaritic, a second-millennium B.C.E. Canaanite language written in cuneiform script on clay tablets; inscriptions of first-millennium dialects very similar to biblical Hebrew; and most recently Eblaite, an early language from Syria whose linguistic peculiarities are still subject to debate.

These discoveries of new languages in the nineteenth and twentieth centuries did not dovetail with Schloezer's original formulation. It became evident that the descendants of Ham, at least those inhabiting the Levant and Mesopotamia, were also Semites when it came to language. Indeed, it is clear that Hebrew and various dialects of Canaan and Transjordan are essentially the same language as are Flemish and Dutch. Even if Canaanites and Israelites were not related by common origins, as some scholars have recently claimed, their written and presumably spoken languages were mutually intelligible. And so, amid considerable debate, Western scholars broadened the family of the so-called Semitic languages, establishing distinct subgroups that share certain linguistic affinities and geographical regions. In that expanded formulation, linguists spoke of clusters of tongues generally described as Eastern Semitic (Mesopotamia), Northwest Semitic (the Levant), and South Semitic (the Arabian Peninsula and Abyssinia). Scholars then proposed a more expansive network of languages. Linguists now refer to the Afro-Asiatic family of languages, a heading that subsumes the languages of Southwest Asia, Greater Egypt, the lands to the west of Egypt, and the Horn of Africa. As linguistic tools become more sophisticated, the cluster of languages sharing common characteristics will no doubt widen. Indeed, that process of seeing language differentiation and diffusion in ever-broader terms is well underway.

Despite a growing recognition of linguistic diversity among speakers of Semitic and related languages, and despite widespread skepticism about the historicity of the Genesis narrative, the earlier notion that the Semites represent, or at one time represented, a distinctive race, or if you prefer, a cohesive subgroup of humankind, managed to persist. The list of Semites proposed by G. A. Barton around the turn of the century and reaffirmed by him in a 1930 publication includes Arabs (by which he meant the peoples of Central and North Arabia as distinct from South Arabia); the Akkadians of ancient Babylonia; Assyrians; Amorites; the Canaanites and their descendants, the Phoenicians; Hebrews (precursors of the Jews); Edomites; Moabites and Ammonites; and various tribes of Aramaeans. In addition to the aforementioned peoples of the ancient Fertile Crescent, Barton included many of the peoples of Abyssinia.

Because they spoke of a remote past before the invention of writing, scholars seeking the origins of the ancient Semites could not rely on contemporaneous records. There is no remote foundational myth, whether oral or written, that ties the origins of a Semitic race or ethnic group to a particular region. Nor, for that matter, are there remains of a material culture that can be labeled distinctively Semitic before recorded history, certainly none that can be traced back nine to twelve thousand years, the time span suggested as the likely period in which the Semites were born. And yet, some scholars remained undaunted in their search for a preliterate Semitic race, a quest that continued well into the twentieth century.

Of particular interest to us is the theory first advanced in the 1860s that Arabia was the cradle of a distinctive Semitic civilization and that bearers of that civilization subsequently migrated throughout the area of the Fertile Crescent, thereby explaining the evolution of the Semitic-speaking peoples and their languages. This theory—or hypothesis, if you prefer the more reserved term—was based on contemporaneous notions of language and nomadic peoples moving from the steppe to the sown. Of all the Semitic languages then known, scholars of the time believed that classical Arabic was the closest to proto-Semitic, the hypothetical language from which all the different Semitic languages evolved. That being the case, they reasoned, that the Arabs (medieval and modern) are the descendants of an ancient race that established the original Semitophone civilization in the homeland of the Arabs—that is, the Arabian Peninsula. Following that, the descendants of these original Arabian Semites left their arid lands and migrated in successive waves to other and more fertile regions of the Near East where other Semitic languages and identities evolved. As the nineteenth-century Arabist Alois Sprenger put it: "All Semites . . . are [the creation of] successive layers of Arabs."

A detailed discussion of the arguments presented by Sprenger and his contemporaries is likely to overwhelm the general reader, particularly the linguistic debate that persisted for some time. Suffice it to say, the only identifiable linkage between the Arabs of today and the ancient Semitophones settled throughout the Near East in ancient times is that they all use(d) languages with broadly shared characteristics. But as a marker of identification and as an emblem of unity, that shared linguistic background has no more weight than would a corresponding claim that all speakers of Indo-European languages have linked identities by virtue of common Aryan origins. Whether linguistic or anthropological, the data do not suggest that waves of Arabs bursting forth from the Arabian Peninsula represent the fundamental and identifiable stock of a so-called Semitic race.

Put somewhat differently: There is no reason to deny that there were, in the general area of the ancient Near East, speakers of specific languages with closely shared linguistic peculiarities, languages which, for the sake of convenience, we refer to as Semitic languages. Nor is there reason to deny that Semitophones were grouped in specific political configurations and developed cultural institutions both unique to their own societies and shared with others among whom they dwelled. All that may be safely conceded. It is, however, another matter to hear learned people speak of the Semites in ethnic and/or racial terms, even today. It may be that the original speakers of a hypothetical language said to have been common to all the earliest Semites—that which scholars label proto-Semitic—represented a particular ethnic group that took root somewhere in the Near East. But that proposed group and the language it purportedly spoke would have stemmed, in any case, from a remote prehistoric past about which we can only speculate. Like the search for the Holy Grail, the search for Semitic origins will always remain an unrealizable quest. One thing is clear, however. Whoever the earliest Semitophones might have been, and whatever the specific nature of their language, neither anthropologists nor historians have any evidence to specify their ethnicity and certainly no license to describe them or later Semitophones in racial terms.

From our vantage point at the outset of the third millennium C.E., it seems a bit odd that less than one hundred years ago the notion of a distinctive Semitic race (often accompanied by pejorative comments about Semites) was widely accepted; and it is even more odd that the notion continues to be accepted today in circles in and outside the Near East. If nothing else, the capacity to envision a stereotypical Semite is testimony to the residual strength of racial theories that first took root among scholars in the eighteenth century and were then applied with evil consequences in the centuries that followed.

POLITICIZING THE SEMITES

Cognizant that racial stereotyping, along with race itself, has become a false start for discussing Near Eastern history or culture, we are still obliged to ask, if ever so warily, what relationship to the imagined Semitic race is claimed by today's Arabs for cultural and political reasons? One can certainly appreciate how Arabs living in their fractious societies may yearn for a sense of common identity that extends back to remote times. By embracing the Semites who are, in essence, the invention of Western scholarship and by accepting the nineteenth-century view that Arabia is the cradle of Semitic civilization, Arabs can issue a call for unity among all those allegedly descended from an ancient Arab/Semite race. Such claims of descent from the early inhabitants of the Fertile Crescent, all of whom are said to be of Arabian origins, enables current Arab regimes to legitimize themselves as modern polities in lands that were at one time settled by their pre-Islamic Arab/Semite brethren.

Saddam Hussein, the recently deposed tyrant of modern Iraq, attempted to establish an Iraqi identity that would transcend the ethnic and religious divisions of his fractious country and at the same time stake his personal claim to leadership of the all-embracing Arab nation. Identifying with Saladin, like him a native of Tikrit, he became at the same time an Arab and a Kurd; claiming direct ties with the Prophet's house, including Ali ibn Abi Talib, the progenitor of the Shiite imams, he became both a Sunnite and a Shiite. If that were not enough to unite the disparate elements of Iraqi society behind him, Saddam produced the trump card that was intended to unify all Iraqis, if not all Arabs. Turning to the ancient Near East, he declared himself heir to Nebuchadnezzar, the Babylonian monarch of the sixth century B.C.E. Citing a past still more remote, he drew sustenance from Hammurabi, the great lawgiver of the second millennium, and from the Sumerians, who inhabited lower Mesopotamia two thousand years earlier. If that were not enough, he portrayed himself as the living representation of the ancient God Tammuz. As the embodiment of Saladin, Saddam was ideally suited to unite the Arabs and the Kurds and then dispose of the new crusaders of the imperialist West, as Saladin had disposed of the Franks some eight centuries earlier. As a relative of the Prophet's family, he would strive to unite the Sunnites and Shiites; and as the analog of Nebuchadnezzar, he would go to Palestine, defeat the Jews, and liberate Jerusalem, putting an end to the "artificial" Zionist state, just as the mighty Babylonian king put an end to the Israelite monarchy 2,500 years earlier. Unfortunately for the Iraqis, Saddam was more inclined to behave like the God Tammuz than the lawgiver Hammurabi.

Among present-day Arabs, the Palestinians have the greatest investment in claims of direct descent from the ancient Arab/Semites. With the rise of modern Zionism, and more particularly the creation of the sovereign State of Israel, religiously driven disputes between Jews and Muslims, and more generally between Jews and all Arabs, have been transformed from polemical encounters over scripture and revelation into an armed struggle over geographical space and historical lineage. In today's highly charged atmosphere, Jews and Arabs alike invoke an ancient past to buttress their claims to the land called by Arabs Palestine (Filastin) and by Jews the Land of Israel (Eretz Yisrael). An unbroken lineage with the peoples of ancient Palestine allows today's Arabs to make a case for the territory they contest with its current Jewish inhabitants, settlers proclaiming their descent from the Israelite conquerors of Canaan in the time of Joshua.

There is by now a substantial body of literature in active circulation linking modern-day Palestine to its most ancient inhabitants. This revisioning of the past first appeared during the British mandate, when Jewish immigrants arriving from Europe reached levels that truly alarmed the Arab populace of the country. By stressing the long and continuous Arab character of their land, Palestinian intellectuals countered Zionist claims, while at the same time they attempted to forge a sense of national consciousness in an Arab society riven by ethnic, regional, and local identities. The importance of this Arab historiography became even more pronounced following the displacement of hundreds of thousands of Palestinian Arabs who fled or were driven from their homes during the fighting of 1947–1948 and then again after the defeat of the Arabs in the 1967 war, which resulted in the Israeli occupation of the West Bank and Gaza. When successive Israeli governments allowed for, and in certain circumstances actively promoted, Jewish settlement in the conquered territories, the imperative to stress the genuine Arab-Muslim character of the land became even more pronounced.

Arabs have never fully appreciated the historic dimension of Zionist claims, its time-honored links to Jewish tradition, and how deeply the long and checkered experiences of the Jewish people are perceived both within Israel and the Diaspora. But they have understood only too well the need to counter the Zionists in the court of world opinion. Facing the Zionist threat, Arabs, Christian and Muslim, have sought to undermine Jewish claims derived from the biblical past by establishing an Arab identity for the Canaanite peoples, the indigenous inhabitants of the land at the time of the Israelite conquest recorded in the Hebrew Bible (ca. 1250 B.C.E.). Seen from that Arab perspective, the later Arab-Muslim conquest of Palestine in the seventh century C.E. united the most recent Muslim Arab arrivals from the peninsula with waves of migrating Arabs who had entered the land and claimed it as their own at some remote time in history. Where such historical license is not enough to legitimize the aspirations of contemporary Palestinian nationalists, some modern Arabs have declared the Northwest Semitic languages of the ancient Levant as forms of Arabic, the equivalent of contending that English is a Romance language and that William the Conqueror's victory at Hastings united the Gallic elements of the European continent with those of the British Isles.

For some defenders of Palestinian nationalism, it is not enough to claim a pre-Israelite "Arab" history of the land that gives their case primacy over that of the Jews. Cognizant of the central role played by Europeans, especially East European Zionists in the settlement of Palestine, Arabs have attempted to sever the links between European Jewry and the ancient Israelites, in effect delegitimizing all Zionist claims based on ancient history. Some Arab writers consider the Jews of Europe to be descended from the

Khazars, a tribe of Central Asian Turks whose ruler reportedly converted to Judaism some time in the eighth century C.E. The extent of conversion among the Khazars is impossible to gauge, and the borders of the Khazar kingdom cannot be established with certainty. But the Khazar realm did include lands in present-day Eastern Europe, hence the claim that European Jewry, or at least East European Jewry, are largely the descendants of converted Turks (as opposed to Jews of Near Eastern origins who first settled on the European continent in Roman times and gradually migrated eastward). Although reputable Western scholars do not take seriously the claim that European Jewry is largely or partially of Khazar origin, that claim continues to evoke a sympathetic response in Arab circles discrediting Zionists settling the alleged land of their forefathers.

Still more bizarre is Kamal Salibi's attempt to sever the Hebrew Bible's link to the Land of Israel. An Arab scholar noted for his studies of the modern Middle East, Salibi has turned his attention to the ancient world and argues that our Hebrew Bible is actually based on an older Semitic tradition that originated in West Arabia. This would mean that the current Judeo-Christian narrative, a story largely situated in Mesopotamia, Syria, and Canaan, was originally a tale of events taking place in, and of persons indigenous to, the original homeland of the Arab/Semites. How then are we to explain the overwhelming number of biblical tales taking place in the Fertile Crescent rather than in Arabia? As always, Salibi is inventive, if not convincing. At a much later time, the Arabian narrative was redacted and reinterpreted by the descendants of Arabians who had migrated to Palestine from their original settlements in the Hijaz region of West Arabia. Our author does not indicate when this historic migration from Arabia took place, but he is sure that the later "Canaanite and Aramaic speaking peoples," whose ancestors came from Arabia along with the original Israelites, made the trek to Palestine before their Israelite neighbors. Salibi does not argue that Jews have deliberately distorted the real account of their origins in what has come to be known as the Hebrew Bible. That long-accepted (but false) version of Israelite history is more likely the result of faded historical memories.

Moving beyond the traditional histories that have shaped Jewish identity from the biblical period until today, a period of well over two thousand years, Salibi asks how the first Israelites, tribesmen in West Arabia, imagined themselves. Citing the Hebrew Bible, he notes that Abraham's kin were known as Hebrews but also declared themselves Arameans, suggesting thereby an ambiguous identity during their stay in Arabia. Since Salibi believes West Arabia was also the original home of the Arameans and Canaanites (the latter designation includes for him the ancient Philistines as well as the other indigenous peoples of the Bible), he suggests the identity of these early Israelites was bound to that of their Arabian neighbors. In such fashion, Salibi transforms virtually all the identifiable inhabitants of ancient Palestine into peoples of Arabian and, by extension, Arab origins. Even the Philistines, a people who invaded Palestine from the Aegean Sea, take their place as legitimate Arabians. By linking the original Israelites with all these peoples, Salibi presents us with a hybrid social group more closely linked to today's Palestinian Arabs than modern Zionist settlers from Europe, recent arrivals without genuine roots in Palestine. But even if one were to acknowledge that some Israelis are in fact descended from Salibi's Arabian Israelites and not from Turkic Khazars, the more legitimate claimants to the Holy Land would be the ancestors of today's Arab Palestinians: the peoples subsumed by the broad label Canaanites and Aramaens, whose presence in Palestine preceded the Israelite conquest of Canaan. By virtue of their ancestry, today's Palestinians have a prior claim to the land they contest with the Jews.

No serious scholar of the ancient Near East has endorsed Salibi's dramatic thesis. To be fair, some influential Western scholars of an earlier generation did acknowledge the importance of Arabia when analyzing the biblical narrative. James A. Montgomery, who specialized in Semitic philology, and the Islamicist D. B. Macdonald both wrote books in the early 1930s linking the Israelites to the world of ancient Arabia. Assuming that the Semites originated in the Arabian Peninsula and then settled in the adjacent Near East in successive waves, and taking note as well of the various Arab tribes mentioned in the biblical text, Montgomery and Macdonald argue that the Hebrew Bible reflected an Arabian milieu as well as that of the Fertile Crescent. But they do not go so far as to claim the Bible or the Israelites originated in Arabia.

Odd as they may appear to serious scholars, Salibi's views may still leave their mark on discussions of current politics. We should not be hasty to dismiss his book as an amateur fascination with the "biblical" past, the idiosyncratic project of an otherwise responsible professor. Salibi's views, or variations of his views, seemingly appeal to a broad if less scholarly audience than historians of antiquity. Some nonbiblicists opine that the extensive Muslim versions of the biblical persons and events originated in some remote Arabian ur-tradition as did the Hebrew Bible, and that the Arabian narrative was then spread by migrating Arab Semites to the lands beyond. Eventually, an altered form of these Arabian myths became part of the Judeo-Christian tradition; it was a reversal of the view commonly held by virtually all Western scholars, that biblical themes in Muslim scripture and tradition are derived, however loosely at times, from cultural artifacts brought to Arabia from the Fertile Crescent.

Salibi's bold venture into uncharted waters can lead readers in still another direction. The privileging of ancient Arabia by a Lebanese Arab serves to authenticate pan-Arabism, that modern political movement that creates, out of new cloth, a distinct Arab nation. By stressing the common bonds of their Arabian origins and not the narrowly defined religious associations that have torn his country apart, Salibi and his fellow Lebanese Christians can become full partners in a larger Arab polity rather than a tolerated minority in the hegemonic ummah or community of Islam. Indeed, Salibi has also written a book situating the Gospels and the historic Jesus in an Arabian setting.

One could then argue that the Christians indigenous to the region have no desire for political independence that might disturb their proud Muslim neighbors. Instead, the Christians could be integrated into an Arab polity that by definition embraces all Arabs equally regardless of religious persuasion. That political outlook is in stark contrast to the Jews, who call attention to the ancient Jewish conquest and occupation of Palestine and justify that occupation and indeed the current occupation of Palestine with the myth of a "promised land" that is actually contrived from an authentic Arab tradition. Salibi's thesis can therefore link the usurpation of (Arab) land by invading Israelite settlers in ancient times to the Zionist settler state of the twentieth century.

SOME LAST MUSINGS ON CURRENT ARAB USES OF THE ANCIENT NEAR EAST

The political leadership that sets the agenda of international relations and the analysts who sit in critical judgment of state policy may well ask if academic historians serve any useful purpose when they interrogate the foundational myths of nations and would-be nations. It is not likely that contemporary politics would be conducted any differently if the political leadership of the Arab world were more cognizant of erudite Western scholarship. Would Arabs abandon the claim of Semitic origins in the Arabian Peninsula and, with that, the current concept of the Arab nation if they were more fully aware of scholarship on the long history of the Near East? Would they modulate their attitudes on the legitimacy of modern Israel if they were better informed of recent archeological and historical debates? One could not imagine the likes of the late Yasir Arafat scrutinizing, or even perusing, detailed analyses of technical publications published in the West, the kind of research that directly informs academic understanding of national myths forged in the modern age. Nor is it likely that the religious establishment of the Arab–Muslim world looks closely at journals published by the Western academy, let alone uses that scholarship to reconsider universally held truths that have united the Muslim faithful and helped keep traditional Arab societies intact over generations.

Academic historians are nevertheless obligated to explore these issues, because misunderstood gleanings from Western scholarship have reached the attention of Arab writers and have been used to formulate political positions that serve the perceived interests of particular Arab states and the Arab nation as a whole. At a practical level, it makes scant difference whether the scholarly debates of the West have been misunderstood or deliberately distorted for parochial needs. What is merely regarded as true in traditional Near Eastern societies can transcend the bare particulars of truth or falsehood; it can occasion dramatic political behavior that proclaims a truth of its own. Those who take serious interest in the region are compelled to investigate the manner in which national and communal identities are forged, if only to understand why polities act as they do. That holds true for Arab/Muslim and non-Arab and non-Muslim communities alike.

2

DEFINING ARAB PALESTINE

Historical Geography, Imagined
Polities, and Sacred Space

Five years after the modern State of Israel was born, a leading American university sponsored a public forum on the Arab-Israel dispute. Some participants, not reconciled to the existence of the Jewish state, spoke instead of the Palestine problem. Among the discussants was an Egyptian professor of international law. When it was his turn to address the audience, he began with remarks that were clipped and exceedingly pungent. He said there is no Israel, only a so-called State of Israel. For him as for all Arabs there is only Palestine. There has been only Palestine in the past. There will be only Palestine in the future.

Given the political climate of the times, one could fully understand what the speaker meant when he referred to the "so-called State of Israel." In that university, which had encouraged a frank and open exchange of views, Israel had been effaced from a map of the world that hung in the international center. As if by sympathetic magic, a clandestine act of vandalism was invoked to undo historical reality. The so-called state, which had no right to be considered among truly legitimate nations, had conveniently disappeared—at least from that map on that wall. Symbolic gestures of this sort were the order of the day among Arabs, be it in the Near East or in foreign settings. For some years after the creation of the Jewish state, Arab representatives, including diplomats, were generally not permitted to engage in public discourse with Israelis, lest any such conversation be understood as acknowledging the very existence of the so-called state and its citizens.

The enforced isolation persisted even after Israel attained full membership in the United Nations. When Arab spokesmen were required to participate in events with Israelis, it was generally behind physical barriers separating the interlocutors, as if the mere sight of an Israeli official would compromise the Arab sense of justice by giving credence to the illegal

Jewish polity. Charles Malik, a leading Lebanese diplomat, found himself in scalding waters when he was photographed bantering with Eliahu Elath, an Israeli diplomat who had been a classmate of Malik's in Beirut some twenty years earlier.

Behavior of this sort may seem exceedingly bizarre in light of what has transpired since. The professor's government not only recognizes the State of Israel as an established fact, but it also has formal diplomatic relations with its one-time enemy. Even the Palestinian Authority, which remains locked in bitter conflict with Israelis, formally recognizes Israel's right to exist. There is, nevertheless, a lingering antipathy to the very concept of a Jewish state in the lands of Islam. Despite steps toward normalizing relations between Israel and its Arab neighbors, the latter remain convinced that Israel was conceived in sin, a foreign entity illegitimately planted on Arab-Muslim soil. Seen in that light, the Egyptian's comment that the land contested by Jews and Arabs has always been Palestine and will always remain Palestine has lost none of its resonance. The Arab-Israel dispute remains, in effect, the unresolved problem of Palestine. But of what Palestine did the Egyptian speak some fifty years ago? What perceptions of historical and geographical Palestine govern Arab and Muslim attitudes today? Of equal importance, what did it mean to speak of Palestine in ages past, and should a discussion of medieval geography and history be particularly relevant to an understanding of current and future developments in the Near East?

PALESTINE BY ANY NAME

The Palestine spoken of today is, by and large, a Christian European invention. More specifically, it is the creation of the great powers that carved up the Ottoman provinces of the Fertile Crescent following World War I. For all intents and purposes, that Palestine represents the area of the mandate awarded Great Britain by the League of Nations and endorsed by the international community in the early 1920s. That is not to say that the name Palestine—or to be more precise, some close variation of that name—does not have a long history that goes back to more ancient times. There is, however, no resemblance between the borders of ancient, medieval, or even Ottoman Palestine and the maps that grace various T-shirts, sweatshirts, jewelry, propaganda posters, and other paraphernalia that have been and continue to be in vogue as fashion statements and/or declarations of support for Palestinian nationhood.

Whether one speaks of ancient Egyptian *Purusati*, cuneiform *Pa-la-sh-tu*, biblical Hebrew *P'leshet*, or Graeco-Roman *Palestine*, the name originally connotes what biblical translators call *Philistia*, the relatively narrow coastal strip inhabited by the *P'lishtim* or Philistines. As distinct from Philistia, the hill country of Canaan and areas to the north were inhabited in biblical times by the Israelites, first in tribal enclaves and later in monarchial polities known as Judah and Israel, the former centered in Jerusalem, the latter in Samaria, modern Arab Nablus. The two cities were situated in general areas called in Hebrew *Yehudah* and *Shomron*, that is, Judea and Samaria, names currently applied by Israelis to the West Bank. When considered as a whole, what had been the ancient Israelite polity became known as Eretz Yisrael—the Land of Israel—meaning the land of all the people of Israel. Were the current situation not so embedded in tragic circumstances, we might savor the delicious irony of it all. The region of ancient Israel's rivals, the Philistines, is today the site of the modern Israeli port of Ashdod, the bustling Israeli city of Kiriath Gat, the greater metropolitan area of Tel Aviv–Jaffa, and a host of other settlements. Modern Israel's densely populated coastal plain represents the demographic and economic center of the Jewish state. On the other hand, in Judea and Samaria, the historic heartland of ancient Israel, the citizens of the modern Jewish state, Jerusalemites excluded, are outnumbered by their Arab neighbors many times over—this despite intensive efforts to promote Jewish settlement in the West Bank since the Six Day War, when a victorious Israel emerged controlling all of Western Palestine between the Jordan River and the Mediterranean Sea.

As for the rest of Canaan, it was inhabited by the indigenous population; these various peoples, like the Philistine invaders, disappeared from the pages of history in ancient times. Given the complicated situation that currently exists, we may wish to consider their early exit from history a fortuitous development, as it spares us of having to be concerned with national liberation movements dedicated to the irredentist claims of the biblical Amorites, Canaanites, Girgashites, Hittites, Hivites, Jebusites, and Perizzites—groups that would no doubt have attracted sympathizers, if not active advocates, among those who champion every peoples' right to self-determination. Taken as a whole, the Land of Canaan clearly extended into what is today southern Lebanon, including Tyre and Sidon, the current sites of major Palestinian refugee camps.

The actual borders of the Israelite state, both within and beyond Canaan, varied from time to time, as did the theoretical boundaries posited in various biblical and rabbinic passages. The smallest Israelite state was the restored polity of the Persian period (ca. 515 B.C.E.), a truncated domain that extended from somewhat north of Jaffa to the border of Ascalon along the sea, and from the northern environs of Jerusalem to the vicinity of Hebron inland. It included no territory east of the Jordan River or Lake

Tiberius, areas that were the enclaves of four Israelite tribes during the period of the monarchy. The greatest Israelite state was the united monarchy under David and Solomon (ca. tenth century B.C.E.). If the biblical sources are to be trusted, the direct influence exerted by father and son extended from the sea to the river (mandated Palestine), as well as Transjordan and much of south and central Syria. Other ancient Jewish polities were situated in domains well within those reported for tenth-century B.C.E. Israel. It is then clear that no single map of the modern state can accurately reflect the diffuse geography of ancient times. When ultranationalist Jews draw precise boundaries of a Greater Israel from the river to the sea, and then add the Golan as well, they take considerable license with the past. Drawing modern maps based on ancient or medieval history is, in any case, a very problematic endeavor, all the more so when mapmaking is driven by ideological concerns. That holds true regardless of who draws the map and for whatever purpose.

As if to recognize the shifting borders and the different names given the land at various moments and by different peoples, some scholars have opted for loose-fitting markers of identification. Hoping to transcend place and time, and not ruffle too many political feathers, they refer to an ambiguous "historical" or "geographical" Palestine. By whatever name and boundaries, the area encompassed by so-called historical or geographical Palestine has always been relatively small and lacking in resources. A land bridge at the crossroads of Southwest Asia and the African continent, Palestine fell to conquering armies and was subjected to many foreign influences, if not domination: Egyptian, Assyrian, Babylonian, Persian, Greek, Roman, Byzantine, Sassanian, Arabian, Turcoman, Mamluk, Mongol, Crusader, Ottoman Turk, and British. Arabs add to this list of intruders the modern Zionist movement, making light of, if not denying altogether, Jewish roots in the land, a history that predates the Muslim Arab conquest by some two thousand years. Many conquerors left a distinctive imprint. They established new settlements, fixed new boundaries, and coined names by which historic Palestine and its various regions and sites would be known for official purposes.

The name Palestine thus appears in Greek and Roman sources where, following a precedent previously noted, it originally signified the narrow coastal strip along the Mediterranean, the area of Canaan that had been inhabited by the ancient Philistines. Similarly, the center of the larger geographical entity carved out by Greek and Roman authorities was known as Judaea after ancient Hebrew Yehudah, the Israelite state that survived with Jerusalem as its capital throughout most of the biblical period (ca. 950–586

B.C.E.). That Israelite state was then transformed (ca. 515 B.C.E.) into the Second Hebrew Commonwealth, a polity destroyed by the Romans after the calamitous war of 66–70 C.E. The Judeans, like their modern counterparts the Israelis, were not always adept at the art of politics, less so of public relations. Foolishly and unsuccessfully they revolted against Roman authority, the last occasion being the Bar Kochba rebellion of the second century C.E. Outraged by Jewish recalcitrance, the Roman governor obliterated the most notable historic markers by which Jews identified their land and its sacred past. Henceforth, Judaea, along with the coastal plain, became Syria-Palestina, that is, the Palestine of Syria. In effect, historic Palestine came to signify a subdistrict of Syria, the latter being the larger administrative unit and a major province of the Roman imperial realm. Although Jews continued to reside in Galilee and other regions of ancient Syria-Palestine, Jerusalem was essentially depopulated of Jews; its sacred shrine, leveled in the Roman War of 66–70 C.E., was replaced by a temple to Jupiter Capitolina. The ancient name by which the city had been known was subsumed in the second century C.E. by Aelia Capitolina, after the Emperor Aelius Hadrianus, thus giving rise to Arabic Iliya, the preferred name that Arab conquerors originally used in referring to the holy city.

As Roman rule evolved, Palestine was reconfigured. By the fifth century, it was divided into three distinct administrative regions, conveniently designated as First (*Prima*), Second (*Secunda*), and Third (*Tertia*) Palestine. The first, situated in the center of the country, running from the sea to the Jordan Valley, was administered from the coastal port Caesarea, whose impressive ruins dot the landscape today. The northern region, Second Palestine, was ruled from Scythopolis, an urban center of truly vast dimensions that stood where the modern Israeli city of Beth Shean is located. The south, labeled Third Palestine, was largely desolate. It included the arid Negev region, parts of the Sinai wasteland, and the extension of the Arabian Desert that lay directly east. Climactic conditions did not allow for extensive cultivation in the south. The region's wealth lay in the caravan trade. Petra, the capital of Third Palestine, a settlement whose major buildings were hewn from the hills of Edom, was one of the cities of the Decapolis, a league of ancient commercial centers situated in what is now Jordan and Syria.

What remains of Caesarea, Scythopolis, and Petra is living testament to their vibrant existence in Roman times, but these magnificent cities were all subordinate to Damascus. The central administration for all three regions was in Syria, a pattern of governance that continued after the Muslim Arab conquest of the seventh century C.E. The shadow of a powerful Syria persisted into Ottoman times and was only lifted when the Palestine mandate was established after World War I. It was only some eighty years ago that the now-familiar map of Palestine was drawn.

Unlike the Palestine of the British mandate, the Palestine from biblical through Roman-Byzantine times, or rather combined Palestines, included parts of the Sinai Peninsula (i.e., present-day Egypt), northern Arabia (currently Saudi Arabia), and lands situated in what is today southern and central Syria. The composite historic Palestine also extended beyond the Jordan River, reaching as far as—and in Solomon's time beyond—Rabbath Ammon (current-day Amman, the capital of the Hashemite Kingdom). Moving north to the headwaters of the Jordan and beyond, historic Palestine included at times the lands east of Lake Tiberius, the elevated plateau known from ancient times as the Golan.

The elastic borders of ancient Palestine have encouraged modern disputes and more are sure to come. Part of the Golan, administered by Israel since its victory over Syria in the Six Day War, is home to some fifteen thousand Jewish residents. For these settlers, as indeed for most Israelis, the Golan is not foreign soil. Rather, it is part of the historic Jewish homeland, having served in biblical times as a territorial enclave for elements of the tribe of Dan. The Golan was also subject to the authority of powerful Israelite monarchies that evolved in the tenth and eighth centuries B.C.E.; the area was, in fact, dotted with Jewish settlements well into the postbiblical period. The ancient rabbis declared it the outer limits of the Land of Israel; its Jewish occupants were thus obligated to fulfill all the commandments that pertained to the Holy Land. Memories of this history were strongly implanted among early Zionist settlers who attempted to establish roots on the Golan Heights in the 1890s. As we shall see shortly, Islamic Palestine also included the Golan. However one configures the borders of historic Palestine, the area of the Golan was, more often than not, part of that land.

On the other hand, later Turkish maps situate the Golan in the administrative district (*w[v]ilayah*) of Damascus. In dividing the Arab provinces of the Ottoman Empire, Britain and France had to decide who was to rule the Golan in the European-inspired map of the modern Near East. Because the principal landowner in the Golan Heights actually resided in adjacent Syria, and his properties extended on both sides of the border, the French argued for and won British approval to preserve the integrity of these private holdings. The line separating British-mandated Palestine from French-mandated Syria was thus drawn at the western limits of the Golan. That agreement underlies the current dispute between Israel and Syria over the Golan lands captured by Israeli forces in 1967.

Despite emotional ties to the Golan rooted in the Jewish past, Israel has returned to Syria most of the territory seized there during the Six Day

War. The ruling of the ancient rabbis notwithstanding, two previous Israeli governments expressed a willingness to return virtually all of the Golan that remains under Israel's control. In 2000, a final agreement did seem within sight, but negotiations broke down over a sliver of territory along the eastern shore of Lake Tiberius. Hafiz al-Assad, Syria's leader at the time, insisted that Israel return to the borders of 1967. As he put it, he wanted to dip his feet into the lake once again—that is, from Syrian soil. From Israel's perspective, the stumbling block, a narrow slice of land measured in meters, is no trivial matter. Retaining the shoreline is a legal safeguard to protect Israel's water rights at a time when water is in high demand and short supply. At this moment, the issue is far from settled.

By no means are all Israelis willing to concede the entire Golan, an area administered by Israeli law, but not quite part of the state. Bumper stickers reading "The nation is with the Golan" can still be seen on the roads of Israel. Some Israelis want to retain the Golan Heights to protect the Galilee. They vividly recall the occasions when Syrian gunners fired at the exposed agricultural settlements below. They are also aware of how Syrian armor, massed along the Heights in 1973, almost penetrated northern Israel. For ultranationalist Jews, the issue extends well beyond defense. Embracing the past, they recall that the Golan was once populated by the ancient Israelite tribe of Dan and that it was home to many Jews in postbiblical times as well. From that perspective, the Golan is no less important than Judea and Samaria, the heartland of the ancient Israelite kingdoms and the center of the postexilic Second Hebrew Commonwealth.

Nor is Israel the only potential claimant of territory within the Golan. Should the border remain contested, one can imagine all sorts of teasing, if improbable scenarios, based on maps of the past. Lebanon already seeks the Shaba' Farms, a tiny enclave of Syrian territory held by Israel along the old armistice lines of 1949. Similarly, the Palestinian Authority could invoke ancient precedent and lay claim to the Golan as an extension of Western Palestine. One hardly expects they will press the issue in the foreseeable future; they might not do so at all. The Palestinians have enough to contend with at present, short of making dramatic demands to rearrange the map of Syria. There is the oppressive Israeli occupation, the battered Palestinian economy, all sorts of problems in the social and political structure of Palestinian society, to say nothing of the unfinished business of securing a viable Palestinian state. Nevertheless, the land east of Lake Tiberius has been part of a greater geographical Palestine in both pre-Islamic and Islamic times. The Palestinians could certainly make a strong argument for annexing the Golan to any future Palestinian state were the congruence of political circumstances and power alignments favorable to promote such a bold agenda.

One ought to be extremely cautious when speaking of historic Palestine and modern politics. Invoking ancient boundaries that shifted with time can open not one but many a can of worms. Consider the lands south of the Golan on the east side of the Jordan River. Were it not for overriding political concerns during and following World War I, Transjordan might have been part of the Palestine mandate. The British were intent on keeping Western Palestine, where they declared their aim of establishing an ill-defined Jewish National Home. The integration of that Jewish homeland within the Arab world was to be negotiated by the Zionists and Britain's Arab allies. Britain's Arab friends would, of course, require compensation. One plan was to link Transjordan to a Greater Syria under Hashemite rule. And so, instead of being part of geographical Palestine as it had been so often in history, the east side of the river was set aside by the British to accommodate a branch of the Hashemite house, their Arabian allies during the war against the Turks. That plan had to be shelved when the French assumed rule of Syria, and Transjordan thus took on an identity of its own. Due to British largesse and political fiddling, a mostly desolate territorial expanse three and one-half times larger than mandated Palestine became an Emirate and then the Hashemite Kingdom of Jordan.

Devoid of natural resources and lightly populated, Jordan has persevered, largely due to the courage and political skill of the ruling family and the loyalty of its highly disciplined beduin army, as well as generous subsidies from Great Britain and later the United States. They have weathered the storm of many challenges in the postcolonial era, including the assassination of Jordan's first king and longtime ruler Abdallah in 1951, the incapacity of his mentally unstable successor Talal, plots to depose or kill his grandson the late King Hussein, the loss of the West Bank to Israel in 1967, a Palestinian uprising in 1970, and an abortive Syrian invasion that same year. Because it is, in certain respects, the most artificial of Arab states, there has been talk of the Hashemite Kingdom's proper place in the larger political framework of the region. Whether all or parts of Transjordan should have been, or should be in the future, part of a Greater Israel, a Greater Palestine, or a Greater Syria, is a question that has been discussed from time to time by both Jews and Arabs.

The early Zionists coveted Eastern Palestine as well as Cisjordan. For one, there was a claim to be made based on history. Central Transjordan, biblical Gilead, had been home to the Israelite tribes of Reuben, Gad, and half of Manasseh. Virtually every Israelite polity in ancient times included the east side of the Jordan until the outskirts of Rabbath Ammon (Amman). The Zionist leadership had no inkling that His Majesty's government would alter the traditional geography of the region and, in doing so, would deny them part of ancient Israel. And while modern Jewish settlement east of the river (and in the Golan) was always rather limited, the entire Jewish leadership continued to look to Transjordan as a place suitable for the Zionist enterprise. During the 1930s, they even negotiated the purchase of land parcels with the then Emir Abdallah. In the end, nothing came of this effort, but the interest was still there. In time, mainstream Zionists understood the emerging realities and concentrated on the demographic center of Jewish settlement west of the Jordan River. That same sense of realism would later lead the Zionist mainstream to accept the partition plan of 1947, even though they had voiced strong objections to various partition schemes in the past.

Revisionist Zionists, precursors of Israel's Likud Party, persisted in their claim that both sides of the river are Palestine and therefore ought to be included in any Jewish state. In the words of the Revisionist anthem: "Two sides of the Jordan; This is ours, and this too." At first, the creation of a truncated Jewish state, limited, as it were, to only part of mandated Palestine, did not discourage the most militant elements of the Revisionist camp. But over time, the demand for Transjordan has become increasingly muted, even in the most doctrinaire Revisionist circles. In that respect, at least, reality has finally tempered expectations among the very aged firebrands of Israel's right. But the notion that the East Bank is Palestine still persists. One recalls that in a previous political incarnation, Israel's Ariel Sharon called for the creation of a Palestinian state in Transjordan (to replace the ruling monarchy of Arabian origins). The West Bank would then be annexed by Israel, creating thereby two legitimate states: one for Jews from the river to the sea (plus the Golan), and one for Palestinians in the extensive lands east of the Jordan. This plan, never realistic or even desirable from the perspective of most Israelis, draws no attention at present from serious people on either side of the divide.

Palestinians have also had ambivalent feelings toward the Jordanian monarchy. During heavy fighting in 1948, the British-trained and -led Arab Legion captured most of the hill country in the West Bank. Following the end of hostilities, Abdallah, the reigning Jordanian monarch, formally annexed his extensive spoils of conquest, including the Old City and eastern sector of Jerusalem, the nearby villages, virtually all the major towns of the West Bank, and the cities of Bethlehem, Nablus, and Hebron (al-Khalil). Henceforth, the Hashemite Kingdom was comprised of Transjordan and the newly acquired bulge carved out of Western Palestine by its army, the Arab Legion. Wedged into the expanded Hashemite state was the heavily populated Jewish sector of West Jerusalem and some previously mixed, or largely Arab, neighborhoods of the western city and its environs, areas that were overrun by Jewish forces during the fighting. The annexation of territory in Cisjordan, made possible by the Arab Legion's successes in 1948, was not the result of an impetuous decision. Abdallah, a descendant of the Prophet's house (*ahl al-bayt*), had long desired to expand his largely desert domain and secure what he considered a proper place for himself and his family in the emerging Near East, be it part of neighboring Syria, an early objective, or, as it turned out, Western Palestine.

The expanded Jordanian state was not the first Arab polity with lands on both sides of the river. Muslim geographers of the Middle Ages refer to an administrative district (*jund*) called Jordan (*al-Urdunn*) that included not only lands east of the river but all of Lake Tiberius and the Galilee region, which is now part of the State of Israel. Al-Urdunn also included the lowlands flanking both sides of the river until the approaches to the Dead Sea, territory that is now shared by Israel, the Hashemite Kingdom, and the Palestinian Authority. That is, the jund of al-Urdunn, whose contours loosely resembled ancient Second Palestine, contained much of the West Bank annexed by Abdallah in modern times. If the king needed a case for annexing the West Bank, he had only to cite the Muslim geographers of the Middle Ages. As it was, the king, with tacit Israeli support, solidified his hold on the West Bank, much to the ire of his immediate Arab neighbors who had their own elaborate visions of a future Near East, be it a Fertile Crescent dominated by Iraq or a Greater Syria manipulated by the authorities in Damascus. In any case, the great losers in the events that transpired were the Arabs of Western Palestine. Rejecting partition for war in 1947–1948, the Palestinians expected to create an Arab state in all the mandated territory. In the end, they were left without any national domain—not even a truncated state in the areas of the mandate seized by Arab armies who fought on their behalf. The failure of the Palestinians to develop a national infrastructure and a leadership that could command the allegiance of a broad cross section of Palestinian Arab society left the indigenous Arabs of Palestine to suffer a disaster at the hands of their enemies and erstwhile friends.

As did the Arab Legion, the Egyptian army invaded Palestine to support the Arab cause. Badly trained, badly led, and badly supplied, the Egyptians performed poorly. At the conclusion of the 1949 armistice agreement, the retreating Egyptians were pocketed in Gaza City and a narrow slice of territory along the Mediterranean coast. There they remained, administering the Gaza Strip until 1967, except for a brief interlude following the Israeli victory in the Sinai Campaign of 1956. Ever since the time of the Pharaohs, the rulers of Egypt had taken a keen interest in Gaza and the coastal region. The so-called *via maris* (highway of the sea), was the most convenient and direct route from northern Africa to Southwest Asia. It also offered the best opportunity to invade Egypt, a land otherwise protected by natural barriers. As a result, Gaza and its environs has long been the springboard for armies moving both east and west. Prior to the 1948–1949 war, the last Egyptian regime to exercise authority in historic Palestine was that of Muhammad Ali, an Albanian officer who took control of Egypt over the first quarter of the nineteenth century. Then, in a direct challenge to the Ottoman Sultan, Muhammad Ali's troops marched along the coast and captured a large swath of historic Palestine in 1832. They held it for some eight years before being forced to withdraw. Moving in the other direction, the Israel Defense Force captured Gaza in 1956 and again in 1967. On both occasions they used the coast road to penetrate and then engulf the Sinai, Egypt's western defense perimeter.

Despite the strategic importance of Gaza and the adjoining coastal areas, the Egyptians made no attempt to declare the territory part of Egypt from 1948 to 1967. To the contrary, they even allowed for symbols of Palestinian national identity, but at no time did they plan for or allow the creation of a Palestinian state. The Palestinians in Gaza had to content themselves with a rump parliament and the formation of the Palestine Liberation Army, both tightly controlled by an Egyptian military governor acting on orders from Cairo. As a result, the Palestinians were denied statehood, even in those areas of the former mandate that remained under Arab control.

Palestinians who harbored hopes for a state of their own found Egyptian rule heavy-handed and distasteful but made no effort to rebel. There was no *intifada*, or uprising, comparable to the stone-throwers' uprising against Israeli authority in 1987, let alone the more deadly confrontations that began in 2000. Jordanian rule was looked upon as a mixed blessing. The Jordanians, in their wisdom, extended full citizenship to the Palestinians throughout the expanded kingdom. In contrast to the Palestinian refugees who settled in Gaza or fled the country for neighboring Arab lands where they remained, for the most part, stateless, Palestinians who made their way across the Jordan, as well as those who remained in the West Bank, were given opportunities for advancement. Many Palestinian notables rose to positions of prominence in the Jordanian government. In time, the Palestinian citizens of the state outnumbered the original Jordanians. Even the east side of the river teemed with Palestinians. And yet, during the nineteen years that Jordan ruled the West Bank, the Palestinians did not rise up or make any concerted effort to establish a state of their own. Keep in mind, Abdallah's annexation of Western Palestine was not formally recognized by a single Arab nation, not even the Hashemite monarchy of Iraq. Initially, only two states in the world community acknowledged the king's bold land grab to be legal: Pakistan and Jordan's patron, Great Britain.

The Israeli conquest of the West Bank in 1967 changed the Palestinians' outlook dramatically. At first, the Jordanian regime retained, with Israel's compliance, considerable influence on the West Bank. This was achieved through an elaborate system of patronage that benefited Israel, local Palestinians, and the Jordanian government alike. The system rested on an assumption shared by the Jordanians and Palestinians, though not expressed, let alone conceded by Israel: namely, that the Israeli occupation, offensive as it was to Muslim sensibilities, was bound to be temporary. As that became less and less likely, and the burden of occupation became more and more pronounced, Arabs living under the Israeli military rule not only challenged Israel's authority, but also sought to undermine the Jordanian regime on the East Bank. In 1970, a series of incidents led to extensive fighting between Jordanian forces and armed Palestinians throughout the kingdom. The rebellion, although quickly and brutally crushed, forced the ruling family to reevaluate its relationship with the Palestinians on both sides of the river. Some within the Jordanian government wished to maintain the Hashemite claim to the West Bank, others regarded the area a potential liability. Taking stock of rising nationalist sentiments among the Palestinians after the first intifada, King Hussein decided to relinquish his claim to the occupied territories. The move signified the monarchy's full support for the future creation of a Palestinian state in part of Cisjordan. The king's only remaining link to what had been Western Jordan was for him to be Guardian of Jerusalem's Temple Mount, a position which recalled the traditional role assigned his ancestors in the holy precincts of Arabia.

There is now a consensus among those who monitor events in the Near East. Virtually everyone believes that at some point in the not-too-distant future, the Palestinians will become an independent nation with a state of their own. The remaining question is how that state will be governed, what its boundaries are likely to be, and how it will manage relations with Israel and the rest of the Arab world. If the Palestinians are allowed to declare a state in most of the West Bank and all of Gaza, they will still be left with less than a quarter of the original Palestine mandate. That is even less than the state envisaged for them by the United Nations partition plan of 1947. With a truncated state and a burgeoning population—the Palestinians are among the most prolific people in the world—they might well look to Transjordan, with its Palestinian majority, as a future target for expansion. The historic jund of al-Urdunn may have contained parts of the

West Bank, but the jund of Filastin, whose name Muslim geographers traced back to the Philistines of the Bible, was an administrative district of geographical Palestine that extended as far as Amman. With that history, the Palestinians of modern times could well claim a sizable segment of what is today the Hashemite Kingdom of Jordan. The Hashemites will not sit idly if challenged on the East Bank. They will respond as they did in 1970. Nor is Israel likely to sanction any Arab attempt to overthrow the present Jordanian regime. When Syria invaded Jordan, Israel signaled Damascus that it was prepared to intervene in order to preserve the status quo. That warning was not taken lightly, even though the Syrians had long dreamed of a Greater Syria dominated by an authority situated in Damascus, as in ages past. After stiff Jordanian resistance, and the appearance of augmented Israeli forces along the Syrian border, the invasion force withdrew.

As a rule, Arab states have been wary when one of their own attempts to radically change the geographical and political map of the region. There is the fear that this will damage Arab unity, and, more particularly, that it will affect the delicate balance of power between Arab states. The last significant move to alter the political map was Iraq's short-lived annexation of Kuwait in 1991, an ill-conceived adventure that shattered lingering illusions of Arab unity and pitted Arabs against one another. Any attempt to reconfigure Palestine and/or the Hashemite Kingdom at the expense of another Arab state will no doubt have a similar effect on an already turbulent region. That said, there is still the danger that rampant ambition fused with ideological fervor may overwhelm political restraint.

THE ORIGINS OF ARAB-MUSLIM PALESTINE

There seem to be enough Palestines in the long history of the Near East to fuel the conflicting territorial ambitions of several Arab nation-states. Jordan, Syria, Lebanon, and the Palestinian Authority all have visions for the future of the Levant. Except for Lebanon, the Arab polities of the region are self-defined Islamic states, though not exclusively governed by Islamic law. Some Palestinian nationalists still give lip service to the concept of a secular-democratic state but, with well over 90 percent of the population Muslim and a powerful movement for Islamic revival controlling the current ruling body of the Palestinian nation, it is inevitable that an emerging Palestine will define itself to be no less an Islamic state than its regional neighbors. One would then think that Muslim revivalists might abandon the map of mandatory Palestine and turn instead to Islamic tradition when staking out present and future territorial claims. Why should the Arabs of Palestine validate a map of Christian Europeans who displaced, by force of arms, the reigning Muslim authority? What if, in the best of all worlds, they turned instead to Islamic geography in order to envision the contours of an emerging Palestinian state—that is to say, not a state limited in size by current or foreseeable political forces, regional and supraregional, but an idealized polity shaped by a vision of the Islamic past? What might a map of that idealized Palestine reveal and how would that map affect present-day political alignments?

Muslims first settled in historic Palestine when Arab tribesmen traversed the frontier of the Arabian Peninsula and conquered the Byzantine lands beyond. None of the medieval Arabic historians refer, however, to a conquest of Palestine (Filastin). The general rubric under which they report the early Byzantine campaigns is *futuh al-Sham*, literally, "the conquest of the Left Hand Land" or "conquest of the North." That is, if a tribesman in Arabia got his bearings by facing the rising sun, the land to his left would be situated directly north of him. Al-Sham thus became the Muslim Arabic term that referred to a large province composed of several subdistricts, a region that corresponded, more or less, to Syria-Palestina of Graeco-Roman times.

Suriya (also Suriyah), the Arabic name for the modern state of Syria, is also attested in medieval sources. One puzzling account indicates that Suriyah, as distinct from al-Sham, included the regions of Palestine (Filastin), Jordan (al-Urdunn), Damascus (Dimashq), and Homs (Hims), but not the area beyond al-Darb (ancient Derbe, the gateway to the Byzantine territory beyond the Euphrates). The land beyond al-Darb was designated al-Sham. Another source simply regards Suriyah as the equivalent of all of al-Sham. The name itself is derived from a Greek toponym, whose etymology goes back to Semitic *Sur*, the city of Sidon situated along the Lebanese coast. Filastin, or Palestine, was one of five subdistricts (jund) of al-Sham. The others were the aforementioned al-Urduun; Qinnasrin, with its capital at Aleppo (northern Syria); Homs (Central Syria); and Damascus (Dimashq), whose capital served as the administrative center for southern Syria as well as all of al-Sham. As did First Palestine in Roman-Byzantine times, early Filastin extended along a narrow coastal strip from Sinai toward the border of southern Lebanon. To be more precise, Filastin extended from Gaza to Acre. The area running north of Acre to the current Lebanese border was administered from Damascus. To the east, Filastin included, as did First Palestine, much of the hill country, and, moving beyond the Jordan, it stretched as far as Amman, the current capital of the Hashemite

Kingdom. Over the ensuing centuries, Filastin also embraced lands that had been part of Third Palestine, including the upper Negev Desert and segments of Transjordan as far south as the Gulf of Aqabah. Based on that historic map of early Islamic times, the current Palestinian Arabs could lay claim to much of Israel and neighboring Jordan, if they saw reason for doing so.

As it turns out, the early Islamic map of Palestine was not engraved in stone. After the defeat of the early Crusaders, who carved Christian kingdoms out of the Holy Land and its environs (1099–1291 C.E.), Muslim Palestine was reconfigured once again. Under the Mamluks, a praetorian dynasty based in Cairo (ca. 1250–1517 C.E.), Filastin, a subdistrict administered as before by the authorities in Damascus, was divided into six smaller regions named after particular cities: Lod (that is Ludd, the original Muslim capital of Filastin), Gaza, al-Quds (Jerusalem), Nablus, Hebron (al-Khalil), and Qaqun. Of these, only the location of Qaqun is uncertain. The contemporaneous geographer Yaqut (d. 1225 C.E.) describes it as either a fortified place near (adjoining?) Caesarea (the capital of Roman-Byzantine First Palestine) or near Ramle (the second capital of Filastin established by the Caliph Sulayman ibn 'Abd al-Malik in 715 C.E.). Juxtaposed on a Roman-Byzantine map of the region, all these cities, and presumably the wider administrative districts they represent, fall within the general boundaries of First Palestine.

The Ottoman Turks who captured historic Palestine in the sixteenth century C.E. rearranged its administration according to five districts (*sanjaq*) with Syria again the seat of provincial rule (w[v]ilayah). When drawing up the map of geographical Palestine, the Turks retained Gaza, Jerusalem, and Nablus, that is, the coast and the hill country, and added Lajjun (exact location unknown but seemingly in the Valley of Esdraelon) and Safed. Gaza, Jerusalem, and Nablus were situated in what had been First Palestine, the region that coincided, more or less, with the Islamic jund of Filastin. Lajjun and Safed were in Second Palestine, that which became part of the administrative district of al-Urdunn after the Arab-Muslim conquest. Responding to changing local conditions, the Ottomans continued to tinker with the component parts of historic Syria-Palestine.

In time, Islamic Filastin lost its discrete geographical identity (along with al-Urdunn), having been replaced by newer configurations of smaller subdistricts. On the eve of World War I, Europeans still referred to Palestine, which they often juxtaposed with references to the Holy Land. This was not so with the Turks, at least not for official purposes. Ottoman maps of the time show an administrative district (sanjaq) of Acre, which more or less corresponds to the medieval jund al–Urdunn, less the lands of the Golan; the sanjaq of Nablus; and the *mutassariflik* of Jerusalem, which was a separate entity, insofar as it was administered from the capital and not by a provincial governor. When combined, the Nablus and Jerusalem regions roughly equaled the old jund Filastin, but without the territory east of the Jordan. The administrative districts of Beirut, Acre, and Nablus were part of the province (w[v]ilayah) of Beirut. The Golan, often part of historic Palestine, was situated in the sanjaq of Damascus; the lands east of the Jordan midway through the Dead Sea were labeled the sanjaq of the Hawran. Transjordan from the southern half of the Dead Sea to the Gulf of Aqabah and the lands extending south into Northern Arabia and west in the southern half of the Negev Desert comprised the sanjaq of Ma'an. These districts were all part of the province (w[v]ilayah) of Syria. The British and French consolidated these districts when they arranged the map that has altered the history of the region—hence, the emergence of modern Syria and Lebanon, the re-emergence of Filastin, and the creation of Transjordan.

With all these geographic and administrative changes, it is clear that invoking the past to stake out specific claims to territory can be a dicey business. There have been numerous Palestines throughout the course of history, each with its own border and administrative structure. There has also been a Greater Syria (al-Sham) that embraced, at different times, what is today Lebanon, Israel, Jordan, the area governed by the Palestinian Authority, and also parts of southern Turkey and northwestern Iraq. If present circumstances are an indication of the future, any attempt to redraw modern borders based on premodern maps is certain to lead to highly diverse and contested claims throughout the region. These claims are bound, in turn, to exacerbate the existing disputes that have already led to much suffering and tragedy.

Among the peoples of the contemporary Near East seeking to legitimize their national domains, the Syrians are likely to draw the most troubling map of what their future state and its satellites should encompass. That is to say, they will draw the map that will most trouble their neighbors. Leaving aside the Crusader interlude, the concept of a Greater Syria that embraces much of Cisjordan, Transjordan, and the Levant has existed since Graeco-Roman times. As often as not, that geographical concept has been translated into historical reality. For ardent Syrian nationalists, the idea of re-creating a domain worthy of being a modern Greater Syria is compelling. The possibility of such a megastate concerns various parties who view an enlarged Syria as destabilizing an already fragile region. Given that Greater Syria would embrace territory that is today part and parcel of other nation-states, any expansion of Syrian influence is likely to be resisted by its immediate neighbors and by Arab states that do not share a common border with Syria but fear any extension of Syrian power. Any Syrian expansion is also certain to draw the attention of those segments of the world community anxious to retain some semblance of stability in the Near East. Under the late Hafiz al-Assad, the Syrians tried to translate the idea of a Greater Syria into a concrete political fact. The results were at best mixed. The Syrians, who had tens of thousands of troops in Lebanon, ruled that weak country in all but name since they helped put an end to the Lebanese Civil War in the 1970s. But they failed to bully Jordan into client status, and their leverage with the Palestinians, which at one time seemed great, has been seriously diminished with the creation of the Palestinian Authority. The Jewish state is a more complicated problem for Damascus. By any yardstick of power, military or economic, the Syrians have more reason to fear Israel than Israel has to fear them. Syria's territorial ambitions thus remain compromised; the advocates of a Greater Syria are likely to be frustrated well into the foreseeable future, if not longer.

In contrast to the Syrians, for whom hope of an enlarged state springs eternal, the Jordanians seem reconciled to the loss of the West Bank. Some might even say there is relief over jettisoning the Palestinians. In any case, the Jordanians have other matters that currently occupy their concerns. The current King Abdallah was an unlikely choice to rule the kingdom. The heir apparent, the able Crown Prince Hassan, was disgraced at the eleventh hour, and the son favored by the dying King Hussein was too young to mount the throne. Abdallah seems to have done well, but he has yet to achieve the stature of his father, a man of political vision and courage, whose reputation increased markedly over time. Nor does the current Abdallah seem as ambitious or proud as his namesake and great-grandfather, the emir and then monarch who wished to redeem the family's honor by acquiring a kingdom worthy of the Prophet's house. At one time Abdallah I had designs on Damascus, but after recognizing political realities, he settled for his desert kingdom. It is difficult to imagine circumstances in which the Jordanian ruling family will invoke history on behalf of territorial expansion in Western Palestine, let alone in what is today Syria. It is more likely that they will be forced to navigate through turbulent political waters in order to maintain their hold on the East Bank. Nevertheless, the royals, if nothing else, have shown themselves to be extremely resilient. The more difficult the situation, the more inclined the family is to close ranks. Moreover, were there to be an actual threat to their rule, the Hashemites could likely count on the support of the West, and, more significantly, their neighbor Israel. In either case, such support is likely to thwart the ambitions of predator states.

Judging by current polls, most Israelis would settle for a state that corresponds to the Israel of pre-June 1967 but with border rectification to include the major highways and the bedroom communities situated just east of the Green Line (that is, the armistice line of 1949). They also demand that Jerusalem remain the undivided capital of the Jewish state, with arrangements to allow for the religious and even political sensibilities of Christians and Muslim Arabs. A sizable portion of Israel's Jews wants to retain at least the major settlements of the West Bank. Most would accept compromises, particularly regarding the smaller remote settlements, if satisfied that it will lead to an end of active conflict with the Arabs. The last government of Israel led by Ariel Sharon adopted a policy of "disengagement," and unilaterally withdrew settlers and soldiers from the Gaza Strip. The current government of Ehud Olmert has embraced a policy of "convergence" in which Israel will withdraw from many parts of the West Bank, establishing the future borders of the state with or without a negotiated settlement. The majority of Israelis are also reconciled to a Palestinian state within Gaza and those parts of the West Bank that Israel does not retain. To be sure, no Israelis trust the current leaders of the Palestinian Authority, Islamists committed in principle to the destruction of the Jewish state. Few Israelis have confidence that any Arab leadership of the future will be able to control the militants among the Palestinians. Be that as it may, only Israeli fringe groups heed right-wing Zealots who call for expelling the Arabs from all the Land of Israel, that is, from the sea to the river. Transjordan has not been coveted by the Zionists for many decades, nor is it likely to be in decades to come. The phantasmagorical Arab fear of a Greater Israel stretching from the Nile to the Euphrates has never been on the Zionist drawing board.

All the aforementioned polities carved out of Greater Syria must balance historic ambitions against the realities of the moment and likely moments to come. None can impose a heavy-handed solution on the others combined; therefore, all have to practice a politics of restraint. The Authority (*sultah*), which represents the interests of Palestine's stateless Arabs, has perhaps the weakest of all hands to play, but its hopes spring eternal even in the most trying of times. Indeed, one might say, the less chance the Palestinians have of succeeding, the more likely they are to abandon compromise. Since the rejection of Partition and the ensuing catastrophe of 1947–1948, Palestinian appetites have included, from time to time, not one but several Palestines: a Palestinian state in the West Bank and Gaza delineated by the pre-June 1967 borders with Jerusalem as its capital; a secular-democratic state in all of mandated Palestine, a Palestinian state in the West Bank and Gaza alongside a secular-democratic state within Israel's 1967 borders, that is, a non-Jewish Israel that will admit the descendants of the Arab refugees who fled that area in 1947–1948; a truncated Jewish state representing the original map of the partition plan of 1947 (complete with a large Arab population); and an Islamic state in all of mandated Palestine in which Jews (and Christians) will be subjected to Muslim law and treated as a tolerated minority governed by the statutes of that law. Most recently, a "new" plan has been advanced to resolve the present impasse and propel the Palestinians toward their long hoped for statehood. Proposed by Palestinian prisoners currently in Israeli custody, figures who run the political gamut of Palestinian politics, the plan has aroused great interest among Arabs. It calls for a two-part solution: (1) a withdrawal by Israel to the 1967 borders (without boundary rectification or consideration of Jewish sensibilities as regards Jerusalem); and (2) the right of Arabs to return to their previous homes in Israel proper. There is not much in this or any of the aforementioned Arab plans that gives Israelis cause for optimism in contemplating the future.

How the geographical contours of Palestine are reconfigured in the future is still a moot question. One thing is clear: Modern history has made a shambles of old alignments and territorial claims; it has also complicated long-existing group identities and loyalties, and not only in the Near East. It is less than two hundred years since numerous German-speaking principalities of central Europe were forcefully combined to form a modern German state with a newly shaped identity that commanded the allegiance of its disparate parts and peoples, twice too often for their own good and that of the world. At more or less the same time, modern Italy was molded from even more diverse regional entities speaking local and regional tongues so different from one another that a common Italian language had to be created to unify them. The forces that occasioned nation building in Europe were centrifugal as well as centripetal. The shattering of the Austro-Hungarian Empire as a consequence of defeat in the Great War initiated a process comparable to that which befell its defeated ally, the empire of the Ottoman sultans. The very heterogeneous population of the Hapsburg Empire included subgroups of extremely diverse linguistic, ethnic, and religious backgrounds. In accordance with Wilsonian principles of self-determination, these subgroups were given license to form nation-states of their own after the war, often amid considerable tension, because once the blanket of empire was removed, the new states had to accommodate mixed populations, not always sympathetic to one another. The rise of the modern nation-state was seen by progressive thinkers as a positive breakthrough in the history of the West. They may have been right. They did not foresee, however, the consequences of a dissolved empire on the continent any more than they foresaw the consequences of the Ottoman collapse in the Arab world. The process of nation building where no nation-states or perhaps even distinct nations existed has not run its course. The democracies of Western Europe are moving toward integration, and may well attract full partners from European lands further to the east, creating thereby a polity that in time might well be unique in the history of the continent. To accomplish that, they will have to lay aside traditional animosities that breed conflict and have bred conflict in the past.

No doubt it would be better for all the peoples of the Near East were they to take stock of reality and reassess their views of the past in anticipating the future of their newly minted national polities. Both geography and history supply enough latitude for serious accommodation among nation-states, if they are prepared to temper the appeal to the past when envisioning sacred and political space for the future. That will not be easy for the Palestinians; they are a people displaced and dispossessed, but they have powerful memories of villages and homes that no longer exist or are occupied by others.

No one has argued more eloquently for the essential Arab character of Palestine and with so much attention to detail and with such great passion than 'Arif al-'Arif, who died in 1973. We should not misunderstand al-'Arif's magisterial project. The acknowledged custodian of Palestinian memory did not undertake six decades of painstaking research on Arab centers of settlement to score debater's points with Zionist spokesmen or ingratiate his people with Western audiences. His voice was that of a Palestinian intended for other Palestinians. His major publications, all written in Arabic, are avidly consumed in the Arab world. By preserving Palestinian memory and recording the history of numerous sites, many left behind by his exiled brethren during the fighting of 1947–1948, he presents the Palestinians with an historical identity and a map with which to reconstitute their national existence. To coin a rather awkward expression, al-'Arif might be considered the quintessential "Arab Zionist."

'Arif al-'Arif was a public official and Arab intellectual, but his particular appeal to the distant and more recent past resonates strongly in all levels of Palestinian society. His work is continued at present through the publication of books and pamphlets calling attention to the history of various Arab families and Palestinian villages, many of which no longer exist. There

is considerable irony in this continuing effort to trumpet the Arab character of the Holy Land These commemorative books remind us of similar
works written by Jewish survivors of the Holocaust to preserve the memory of their destroyed life in the villages and hamlets of Europe. There is,
however, a marked difference in these literary enterprises. The Jews, many
of whom have begun life anew in Israel, mourn a world they neither expect nor, for that matter, wish to re-create in its original geographical setting. For the Arabs of Palestine, the books promote a world that should, indeed will, be reborn.

3

"MY LAND [*BILADI*]"

The Formation of Palestinian National Consciousness
and the Quest for a Modern Nation-State

Given the ambiguous geography of Palestine in Muslim times, we might well ask what, if anything, defined Palestinian identity from the Arab conquest until the rise of modern nationalism. In other words, who were the Palestinians, if we can, indeed, speak of Palestinians before the twentieth century?

The surest mark of identity among Arabs is the importance attached to extended names. Naming in the Near East became a rather complicated process designed to honor ancestors and preserve a sense of solidarity among kinsmen. Before Arab practice adopted modern European conventions by stressing only proper and family names, the extended Arab name consisted of at least four, possibly five, six, or even seven elements. Usually, a first-born male child would be called after his grandfather, say Muhammad. In addition to his proper name, the aforementioned Muhammad would be given a patronymic at birth, that is, a prefixed nickname in which the name of his future first born son was designated, usually after the newborn's father, say 'Abdallah. And so, the most recent male addition to the extended household was called Abu 'Abdallah, Muhammad (that is, Muhammad, the father of [Abu] the [future] 'Abdallah). A third element of the name preserved the genealogy of the family. Hence, Abu 'Abdallah, Muhammad became ibn (son of) 'Abdallah ibn Muhammad, often with many generations of paternal ancestors added. Family lines, whether real or imagined, were traced back to remote times. Muslims thus claim the Prophet's genealogy began with Ishmael, the son of Abraham and the progenitor of the Northern Arabs. Such Arab family trees can be compared with the genealogical lists of the book of Genesis, which signified to readers of biblical scripture links between various peoples of the world and their distant ancestors.

An Arab tribesman, or someone affiliated with an Arab tribal group, would also be identified by ties of kinship, say al-Tamimi, "the Tamimite," after the tribe of Tamim or, as in the case of the contemporary Jordanian monarchs, al-Hashimi, after the Banu Hashim, Muhammad's clan. Other nicknames might appear to record an unusual physical feature or trait, such as "the One Eyed," "the Ambidextrous," or, as one caliph was called, "the Ass," not for lack of intelligence but because the wild ass of the desert was a symbol of pride and fortitude. A family's occupational status might also be added as a marker of identification, for example, al-Khayyam, "the Tent Maker." Designations of this sort did not always apply to the person so named—not everyone named Goldsmith actually smelts and fashions precious metals, nor does every Baker produce breads and pastries. The occupational marker is often no more than a footnote to family history, if that.

Most important for our purposes is the element of the name that signifies links to a particular region, or a more narrowly defined location. Here, too, we must be careful not to read too much into the pattern of naming. A geographical designation, say al-Jaza'iri, "a man of al-Jazirah" (a large province abutting medieval Iraq), did not necessarily mean that the bearer of this name actually was resident in that province or that he was even born there. It does indicate, however, a real or desired family connection and, beyond that, a sense of meaningful identification with a particular place. Unlike Americans, who might not be aware that their family names are actually derivative of places where ancestors lived in foreign climes, Arabs took keen notice of geographical markers and wore them proudly.

It is surprising, then, that in the vast compendium of Arabic biographical literature, a body of material that contains tens if not hundreds of thousands of names, often with extensive genealogies, we have yet to come across a single reference to an individual whose genealogical origins mark him al-Filastini, or al-Filasti, "the Palestinian." Yaqut's multivolume geographical dictionary (*Mu'jam al-buldan*), a work penned in the thirteenth century C.E., contains thousands of entries, often accompanied by the genealogical names to which each place name gives rise. Most often, he cites examples of individuals bearing that genealogical label. When writing under the rubric Filastin, Yaqut indicates that a Palestinian should be referred to as al-Filasti, but oddly enough, the great geographer and genealogist gives not a single example of anyone so-named. In the equally vast historical literature of premodern times, we have found only one individual bearing a geographical affiliation to Palestine, in that case al-Filastini. There are numerous Iraqis, Masris (Egyptians), Shamis (Syrians), Maghribis (North

Africans), Andalusis (inhabitants of the Muslim Iberian Peninsula), and the like. Each of these is a name derived from a large, self-contained region of the Islamic world, the vast territorial expanses that were considered truly major provinces. An exhaustive search of the literature, both printed texts and manuscripts, may well yield additional Palestinians, but the virtual absence of Filastini or Filasti, and for so long a time, requires some additional comment.

The absence of these last genealogical markers does not imply at all that there was no Palestine in the Muslim geography of premodern times. Perhaps Filastin—unlike, say, Syria—was too small an administrative entity to serve as a significant marker of identification. At the same time, its geography might have been too all-embracing for local inhabitants to identify as their native abode. When identifying with a particular place, most Arabs preferred to be linked with smaller settlements. Genealogical markers derived from cities, towns, and villages, including those in Palestine itself, are far more numerous than names linked to the major provinces of the Islamic realm. Some examples are Baghdadi, Dimashqi (Damascus), and Halabi (Aleppo), and within Palestine, Nabulsi (Nablus), Qudsi (Jerusalem), Tabarani (Tiberius), and Khalili (Hebron), to name but a few. Still more numerous are names derived from sections of cities. Even small, self-contained neighborhoods frequently appear as genealogical labels. The Khatib al-Baghdadi's monumental history (*Ta'rikh*) of Baghdad, in reality a biographical dictionary that fills fourteen volumes in the printed edition, frequently reports the subject's full name. We discover among the more than eight thousand entries many Iraqis and, to be sure, many more Baghdadis, but far more individuals are identified according to specific neighborhoods—even the nooks and crannies of the city are well represented. That tendency to identify with more narrowly defined locations (as well as discrete ethnic and family groups) remains powerfully imbedded in the consciousness of today's Arabs, including the Palestinians. We have already noted that from the very outset of Islam, there has been a tension between the idealized concept of a universal Islamic community (ummah), and the reality of highly diverse Muslim societies with local, ethnic, and linguistic loyalties. The same tensions existed within circumscribed geographical locations and even within cities and towns, as discrete neighborhoods demanded loyalty of their inhabitants. Before the creation of the modern nation-state, Arabs tended to identify most closely with their families, extended clans, and their urban neighborhoods and rural villages. Now more than ever, they adopt a range of multiple identities. Despite a newfound sense of nationhood, residual loyalty to a smaller societal unit remains extremely powerful, more

powerful indeed than many, if not most, current observers are wont to acknowledge.

What does this suggest about today's Palestinians? It seems remarkable
that without ever having had a national polity, language, or historic identity
that could be described as distinctively Palestinian, the current generation
of Palestinian Arabs has literally invented and legitimized Palestinian nationhood. It was only some thirty-five years ago that the then Prime Minister of Israel Golda Meir asked to be shown a representative Palestinian, as
if to say, there is no Palestinian nation to speak of and, therefore, there are
no Palestinians. No serious Israeli, reflecting the current state of affairs,
would embrace such a view. Palestinians have succeeded in forging a sense
of nationhood that for the moment transcends the divisiveness of local Arab
society, an accomplishment of considerable magnitude that generates enormous emotional force.

THE GROWTH OF PALESTINIAN NATIONAL
CONSCIOUSNESS: ORIGINS TO 1967

How has that sense of national consciousness managed to evolve in a society marked by multiple identities and allegiances? What were the internal
and external stimuli that gave shape to Palestinian self-imagining? What was
the convenient point of departure, the moment at which one can begin to
trace the evolution of the modern Palestinian nation, and how have residual memories, real and invented, influenced this proud Arab people as they
have moved toward the statehood that they and their well-wishers have long
desired?

Of the many works that address these queries, directly or indirectly—
a bibliography in European languages alone would fill all the pages of this
chapter—two are particularly noteworthy: Rashid Khalidi's *Palestinian Identity* (New York, 1997) and Yehoshua Porat's two-volume study, *The Emergence of the Palestinian-Arab National Movement 1918–1929* (London, 1974)
and *The Palestinian Arab National Movement 1929–1939* (London, 1977).
The former is an interesting and highly reflective intellectual history, the
latter a thorough and richly detailed study of the evolution of Palestinian
politics and society. The two books, one written by an Arab, the other by
an Israeli, complement each other and form a convenient starting point for
any serious investigation of Palestinian nationhood.

Khalidi, the scion of an eminent Palestinian family long distinguished
for intellectual pursuits and public service, begins his investigation in the

late Ottoman period. That is, he starts with the last quarter of the nineteenth century, an age marked by substantive changes in the heartland and Arabic-speaking provinces of the empire, many of them stimulated by the challenge of Europe and the desire to imitate European institutions. The author is too responsible an historian to claim that a distinctive Palestinian national consciousness congealed at the time. Nor is he about to join those scholars who suggest an 1834 uprising that broke out in Palestine's central highlands represents the first putative stirrings of national sentiment. The 1834 revolt was occasioned by the forced conscription of the local peasantry. By filling the ranks of the governor's army, the fellaheen (*fallahin*), or rural agriculturalists, would have become cannon fodder in a war not of their choosing and hardly to their liking. In effect, they had become pawns in a conflict between the Albanian family that ruled Egypt and Palestine and the Ottoman Sultan who was in theory, though not in fact, their sovereign. However much one sympathizes with the plight of the peasants and perhaps even the landowners who needed them at work rather than dying in some distant campaign, one cannot detect any sense of Palestinian national consciousness from these rebellious stirrings. The very notion of a nation-state or even a nation did not exist in the Near East of the 1830s. Indeed, despite continued nineteenth- and early twentieth-century references to Filastin and Falastin in official correspondence, writings, and speech, Palestine did not reemerge as a discrete geographical or administrative entity until the British mandate took hold in the 1920s. Some may wish to argue that the uprising of 1834 represents at least the expression of protonationalism, but by the same token, that argument could be made for regional or local revolts taking place at any time in the Fertile Crescent and beyond. For those seeking to identify the onset of Palestinian nationalism, 1834 is a nonstarter.

It is true that Khalidi notes the role of the peasantry, but his peasants lived half a century later and more; their concerns were not forced conscription but the Zionists who purchased the lands they tilled from absentee Arab landlords, thus setting the course for a major dispute and then conflict between Arabs and Jews. Whatever their grievance, the rural Arabs cited by Khalidi did not articulate a sense of national consciousness at the onset of the Zionist project in the 1880s, nor were they likely to have displayed feelings of solidarity that bound them inextricably to their fellow countrymen. Their allegiances were much more narrowly defined. If anything, there was a growing rift between the rural population and the leading families of the cities and towns. A wider declaration of national purpose was left to the urban notables, worldly individuals who sowed the seeds of a Palestinian identity that would evolve over the following decades.

When the Ottomans established a separate district (*mutassariflik*) of Jerusalem in 1887, a political move that was part of a more extensive plan to divide Greater Syria, they gave the local officials direct access to the Istanbul government. These officials were in turn largely recruited from local Arab notables (*a'yan*). Unlike Damascus and other provincial capitals where large numbers of Turkish officials were posted, Jerusalem had an administration that was distinctively Arab in character and indigenous to that specific setting. The same was true of Nablus, the third-largest urban settlement in Ottoman Palestine after Jerusalem and Jaffa. Many leading Nabulsis had been educated in Istanbul, and some were even schooled in Europe, both of which were valuable assets. Not so tightly knit to great families capable of wielding political influence, the leading men of Nablus were trusted by the Ottomans to comply with official policy and were thus much sought after by the last sultan to administer the affairs of the city. That trust aside, the Nabulsis, like the Jerusalemites and others, championed the cause of the Arab nation.

We must be careful, however, when speaking of the roots of a distinctive Palestinian nationalism. In the early twentieth century, Khalidi's Palestinians were still part of a wider Arab national movement, a collection of individuals and groups who identified with an extended region that embraced inter alia territories that would later become the mandates of Syria, Lebanon, Palestine, and the British-controlled Emirate of Transjordan. In sum, a distinctive Palestinian nationalism evolved out of what was originally a more broadly conceived sense of the Arab nation. In the Arabic-speaking provinces of the Fertile Crescent, a new if loosely defined Arab feeling of commonality was being shaped by an Arabic print culture that first took root in the nineteenth century. In addition to an efflorescence of Arabic letters, a very lively press discussed the vital issues of the day and disseminated news of the Arab provinces and the world beyond. In such fashion, developments throughout the Ottoman realm and even Europe came to the attention of eager readers. Among the various topics discussed by Arab intellectuals and public figures was the problematic relationship between the Arabic-speaking peoples of the Ottoman Empire and the ruling Turkish Sultan.

Reformist Turks were well aware of tensions generated by nascent Arab nationalist sentiment. The Young Turks, revolutionaries who challenged the established authority of the reigning sultan in 1908 and then deposed him the following year, perceived of an Ottoman Empire that could accommodate all of its Arabic-speaking subjects. Christians as well as Muslim Arabs would embrace and be embraced by an accepting form of "Ottomanism" that transcended more narrowly defined loyalties to villages, towns, regions, and ethnic and religious groups. Leading Arab nationalists who were in contact with the Young Turks spoke at first of reform and even autonomy within the Empire, but not of total independence, let alone clearly defined individual Arab states or protostates. The initial Turkish concern for Arab sensibilities did not lead, however, to a greater acceptance of the Arabic-speaking peoples and their needs. Reforms were not forthcoming; quite the opposite occurred: The revolution of 1908 led to the increasing Turkification of the Ottoman state, both in the imperial heartland and beyond. As a result, the majority of the Arab nationalists, aware of the continuing success of national movements in the rebellious Balkan provinces, considered opposing the imperial order. But it was only during the Great War of 1914–1918 that a loose coalition of Arab tribesmen and leaders actually revolted against the sultan. They did so at the behest of the British, who promised them some form of independence within Arabia and the Ottoman provinces of the Fertile Crescent. When the Ottoman Empire collapsed after World War I, Arab concerns turned to unfulfilled promises and European colonial rule. Even then, the talk was not of a series of independent Arab states but of a single Arab-led government centered in Damascus. Regarding the Palestinians, it was only when the British reestablished Palestine as an administrative entity with clearly defined borders that the local Arabs created a distinctive political movement of their own with broad appeal and, most important, explicit territorial claims.

Still, any meaningful discussion of modern Palestinian nationalism begins with the period and the society that attracts Khalidi's attention: the late nineteenth and, more particularly, the early twentieth century. The world that fascinates this author is that which has captivated his extended family. For generations, his relatives have been gifted men of letters. Not surprisingly, his interest in writing about Palestinian nationalism draws him to intellectual history that he presents in a lively and engaging fashion. Building on his doctoral dissertation and other researches of the 1970s—projects on nationalist stirrings in Syria, Lebanon, and Palestine before World War I— he fashions a compelling narrative constructed from a wide range of literary sources. The author has pored over newspapers, journals, memoirs, and of special interest, private correspondence, much of it rare material found in the family's magnificent Jerusalem library. The project was originally conceived to be a comprehensive history of Palestine going back two centuries, as if there were throughout that period a discrete geographical entity of that name and a more or less distinct Palestinian people to match. Unforeseen circumstances forced Khalidi to reduce the scope of his broad inquiry. He was called back to the world of politics where he had spent several years early in his career.

The Khalidis are not only men of letters. This family, which traces its Jerusalem roots back generations upon generations, also takes seriously the notion of public service. They are true exemplars of Arab notables if one thinks of notables in the best sense of the term. The son of a diplomat, Rashid Khalidi first served his people as an official in the Beirut nerve center of the Palestine Liberation Organization (PLO). The experience exposed him to the corruption and highhandedness of the political leadership, which he acknowledged in public forums—an act of no small courage. After leaving politics, his energies went into research and teaching, primarily at the University of Chicago where for some years he served as director of its prestigious Center for Middle East Studies. (He is now situated at Columbia). A most eloquent and effective spokesman for the Palestinian cause, his frequently sought commentary on regional issues is always informed by a historian's perspective. When he was about to embark on his aforementioned history of modern Palestine in the early 1990s, he accepted, if somewhat reluctantly, an invitation to serve as adviser to various Palestinian peace delegations. Although his return to politics in no way signaled abandoning his academic career, the ambitious history of Palestine that he contemplated gave way to a truncated study tracing the construction of national consciousness in what might loosely be described as a period of nascent Palestinian nationalism. In essence, the author's detailed narrative ends with the years shortly after World War I, that is, with the onset of mandatory rule. A last segment titled "The Disappearance and Reemergence of Palestinian Identity" brings the story up to date, if in a rather sketchy fashion.

Although Khalidi sees modern Palestinian identity as an evolving phenomenon, his readers might well conclude that it was already established before the onset of British colonial rule and the challenge of increased Zionist settlement and organization after the Great War. Seen from that perspective, the Palestinian nation has not emerged merely in response to those powerful external stimuli but is at heart the earlier creation of a people linked by deep yearnings for self-rule in a distinctive land they call and have called their own over generations.

Arab nationalists today may owe a great deal to the early intellectuals of whom Khalidi writes with such respect and affection. There is, nevertheless, a gap between intellectuals of late Ottoman times musing broadly or discussing specific issues of the moment and a political movement whose clearly articulated program has captured the imagination and, more important, the loyalty and active participation of an entire people. Contrary to Khalidi's claim that by the early part of the twentieth century much of Palestine's (Muslim Arab) population imagined itself as a political community with clear boundaries and rights to sovereignty, there does not seem to be convincing evidence of a Palestinian nationalist movement with distinct territorial claims before World War I. Neither his nor any other data reveal that there was in late Ottoman times a movement capable of mobilizing many, if not most, of the elements of Palestinian society in common cause, or indeed that there was a cause commonly perceived by all Palestinians. There was surely none capable of uniting them in polity. What Khalidi describes are at best seedlings or perhaps only seeds that slowly grew into the energizing force of today's Palestinian nationalism. He says as much himself when he writes, "Local patriotism could not yet be described as nation-state nationalism," and then adds, "The prerequisites for modern nationalism did not yet exist, notably the means for a political leadership to mobilize large numbers of people and rapidly win them over to a single set of ideas, especially the idea that they partook of the same fate and were a single community" (32). In the end, Khalidi notes that the evolution of national consciousness among the Palestinians has been painstaking, uneven, and marked by competition with other loyalties. Arguably, that is true even today. Be that as it may, the seeds or seedlings of what was to become a genuine Palestinian nationalism were likely sown or planted by Khalidi's intellectuals of the time.

Whether those seeds would have sprouted if the Ottoman Empire had survived and altered its relations with the Arabic-speaking provinces—that is, if it had given the latter, particularly the peoples of what had been a greater Syria, a larger share in the administration of the state and a degree of real autonomy—is an open question. As Khalidi believes the nationalist program was broadly conceived even then, his answer to that question is likely to be yes. Some might argue otherwise. In either case, we are dealing with conjecture. Allowing for that, we might wish to consider another contrafactual possibility. What might have happened if Britain had obtained a mandate for the entire Levant and reconstituted much of historic Greater Syria with its capital in Damascus? Would the peoples of the Palestinian subdistricts have assumed a Syrian national identity, and if so, would that have superceded any local patriotism among Arab nationalists? Amin al-Husseini, the firebrand Palestinian nationalist who vociferously opposed British rule and Zionist settlement from the 1920s through the 1940s, was in premandatory times an advocate of Syrian nationalism. After the British installed their ally, the Emir Feisal, as king of a fledgling, semi-independent

Arab government in Damascus, an event that took place in late 1918, many Palestinian notables favored becoming part of a new Greater Syria. In 1920, there was a wave of boisterous and even bloody demonstrations combining anti-Jewish sentiments with support on behalf of Feisal and unification with Syria. The entire venture collapsed when, shortly thereafter, the French supplanted the British and took control of Syria and Lebanon, thus aborting any prospects of a truly independent Arab state in the Levant. Uniting under a Syrian banner was no longer a realistic option, but there were Arabs, Palestinians among them, who referred to the region of the Palestine mandate as "Southern Syria" and were still willing to pursue the goal of union in the early 1930s.

In contrast, there were notables opposed to union from the outset. Was their opposition influenced by long-held historic feelings to a land called Filastin? Put somewhat differently, did Arabs raised in late Ottoman Palestine display palpable loyalty to such a land, as Khalidi strongly suggests? If that were indeed the case, how did these loyalties compete, if at all, with powerful attachments to specific villages, towns, and tribal domains? What special allegiance, if any, did the inhabitants of modern Palestine have to an ancient land steeped in monotheist history and revered by Jews and Christians as well as the Muslim faithful?

Khalidi has much to say about the special importance of Jerusalem and more generally of Palestine as a land sacred to Muslims. About that, much has been written over the ages. For a millennium and more, Muslims have resonated to traditions of particular holy sites and, by extension, to a geographically ambiguous "Holy Land" (*al-ard al-Maqdis* or *al-ard al-muqaddasah*), a territorial expanse that Arabic geographers equated with the jund of Filastin, that subdistrict of Muslim Syria known in Graeco-Roman times as First Palestine (see chapter 2). However much loyalty Filastin elicited among the local inhabitants, in traditional Islamic literature, the sanctity of the individual sites, places such as Jerusalem (al-Quds) and Hebron (al-Khalil), transcended that of the land as a whole. There are no known tracts titled Fada'il (The Virtues of) Filastin, or even Fada'il al-ard al-Maqdis or Fada'il al-ard al-muqaddasah. Narrowly defined Muslim visions of Holy Land geography did not encompass the Islamic subdistricts of the north and south, areas that were included in mandated Palestine and that in Graeco-Roman times corresponded to Second and Third Palestine. On the other hand, the definitions of al-ard al-muqaddasah preserved by early Qur'an commentary (al-ard al-muqaddasah is first mentioned in Qur'an 5:21 in connection with the Israelite conquest of Canaan) refer to Greater Syria;

the geographically limited [jund of] Filastin; other areas in Transjordan; the city of Jericho; and even the holy ground of Mount Sinai, which by any account is not part of historic Palestine.

The traditional Muslim mapping of the "sacred land" and the map of Palestine that was ultimately embraced by a modern Arab nationalist movement reflect geographical conceptions of a very different sort. Still, that does not diminish the emotional appeal of modern Palestine as holy land to Muslims now seeking a state. Early on, Arab nationalists were genuinely moved by the sacred character of the land and were prone to cite that sacred character in articulating their claims, especially when these claims confronted Zionist activity.

In 1910, the Zionists arranged for the purchase of land in al-Fulah, gateway to the fertile Jezreel Valley. Now the major Israeli regional center known as Afula, al-Fulah (understood by medieval Muslim geographers as an Arabic toponym meaning "the bean") has a long history dating back to the fourth millennium B.C.E. That ancient history was, of course, unknown to Arabs at the time of the proposed sale. What Arabs identified at al-Fulah were the remains of a Crusader fortress called la Feve, "the bean," a place purportedly captured by Saladin in his war against the Franks. To have reclaimed this place with Muslim blood in the twelfth century only to sell it back in the twentieth to unbelievers, in this case Jews, was regarded as a sacrilege that undermined Muslim hegemony over sacred land. As a result, the transaction became a cause celebre among the local Arab notables, and they pressed the issue with the Ottoman authorities, but to no avail. The incident may speak to the nationalist concerns of present-day Palestinians; it may have affected the local patriotism of Arab notables in 1910–1911. But would the sale of this land parcel to Jews have drawn as much original attention had it not been the al-Fulah of Saladin's campaign to rid the Holy Land of unwelcome infidels eight centuries earlier? The debate over al-Fulah raises the broad question of how religious sensibilities impinged on the formation of a nascent Palestinian national consciousness.

Even before the upsurge of Zionist immigration at the outset of British rule, there was much to rankle the religiously sensitive Muslims in Greater Syria's southern regions. By the mid-nineteenth century, Europeans and Americans as well had rediscovered the Holy Land; some fifty years later, they peppered the landscape. While these foreigners spoke of the Holy Land, they also referred out of habit to Palestine, thus giving added life to a geographical label no longer used for administrative purposes by the ruling Turks (see chapter 4). Whether in Palestine or the Holy Land, men and women of means, stimulated by curiosity and a need to travel the world, retraced the steps of their biblical ancestors in grand style. Others came as pious pilgrims, their path made easy by steamships that safely sailed the Mediterranean and reputable travel agencies with local branch offices like that of Thomas Cook. European missionaries were added to an already sizable mix of Christian clergy. With the foreign missionaries came private schools with Christian subject matter and European curriculums. The Europeans also brought with them Western banking and business acumen. The introduction of a railroad, made possible by the invention of the steam engine in the West, reduced travel time between certain parts of the country and linked the Holy Land with Arab lands beyond. Be it for business, pleasure, or religious purposes, the land of three faiths became more easily accessible to those seeking to visit or reside permanently. By the end of the last quarter of the nineteenth century, Palestine, a rather sleepy backwater of the Ottoman Empire, was clearly experiencing change, much of it clearly influenced by increased contacts with the West.

To protect their varied interests in the Holy Land, the European states were able to establish consulates in Jerusalem. Among their various concerns, the consuls took a keen interest in the long-rooted Christian communities that graced the local landscape. Disputes among diverse Christian groups led to the intervention of the European powers who, identifying with different disputants, interfered in what should have been solely the concern of the Ottoman administration. The sultan, much weakened by a broad chain of events within the Ottoman Empire, was in no position to dismiss European interference. And so, Palestine was increasingly exposed to direct as well as indirect foreign influence.

There were also learned Jewish scholars and pietists of various sorts that made their way to Palestine, called by them "the Land of Israel." Some stayed permanently; some lived off a dole provided by Jewish communities abroad. A chief rabbi was appointed by the Ottomans in recognition of the growing numbers of Jews and their rising communal needs. Wealthy Jewish benefactors from Europe took direct responsibility for establishing a host of Jewish institutions while supporting others already in existence. These included hospitals and schools based on modern European models. Then there were the early Zionists who established new settlements rather than live among their Muslim and Christian neighbors in the established religious centers of Jerusalem, Safed, Hebron, and Tiberius. In 1909, the all-Jewish city of Tel Aviv was founded on sand dunes directly south of Jaffa, the main port of Ottoman Palestine. In short order, Tel Aviv became a heavily populated, thoroughly modern city that rivaled its Arab neighbor.

By the mid-nineteenth century, the Muslims were a minority in Jerusalem. In the city that Muslims declared to be equal in status to Mecca and Medina—the holiest of all cities in the Islamic world—the Jews had become the largest group, followed by the Christians. By 1865, fully half of the city population was Jewish. New Jewish and Christian quarters sprang up; old religious buildings were refurbished. The community of unbelievers, hitherto held in quiet contempt by the Muslims, was showing signs of unexpected vigor while the Ottoman authorities did nothing. The influx of Jews from Europe was especially troubling as the Zionists did not hide their intention of reconstituting the Jewish people in its ancient homeland, a project that Arabs everywhere understood to mean the creation of a distinctive Jewish polity with its own institutions and even its own language. These new arrivals were not the Ottoman Jews who knew their place as a minority within the Islamic empire and, as a result, kept a very low political profile. The potential of the Zionist threat was well understood, not only by the local Arabs, but also by Arab nationalists in other regions of the Near East. It also troubled the central authorities in Istanbul, who did not need another strident minority to add to their mounting minority problems elsewhere in the empire—the sultan was then struggling to hold onto the last Ottoman provinces in the Balkans.

Before the outbreak of the Great War, there were some eighty thousand Jews in historic Palestine, more than three times the number before the Zionists began arriving in 1882. In addition to the Jewish city of Tel Aviv, some forty new Jewish settlements were established largely on lands bought from absentee Arab landlords. The Jews also brought industry and European business management that Arab entrepreneurs found threatening. With the influx of Christians, modern anti-Semitism came to the region. Arab Muslims and Arab Christians were now able to weave European images of demonic Jews into their anti-Zionist representations. In accordance with these imported stereotypes, the Jews were pictured as controlling international financial markets and otherwise exercising power over foreign governments. These stereotypical images would be augmented decades later by propaganda materials directly obtained from Nazi Germany. While some Arab notables sought an accommodation with the Jews, the overwhelming majority did not. The opponents of Zionism circulated petitions to restrict Jewish immigration and land sales, but without success. If the budding Palestinian national movement required a stimulus, it needed only to look to the new Jews of Palestine, particularly after 1904 and the second wave of Jewish immigration that brought the cadre of political activists who would become the founding fathers of the Jewish state some forty years later.

There were, to be sure, advantages to opening up the Holy Land to foreigners and foreign ideas. As the Ottoman sultans had discovered in Istanbul, there was much to learn from the West about negotiating life in the modern age. Forward-looking Palestinian notables actually enrolled their children in foreign schools, thus augmenting their traditional Islamic learning and preparing them for leadership roles in an increasingly complex society. Some sent their sons abroad. The world of Palestine's Arabs was changing in ways that just a short time earlier would have been inexplicable. For instance, when the French consul in Sidon made an official visit to Jerusalem in 1701, the local population was in an uproar. The very sanctity of Islam's third holiest city had been breeched. Never since the conquest of Jerusalem in the seventh century C.E. had Muslims allowed an unbeliever to establish a diplomatic presence there. They expressed the fear that the visit of the consul could presage nothing less than a return of the hated Crusaders. No doubt, similar resentment of foreigners was widely felt throughout Palestinian society, particularly among more conservative religious elements.

As the Ottoman Empire entered into its final decades, there was considerable unease among the natives. The reaction to these disturbing changes was amplified after the issuance of the Balfour Declaration and the British conquest of Palestine in 1917, and then again during the process of establishing the mandate in the early 1920s. Arguably, these external stimuli proved equally important, if not more important, to the formation of Palestinian political identity than any residual feelings Arabs may have shared for any Filastin of the past.

The Balfour Declaration, framed after extensive discussions between Zionist representatives and the British Foreign Office, was an extraordinary example of diplomatic obfuscation. The terse statement issued by Lord Balfour began by stating that His Majesty's government favored establishing a Jewish national homeland in Palestine and was prepared to work on behalf of that objective. Left unstated was the nature of this Jewish polity. Zionist negotiators preferred specific mention of a Jewish state but were dissuaded from pressing the issue. The declaration ended by indicating that the British were not in favor of any project that may prejudice the civil and religious rights of existing non-Jewish communities in Palestine (read: Christians and Muslims). A final clause refers to Jewish communities elsewhere. The diplomatic history of the document and its importance to Zionist plans does not concern us here. Likewise, we are not concerned with other serpentine and duplicitous initiatives undertaken by the European powers—each anxious to claim a part of the expansive Ottoman state—nor with the British correspondence with the Sharif Hussein (1915–1916), the guardian of the Islamic holy sites in Arabia, to whom the British made suggestive promises of independence in return for Arab cooperation against the Turks. These matters and the broad political history of Arab and Palestinian nationalism have been discussed repeatedly in a vast and still-growing literature. Our interest here is the reaction of Palestine's Arabs to the declaration and how it affected their sense of nationhood and the course of their national aspirations.

Although the document did not specify that the Jews would be allowed to establish a nation-state, the omission of any reference to the political rights of the Arabs in the second clause made it abundantly clear that the Jews, who at the outbreak of the war probably represented a minority of no more than 12 percent, could claim political hegemony over the majority population. From a Palestinian Arab perspective, the ambiguous "national homeland" imagined by Britain and the Zionist leadership was not likely to be a secured cultural space or even an autonomous region within a larger Palestinian polity. When General Allenby, the commander of the British Expeditionary Force, marched into Jerusalem less than a month after the declaration was issued, Arab fears that had germinated during the final decades of the Ottoman Empire seemed to take on a life of their own.

Such fears were intensified during the next two decades. Great Britain formally received the League of Nations mandate to administer Palestine in 1922, and renewed waves of Jewish settlers from Europe—most of them ideologically driven by the Zionist dream—streamed into Palestine during the early 1920s. As a result, the Jewish population climbed to a hundred and fifty thousand by 1927. The total number of settlements grew from around forty or so in the prewar years to 111. It is no small wonder that the Arabs of Palestine found the incentive to establish a locally based nationalist movement and a political agenda that resulted in occasional spurts of violence against both the Jews and the mandatory authorities. The conditions of the early postwar period led to the real genesis of Palestinian national consciousness and militant Palestinian nationalism. Matters boded worse for the Arabs as additional waves of settlers arrived from Poland beginning in the early 1930s, and a flood of refugees escaping Nazi Germany made their way to Palestine starting in 1933. By 1936, the year Arab nationalists fomented an uprising that plunged Palestine into three years of bloody conflict, the Jewish population had swelled to more than four hundred thousand, including some two hundred settlements. It was, however, not only a question of numbers. The Jewish community, known as the Yishuv, was well on its way to creating a state within the mandate. Much of the infrastructure of the future State of Israel was already in place and functioning long before 1948. All that captured the attention of Palestine's worried

Arabs. One should not dismiss long-standing Arab associations with the land or make light of the earliest stirrings of local patriotism in Ottoman times. Nevertheless, the Palestinian nationalist movement was able to mobilize as it did in the interwar period, because it was shaken by the encroachment of foreigners seeking rule and actually ruling: Jews, mostly from Europe, seeking to establish a state of their own and British colonial administrators wishing to maintain an imperial presence.

It is not surprising that Yehoshua Porath focuses his narrative of emerging Palestinian nationalism on the events between 1918 and 1939—between the end of the "war to end all wars" and the beginning of the great conflagration to which the postwar peace process led. Until his retirement, Porath was a distinguished professor of modern Near Eastern history at the Hebrew University. Among his colleagues, he had a well-deserved reputation as an indefatigable researcher. His two-volume tour de force covers 820 pages and uses a vast array of sources, primary and secondary. In addition to the kinds of Arabic works cited by Khalidi, Porath made extensive use of materials in Hebrew. He perused numerous official publications and scoured a wide array of archival sources, among them the Israel State Archives that preserve the documents of the chief secretary of the Palestine government, the Arab Executive Committee, the Supreme Muslim Council, and the papers of various Arab notables. He made extensive use of the enormously rich Central Zionist Archives, the Haganah Archives, and the Public Record Office in London that contains the papers of the British Colonial, Foreign, and War Offices, as well as those of the Cabinet. After a lengthy introduction that covers the period of Khalidi's interest, the author methodically works his way through the interwar years, presenting an enormously rich and detailed picture of the social and political dynamics of the emergent Arab nationalist movement. The result is a seemingly exhaustive study of how Palestinians shaped nationalist ideology and confronted the dual threats of Zionism and British rule.

Oddly enough, there seemed to be a very brief moment when a few leading Arab nationalists (though not the mainstream, and certainly not the Palestinians) were prepared to discuss a Jewish national home. What could have led to such discussions? Might mere talk of Arab-Jewish cooperation have enhanced the goals of Arabs seeking to establish a regime of their own in Arabia and the former Ottoman provinces of the Fertile Crescent? These queries invite an ironic, perhaps even whimsical observation. European anti-Semitic propaganda, which had taken root among the Arabs, and Zionist diplomatic successes in Europe and the United States might have left some sophisticated Arab leaders with the impression that Jews could directly influence the political behavior of great nations. With the European powers meeting to inscribe the peace and redraw the map of the Near East at the conclusion of the war, Zionist support for an independent Arab polity might have been seen as extremely beneficial to Arab nationalist aims. In that respect, there was something to be gained in currying favor with the fledgling but highly aggressive Zionist movement. In late 1918, the Emir Feisal, would-be ruler of a Greater Syria, met with Chaim Weizmann, the most visible and diplomatically astute Zionist leader of the time. The result was a signed agreement pledging Arabs and Jews to support each other's nationalist projects: namely, carrying out the provisions of the Balfour Declaration in Palestine and establishing an Arab state (in territories other than Palestine). In an addendum, Feisal declares the agreement conditional on Britain satisfying Arab expectations of that future state. In sum, the emir declared that Jews had a real stake in supporting Arab nationalist ambitions.

Feisal would later exchange letters with Felix Frankfurter, a leading American Jew, bringing him up to date on his negotiations with Weizmann and the European Zionists. In March 1919, the noted Arab leader reiterates his full support for Zionist aims. He speaks of two (nationalist) movements complementing one another and expresses gratitude for Zionist support of the Arab agenda. Feisal then adds a disquieting note that bears witness to reality on the ground. There are less informed and less responsible people who ignore the needs for Arab-Jewish cooperation. Instead they try to "exploit the local differences that *must necessarily arise in Palestine* [italics ours] in the early stages of our movements." The emir then regrets that Arab and Jewish aims have been misrepresented to the peasantry of both societies in order to "make capital of what they call our differences." Feisal goes on to declare that these differences (a clear acknowledgment that there were in fact differences) are not based on principle but on matters of detail. As such, they can be easily adjusted by mutual goodwill. He then assures Frankfurter that *nearly all of them* will disappear with fuller knowledge. The letter ends with still another call for mutual assistance. Representing the American wing of the Zionist Organization, Frankfurter, who would achieve great fame as a Harvard law professor and later as a Supreme Court justice, endorsed the emir's sentiments and drew reference to the Paris peace conference that was to chart the future of the Near East. Diplomatically attuned Arabs were no doubt aware that the United States had emerged as a world power after the war and that President Wilson was determined that his country should play a direct and vital role in international affairs. They were also no doubt aware of Wilson's openly declared support for fulfilling nationalist aspirations as a matter of justice and as part of a new and harmonious world order. Having Zionist support in the United States and in international forums could then have played a significant role in bringing Arab hopes to fruition. As it was, the international bodies rejected the immediate implementation of both Jewish and Arab nationalist agendas. There was no Jewish homeland, let alone state in Palestine, and no independent Arab state in what had been the Arabic-speaking provinces of the Fertile Crescent. With that, any Arab calls for accommodation with the Jews, which seem at best a ploy, gave way to new political realities. By summer, Feisal was backtracking from his earlier stance as he fully appreciated the strength of Palestinian opposition, and more generally Arab opposition, to the Zionist project.

Palestinian historians, seeking to preserve the purity of Arab nationalist visions, have depicted Feisal's seeming embrace of the Zionist cause as nothing more than a call for religious harmony in a thoroughly Arab Palestine. To their thinking, the agreement resulted from an offer, communicated orally by Weizmann, that the Jews had no intention of establishing a government of their own in Palestine and would instead help develop the country so far as that would be possible without damaging legitimate Palestinian interests. Were that not enough to qualify Feisal's response to the Zionist leader, the emir is also described as having been under enormous pressure to adopt immediately a conciliatory attitude to the Zionists in accordance with British policy. It is thus suggested that left to his own devices and in full consultation with other nationalist leaders, especially his father the Sharif Hussein, Feisal might have refused to sign any agreement with the Zionists, even one that seemed relatively innocuous.

Arab historians also focus on the text of the agreement, recorded in English by the legendary T. E. Lawrence who served as interpreter; only the codicil with Feisal's reservations is written in Arabic. Historians are convinced that the published text is a loose and somewhat misleading paraphrase of the original; a summary of extended conversations. What can be explained as perhaps an act of political expediency by an Arab leader thus becomes still another case of Arab victimization at the hands of unscrupulous European diplomats—if true, that story would have had ample precedent given the duplicitous negotiations of the time. But not every event in the unfolding history of the modern Near East is a footnote to a broad conspiratorial narrative. Conspiracy theories, particularly the more titillating ones, have a tendency to transcend embarrassing details. Assuming that Feisal was duped by Lawrence, and perhaps Weizmann as well, what is one to make of the Feisal-Frankfurter letters? The Frankfurter exchange would seem to undercut any notion of a conspiracy that distorted the actual views exchanged between Weizmann and the emir. In his letter to the American lawyer, Feisal refers to meeting with Zionists at the peace conference and witnessing them as they presented their case. Were that so, the Arab leader had to be well aware of persistent and well-reported Zionist demands for an independent Jewish state in Palestine. Then as now, the Zionists were hardly bashful in promoting their agenda. Whatever the truth regarding the Feisal-Weizmann agreement, the talk of cooperation between Zionist representatives and a most prominent Arab leader melted away. Arabs, experiencing growing frustration over their aborted nationalist ambitions, were in no mood to acknowledge the Zionist project regardless of how innocuously it might be defined.

Having divided historic Greater Syria into Lebanon, Syria, Palestine, and the Emirate of Transjordan to suit their own purposes, the British and French undid some 1,300 years of Islamic history, in addition to tampering with a more ancient geography. By shaping a modern Iraq from three disparate Ottoman provinces, each with a majority population that bore suspicion of, if not animosity to, the people of the other provinces, the British created a future nation-state that has been ruled only by the imposition of strong centralized, authority and more recently by a horrific tyranny. But Feisal now had a country to rule. After failing to secure a throne for him in Damascus, the British simply ensconced the Arabian Hashemite in Baghdad. The Arabs of Palestine, denied a Syrian option that spoke to the logic of history, accepted the borders of the recently established mandate and went about the task of developing an indigenous nationalist agenda designed to produce an independent Palestinian state. Adamantly opposing Zionism and British colonial rule, they began to set the foundations of their own specific nationalist vision.

Critics of Britain's vast colonial enterprise have often accused His Majesty's government of deliberately "blundering" their way into an empire and then ruling their new subjects through a carefully conceived policy of "divide and rule." In regard to the Palestine mandate, the Arab and Jewish communities were already divided and, despite social and professional contacts, Zionists and Arab nationalists were moving along very separate paths. For the British ruling authorities, the deep and growing chasm between Jewish and Arab societies was a hindrance rather than a help to stabilizing the country. The expansion of Jewish settlement and the rapid development of Zionist enterprises during the interwar period is described in the second section of this book; the growth of national consciousness among the Palestinians and, related to that, the evolution of a national movement that actively challenged both Zionist claims and British rule are our immediate focus.

Oddly enough, the British themselves paved the way for the emergence of Palestinian self-identity and with that the mobilization of a nationalist movement. By allowing both Arab and Jewish communities to develop their own institutional structures, mandatory officials gave Zionists and Arab nationalists alike the opportunity to define themselves and their political objectives. Operating under British rule were the Arab Executive Committee; the Supreme Muslim Council, which sponsored a number of political parities and associations; various groups representing the interests of the rural notables; the Muslim-Christian Association; and similar political and cultural organizations. The ruling authorities also broke precedent and established a Grand Mufti, a supreme Muslim jurisconsult, with a seat in Jerusalem. With that, they recognized that mandatory Palestine was, from an Islamic point of view, what it had come to be de facto: a juridical entity separate from that of Greater Syria. From an Arab perspective, the task was how to translate the new political situation into the staging ground for a true nationalist movement.

The great problem facing Arab nationalists in the interwar years was that of promoting a common sense of identity and fostering expectations of a common destiny. That task required educating a new generation of Arabs who were coming of age. Here, too, the nationalists were assisted by the British authorities who were intent on creating a complex school system coordinating both private and an expanding public education. There were, as before, three school systems: (1) a Jewish network of schools where the language of instruction was Hebrew (in ultraorthodox schools run by Jews of European ancestry, a strictly religious curriculum was rooted in classical Hebrew and Aramaic Jewish texts that were explicated in Yiddish); (2) an Arab public and private school system where the language of instruction was Arabic; and (3) a private school system, based on European models and often run by foreign Christians, where classes were taught, as a rule, in English or French. The foreign schools, most often run by church-affiliated groups, appealed to Christian Arabs, but also to Muslims seeking an education with which to successfully encounter the modern world. A smattering of Jews enrolled in foreign private schools; a small number of Arabic-speaking Jews attended Arab schools. The Armenians, anxious to preserve their language and religious heritage, had their own private school system in Jerusalem.

The growth of education was already evident in late Ottoman times. Following the Young Turk Revolution of 1908 and the accompanying demands for widespread reform, the sultan opened a public school system in which the language of instruction was Arabic rather than Turkish. The

British in turn accelerated this trend. In 1914–1915, there were altogether ninety-eight Arab government schools with less than 2.5 teachers for each school. Nearly 7,000 boys and 1,400 girls were in attendance; the sum total of 8,248 pupils represented about 11 percent of the school age population. When one adds the traditional Arab religious schools and various private schools available to young Arabs seeking a more secular education, the total of both Christian and Muslim Arab students must have been somewhat higher. Under Ottoman law, the state schools offered five years of education beginning at age seven.

In 1922–1923, the first year of the mandate, the number of public schools increased to 314, and the number of pupils to almost twenty thousand, but given the high birth rate, the percentage of public school students relative to the school age population remained more or less the same. Muslim private schools accounted for an additional 2,287 students; Christian private schools added some 12,000 more. The total number of students in the Arab sector relative to the total population of school age children was on the order of 22 percent; the years of schooling now went from ages seven to eleven to ages five to fourteen. By 1948, the year in which the mandate came to an end, Arab public schools enrolled more than a hundred thousand students, some 30 percent of the Arab school age population. Private school statistics are not available for that year, but two years before (1945–1946), Muslim private schools enrolled some fifteen thousand students and Christian schools some twenty thousand more. In sum, by the mid- to late-1940s, approximately 40 percent of the Arab school age population received at least an elementary school education—a remarkable advance since the advent of British rule. By way of contrast, the number of Jewish school children enrolled in 1945–1946 was approximately 110,000, but the total Jewish population was only about 600,000—that is, slightly more than half the Arab population—and with a much lower percentage of school age children.

The intent of the Ottoman public schools was to inculcate loyalty to the concept of the Ottoman Empire and allegiance to its ruling authority, the sultan, who was also proclaimed heir to the Arab caliphate. The mandatory authorities imposed no such ideological freight on the Palestinian public school system; the schools did not go out of their way to inspire patriotism to king and crown. Pupils were not expected to emerge as native versions of proper Englishmen, produced according to templates borrowed from British grammar schools, let alone the likes of Eton and Harrow. Both Jewish and Arab communities were allowed to run their schools in their respective languages and with full consideration of their specific cultural needs. Both communities were thus given the opportunity to produce a highly educated youth whose minds might be shaped by distinctive nationalist ideals.

When it came to education, the Arabs tended to lag behind the Jews. The majority of Arab schools offered only elementary education and on the whole lacked adequate funding. At the start of British rule, there were only six lower secondary schools, all situated in the major towns and cities: Jerusalem, Nablus, Hebron, Jaffa, Haifa, and Gaza. Two higher secondary schools, the Arab College and the Rashidiyah, were situated in Jerusalem; another was soon established in Nablus. By the end of the mandate, the number of lower secondary schools had grown to twenty and the high schools to eight. As there was no university education, teachers were recruited among those who successfully completed a postsecondary schoolteacher's course that took two years. Occasionally, learned university graduates who studied abroad were employed in the Arab system. Practical subjects such as mathematics, science, and some European history were taught, but the Arab curriculum in the secondary schools consisted largely of courses in Arabic language, literature, and civilization.

Some Arab intellectuals complained that the public school system was in the hands of the government, and as it allegedly produced compliant Arab youth, it favored the Zionists, whose private secondary schools were modeled on the most advanced European gymnasia. The Jewish high schools featured a full complement of courses in mathematics, biological and physical sciences, and foreign languages and history, including a four-year option in Arabic and Islamic civilization favored by many students. Some Arabs also complained about private schools founded by Christians from abroad. In the 1940s, there were eleven Arab public schools in Jerusalem, seven private Arab schools, and no fewer than forty foreign-run schools. One may assume then that the majority of Christian Arab students and not a small number of Muslims in the Holy City and its environs received their primary education from European or Eastern Christian-linked institutions. That was not true, however, in the more heavily populated Muslim areas of the country and certainly not in the rural hinterland where Muslim religious tradition resonated strongly and suspicion of foreigners was palpable.

Under any circumstances, the logic of the Arab complaint is not entirely clear. Granted, the Jewish and European schools were given considerable slack in establishing their curricula. But Arab educators could have experimented more widely with their own offerings and the manner in which they were taught, especially in the private schools. They certainly could have put more emphasis on mathematics, science, and foreign civilizations; above all, they could have promoted higher standards. It is of course true that the non ultraorthodox Jewish school system reinforced Zionist ideology, but Arab nationalists did the same in educating their pupils. The students of the Arab schools, whether public or private, did not passively acquiesce to the mandatory regime, nor were they taught to react tepidly to the Zionist aim of creating a Jewish state in their native land, as some Arabs maintained. The British have been criticized by all sides for the manner in which they ruled Palestine, but one can hardly imagine a single public school system with a fairly uniform curriculum for Muslims, Christians, and Jews, or one in which private schools were placed under like constraints. Similarly, there was no way the government could have established a unified school system in which Jews, Arabs, and non-Arab Christians all sat in class together. What would have been the language of instruction? How would a curriculum catering to all these students have done justice to the broad cultural needs of the different communities? Would Arabs who complained about the education of their youth have compromised the religious and cultural orientation of their communities if asked to experiment with a national school program that shortchanged Arabic language and civilization in favor of a broad course of study? The only alternative was a divided school system that allowed all of Palestine's communities to educate their own youth. As a matter of principle, that was hardly reason for Arabs or Jews to protest.

There were, however, matters that might have distressed quite a few Arab intellectuals. The Jewish and foreign schools were better funded than the public schools in the Arab sector. They were less dependent on tight budgets fixed by the mandatory regime. Jewish communities everywhere had long been accustomed to financing their own social services, including education. This was seen as a collective responsibility; no able Jew was exempt from contributing to the welfare of coreligionists. Zionists could also count on sums of money from Jews abroad; some of those funds came from rich benefactors whereas others were obtained by agencies employing an army of volunteers that solicited countless small contributions. In contrast, Muslims had always preferred that individual patrons or the governing authority underwrite society's needs. Giving to charity was an individual rather than communal concern. Even today, and even among Israel's Arabs, it is difficult to levy and collect significant tax revenues to service municipal projects in Arab townships. While Palestinian Arabs waited for the British to establish a national university—none was forthcoming—the Jews founded a university of their own in 1925. Drawing inspiration from contemporaneous German higher education, the newly founded Hebrew

University in Jerusalem was initially staffed by holders of European doctorates. During the 1930s, the Jewish university was greatly enriched by refugee scholars fleeing Nazi persecution, creating virtually ex nihilo a world-class faculty and research staff. The holdings of the Jewish National Library, which was in effect the university library, were becoming comparable to those of major research institutions abroad. In addition to the university and the Jewish National Library that serviced it, an advanced technical school specializing in science and engineering was opened in Haifa, and a major scientific research institute and center of agricultural science took root to service the needs of an increasingly modern Palestine. With nothing comparable in their own sector, a number of Arabs attended the Jewish university; because the language of instruction was Hebrew, their opportunities were limited. Even after 1949, when the West Bank was ruled by Jordan and Gaza by the Egyptians, Arab Palestinians had to travel abroad to receive a university degree. Ironically, the current universities of the West Bank, many of them expanded from junior colleges, were created with the permission, if not the encouragement of the Israeli occupation authorities after the 1967 war.

Still, Arabs lost no opportunity under the mandate to use the increasing number of schools and pupils—including the upsurge of education within the rural areas where illiteracy had previously been rampant— to promote a Palestinian identity and mobilize Arab youth for the conflict with Zionism and British rule. In that respect, the Arab schools of the mandatory period foreshadowed those of the Israeli occupation a generation and more later. Students participated eagerly in the strikes and civil disobedience of the 1930s; in 1936, following the outbreak of the general revolt, the schools were closed for six months. Formal schooling was supplemented by educational clubs that sprang up in virtually every town and large village. These, too, were hotbeds of Palestinian patriotism. The clubs that were widely popular among educated Palestinians functioned much as community centers do today. They had sports facilities of a sort, libraries, and varied cultural activities, which often reinforced the links between the Palestinians and their land throughout the course of history, whether real or imagined. The same pride in the Palestinian heritage could be found in the Arab Boy Scouts, a movement loosely modeled after the enterprise initiated by Britain's Robert Baden-Powell early in the twentieth century. Public libraries, which opened in all the major urban areas, also featured programs that reinforced nationalist sentiments and provided a wide range of reading materials that promoted a broadly based Arab culture.

What was still lacking, or so it seems, was a comprehensive narrative that tied the current generation of Palestinians to a more ancient history of the land that some Arab intellectuals insisted had been theirs from time immemorial. The broad outlines of this narrative have been discussed earlier (see chapter 1) and will emerge again later when we turn to recent biblical scholarship and Arab nationalist claims. Suffice it to say, Palestinian intellectuals were keen to provide a story of their people and the land that could compete with the more familiar tale (at least to Western audiences) of the ancient Israelites in the Hebrew Bible. The biblical narrative was the quintessential expression of Zionist aspirations and the basis of Christian support for the Zionist program. To be sure, the Muslims who represented some 90 percent of all Arabs had a proud history of their own with which to lay claim to the Holy Land. The account of the Arab/Muslim conquest of Palestine in the seventh century C.E. is told by them with evident pride and with the aim of establishing a significant, if all-too-obvious, link to the Arab/Muslim past. How could one deny the Arabs some 1,300 glorious years in the land they contested with Zionist interlopers who first appeared on the scene in the nineteenth and twentieth centuries? But as the Zionist narrative, which was embraced in part by the Christian world, began with Abraham and the children of Israel, Arab Muslims whose ancestors conquered Palestine in the seventh century C.E. had to portray themselves as having still earlier connections to the Holy Land—that is, a history that predated the Israelites. And so, Palestinian historians pictured their ancestors as the last of several waves of Arab Semites that entered Palestine and other countries of the Fertile Crescent from Arabia. Put somewhat differently, as the historians claimed all Semites to be Arabs who originated from the Arabian Peninsula, the indigenous peoples of the land conquered by the ancient Israelites were in fact all Arabs and therefore kinsmen to the current generation of Palestinians, be they Muslim or Christian.

It is rather doubtful that this intellectual artifice resonated widely among the less educated, particularly the Muslim Arabs whose historical imagination was closely linked to Islamic experience. The Egyptian textbooks that were used in the Arab school system until the 1940s drew no special attention to so ancient a legacy. Arabs showed little interest in the rising tide of archeological excavation that uncovered the land's hitherto unknown pre-Israelite history. During the Palestine mandate, the Department of Antiquities was run by British administrators and a largely British professional staff. There were, in addition, numerous foreign institutes devoted to archeology and biblical studies. At the Hebrew University there was great interest in the history and topography of Palestine. From the outset, university archeologists and text scholars were at the forefront of modern research. There was, however, no Arab-sponsored archeology or even Arabs in charge of digs; nor was there a concerted effort by Palestinian Arabs to master the languages of the ancient civilizations they now claimed as their own. Neither was there much public fascination among Arabs with the newly discovered past of ancient Palestine. The Rockefeller Museum, one of the finest institutions of its kind in the Arab Near East, was not visited by throngs of Arabs; no daily field trips of Arab schoolchildren marched through the exhibition halls soaking up the remote history of the land they contested with the Zionists. Even the Islamic monuments do not seem to have been of great interest to Muslim Arabs. Aside from the noteworthy structures surmounting the Temple Mount in Jerusalem, the Ibrahimi Mosque of Hebron—which is said to encase the tombs of patriarchs and matriarchs, revered by Jews and Muslims alike—and a few shrines and grand mosques situated throughout the country, there was little in the way of Palestine's topography that elicited a broad response from the vast majority of its Muslim Arab population. The surviving public architecture of the Muslim past did not elicit curiosity, let alone comment, nor did the hundreds if not thousands of Arabic inscriptions that testified to Muslim rule. To this day, the Islamic Museum on the Temple Mount is less an educational institution than a repository of mostly unexamined cultural artifacts.

Still, the Arabs of Palestine were not about to surrender to foreigners the land they had ruled for so long. The Palestinian Muslims of the interwar period needed no narrative that established them in their country before the ancient Israelites, nor did they need a geographical Palestine in premandatory times with borders that coincided with the land's new boundaries. It was enough to know that they were ruled by foreigners from Europe, heirs to the Crusaders of old, and that they could be ruled in the future by Jews, a people broadly condemned in Muslim tradition for their failure to recognize the legitimacy of Muhammad's prophetic calling. How could Muslims conceive of being ruled by a Jewish community that had for so long complied so sheepishly with Muslim rule? The very thought of Jews behaving confidently, indeed aggressively, was jarring to Muslim sensibilities, and for good reason. Arab Muslims correctly understood that the Zionist project, if brought to conclusion, would result in a complete reversal of their religious and political expectations. In sum, a world that was honed on the anvil of a thousand years and more of Islamic history would be turned upside down. Therein lay the powerful appeal of an evolving Palestinian nationalism and calls for action against the enemy. For Christian Arabs, the issue was largely one of an idealized Arab nation against a non-

Arab interloper, but for Muslim Arabs—that is, for the vast majority of Arabs—Palestinian nationalism was increasingly seen as a movement protecting Muslim as well as broad Arab interests.

When Palestinian Arabs initially took to the streets in open protest, the direct circumstances that elicited their anger had less to do with Zionist challenges to a universal Arab nationalism and more to do with a Jewish challenge to Islam. Arab nationalists did not seem overly exercised because a thoroughly Jewish city, Tel Aviv, had arisen in what had at one time been the Philistine/Canaanite coastal region. Arabs were not especially concerned that Zionists had chosen to settle in the pre-Islamic homeland of the Palestinians' newly embraced ancient Arab ancestors. Initial building on the sand dunes south of Jaffa did not result in significant dislocation of Arab peasants who had worked their fields for generations, as would be the case when Jewish agricultural settlements were established on lands obtained from financially pressed Arab absentee landlords. In any case, the initial flash point was the religious topography of Palestine; the areas of most serious disturbance were the holy cities where Jews and Muslims shared sacred as well as physical space: Safed, Hebron, and Jerusalem.

Of particular interest are the riots that arose from controversies surrounding the Jewish use of a narrow street astride the Western Wall of the Temple Mount. Jews were long attracted to that place, for it was all that remained of their ancient house of worship, the eternal symbol of their national existence. For those who embraced the faith of the patriarchs, there was no holier ground on earth. Not surprisingly, pious Jews often came there to pray. Although the street was owned by Muslims and the Temple Mount was administered by a Muslim charitable foundation, there was no Muslim objection that Jews came to offer private devotions at the wall. What aroused the Muslims were Jewish attempts to convert the area into a temporary synagogue for public worship at festivals (days of the year when Jews of old came to offer sacrifices at the temple) and during the High Holy Days, especially the Day of Atonement (when in ancient times the High Priest entered the Holy of Holies on the Temple Mount to intercede with God on behalf of all the faithful). The conversion of the street into a synagogue, even one that was temporary, was against the spirit, if not the letter, of Islamic law, which prohibited, in theory, the creation of new Jewish (and Christian) houses of worship and, above all, condemned public displays of the Jewish (and Christian) faith. As a rule, the Muslims were quite lax in enforcing legislation against Jews and Christians, but the threat of an emerging Zionist polity breathed life into old prejudices and standing legislation that had been taken for granted.

Attempts by Jews to purchase the land adjacent to the wall under the Ottomans and in the premandate phase of British rule failed for various reasons. However, with judicious bribes, the Jews managed to bring benches and arks containing Torah scrolls. In such fashion, they were able to carry out communal worship and not simply recite occasional prayers. The rather lax attitude of the Muslim authorities changed with the advent of British rule and the emerging threat of the Zionist movement. When Jews insisted in 1920 that they and not the Muslim charitable trust repair the outer section of the wall and beyond—that they be given legal possession of the wall and the narrow street along its path—Muslim fears were aroused. The British for their part did not wish for any change in the status quo and so the Jewish request was denied, but the Arabs drew their own conclusions. Possible Jewish acquisition of the wall was seen as a first step toward the takeover of the entire Temple Mount. Muslims even feared Jews might wish to demolish the al-Aqsa mosque and various adjoining structures in order to rebuild the holiest of their own holy shrines. Some might think it quite a stretch to go from hauling benches to the wall to partake in communal prayer (a rather modest if provocative act) to leveling one of the three holiest places in the world of Islam in order to make way for a reborn Jewish temple. But one should never underestimate the power of imagination in the Near East. Muslims thought they had good reason to suspect Jewish intentions given the aggressive stance of the Zionist movement in acquiring Arab property and the long-standing Jewish dream of reestablishing God's House as in days of yore. The Arabs pressed the government to prevent Jewish acquisition of the wall area. Not wishing to open a can of worms, the British authorities complied with their demand.

Arab Muslims, represented by the newly formed Supreme Muslim Council (SMC), pushed the issue still further. Lest the long-established custom of bringing benches to the wall be understood as some sort of incipient squatters' rights, the Arabs sought to prevent the practice in 1922, 1923, and 1925. Once again they succeeded with the authorities, and finally a definitive ruling was issued in favor of the Muslims. Undeterred, the Jews in 1926–1927 again sought to purchase land adjacent to the wall but were unsuccessful. Nevertheless, Jews continued to bring their benches; more than that, they also brought partitions necessary for separating male and female worshippers, as required by orthodox tradition. The partitions were removed in midservice by the mandatory police, but the die had been cast by the seeming provocation. The SMC used the incident to resuscitate a Palestinian nationalist movement, hitherto marred by internal dissension. By focusing on the Temple Mount, they invoked a theme that had broad appeal to Arab Muslims from all walks of life and in both urban and rural areas. Zionism was not simply an obstacle to Arab nationalist yearnings; it had become a direct threat to Islam and Islamic institutions. When the British authorities waffled on exactly what Jews would be allowed to do in the plaza adjacent to the wall, the Mufti Amin al-Husseini was bent on a daring course of action.

The immediate pretext was a demonstration by a right-wing Jewish youth movement at the wall in 1929. The day was the ninth of Av when Jews commemorate the destruction of the temple in Jerusalem and other calamities that befell them throughout the ages. Within a week, there were widespread disturbances in which scores of Jews were murdered in the traditional communities of Safed and Hebron. Although there were Arabs who sheltered Jews in Hebron, the town was soon emptied of a population that had lived there continuously since biblical times. For their part, the British wrote off the disturbances as a response to Zionist provocation, as if a symbolic gesture by some high-spirited Jewish youth justified taking the lives of nearly a hundred innocents. The Palestinian leadership, mindful of the need to answer to the British authorities, denied any responsibility for the breakdown in public order. Still, there was a price to be paid. A number of Arabs were brought to trial and three were hanged, much to the dismay of an enflamed Arab population. In the end, the events of 1929 had a telling effect on the nationalist movement. The Arab Executive, represented by urban notables who had resisted pressure to be more confrontational with Britain and the Zionists, now found itself vying with young firebrands, all of them Muslims. That competition between a traditional and entrenched leadership and mostly youngish activist elements has remained a feature of the Arab nationalist movement until this day. Most importantly, the controversy over the Temple Mount (Hebrew *har ha-bayit*) or the Noble Sanctuary, as it was called in Arabic (*al-haram al-sharif*), moved a nascent Palestinian national movement from a discussion of self-determination and majority rights—concepts borrowed from the political vocabulary of Europe—to a more familiar defense of Islam and Islamic territory against the Jews.

One should not be misled into thinking that the Christian Arabs, who were themselves divided, were swept aside by the tide of events. To the contrary, their antipathy to Zionism ran as strong as ever. Their commitment to a more universal Arab nationalism in Palestine and elsewhere remained largely unshaken. Following 1929, there was a concerted effort to bridge the gap between Arabs of different faiths and to shore up the Palestinian Arab movement; more specifically, it was to strengthen the organization known as the Muslim-Christian Alliance (MCA). The attitude of the

Christians was quite complex, reflecting as it did significant differences and historic rivalries among their different sects. There was also suspicion of Muslim intentions. In Syria, a nationalist revolt against French rule included bloody anti-Christian incidents, a development that caused misgivings about Arab nationalism among some Palestinian Christians. There were also a few anti-Christian incidents in Palestine itself. Although decidedly less dramatic than the Syrian encounters, they still caused consternation and internal debate among the Christians, but they did not close the door to cooperation with the Muslim majority. From the Muslim side, there was fear of Christian missionary activity, now seen as even more threatening because the country was ruled by unbelievers. Despite some misgivings about the Muslims, the Christians threw in their lot with their fellow Arabs. Their opposition to Zionism and their desire to identify as Palestinians carried the day.

Although they represented only about 10 percent of the Arab population, the Christians played an important role in the development of Palestinian nationalism. They brought organizational skills and a greater familiarity with the ways of the non-Muslim world. Many were at home in European languages and cultures. Throughout the checkered history of the nationalist movement, Christians with roots in the Near East conveyed Palestinian aspirations to the world beyond, most often with great eloquence and no small measure of success. George Antonius in the 1930s (as part of a broader Arab nationalist agenda), Nicola Ziadeh and Albert Hourani (briefly) in the 1940s, and Hanan Ashrawi and Edward Said after the Israeli occupation of the West Bank in Gaza in 1967 all found eager and receptive audiences outside the Arab world.

Despite outward manifestations of unity, the Palestinian movement of the 1920s remained badly divided, its sense of national consciousness not yet fully formed. Given an option to participate in government bodies, Palestinian leaders chose instead to boycott most institutions of self-rule. By refusing to participate in elections, the leadership successfully imposed its boycott against the government at the highest levels, but the Arabs still had to do business with the British authorities on a daily basis. In effect, the shortsighted leadership denied itself and the evolving Arab nation it claimed to represent an official voice. When the leadership finally decided to participate in some sort of a representative council, they found themselves thwarted by the bloody riots of 1929.

Even the antagonism to Zionism, perhaps the most powerful engine for Arab unity, did not produce a blueprint for success. The Arab leadership could hardly prevent contact with a growing Zionist community. In good times, the burgeoning Jewish sector presented Arabs with opportunities for much-wanted employment. When economic conditions spiraled downward, absentee Arab landlords, strapped for funds, found it necessary to sell off lands, thereby displacing rural agriculturalists whose families had continuously worked their fields since Ottoman times, but without any proof of ownership. A thorough study of land transfers during the interwar years reveals an extraordinary degree of cooperation between Arab nationalists and Jewish land-purchasing agents, particularly during the 1930s. Virtually the entire Arab Executive, the self-declared and controversial supreme body of the nationalist movement, was involved in selling land to Jews. More often than not, these were clandestine sales involving third-party agents to avoid the embarrassment of disclosure.

Changed conditions during the 1930s reinvigorated the nationalist movement and led ultimately to the open revolt of 1936–1939. The rapid upsurge of Jewish immigrants fleeing anti-Semitism in Eastern and Central Europe alarmed the local Arab populace. Concurrent with that, the worldwide depression led to increased land sales among cash-starved Arab notables. The results were distress among rural Palestinians displaced from their lands and considerable fears among those who still worked their fields but without the security of ownership. Jewish labor, now more readily available, also displaced Arabs from coveted jobs they held in the Jewish sector. With the rise of Fascist powers in Europe, the situation turned increasingly tense. The British, anxious to secure Arab support throughout the region in the face of a growing German threat, sought to stymie the Zionist project while at the same time groping for short- and long-range political solutions that might satisfy both parties. A plan to partition the country into respective Arab and Jewish polities was suggested in 1937 but rejected in part or whole by the leadership of both communities. For Arabs, the immediate issues were Jewish immigration and land sales. For Jews, it was the ingathering of their brethren, made refugees by changing conditions on the European continent. Arabs were no doubt aware that massive numbers of Jews were making their way to Palestine, giving the Jews an absolute majority, and that the Zionist leadership might boldly call for the establishment of a Jewish state. The worst fear of the Arabs would then be realized. The British authorities were certainly cognizant of what unrestricted immigration might bring in its wake. In order to stem the tide of Jewish settlement, questions were formally raised about the absorptive capacity of Palestine. These queries occasioned debates on the demography of the country in ancient times when it was presumed to be heavily populated. Jewish scholars and scientists amassed evidence to show a country of several millions in times past; those favoring the Arabs argued that the land's absorptive capacity had already been or was soon to be reached. This was no mere intellectual exercise; the issue of who was to settle Palestine and in what numbers was freighted with political importance. Clearly, if Jewish immigration were to be halted or even slowed to a trickle, there would be no basis for fulfilling the Zionist program that called for a Jewish state in all of Palestine.

The creation of a Jewish state was, in any case, a potential and not immediate threat. On the other hand, the land sales of the time altered the Arab character of Palestine and caused direct hardship for some of the peasantry. In the 1920s, lands were largely sold by absentee landlords from neighboring countries; the transfers were by and large of sizable but uninhabited plots. In the 1930s, locally based landowners sold cultivated lands from under their tenant farmers. The actual number of Arab agriculturalists forced from their fields was relatively small, numbering at best a few thousand. But the broad implications of the land sales were clear and the prospects of massive future dislocation were taken seriously. The government was pressured to restrict the transfer of land into Zionist hands. In the meantime, the Arab leadership openly encouraged tenant farmers not to leave. Jewish agents discovered that some forms of financial compensation encouraged the migration of peasants willing to take their chances in cities and towns. Peaceful demonstrations organized by the Arab leadership did little to stop land sales, and tension persisted. Militant elements of the nationalist movement encouraged a more forceful response, and so the ground was laid for the Arab revolt of 1936–1939. Organized, armed resistance shaped national consciousness and became part of the nationalist platform.

4

THE CALL TO ARMS

A Mark of Palestinian Nationhood

In December of 1935, a general strike was declared in the Arab sector. Shortly thereafter, the Higher Arab Committee was formed to coordinate the politics of the moment that soon gave way to armed resistance that caught the Arab notables off guard. The initial violence against British rule was fomented by urban toughs in Jaffa, many, if not most, drawn from elements migrating from the rural countryside. Arab towns and cities had significant populations of transplanted rural Arabs anxious to take advantage of what had been a growing economy. But the focus of the revolt soon shifted. When the economic difficulties caused by a worldwide depression were exacerbated by the general strike, rural Arabs who had formed the Arab urban lumpen-proletariat returned to their native abodes. For the next six months, armed bands of Arabs, the hard core drawn from the rural villagers and beduin clans, attacked the British and Jews alike. The marauding units were organized along regional lines in accordance with local loyalties that vied with a larger sense of national identity and purpose.

Although the strike fizzled out within the year, the violence continued; indeed, it expanded into a general uprising. It is worth noting that the revolt was coordinated by Palestinian exiles in Damascus, and that the rest of the Arab world threw its support behind their Palestinian brothers. The Palestine problem was now taking on the dimensions of a broad problem for the entire Arab nation. The iconic figure of the uprising was the charismatic 'Izz al-Din al-Qassam, a Syrian religious scholar situated in Palestine who was killed in the fighting that included volunteers from neighboring Arab countries. The revolt, which led to expressions of support throughout the Arab world, might also have produced a Palestinian national consciousness able to transcend the divisive structures and sensibilities that still characterized Palestinian Arab society. In the end, that proved not to be the case.

The revolt, now largely centered in the Palestinian highlands that gave the rebels better cover, was conducted by disadvantaged Muslim peasants and beduins. Long mistreated by Arab townsmen and urban dwellers, the rebels, having experienced a real sense of agency, soon became the vanguard of a social protest movement aimed at their fellow Palestinians. They demanded funds from financially strapped Arab merchants and citrus growers while at the same time, they withheld rents and debt payments; many patrons and creditors feared venturing into the villages spawning the current phase of the revolt. Many Palestinians considered the rebels men of pure heart combating the British authorities, the Jews, and the greedy and unresponsive notables and absentee landowners who refused to shoulder their Islamic obligation to war against the unbelievers. In contrast to those Arabs who viewed the revolt from the sidelines or, worse yet, left the country to avoid the increasingly dangerous climate, the rebel combatants were referred to as *mujahidin*—"fighters for the faith." In this respect, the Arab revolt followed a pattern that can be observed repeatedly throughout Islamic history. In order to legitimize rebellion against established authority, socially disadvantaged Muslims have always defined their protest in broad religious terms.

Having begun by attacking the unbelievers in the name of the Palestinian nation, the rural poor then directed their hostility against fellow Arabs who did not obey the call to arms. These included figures of authority who had long taken advantage of the lower stratum of society: village headmen (*mukhtar*), urban notables, local merchants, and the like. Many of these merchants sustained grievous economic losses during the abortive general strike and were not prepared to risk further losses, let alone forfeit their lives by taking to the hills to do combat against the ruling authority. Influential Arabs faced the unwanted prospect of having to defend themselves from the cruelty of fellow Palestinians who seemed more committed than they were to the nationalist cause. The ensuing violence threatened to tear Arab society apart, and with that, the evolving nationalist movement. Divisive feuds between leading families became even bitterer and at times exceedingly violent; grievances hitherto swept under the rug reemerged in full fury. It so happens that the rebels were virtually all Muslims and from the more conservative religious elements of society. Not surprisingly, the Islamization of the revolt brought about a hardening of the religious arteries and with that a demand for compliance with traditional Muslim sensibilities. Modest attire was now required for Muslim and Christian women alike. More important, the rebels actually turned against individual Arab Christians, a number of whom were killed. The Christian villages themselves were spared, however, by the intervention of the supreme Muslim religious authorities. The Druze, an offshoot sect of Islam, did not fare as well. Their villages along Mount Carmel were attacked systematically. The war, initially against the British and the Jews, had turned into a destructive internecine conflict in which local and ethnic alliances were undermining the loosely formed Palestinian nation. In a sense, the Palestinians never recovered from the revolt and were thus unable to meet the Zionist challenge of 1947–1949 when two prospective states hung in the balance: the nascent State of Israel and the aborted national project of the Arabs of Palestine.

The widespread violence, seemingly unchecked, called for the decisive intervention of the mandatory authorities. Two years after the outbreak of the revolt, the British threw the full force of their military and police against the rebels. The authorities, showing little restraint, crushed all resistance within a year. In addition to suffering battlefield deaths, a noble sacrifice traditionally worthy of epic poems, scores of rebels were hung in public, an ignominious fate that brought great shame. Brutal as the British had been, in the end more Arabs were killed by fellow Arabs than by the mandatory forces.

At first glance, it would seem the rebellion was a failure, particularly because it exacerbated profound divisions in Arab society. And yet, the rebellion resulted in specific gains from which Palestinians might have derived considerable satisfaction. The initial military operations seriously disrupted the rhythms of daily life, as roads were as unsafe as they had been when beduins controlled the countryside during much of the nineteenth century. The general instability gave the rebels a sense of real power and the authorities cause to wonder. Faced with Arab intransigence in Palestine and with open support for the Palestinian Arabs in surrounding countries, the British published a white paper in 1939 curtailing Jewish immigration. Indeed, the problem of Palestine had come to transcend the strivings of the Yishuv and the local Arabs. The impending war with Germany had moved the Palestine problem into a larger political arena, one involving the entire region. It was now in Britain's interest to downplay Zionist aspirations and promote a broad policy toward the Arabs that would protect British imperial interests. Still, one could argue that the Arabs of Palestine never fully recovered from the revolt of the 1930s and the damage it wrought to nascent Palestinian institutions and self-governance.

With the outbreak of hostilities shortly thereafter, British attention was diverted to combating the axis powers in North Africa and Egypt, and the nationalist agendas of both Jews and Arabs were essentially put on hold.

Having escaped the Nazis by immigrating to Palestine in the 1930s, many Jewish refugees foresaw a possible onslaught of German armies encamped in Egypt's Western desert. Zionist leaders vowed to continue pressing for a Jewish state, but with the Nazis as a common enemy, they also pledged support to Britain against the axis. A miniscule clandestine group of Jews, known as the Stern Gang, sought to continue the struggle against the British authorities and was responsible for high-profile acts of assassination and mayhem; for the most part, the Zionists put aside their grievances with the British and took on the Nazi menace. Jewish industry and technical skills were put at the disposal of the British troops in Palestine. Several thousand Jews joined the armed forces and served in a variety of noncombat roles. Others, no longer willing to be passive bystanders to their fate, volunteered for an elite fighting unit, a Jewish brigade that fought with the British Eighth Army, thereby creating the experienced core of commissioned and noncommissioned officers that would lead the Israel Defense Force after the creation of the Jewish state.

On the whole, the Arabs of Palestine and neighboring countries displayed a more cautious attitude. Most cooperated with the British and enjoyed the economic benefits of a booming war industry that was starved for labor as they waited for a victor to emerge in the struggle that was unfolding. However, not all were inclined to wait. As the Germans had no colonies in the Arab world, some Arabs found no reason to dismiss them out of hand. A pro-axis insurrection in Iraq supported by the Mufti of Jerusalem was put down quickly by the British; similarly, the king of Egypt who had been in contact with foreign agents was summarily forced from his palace by the Egyptian ruling party and British tanks. In Palestine, which had become a military camp, there was little room for anti-British forces to maneuver; and so the Mufti, already persona non grata because of his role in inciting Arabs to violence, fled to Germany, where he spent the war years hosted by the axis.

At the conclusion of hostilities and the triumph of the allies, both nationalist movements sought concessions from the British, now hard-pressed by the cost of maintaining their empire. Resistance to British rule intensified in both camps, and Palestine required a hundred thousand British troops to keep order, a staggering military presence given a total population of fewer than two million souls. The British were also under intensive moral pressure to resolve the Palestine problem. The war had seen the decimation of European Jewry. Six million were dead—fully two-thirds of the prewar population—and countless others roamed about a ravaged continent with no place to go. With the conscience of the world stirred, the openly declared Zionist hope was to send the displaced Jews to Palestine. The larger objective was to establish there some form of Jewish state that might integrate the flotsam and jetsam of Jewish humanity who had somehow survived the fate of their coreligionists. Governments that had previously turned a blind eye to the plight of the Jews and a deaf ear to pleas to save at least a remnant of them now pressured Britain into taking action. The Arabs who had no hand in the destruction of European Jewry would be asked to compromise their own strongly expressed national aims.

A committee was sent by the newly formed United Nations Organization (UNO) to investigate the Palestine problem. The committee members, drawn from a number of countries, concluded that the best solution was to partition of the country into respective Jewish and Arab states. Each polity was designed to have a majority of its own, although the proposed Jewish state would have contained an Arab minority of no less than 47 percent. The Zionist leadership grasped the historic moment and accepted that half a loaf of bread, even with a large Arab population, was better than none. The Arabs refused to accept partition even after a vote to divide the country carried in the General Assembly signaling the international community's approval of the plan. As before, the Arabs of Palestine took to arms; as before they were denied success. Although they had an initial advantage in manpower and could, given the geography of Jewish settlement (see chapter 11), blockade various major Jewish centers, including Jerusalem, the Arabs could not defeat the Zionists in the months leading up to partition and thereafter. Unable to fully mobilize their resources, riven by dissent, overconfident to a fault, and subverted in their efforts by neighboring Arab states with designs of their own, they were defeated by the Jewish militias even before the last British troops withdrew from the country. When the State of Israel was declared in May of 1948, it remained for the armies of the Arab states to impose an Arab solution on Palestine. They invaded what had been the territory of the Palestine mandate, but all except Jordan's Arab Legion were defeated. An Israel larger than that called for by the partition plan came into being with the armistice agreements of 1949.

For the Arabs, and most especially for the Palestinians, the decision to reject the 1947 UNO resolution to divide Palestine was a disaster of monumental proportions. No Arab state of Palestine was created; Palestinian society was shattered; and hundreds of thousands of Palestinian Arabs were driven or forced by circumstances into exile. Even the territory of Palestine that Arabs managed to retain was ruled by non-Palestinians. As is noted in the previous chapter, Abdallah I, whose British-trained Arab legion fought the Israelis to a standstill in the western hill country, annexed the area to his kingdom across the Jordan River. The invading Egyptian army, which retreated into a narrow strip along the Mediterranean coast, did not see fit to promote a legitimate Palestinian authority therein. The Gaza Strip, soon swollen with myriad Palestinian refugees, was turned into a haven for smugglers and later saboteurs and terrorists crossing into Israel.

The circumstances of 1948–1949 were called by the Arabs "the catastrophe" (*al-nakbah*). At first that designation, which also carries the meaning "disgrace," referred to the plight that had befallen the entire Arab nation; in time it came to refer to the special circumstances of the Palestinians, many of whom were left homeless and most of whom remained stateless as a consequence of Israel's victory. Apportioning moral responsibility for the plight of the Palestinians and interpreting the significance of the Nakbah in arresting the national goals of the Palestinian Arabs has become a major subject of scholarly and political discussion for Arab nationalists and Zionists alike.

For Palestinian intellectuals, the Jewish state was conceived in "original sin," a heavy moral burden for all Israelis to carry. The very creation of Israel was a travesty. What right did the Jews have to establish a sovereign polity in what had been Muslim land for thirteen centuries and Arab qua Canaanite land in most ancient times? Only the undoing of the Jewish state would result in a proper solution to the ongoing Palestine problem. Over the years, reflective Arab writers and politicians have come to understand that, given political realities, there is nothing the Palestinians or the Arab states in concert can do redress the basic injustice that has overwhelmed them and left them enraged—at least not for the foreseeable future. And so they remain resigned to the temporary existence of a foreign government on Arab/Muslim soil.

To be sure, mainstream Israelis are inclined to view the events beginning in November of 1947 and continuing until 1949 rather differently. The fighting that resulted in the first fully established Jewish polity after nearly two millennia of statelessness was referred to as the "War of Liberation" (*shihrur*). In the official Jewish narrative, Israel was pictured as a David taking on the Goliath of the Arab world, outmanned, outgunned, but with the spiritual resources to carry the fight against an enemy lacking unity and common purpose. In the course of fighting, hundreds of thousands of Palestinians fled largely at the behest of their leaders, their places eventually taken by ingathered Jewish exiles. For more than two thousand years, the world had persecuted the Jews and denied them an authentic political identity. That was now made right by the international acceptance of a Jewish state on the very soil of Israel's venerated forefathers. If the Palestinians had failed to achieve statehood, it was not Israel's fault. Nor is Israel responsible for the dispersion of the Palestinians. Had they and their Arab brothers accepted the partition plan as a moral compromise, they would not be stateless, nor would any have to be homeless.

Beginning in the 1980s, revisionist historians in Israel began questioning the moral pillars upon which the foundations of their society were built. Accessing hitherto unavailable archives, they draw a murkier picture of the emergence of the Jewish state, one that allowed Arab nationalists to rejoice, as now there were even Jews who thought Israel was conceived in sin. It is difficult to refer simply to revisionist historians because these historians do not speak with a single voice, perhaps less now than ever. A few are anti-Zionist. Their vision of the rise of Israel is not much different from Arab historians who regard the very creation of the Jewish state as reflecting a failure of moral and political nerve in the West. Looking to the future of the region, these anti-Zionist revisionists hope for a binational state of some sort, be it an Arab polity that fully accepts Jews as citizens or a polity of Jews and Arabs that bears no special responsibility for world Jewry. There is, however, little discussion of practical issues that would arise were such a state to be created in the most unlikely of scenarios. Other revisionists remain staunchly Zionist but are critical of Israeli governments, past and present, for not going far enough in attempting to reach an agreement with the Palestinians and other Arabs, as if such agreements only required a more concerted effort on the part of Israel's leaders. From this revisionist perspective, the Arabs were very willing to court peace, but Israel was always reluctant. The evidence for this assumption is in all cases highly questionable and tendentiously driven. Interestingly enough, there were no data available from Arab archives to support these claims; indeed there may be no detailed Arab paper trail concerning clandestine attempts at negotiations in the years immediately after the 1948–1949 Arab-Israel war.

Some "new" historians have attempted to undermine the myth of Israel's weakness in 1948–1949, pointing out—and rightfully so—that at the conclusion of the war, the recently founded Jewish state had more men in arms and was better equipped than the combined forces of their Arab enemies—a concession that bleaches white the precarious situation in which the Zionists found themselves during the earlier stages of the conflict. Lest one forget, 1 percent of the entire Jewish community of Palestine was killed in the fighting, a number equal to three million Americans today. Those battlefield losses, often the result of untrained and ill-equipped men and women being hurled into desperate combat, still sears the memory of the aging veterans who participated in the futile attempt to take the fortress of Latrun and similar engagements.

Perhaps the most trenchant criticism of the Jewish narrative concerns the Arab refugee problem. Here the revisionist historian Benny Morris refutes the idea that the Palestinian Arabs fled the land only because their leaders advised them to do so or because they elected to do so. In a careful reconstruction of the stages of the Arab flight, he demonstrates that there were moments when force was used to clear the field of any Arabs, and barring their return became a matter of subsequent policy. These contentions were not revelations by any means. It had long been known that the Jewish defense forces felt impelled to reduce the danger to themselves and the areas of Jewish settlement by expelling Arabs who stood in the way of clearing a straight path from one Jewish community to another. But the accusation took on special meaning at a time when Israeli opinion was sharply divided as regards the Arabs and when many Israelis were prepared to look deeply into their hearts in search of a morally acceptable solution with the Palestinians and those Arab states still technically at war with Israel. The revisionist historians are now in retreat, especially within Israel itself, but their effort has occasioned considerable soul-searching among many Israelis. A major television series reexamining Israel's War of Liberation was screened. A commission of educators met to consider writing schoolbooks that would offer a new and more morally complex narrative of events. The commission's deliberations stimulated a wide debate among Israelis, some of whom felt that the new scholarship had been used to diminish Israel's moral basis and legitimacy.

Thoughtful Arab historians have embraced the revisionists, but they have not called for a new look at how the Palestinians and the Arab states conducted their own affairs during the critical years shortly before and after the creation of the Jewish state, let alone during the decades that followed. There is yet no revisionist school of Arab historiography. Instead, Arab historians continue to focus on Palestinians as victims, incapable of charting a courageous and pragmatic course in their own self-interest. Should they be questioning whether the Palestinian leadership of the 1940s and 1950s bears responsibility for failing to defend their people and allowing the collapse of Palestinian national institutions? Should they reflect on why the Palestinians remained largely quiescent as Jordan gobbled up the West Bank, and Egypt held on to the Gaza Strip? Should they be writing about what might have happened if Palestinian leaders made detailed overtures to the Jewish state following the 1967 war in an effort to persuade their enemies that they were now prepared to accept a two-state solution, provided one of the states was a sovereign Palestine? There is no reason to believe that the Israelis would have rushed to embrace the Palestinians, but such a move could have paved the way for serious reflection and perhaps a change in Israeli policy, especially as none of the constituted Arab states was willing to consider any sort of peace with Israel at the time. There is something surreal about knowledgeable and highly reflective Arab intellectuals declining to revisit the policies of the past with a truly critical eye. Perhaps the trauma of the Nakbah has been too overwhelming; perhaps the seeming resignation of the Palestinians to the fate that overcame them has been too painful and scarring a memory.

There is little question that for the Arabs of Palestine, the Nakbah was a catastrophe in the full meaning of the word. By the time the armistice agreements were signed in 1949, the coastal city of Jaffa, perhaps the most cosmopolitan and westernized of all Palestinian Arab cities, had been emptied of virtually all its Arab inhabitants. Of some seventy thousand Arabs, barely three thousand remained. Passing through the city today, one still encounters the rubble of the northern neighborhood; the only building still standing there from pre-1948 is a refurbished and gracefully elegant mosque that creates an eerie skyline. The center of Jaffa is currently populated largely by Jews who were at best some 30 percent of the population before the war. Beginning in the 1960s, Jaffa underwent a revival as some old Arab quarters were converted into upscale neighborhoods, the old villas eagerly sought by wealthy Israelis. The port area, which was once a point of entry for so many visitors and a place of commerce and trade, was converted into a tourist attraction. Far to the north, in the bustling seaport and industrial city of Haifa, virtually all the Arabs fled what had been a mixed city. All but three to four thousand remained behind from a prewar Arab population— perhaps twenty times that number. The once-vibrant coastal cities that were Arab Palestine's window to the Western world became part of the urban setting of the new Jewish State of Israel.

In Western Palestine, the largely Arab city of Safed was emptied of its inhabitants. As part of Israel, it became an artists' colony and many years later a shabby absorption center. Similarly Tiberius, a city whose population was more or less balanced between Muslims and Jews, became an all-Jewish city. Along the corridor connecting Jerusalem and the coast, Jewish forces drove the local Arabs out of Lydda (*Lud*) and from the city of Ramle, which had been built by the Umayyad caliphs in the eighth century C.E. to serve as the capital of Arab Palestine. Both places were without Jews on the eve of hostilities; few Arabs remain in what are now Jewish towns.

Like the country itself, Jerusalem, the Holy City, was divided. The Jewish quarter of the old city, the most sacred of all territory to Jews, was lost to Jordan's Arab legion and only regained, largely in ruins, after the 1967 war. Thanks to the fighting skill of the legionnaires in 1948–1949, the Arabs retained all of the old city and the entire eastern part of Jerusalem. On the other hand, the mixed neighborhoods and Arab quarters of the largely Jewish western city and its environs fell to Israeli forces. The result of the fighting in and around West Jerusalem was a massive exodus of the Arab population. The few Arabs who remained eventually became linked to the local landscape and society. A case in point is the Muslim Arab village of Beit Safafa, which was cut in half. The mosque and the surrounding area, which remained on the Jordanian side of the border, bore all the telltale marks of a traditional Arab settlement. What remained of the truncated village on the Israel side was soon transformed into an urban setting with modern houses. Israeli Beit Safafa is in fact indistinguishable from the rest of the Katamon quarter in which it is situated, except for the frequent patter of Arabic and the appearance of elderly residents dressed in traditional Arab garb.

Perhaps the greatest upheaval to Arab society was in the rural areas captured by the fledgling Jewish army. More than three hundred villages were abandoned, many plowed under never to be seen again except for an occasional ruin or solitary building that serves as a constant reminder of what had once been. Many villages live in on memory, but only the elderly can remember exactly where they were and what they looked like. Occasionally there are sad, if not grim, reminders of a past lamented but not forgotten. For example, the Arab village of Shaykh Mu'nis was situated north of the Yarkon River near Tel Aviv. It is now part of the sprawling campus of Israel's largest university. All that remains of its earlier history is "The Green House," the villa of the village headman that serves as the faculty club, a ghostly reminder of what befell the Arabs of Palestine because of a war they eagerly sought.

During the Aqsa intifada, the uprising that began in the fall of 2000 against the Israeli occupation, signs appeared bearing the names of Arab villages that disappeared with the creation of the Jewish state and the exodus of the local Arab population. The signs were held during ceremonies by schoolchildren, who by their appearances seemed too young to have protested the Israeli occupation in a more emphatic manner. This use of symbolic paraphernalia was not an isolated occurrence. Nor was the use of nationalist symbols limited to formal political protests. As if to emphasize the deep-rooted historic claims to Palestine claimed by Arab nationalists, enterprising Palestinian merchants marketed a particular variety of beduin cloth in East Jerusalem. The material was advertised as having been embroidered by Arab women as they have embroidered fabrics in Palestine for the past five thousand years. An expression of Arab sovereignty less dramatic than armed resistance, the marketing of crafts said to reflect an Arab-Palestinian tradition of five thousand years is, nonetheless, an indication of profoundly held beliefs that an identifiable Arab people inhabited Palestine from almost time immemorial, the Arab exodus of 1948 notwithstanding.

By the conclusion of the fighting in 1948, perhaps one-half of Palestine's Arabs had fled or been uprooted from their homes, creating thereby an immense refugee problem that remains a tragic dilemma almost sixty years later. The dimensions of the catastrophe are not merely in the numbers. The social fabric of Palestinian society was ripped apart. The rural villages of Palestine were largely self-contained and relatively homogenous social units held together by clan or extended family loyalties. Even short distances between villages and between villages and the nearby towns were sufficient to keep these local societies intact and distinct from one another. There was a sense of belonging, a sense of order, a sense of continuity, and, for the most part, a sense of stability. The exodus and subsequent relocation of rural Palestinians, many to teeming refugee camps both within the old lines of the mandate and beyond, changed completely modes of social interaction. In particular, the young had to redefine their relationship with their elders and their new and strange neighbors. Placed on the dole, many refugees remained idle, their dignity shredded by unforeseen circumstances. At first, the village notables were regarded as spokesmen for their people in the camps, but their authority eroded in time.

The traditional urban leadership that did not flee the fighting for safer climes abroad was powerless to stem the tragedy as the Jordanians and Egyptians seized control and ruled whatever territory of the former mandate was not absorbed by the Jewish state. Even before the fighting broke out, Palestinian interests were subverted by neighboring Arab countries anxious to promote their own interests. The Palestinians thus became victims of inter-Arab rivalries. But if nothing else, the Arabs of Palestine proved exceptionally resilient. In time, the refugee camps became extremely crowded urban settlements with permanent housing. The more enterprising Palestinians learned how to negotiate with their Jordanian and Egyptian patrons and how to adjust to changed economic realities. Despite the deplorable circumstances, Palestinians retained their identity and their dreams of return.

More than a hundred thousand Arabs remained in the areas originally assigned to the Jewish state or absorbed by it during the fighting. They were quickly made full citizens of Israel with rights to representation in the country's parliament. However, given the military situation, they were shackled by security regulations until 1966. To this day, the Arab citizens of Israel, now some 1.2 million, have ambivalent feelings about their awkward relationship with Jewish society and with the Jewish state that demands their allegiance. Given a choice, it appears they would prefer a binational state within Israel or, at least, the de-Judaization of the Jewish state. In a sense, these Arab citizens remain strangers in their own land. Before 1967, the neighboring Arab states forbade them from crossing the border, thus denying Israeli Arabs access to their brethren in the West Bank, Gaza, and beyond. Israeli Muslims were not even permitted to perform the rites of pilgrimage at Mecca, an obligation demanded of all the faithful. Since 1967, the Arabs of Israel have cultivated close ties with those of the occupied territories and lands subsequently administered by the Palestinian Authority. However, while Israel's Arabs proudly wear the label Palestinian, there is at present no great desire among them to become part of a Palestinian polity in the making.

Following the armistice agreements of 1949, Palestinians who remained in the West Bank and Gaza or in refugee camps in neighboring Arab lands anticipated returning to their homes. Various clandestine groups and formal associations took root, largely inspired by younger Palestinians, men such as Yasir Arafat, George Habash, Khalil al-Wazir, Salah Khalaf, and others who became the vanguard of the movements in the Palestine Liberation Organization (PLO) established in 1964. The younger nationalists replaced the elderly urban notables who for generations controlled the pulse of Palestinian politics. The old Arab Higher Committee, which still existed in its Beirut exile, was essentially powerless, never again to play a role of political importance. During the early to mid-1950s, Palestinians launched cross-border incursions into Israel, mostly acts of sabotage. The Israelis responded with reprisal raids, an attempt to make it clear to those responsible for public order that the situation would not be allowed to continue. Thereafter, those who controlled the Palestinians usually kept them on a short leash. By the early 1960s, the Arab world, which was beset by internal rivalries, turned once again to the question of Palestine. Meeting in Cairo in 1964, representatives of the Arab states renewed their commitment to the Palestinian cause and created an umbrella organization of Palestinian groups whose goal it was to liberate their homeland. The decision of the Arab League to form the PLO was less the result of renewed sympathy for their stateless brothers or of any concrete plan to liberate the territories that had been lost in 1948–1949; rather it was an attempt to maneuver through the treacherous waters that were enveloping the Arab nation-states. For the Egyptians, who dominated but did not control Arab politics, the PLO was an instrument by which to manipulate Palestinian activity to avoid a major conflict with a powerful Israel. It also served to deflect Syrian criticism that Egypt had abandoned the Palestinians. Not to be outdone, the Syrians backed an aggressive group within the PLO, Fatah (*al-Fath*), a reverse acronym for *Harakat Tahrir Filastin*, "The Movement for the Liberation of Palestine." Fatah was founded in 1958 by a group of Palestinians from Gaza who had studied in Egypt. Inspired by the success of the Algerians in taking the fight to the French, they espoused a position that ran counter to the conventional wisdom then prevailing among the Arab nation-states and most Islamic revivalists. Whereas it was thought (particularly after Israel's spectacular military successes) that the liberation of Palestine required real Arab unity before engaging the Zionist foe, Yasir Arafat and the leaders of Fatah saw liberation coming as a consequence of a direct and immediate confrontation. This does not mean that any of the Arab states were prepared to back an all-out conflict against Israel; rather, they would use the more militant factions of the PLO to establish their own credentials as Arab nationalists and defenders of the Palestinian cause. Only the Jordanians were wary of the resurgence of the Palestinians, and for good reason. A beleaguered Hashemite monarchy, home to a vast Palestinian population (more than 50 percent of the kingdom) and pinched between a powerful Syria and an even more powerful Egypt, was cause for concern, especially after the overthrow of their Hashemite cousins in Iraq during the fateful summer of 1958. The last thing King Hussein needed was a confrontation with Israel over Palestinian incursions.

The PLO, emboldened by the support it received, was resolved to pursue its own agenda. That agenda was first formulated in 1964 in a document that has come to be known as the Palestinian National Covenant (*al-mithaq al-qawmi al-Filastini*). The document begins by placing the land of Palestine within the broad framework of the Arab world. Palestine is thus declared an Arab land bound by strong national ties to the rest of the Arab nation-states, who along with Palestine constitute an all-inclusive Arab homeland. The Palestinians are thus seen as a discrete group but part of a transcendent Arab nation. Of what Palestine did the PLO speak? The borders are those of mandatory times and are regarded as indivisible, a clear indication that partition would not be recognized and that there could be no two-state solution as envisaged and voted upon by the United Nations. Hence there could be no State of Israel. In a subsequent article, the charter states explicitly that the 1947 partition is illegal and remains illegal regardless of what has transpired. That is because the division of Palestine was contrary to the will of the Palestinian people and at odds with the United Nations charter that calls for the right to self-determination. Similarly, the Balfour Declaration is declared null and void. In any case, Jewish claims to Palestine based on historical and religious ties are declared incompatible with the facts of history. Judaism is a religion; as such, Jews are citizens of the states to which they belong and cannot have national aspirations of their own. With that, the covenant declares that Jews lack a real history that ties them to the Holy Land; the Zionist state is an artificial entity. There can only be an Arab Palestine.

Having established the geographical parameters of the Palestinian state, the charter goes on to specify that the Palestinian people alone have the legal right to determine the character of the polity that will be created after liberation. These Palestinians are then defined as Arab nationals who until 1947 resided in Palestine, so there is no difference between those who remained behind on Palestinian soil and those who were forced into exile. All subsequent offspring with Palestinian fathers are considered Palestinians, whether born in Palestine or elsewhere. In sum, all Palestinians—whether in Israel, the West Bank, Gaza, or in exile—are entitled to return to the homeland. But what was one to do with current Jewish citizens of the State of Israel? What was to be their fate once Palestine was liberated and restored to its rightful place among the Arab nations? All Jews of Palestinian origin (i.e., those in Palestine before 1947) were to be accepted as Palestinian citizens, provided they showed loyalty to the Palestinian polity and were prepared to live in peace with its Arabs. The presumption here is that the massive number of Jewish immigrants who arrived after 1947 would have to depart. An emended 1968 charter considered only Jews who were in Palestine before the Balfour Declaration of 1917 as potential Palestinian nationals. As the operative phrase was "before the Zionist invasion," one could argue that the covenant implied that Jews who arrived after the first Zionist settlers in the 1880s would be denied the right to settle in Arab Palestine.

All Palestinians, regardless of where they might be situated, were then asked to close ranks and prepare for armed struggle (various strategies are suggested) against the forces of Zionism and imperialism in order to liberate the homeland. The covenant goes on to stress the links between Palestinians and other Arabs and the responsibility of all Arabs to the Palestinian cause. Clearly, there could be no compromise with the Zionist enemy except on Palestinian terms. For all the bluster and the heralding of guerrilla warfare, the PLO, restrained by the Arab states, achieved little in its military confrontation with Israel. All that changed with the 1967 war.

AFTER THE SIX DAY WAR: FROM 1967
TO THE INTIFADA OF 1987

Since the creation of the modern Israel, no single event has had a greater impact on the Arab-Israel dispute than the war of June 1967. Within hours, Israel's air force decimated the combined air fleets of the major Arab confrontation states. Within a day, Israeli ground forces sealed off and captured the Gaza Strip along with al-Arish, the capital of the Sinai Peninsula. Within three days, all of Sinai was in Israeli hands, and troops of the Israel Defense Forces (IDF) were seen wading in the Suez Canal. The 1967 war marked the third time that Israel had captured vast territory from the Egyptians in Sinai. In both 1948 and 1956, the army of the Jewish state had routed the Egyptian defenders, only to withdraw after extended negotiations following the hostilities. The Jordanians, misled by Egypt and pressured into battle on the first day of hostilities, lost the entire West Bank of the Jordan, the territorial enclave they had annexed as the spoils of the 1948–1949 war. Three days later, the Syrians who belatedly entered the fighting were pushed off the Golan Heights that overlooked northern Israel. When a cease-fire was finally declared shortly thereafter, columns of the Israel Defense Forces were within artillery range of the Damascus suburbs. The swift and decisive Israeli victory was heralded as a triumph of human resources, an electrifying example of the superiority of a modern society with roots in Western culture and espousing Western values. With their remarkable feat of arms, the Jews had gone from being quintessential victims to quintessential conquerors. According to a humorous quip circulating at the time: Who would have believed after the Second World War the Japanese would become the world's businessmen and the Jews the world's fighting men?

On the Arab side, what started out in mid-May as an Egyptian effort to secure bragging rights as the defender of Arab honor soon gave way to a risky adventure in which Nasser hoped to restore full Egyptian control to the Sinai Peninsula and the Straits of Tiran, the narrow body of water that commands the approaches to the Gulf of Aqabah (see below). By the beginning of June, the Egyptian-inspired crisis was transformed once again. This time the issue was not Egypt's right to reoccupy Sinai with military forces or deny Israeli shipping passage through the straits; the very existence of Israel was made an issue as Nasser threatened to put an end to the Jewish state and replace it with a sovereign Palestinian polity.

For three weeks prior to the outbreak of hostilities, the Arab street and the world at large were treated to a carnival-like atmosphere in which all sense of reality was overwhelmed by unbridled Arab expectations. In contrast, the Israeli public, unaware that its armies stood poised to register a great victory, were confused by the seemingly inept response of Israel's political leadership and depressed by what they thought was the world's lack of concern. They were not privy to the deputy chief of staff's candid assessment about the expected outcome of the war. Speaking for Israel's generals, Chaim Bar-Lev anticipated a swift, decisive, and elegant campaign. Arab expectations, so high in the weeks leading up to the battle, were pumped up still further during the first day of the hostilities. While the Israel Broadcasting Service revealed nothing of the fighting, Cairo radio boasted of victories, on Israeli soil no less. As hard news from the front trickled in, Arab euphoria was replaced by a sense of enormous disquiet and then overwhelming shame. Arabs who had access to the world's media quickly discovered the immensity of their defeat. The disparity between the boasting of their leaders and their fate on the field of battle made proud Arabs the butt of humiliating jokes everywhere. In contrast, the hated Zionists who occupied Palestine were heralded as a nation of true determination and purpose.

In 1949, the Arabs claimed that they were betrayed by corrupt leaders, a straightforward if inadequate explanation for their defeat and the loss of Palestine. In 1956, Israel routed Egypt in the Sinai War, a military campaign that was concluded within a few days. As in 1967, the swift and decisive Israeli victory captured the imagination of military planners everywhere; the so-called "Hundred Hour War" became a textbook case of mobile warfare that was studied in the staff colleges of the West. This was not the case in the Arab world, where the colossal defeat of the Egyptian army was transmuted into a great Arab victory. Egyptians were told that their army was not beaten by Israel, but that it withdrew from Sinai and Gaza to face the real enemy: not the Jews, who they could have defeated handily, but the Anglo-French expeditionary force that colluded with the Jewish state and invaded their country. When Israel was forced to withdraw from Sinai and Gaza in 1957 because of intense pressure from the United States, the path was paved for declaring the Sinai War a major Arab victory, commemorated no less by a magnificent monument that graced the approaches of al-Arish. There were, however, political conditions attached to the Israeli withdrawal: the demilitarization of the peninsula; the stationing of United Nations forces on Egyptian territory as a buffer between the opposing armies, still technically at war; and the opening of the Gulf of Aqabah to Israeli shipping. Imposed as they were, all these conditions rankled the proud Egyptian leadership. Nevertheless, the Sinai disaster was reshaped into an Arab success. No such revisioning of history was possible in the aftermath of June 1967. The Arab world was in shock. Perceptive critics bitterly assailed the phantasmagoria of traditional Arab politics. For a very brief moment, some Arabs even doubted the efficacy of Islam. In contrast, Israel came to be seen by everyone—Arabs included—as a major military power able to defeat any single Arab army or all their forces combined. For the Arab confrontation states, a new, unexpected, and threatening reality had been created by Israel's swift victory.

The Six Day War, which dramatically affected Arab perceptions of the Jewish state, also changed the Palestinian role in the Arab-Israel dispute. At the conclusion of the fighting, Israel controlled both the West Bank and the Gaza Strip, areas that were part of the Palestine mandate and heavily populated with native Palestinians. Once again, the Palestine problem was moved to the forefront of the Arab agenda. With their Arab supporters disgraced and in disarray, the Palestinians, who had been held on a short leash by their Egyptian, Syrian, and Jordanian handlers, were finally given greater license to pursue their political objectives and redeem Arab honor. Bowing to pressure for action but unable to act themselves, the Arab nation-states gave the Palestinians a freer hand to engage the Zionist enemy in the occupied territories and Israel proper. With that development, a stateless Palestinian society renewed its sense of purpose with increased energy and began to display the symbols and institutions of an emerging nation.

In the early 1970s, some Israeli geographers became interested in how Palestinian society conceived of itself. More particularly, they wished to determine the relationship between local, regional, and national identities. To that end, they sent out teams of researchers to rural villages in the West Bank, the kinds of Arab settlements where the pull of the local identity was most likely to conflict with a national identity that would transcend all other allegiances. In the end, they discovered that rural Palestinian society cohered within concentric circles, all fairly self-contained and in many respects self-reliant. The need for manufactured goods and other services might send rural villagers to nearby villages and towns; similarly neighboring townsmen might have to satisfy certain needs in nearby cities, but by and large, rural Palestinians did not establish strong links with other communities or fully articulate a sense of nationhood. To the contrary, they were often deeply suspicious of urban society. They owed primary allegiance to their own extended kin, their elders, and the powerful landowners to whom they were beholden. A reflective Israeli academic, put in charge of Arab affairs for the West Bank's military government in 1978, called for a league to serve the interests of all rural Arabs. The idea, which never bore fruit, was to loosely unite the villagers and establish a counter-weight to the larger towns and cities where active Palestinian nationalists were more firmly rooted.

It behooves us to ask how deeply a sense of national consciousness was ingrained even in the psyche of politically sophisticated urban elites. Had the bonds of national unity thoroughly swept aside all other identities and traditional allegiances between the catastrophe of 1948 and the rout of 1967, as well as in the years immediately thereafter? Put somewhat differently, if a transcendent sense of nationhood resonated among urban Palestinians, how is it that the Jordanians and Egyptians ruled so effortlessly over the Gaza Strip and West Bank before the Israeli conquest? One can readily understand the reluctance of Palestinians to pursue the path of open and sustained violence against the ruling Egyptian and Jordanian authorities. They appreciated the political advantage those authorities wielded and understood very well that the security forces would likely respond with devastating brutality. But that does not explain why Palestinians accepted Jordan's annexation of the West Bank without significant political protest or, in most instances, no organized protest at all. How is it that so many prominent nationalists—members of leading Palestinian families who accepted their new Jordanian citizenship—willingly sought administrative positions, including cabinet posts, under their Hashemite patrons? That is, they abandoned pursuing their own nationalist agenda to do the bidding of an Arabian family transplanted by the British on the desert wastes east of the Jordan River? Conversely, how is it that the emotive force of a distinctive nationalism has become so powerful and ubiquitous in all levels of today's Palestinian society? Rural and urban Palestinians alike have joined militant organizations and willingly shed their blood on behalf of the idealized nation. Palestinians may still not be united in policy or outlook, but they stand together as a people. What caused this Palestinian identity to congeal, within a generation no less? If these were indeed legitimate questions, the answer would seem to be Israel, more particularly the Israeli occupation. More than anything else, the very presence of a Jewish authority on sacred Muslim soil served to stimulate national consciousness and develop a greater sense of unity in the territories and the Palestinian Diaspora. An evolving sense of common cause has allowed Palestinians to increasingly mobilize their human resources toward a single objective: putting an end to the humiliating occupation and establishing a state that represents all Palestinians. The growth of Palestinian nationhood in the wake of the unexpected 1967 rout remains, four decades later, a slow and painful but certainly ongoing process.

Neither the Israelis nor the Palestinians anticipated the June war, nor did they prepare for its outcome. Although various Arab writers have embraced the notion of an Israel poised to establish territorial hegemony over all mandated Palestine, the truth is both the war and, more particularly, the post-war situation caught both Israelis and Arabs by surprise. Within days, the Zionist state had to establish a relationship with millions of Palestinians in the conquered territories. In Gaza, the Israelis could fall back on lessons learned during their occupation of the strip in 1956–1957. Many Palestinian leaders who had worked with the military administration after the first Sinai War were still in place; Israel could also draw advice from its own political officers who had ruled Gaza nine years earlier. The West Bank was a different matter altogether. For nineteen years, there had been no contact between peoples on opposite sides of the "green line" that separated Israel from the Arab areas west of the Jordan River. The same was true of Jerusalem, a city divided into east (Arab) and west (Jewish) sectors that were inviolably sealed. Only diplomats and Christian pilgrims were allowed to cross from one side to the other.

When the barriers separating the Jewish and Arab cities came down, Jerusalem was united once again, albeit with distinct Jewish and Arab neighborhoods. Within days, traffic was open to both sides of the city; Jews and Arabs revisited old haunts and relived old memories. Soon all of the occupied territories were open to Israeli traffic; similarly, Arabs could visit Israel. The hostility of the past was subsumed by an unusual sense of curiosity, particularly among citizens of the Jewish state. Every weekend, the roads were jammed with Israelis retracing the route of the IDF's campaigns against the Egyptians and Syrians and/or "doing the [West] Bank," which included visiting sacred Jewish sites in and around Jerusalem's Old City, Hebron, Bethlehem, Nablus, and the like. They were soon joined by hordes of Jewish and non-Jewish tourists from all over the world. Israel's Arabs also took the opportunity to reconnect with relatives from Gaza and the West Bank. Arabs from the territories reciprocated, visiting their Israeli kinsmen for the first time in two decades.

The initial mood in Israel was euphoric. To begin with, there was relief that the worst fears had not materialized. The Jewish state would endure, not only for the foreseeable future but for untold generations to come. Because it was so decisive, the stunning Israeli victory gave rise to absolute confidence in the IDF, the nation's citizen army. With that confidence there were hopes, if not expectations, that the Arab-Israel conflict would be brought to a conclusion sooner rather than later. Surely, the Arabs now understood the futility of engaging Israel's modern society in games of modern warfare. Surely, Egypt, Jordan, and Syria would be anxious to reclaim vast territories lost by their defeated armies. A popular Hebrew song written shortly after the war and titled "Tomorrow" spoke of a new age marked by peace and harmony between old combatants, as if the issues that separated the two parties had been or could be resolved by a political logic dictated by force of arms. Post-war Israel became deluded with the prospects of an immanent and enduring peace, just as the Arab world had deluded itself into thinking Israel would succumb in an all-out war.

During their frequent jaunts through the Arab territories, Israelis were misled by the open banter of Arab merchants eager to make sales and smiling children who seemed to wave at each passing car and tour bus as if welcoming new friends. Some alert travelers discovered that the ceremonial waves were occasionally accompanied by the "pebbling" of their cars as they drove by, a forerunner to the serious stone throwing that would begin years later during the first intifada, the Palestinian uprising of the late 1980s. From the outset of Israeli rule, Arabs took offense at having to deal with the administration authorities. They had less difficulty with the Arabic-speaking officers, especially those Jews who not only understood the language of the Arabs but also their body language—that is, Israelis who were fully conversant with Arab culture. But most of these Israeli administrators, many of whom were raised in the Arab world or in Arabic-speaking environments, were served by subordinates or responded to superiors who did not recognize—or worse yet, cared not to recognize—Arab sensibilities. A cultural gap marked Arab-Israeli relations, even in the quiet years shortly after the June 1967 war.

Headmen of Arab villages and towns attempting to see the local or regional military official on vital business were kept waiting in anterooms by teenaged Israeli woman soldiers immodestly attired—so it seemed to the Arabs forced to gaze at miniskirts and blouses with rolled up sleeves. It was one thing to do business with wizened warriors of the powerful Israeli army, but it was quite another to confront such women who addressed proud Arab males in a hastily acquired Arabic, all too often without sufficient respect for their station or manhood. After carefully cultivating a tribal leader and getting him to agree to water pipes on tribal land, an Israeli officer responsible for local beduin affairs found his work subverted by the military governor of the West Bank. This orderly individual wished to place meters on the pumps to measure and then charge the tribesmen for water they consumed, a concept totally foreign to the beduins who had always believed that water, like air, is God given and free. The owner of a hotel in the Arab sector of Jerusalem recounted to a visiting American Arabist how he came to discover that the Israelis lacked true culture. He recalled that in the days of the Jordanians, when the tax collector called upon him, he would entertain that official with coffee and cakes while they discoursed at length about Arabic poetry and the world at large. At the end of the evening, the Jordanian opened two attaché cases into which the proprietor placed two sums of money: the first for the government, the second to cement goodwill with the tax collector. The Israelis knew of no such social pleasantries or private financial arrangements among friends; they insisted that the hotel produce actual receipts. The Arab proprietor considered that a breech of good manners and a sign of bad faith. Israelis descending in droves on Arab markets tended at first to buy everything without bargaining, an insult to an Arab's sense of social relations. Having discovered the propriety of bargaining, Israelis—normally of brusque nature—haggled endlessly with Arab merchants whether or not they intended to make a purchase. Judging by a wealth of anecdotal evidence, incidents of this sort were multiplied many times over. Sophisticated Arabs could dismiss such behavior as ignorant or at worst uncouth, but others saw it as a deliberate affront.

It was not that the Israelis lacked interest in Arab culture. At first, many were fascinated by an Arab world that unfolded before them, especially citizens of the Jewish state born in mandatory times. Memories of previous contacts between the two societies, dimmed by two decades of separation, were rekindled with each new contact. The same interest in Arab culture and society was found among Jews from Arab lands and survivors of the Holocaust, who arrived after the birth of the state and the severing of contact with the surrounding world. In Israel, tens of thousands of Jewish immigrants from Arab countries were intrigued by new neighbors with whom they could converse in their native tongue. Arabic was traditionally taught in Israeli high schools as a second foreign language after English. The army also maintained Arabic-language schools for its intelligence branch officers. In Israel's universities, Arabic and Islamic studies were long regarded as a staple of the curriculum. At any given time, hundreds of students majored in Arabic language and literature, Islamic civilization, and medieval and modern Islamic history. Staffed by some of the most prominent Arabists in the Western world, Israel's institutions of higher learning were universally recognized among the great centers of modern Islamic studies.

Many Israelis were overwhelmed by the unexpected exposure to Arabs and their culture and avidly sought books on Islamic civilization. More diligent Israelis actually enrolled in Arabic language classes; but Arabic is a difficult language, even for speakers of Hebrew. It requires considerable time and effort to master, and so interest soon tailed off. Instead, the Arabs registered for Hebrew classes, as that language became necessary to transact daily business with the Israeli authorities as well as with Israeli clients. In addition, thousands of Arabs learned Hebrew informally when they came across the green line to work in construction and a host of other jobs that went unfilled because of a labor shortage in the Jewish sector. Still others would come to learn Hebrew in Israeli prisons. We should be clear about Arabs who speak Hebrew: Unlike Israelis, most did not attempt to learn the language because they were intellectually curious about their neighbors and their neighbor's culture. Their concerns were entirely pragmatic. Still, the Arab engagement with Israeli society has had a far-reaching effect on relations between the two peoples.

The Six Day or June 1967 war gave rise to what Israelis called the "victory industry." Not only was a stagnant Israeli economy revived, but the growth rate ranked among the highest in the world. Within twenty years or so, Israel's standard of living competed with that of various industrialized countries in Western Europe. The Palestinians were at first recipients of this economic boom. Thousands, then tens of thousands, and ultimately more than a hundred thousand Arab laborers found daily employment across the old green line. Large Arab families where one or two sons worked for trivial wages were sending all their male offspring to work. Some Arabs received regular contracts, including benefits, which were and continue to be ample in Israeli society. Most were recruited informally to work construction jobs or engage in menial labor that Israelis were no longer willing to undertake. Their wages were significantly less than those that would have been paid to Jews performing the same tasks. Still, large Arab families, whose adult males were all employed in Israel or by Israelis, could pool their resources and advance themselves as never before. Many social and economic barriers came down for enterprising Arabs taking advantage of newfound opportunities. In the agricultural sector, Arab farmers were instructed by Israeli agronomists on how to increase their yields. To be sure, not all the farmers wished to break with traditional methods or grow different crops, but those who took the advice of the agricultural experts prospered. Not wishing to flood the Israel market with cheap Arab produce—many Israelis who had access to Arab market stalls shopped there on a regular basis—the occupation authorities reopened the bridges across the Jordan River. People and goods came and went to and from the rest of the Arab world, thereby solving a potential economic problem and relieving the caged feeling that gripped many Palestinians. In general, most Palestinians who had never had any contact with individual Israelis discovered the human side of the enemy. Seeing the relative freedom in which Israelis lived, they also came to realize that they as Arabs had greater license to express their displeasure than they previously had under Jordanian or Egyptian rule. That did not salve, however, the growing humiliation of being ruled by nonbelievers of such a different culture. Some Arabs, much at home in the Western world, enjoyed the intellectual company of Israelis, particularly those in left-leaning circles who sympathized with Palestinian aspirations. But when it came to politics, the newly established familiarity did not collapse formidable barriers to understanding. That was true in all levels and segments of Palestinian society.

Before 1967, Palestinians seeking higher education were forced to go abroad. With travel somewhat burdensome following the war, a few sought to enroll in Israel's prestigious universities, but the social and intellectual adjustments were daunting. Classes were conducted in scholarly Hebrew; assignments were heavily larded with English-language readings. The curriculum also tended to be more theoretically oriented than that of Arab universities. The occupation authorities therefore allowed the creation of several Arab universities in the West Bank and Gaza, institutions of higher learning that shortly became hotbeds of Palestinian nationalism. The new universities were the incubators of dissidents who vehemently and at times violently opposed the Israelis and the occupation. They also produced a generation of future technocrats who could run the many Palestinian institutions that began to sprout in the territories. These individuals could and would no doubt shape any future Palestinian state. Not having anticipated the June 1967 war, let alone the conquest of the West Bank, Israel lacked a strategic plan for dealing with the newly acquired territories and their inhabitants. The defense minister who became the iconic figure of Israel's victory, Moshe Dayan, declared shortly after the cessation of hostilities that his government was prepared to return the fruits of its conquest. The only thing he and his people requested was a telephone call from the Arab world signifying a desire to formally end all hostilities and accept the Jewish state as a legitimate partner in the Near East. It is highly unlikely that such a call or comprehensive peace treaty would have resulted in a complete Israeli withdrawal from the former lands of mandatory Palestine. Nevertheless, aside from the Jerusalem metropolitan area and Gush Etzion—a small bloc of Jewish farms south of Jerusalem that had been lost to Jordanian forces in the 1948–1949 war and then reclaimed by the original settlers and their offspring—there was at first no effort to promote Zionist settlement in the conquered territories. In the flush of victory, Israel might very well have been satisfied with minor border rectification. But the proverbial phone call never came. Quite the opposite; faced with the enormity of their defeat, the Arab states preferred intransigence to surrender of any principle. As a final peace continuously eluded Israel, settlement of the West Bank began in earnest, sometimes with and sometimes without the active encouragement and support of the Israel government then in power. There are currently some 230,000 settlers to muddy the political waters. Their very presence is a major stumbling block to any resolution of the Arab-Israel impasse.

As the occupation continued, the Israeli authorities found themselves in a quandary. It was one thing to provide security and coordinate the needs of the populace with a coterie of Arabic-speaking officers; it was quite another to handle the innumerable transactions of daily life. Unlike the Americans who devastated the ruling Baathist infrastructure in the wake of the second Gulf War, Israel retained much of the previous Jordanian administration. That suited the Jordanian monarch King Hussein, who feared that the creation of an independent Palestinian leadership in what had been the western region of his kingdom might foreclose his options to return or even subvert his rule in Transjordan, where Palestinians represented better than half the population. Seeking to retain political influence in the lost territories, the Jordanian government exerted its patronage by continuing to pay the salaries of all civil servants in the West Bank. The Israeli administration also put the civil servants on its payroll, so they received two salaries, much to their delight. Nevertheless, as time passed, the Palestinians of the West Bank began to distance themselves from their erstwhile king. Even those situated in Transjordan began to challenge the monarchy. In September of 1970, East Bank Palestinians affiliated with the more radical groups of the PLO fomented a rebellion against the king. They misread completely the realities of power. There were many snide jokes: about the king's height, which confused his physical and political stature (the Hashemites tend to be very short); about the portrayal of him as rabbit; and about his being called the Mayor of Amman, as if his influence did not extend beyond the capital, if that. These and other disrespectful acts only served to show how little the Palestinians understood the king's surfeit of personal courage and capacity for bold action. The insurgency was brutally suppressed by the Jordanian army in what came to be known as "Black September." In an ironic twist, many Palestinian militants crossed the border to seek captivity in Israel rather than face Hussein's beduin army. Over time, the Jordanian ruling family was forced to reconsider its relationship to the West Bank and the Palestinians. Within Jordanian ruling circles, what had previously been unimagined was eventually discussed in all seriousness. Should the Jordanians continue to press their claims to territories lost in the

June 1967 war? Would the return of the West Bank to Jordan be a liability or an asset to the Hashemite rulers?

As the years passed and the occupation continued, the Palestinians became increasingly independent of the king's influence. They created and administered institutions and designed national symbols to service their own needs, creating thereby the foundations of an anticipated Palestinian state. A popular Egyptian patriotic song, "My Country" (*biladi*), was adopted as a national anthem. The Palestinian flag was displayed widely though it was officially outlawed, and pictures of Arafat graced the walls of many homes. The Dome of the Rock, the great Muslim religious shrine sitting on the Temple Mount, became an icon of Palestinian identity, the quintessential symbol of a glorious past. The schools, relieved of the shackles of Egyptian and Jordanian oversight and given considerable leeway by Israeli educational officers, promoted a national message in all classes beginning with kindergarten. Palestinian writers within the territories and in exile produced extensive literature extolling the nation and making a virtue of resistance to the occupation. Classical texts describing the merits of the Muslim Holy Land were reprinted and distributed with an introduction that addressed the current needs of the emerging nation. Political theater bearing nationalist messages delighted sophisticated audiences. On occasion, the Israel authorities censured the press; they also prohibited importing more inflammatory writings, but overall these efforts were halfhearted. In that respect, the Palestinians under Israeli occupation had more freedom of expression than they had under Arab control. Professional associations, including women's organizations, became more prominent; labor unions grew in strength; student organizations were formed in the newly established Palestinian universities. As all these groups crossed family and clan lines, more narrowly defined allegiances gave way to a greater sense of national unity, made all the more possible by the concurrent weakening of the great landowners and family notables. The flight of the Palestinians in 1948 created a more level playing field in Arab society for those Palestinians who remained behind in the Jewish state. A similar phenomenon was underway in the areas under Arab control. Not surprisingly, Israel's Arab minority gave verbal support to their brethren across the green line.

A few Israelis continued to hope for a peaceful solution in which the king would reclaim the West Bank and make it secure for himself and Israel as well. However, circumstances were moving in the opposite direction. The issue of Jordanian sovereignty was finally resolved in 1994 when King Hussein, realizing there was no going back to the past, gave up all rights to the West Bank except his role as guardian of the holy shrines in Jerusalem.

The king's hand had been forced by the turn of historic events. Following the 1993 meeting on the White House lawn—in which Israel's Prime Minister Yitzhak Rabin, and the head of the PLO, Yasir Arafat, shook hands in a sign of mutual recognition—the entire world recognized that Palestinians were both entitled and en route to independent statehood. It had taken a quarter of a century, but even Israel's leaders accepted the urgency of resolving the conflict with the Arabs based on fulfilling Palestinian aspirations for statehood. The Israeli occupation was about to come full cycle, or so it seemed.

It is unclear whether anyone could have predicted, a quarter of a century earlier, the circuitous course of events leading to that moment. Immediately after the 1967 war, the Palestinians in Cisjordan, as well as their leadership abroad, were faced with the reality of unanticipated Israeli rule. After the shock of Israel's victory had settled, it became apparent to them that no diplomatic initiative would put an end to the occupation, at least none that could have been acceptable to both Israel and the Arab nations still technically at war with the Jewish state. It was also apparent that, for the foreseeable future, no Arab government acting singularly or in concert with other Arab states could defeat the IDF on the field of battle. Even if that were somehow possible and the Arabs triumphed, there was no guarantee that the Palestinians would be granted a truly independent state of their own. Whether achieved peacefully or on the battlefield, the end of Israeli rule in the West Bank and Gaza might very well have resulted in the return of the Egyptian and Jordanian authorities, none of whom showed any particular sympathy for Palestinian statehood when they ruled segments of what had been mandated Palestine. But that is all speculation. In the days, months, and years following the 1967 war, only the Palestinians acted boldly to confront the most powerful state in the region.

Given license by Arab governments to operate more freely than before, various constituents of the PLO, the umbrella organization of the Palestinian nationalist movements, undertook direct action against Israel, both in the Jewish state and in foreign settings. Pledged to put an end to the illegal Zionist entity by force, Palestinian militant groups promoted a series of high profile operations that attracted world attention and, more especially, the admiration of the Arab street. Finally, Arabs had acted in a proud fashion that drew notice to the plight of their own, the stateless Palestinians. Truth be told, the cross-border raids—mostly from Jordan—caused little property damage and no significant loss of Israeli life. Many of the Palestinian fighters (*fada'iyin*, referred to in the press as *fedayeen*) gave up quickly after encountering the first Israeli patrols; those prepared to do combat were, more often than not, hunted down and quickly killed or captured. Seeking to establish a profile for the infiltrators, the IDF studied the fedayeen taken captive. The majority had a minimal education and little awareness of the broad political issues underlying the dispute with the Zionist state. Nor did they seem to have a fully developed sense of national consciousness. They saw themselves as Arabs fighting against the Jews. Nevertheless, the PLO discovered the power of the world media to dramatize its case. The exploits of the fedayeen were magnified for the foreign press. In one instance, a journalist was allowed to accompany a raid that was in reality a mock battle staged on the Jordanian side of the border. Slowly but perceptibly, the plight of homeless and stateless Palestinians captured the world's attention as had that of the Jewish refugees following the Second World War. The infiltrators were merely attempting to redress the terrible fate that had befallen the Palestinians when the Zionists drove them from their lands and left so many of them to subsist on handouts from international relief agencies. Surely, the world owed the Palestinians a stake in their own future. Surely, the Palestinians had no less right to their cherished homeland than the Jews.

Much of this moral capital was squandered by the Palestinians in a series of daring and violent acts: hijacking and blowing up commercial airliners; killing innocent travelers who happened to be in the wrong place at the wrong time; enticing gullible foreign women to unknowingly carry explosive devices on aircraft; commandeering a cruise ship and then blithely tossing a wheelchair-bound passenger overboard; and ultimately, the most daring act of all, the murder of Israeli athletes at the 1972 Olympic games in Munich. However much the world recoiled from the more excessive acts of violence, the Arab world applauded the audacity of the perpetrators, and the stock of the PLO rose accordingly.

Within Israel itself, the militants at first proved rather inept. During the first year or so of the occupation, a series of explosions went off in various public places in Jerusalem. The only casualty in the so-called "Night of the Grenades" was a man mistaken for an Arab and beaten by an outraged group of Jewish thugs. A second explosion in a supermarket resulted in the death of two foreign students from Latin America. Subsequent events produced greater losses of property and life as the explosive devices became more sophisticated. The Israelis were quick to grasp the significance of developments. Access to public venues required the search of handbags, shopping baskets, and the like; the public was instructed to spot suspicious objects that might be explosive devices; security at airports was extraordinarily tight. Roadblocks were established everywhere to intercept potential terrorists before they reached their intended targets. Arabs going from place to place found their movements increasingly restricted. Crossing the bridges from Jordan was a particularly long and arduous process, as Israeli security personnel carefully examined every vehicle crossing the border. In the summer months, Arabs might have to stand for hours in the broiling heat; in the winter, there was the cold rain. The occupation, seemingly without end, had grown from wearisome to humiliating and then unbearable. When the first intifada broke out in 1987 and Arabs rioted in the streets, the Israeli army was given license to break bones in an attempt to stanch the rebellion. Faced with problems of security, the authorities periodically closed the checkpoints leading to Israel, thus depriving tens of thousands of Arab laborers of a livelihood. When the violence did not subside, guest workers were brought from Europe, Asia, and Africa to replace Arab labor, causing devastation in the economy of the West Bank and Gaza. Although deemed necessary by those responsible for Israel's security, these moves proved counterproductive. The collapse of the Palestinian economy produced even greater resentment and set the stage for religious revival; in turn, the large numbers of guest laborers, many of whom overstayed their welcome to work illegally, put great strains on the social fabric of Israeli life. Israelis and Palestinians alike were trapped in a cycle of violence and declining civility. Each passing year of the occupation fueled the fires of Palestinian nationalism. Above all, it stimulated Palestinian society to mobilize in common cause as never before and at many levels of society. Slowly but surely, the preconditions had been set for the emergence of a Palestinian nation united in common cause. Faced with the overbearing presence of Jewish control, the Arabs of Palestine tended to sweep under the rug the many differences that divided them.

Still, nearly three decades after it declared its goal of liberating Palestine by force of arms, the PLO was unable to make any headway in achieving its aims. Quite the opposite, Egypt had entered into a formal peace agreement with the Jewish state in 1979, and by the late 1980s there was serious talk of resolving the Arab-Israel dispute, among Arabs no less. In an unexpected fashion, peace was now on the international agenda, but Palestinian statehood was stalled and the PLO was accountable. The PLO had always been at a disadvantage within the occupied territories. It had its trusted agents throughout the West Bank and Gaza, and it exercised considerable leverage as a result of the vast sums of money it controlled. But the leadership had been forced from one Arab country to another, most recently to distant Tunisia, a humiliating exile occasioned by the Israeli invasion of Lebanon in 1982. The disparity between the exiles' relative prosperity and the difficult conditions under which the occupied Palestinians lived did not escape notice in the West Bank and Gaza. Publicly, the Palestinians who remained in the ancestral homeland expressed full support for the bold lions in exile; privately they held many of them in contempt. When the first intifada erupted in December of 1987, it soon became clear that this was a spontaneous uprising by an occupied population that had been pushed too far. Observing the momentum generated by people taking to the streets in defiance of the IDF, the old guard attempted to co-opt the intifada from afar, only to be rebuffed. The die had been cast. A younger and more militant leadership would arise in the territories, within both the PLO and the new Islamic organizations that were emerging in the West Bank and Gaza.

The Islamic organizations would completely alter the nationalist mantra of the PLO. Perhaps the most remarkable aspect of the 1964 covenant and the PLO's later versions of 1968, 1973, and 1977 is their thoroughly secular character. One is taken aback by the lack of references to Islamic tradition, especially because Arafat and some other PLO leaders had a history with the Muslim Brotherhood. As articulated in the PLO covenants or charters, the legitimacy of Palestinian claims is not rooted in the Qur'an or in subsequent Islamic texts, but is instead based on the concept of the Palestinian people taking their proper place within the larger and all-embracing Arab nation. The only document cited in support of Palestinian rights is the United Nations Charter, which calls for the right of self-determination for all peoples. The secular character of the original covenant allowed the PLO to take the propaganda lead following the 1967 war. With the Palestinian problem once again in the international limelight, Arafat and his cohort peddled the notion of the "secular democratic state." Israel would be dissolved, by force if necessary, but this would not lead to a hegemonic Arab/Muslim polity. In place of Israel, by definition a Jewish state, a Palestinian polity that honored all the values of the Western world would arise: There would be no imposition of religion in the democratic state to be formed. Such declarations were quickly looked upon by foreigners seeking a solution to a seemingly intractable moral dilemma as a sign of Arab moderation and a hopeful approach to resolving the Arab-Israel conflict. The new line quickly gave rise, however, to spirited discussion among the Palestinians who feared a slippage in their uncompromising resistance to the Jews. In numerous memoranda and published views, it was made clear that the secular democratic state would be a thoroughly Palestinian Arab state, but for rhetorical purposes, the concept would be allowed to stand without commentary. In any case, there was no such model state, nor was there ever any such model state in the entire Arab world. Israelis understood very well that the PLO's vision of the future was merely a ploy in the present. Even if such a state came into being, according to the principle of "one man one vote," the Arab majority would have its way in all matters. Nevertheless, all that discussion seemed to compromise basic Islamic beliefs. The secularist formulations of the PLO, taken together with the ineptness of their military confrontation with Israel—to say nothing of the corruption of their leadership—paved the way for militant Islamic organizations to challenge the entrenched leaders.

5

THE ISLAMIC MOVEMENT

*Traditional Islam and
Palestinian Nationalism after 1987*

The failure of the Palestine Liberation Organization (PLO) to make significant progress in achieving Palestinian statehood left the field open for new players and ideas about nationhood and a future Palestinian state. Foremost among these new players were various Palestinian organizations closely linked to Islamic revival, a movement or phenomenon often referred to by Westerners as Islamic fundamentalism. Even before Muslim terrorists destroyed the World Trade Center in September of 2001, the Western media devoted considerable attention to the resurgence of Islam. Since 9/11, there has been a virtual deluge of so-called expert commentary on Islamic movements, much of it highly inaccurate and misleading.

The very term "fundamentalist" is awkward if not inappropriate; it confuses Muslim revivalists with Christian Protestants who insist on the literal interpretation of scripture. While all Muslims believe the Qur'an to be the word of God, they read and understand the text with the aid of numerous commentaries and legal texts that elucidate its meaning. Without this vast body of literature and the popular oral tradition to which it has given rise, much of Muslim scripture, a composite of prophetic revelation, legal dicta, and didactic references to a monotheist past, would be largely unintelligible, even to those with a superb command of classical Arabic. Indeed, the license to freely interpret scripture and to expand that interpretation gives revivalists room to maneuver in the modern world. Were they restricted to a literal reading of the Qur'an, they would have no way of addressing the wide concerns of present-day Muslims. Anyone analyzing revivalist thought is therefore obliged to consider the broad interpretive enterprise that gives the Qur'an meaning for all the faithful regardless of place and time. Unfortunately, too many people addressing the complex issues before us have no convenient point of entry into this vast corpus of written and oral texts. That being the case, they are unable to penetrate the ideological realm of the revivalists. It goes without saying that their inability to get to the heart of revivalist thought and thereby unpack its militant declarations complicates life, especially for those who are inclined to rely on such experts to enlighten the public, or worse yet, make government policy. There is much more to the resurgence of Islam than the Western public has been led to believe.

Similarly, we should not be misled into thinking, as the public did for a long time and some people still do, that all Islamists (as the revivalists are most frequently called) are insulated from modern culture or completely resistant to it. The familiar images of the unworldly and unyielding Taliban and of Muslim children suffering from the intellectual sclerosis of Qur'an schools mask the true face of Islamic revival, certainly as we encounter it among present-day Palestinians. The spiritual leadership of the Palestinian Islamists may be supplied by classically trained Muslim imams, but the daily activities of the various militant groups are coordinated by individuals much at home in modern technology and ideas. Fathi al-Shiqaqi, leader of Islamic Jihad before his assassination in 1995, was a doctor of medicine who boasted of his passion for Western literature. His successor, Ramadan Shallah, a former "secularist" like many converts to the movement, was at one time a professor of political science in the United States. The late 'Abd al-'Aziz al-Rantisi and Mahmoud Zahar, two leading political figures in Hamas, were trained to be physicians. The nerve center of Hamas in Gaza's Islamic University is not the faculty of theology but that of the natural sciences, where Zahar has been dean. Like other Islamist movements, Hamas has filled its leadership with engineers, physicians, pharmacists, computer-literate technicians, and the like. In that respect, one would be hard-pressed to draw a distinction between many leaders of Islamic revival and those of the so-called secular nationalist camp.

As for the Islamist shock troops, many live in wretched refugee camps and poor rural villages, but not all come from impoverished and/or intellectually disadvantaged families. The powerful appeal of Islamic revival may be linked to diminished opportunities, many of them economic, but that appeal will not lessen if just the material life of Palestinians improves. The community's wide acceptance of Islamists who condemn Israel, the imperialist West, and a godless and amoral Western culture taps into a profound malaise found in all social and economic levels of Arab Palestinian society. The wide-ranging appeal of the Islamists is rooted in feelings of rage generated by an inability to reverse three hundred years of foreign encroachment—

the humiliating Israeli occupation being only the latest and perhaps most cruel humiliation of all. Regardless of their socioeconomic standing, all Palestinian Muslims see the current situation as absolutely incongruous with long-standing expectations based on a thousand years of mostly uninterrupted Muslim triumphs before the advance of the West.

It is no small wonder then that Muslims wish to return to the past and, among other things, redress the injustice represented by the very existence of a Jewish state within the boundaries of "historic" Palestine. To that end, many Palestinians have entrusted their future to militant Islam. They have recently affirmed that choice in a democratically held election for the Palestinian parliament, which surprised all observers including the Islamist leadership.

How should we profile these militants? What induces their specific sense of Palestinian consciousness and their particular vision of a future Palestinian state? Does their approach to the Zionist entity, the pejorative euphemism by which they refer to Israel, differ from mainstream Palestinian nationalists, and if so, what are the implications of their views for the future of Jewish-Muslim relations? Put somewhat differently, is there an Islamic solution to the Arab-Israel dispute that some if not most Israelis can live with, however uncomfortably? Or is Islam itself the most identifiable drawback to any such solution? That is, does the Islamic solution call for the very dissolution of the Jewish state? And if so, can Islamists show any flexibility in the short or long term regarding the existence of a foreign Jewish polity on sacred Muslim soil? With the Islamists representing more than half the Palestinian legislative assembly, these are no longer theoretical musings. We are much in need of clues regarding the future outlook and behavior of Palestine's Islamic revivalists.

As with all revivalist movements in the long history of Islam, a declared reverence for the past is the key to understanding the present and anticipating the future. As noted previously, traditional Muslims have never held the past to be distinct from contemporary life. To the contrary, Muslim experiences from the most remote times have served and continue to serve as models that guide Muslim thought and behavior. That being the case, we are left to ponder how Islamists so rooted in the past can be so conversant with modern science and technology. On the whole, those who acknowledge that many Islamists are genuinely attracted to the modern world—and thus consider them serious partners for future dialogue—often misunderstand the nature of the attraction. One cannot deny that the physicians and engineers who help direct Islamic movements promote the practical importance of Western medicine and technological advances (what in Arabic is known as "mashiniyat," the wondrous world of machines), but neither they nor their religiously trained colleagues embrace the freedom of inquiry that girds scientific innovation. The scientific revolution in Europe, which gave the West dominance over the Islamic Near East, was occasioned by a perceived license to discard long-held beliefs. The individual and institutional capacity to abandon old paradigms and design bold research that represents new departures is in fact the hallmark of modern science. It is also the hallmark of innovative social engineering that has transformed Western societies in the modern age. Of equal importance, there has been a revolution in the way reflective Western historians have produced complex historical models to explain the past and adjust to the realities of the present. That is to say, in the West, revolutionary impulses lead to radical breaks with the time tested and familiar. Revolutionary change is by its very nature transformative and, in the best of cases, beneficial to society.

Traditional Arab Muslims are inclined to view transformative change rather differently. For them, dramatic breaks with the past are possible openings for diminished religious authority and broad-based heresy, a concern that is reflected, however subtly, in the Arab school system, where the authority of the teacher and curriculum go largely unchallenged and, all too often, unchanged. There is much rote learning and not enough encouragement of independent thinking. Even at the more advanced grades, schools do not encourage students to test their analytical abilities and solve problems by means other than those learned by repeating the same exercises or memorizing the same data. Nor is there a pronounced effort to stimulate genuine interest in foreign cultures, be it in the realm of history, literature, art, or music. Given that restrictive rearing and the outlook it generates, traditionalists are able to absorb modern medicine and technology, but they are far less prepared to sustain theoretical research at a high level or engage other civilizations out of genuine intellectual curiosity.

For the most part, Muslim revivalists do not like to wax philosophical, be it about their world or the worlds of others. As physicians, pharmacists, engineers, and the like, they value quick and efficient solutions to problems they can readily identify. Regarding that, technology has served the militant Islamists and served them well. Their leaders communicate from clandestine locations by cell phone; they send out missives by fax; distribute sermons on cassettes; manufacture explosive devices with knowledge obtained in chemistry classes; and produce primitive artillery in metalwork shops. They can do all that because this kind of resourcefulness does not depend on challenging traditional patterns of belief and behavior.

Islam is well suited to Arabs who seek practical and immediate solutions. Religious law orders daily life from the moment of waking to that of sleeping and prescribes behavior for all sorts of contingencies. Nor are the lives of true believers overly encumbered by spiritual doubt or uncertainty; their path is well plotted. Staying on the straight and narrow may not bring material rewards in this life, but it gives all observant Muslims the absolute dignity of complying with God's wishes. In unsettling times, there is much comfort in knowing and occupying high moral ground. The certainty of it all gives the Islamists an edge over reflective secular Arab rivals and a tactical advantage over Western enemies who are beset, all too often, by ambiguity and indecision bred of moral relativism.

Among current Muslim revivalists, including Palestinians, firm convictions are most often linked to didactic lessons learned from a distant past. That comes as no great surprise. Historical memory has always been the cement that binds the faithful in bad times as well as good. Until the encroachment of the West and the establishment of a Jewish state on sacred Muslim soil, the past conjured up visions of Muslim polities that rivaled the Roman Empire. That was a sign of Allah's favor. There were, to be sure, disturbing moments as well, historic developments that challenged the self-confidence of the Muslim body politic. Even people who embrace a triumphant outlook, as did the Muslims of the Arab world, can feel beset from time to time by the vicissitudes of history. In unsettling times, there have been calls for new directions. And so, beset by crises that disturb the equilibrium of traditional society—whether the result of foreign encroachment or internal stresses and strains—Muslims, ordinarily resistant to change, have invoked the past in attempts to reform or completely restructure existing societies.

But even these revolutionary appeals to dramatically transform Islamic society and/or combat external enemies have not called for bold new departures. Islamic revolution does not signify radical political innovation and/or dramatically new social engineering as did the French and Russian revolutions, momentous events often cited by Arabs looking to Europe. To the contrary, Islamic revolutionaries preach a return to the origins of Islam, an age of pristine religious behavior, admirable politics, and triumphant warfare over enemies, the Jews among them. For Islamic revival to succeed, the wheel of history must revolve completely back to the starting point.

What does this reliance on the past tell us about Islamic militants and present and future developments in the Near East? Or, given our interests here, how does embracing the past shape Palestinian national consciousness and visions of the future Palestinian state? Surprisingly, indeed paradoxically, being enfolded in the past gives current militants considerable leeway in combating Zionism. On the one hand, believing Muslims have long invoked history in order to change Islamic societies by whatever means necessary, including the use of brutal force. The recent activities of the Taliban in Afghanistan and the Islamists of Algeria, whose actions have resulted in more than a hundred thousand deaths, are cases in point. On the other hand, Muslims have also invoked history to discourage taking up arms against an implacable enemy when the odds for success are deemed exceedingly long. They have even cited the past to discourage active rebellion against a Muslim authority that guardians of the faith consider unjust and unwanted. In numerous Muslim traditions, the Prophet himself advises the faithful to curb their appetites for combat and justice until a more propitious time. A premature campaign against the unbelieving enemy or against a Muslim tyrant can lead to a failure that will set back still further the cause of the righteous. When military adventures are unlikely to succeed, prudence dictates that swords remain sheathed.

Moreover, rebellion, even in a just cause, can give rise to dangerous circumstances. In an evolving Islamic political theory, tyrants were considered preferable to rebels who might produce anarchy and the total destabilization of Muslim communities. Hence, would-be champions of change, confident of their moral position, could still sit on their hands and, citing historic precedent and law, delay taking action. Over the course of Islamic history, such an attitude and agenda suited potential rebels filled with rage but lacking resolve; or more charitably put, it was favored by rebels blessed with a surfeit of good tactical sense and an appreciation for long-range strategic planning. In sum, traditional Muslims, including today's Palestinian militants, can, in all good conscience, read the past as a guide to action or inaction depending on the exigencies of the moment. They can choose rebellion or accommodation and still be devoted Muslims.

The long history of the Islamic revival is filled with stories of premature rebellions—abortive insurgencies launched with enormous bravado, usually destined to failure. The more successful champions of the faith fully understood the realities of power and bided their time until success could be assured. The most noteworthy case of political restraint is perhaps that of the Abbasid caliphs, true revolutionaries who restored the Prophet's family to rule in the eighth century C.E. and then shaped Islamic political culture as no Muslims had since Muhammad himself. The Abbasids, kinsmen of the Prophet, understood only too well that long-range goals often require careful planning and, above all, delayed gratification. They built a clandestine revolutionary apparatus and waited almost fifty years before unfurling the celebrated black banners of their cause. The long period of gestation that preceded their open revolt elicited much criticism in retrospect, especially from those Muslims who were willing to accept martyrdom in a just cause while the Abbasids kept a low if not invisible profile. The new rulers had much to explain for their seeming inaction at the time, but unlike their critics who had to be satisfied with memories of failed uprisings, the Abbasids, given their patience, created a dynasty that was to last some five hundred years.

MODERN REVIVALISTS: THE MUSLIM BROTHERHOOD (*IKHWAN*) AND PALESTINE

The Palestinian Islamists thus have two models they can follow, both deeply rooted in Muslim experience: temporary accommodation based on the realities of power, and an open revolt regardless of the odds of success. Until the Iranian revolution, which served as a powerful symbol of successful Muslim action, revivalists in the modern Arab world tended to avoid truly epic confrontations in highly unfavorable circumstances. The Muslim Brotherhood (*Ikhwan*), which has so powerfully influenced Palestinian nationalism, is one example of a revivalist movement that has cautiously navigated through the troubled waters of modern politics. Founded in 1928 by Egyptian schoolteacher Hasan al-Banna, the Ikhwan espouses the creation of a true Islamic polity. To that end, it has opposed established secular government and called instead for Arab polities ruled by traditional Islamic law (*shari'ah*)—that is, Islamic states. Ultimately, the regional states would be replaced by a universal Islamic community based on the ummah of the Prophet Muhammad. Despite its radical agenda, the brotherhood has tended toward caution. When the authorities used force against the movement, its leaders opted for a lower political profile. Rather than seek a decisive showdown with the powerful forces of the state, a tactic that would serve no redeeming purpose, the brothers have chosen to bore quietly and deeply within the ruling society by infiltrating government agencies and private and public professional associations. That was particularly true of the Palestinian branches of the movement, the forerunners of today's Islamic militants.

After the Nakbah, the catastrophe of 1948–1949, the brotherhood was highly critical of the role played by the secular Arab states, accusing them of sending ill-equipped and ill-trained armies against the Zionists. This broad complaint mirrored the general view of the Arab public. But the Islamists went further in their analysis of Arab failure. Negligence and ineptitude were not the only or even basic causes of the Palestine fiasco; it was rather the secular nature of the modern Arab nation-state. The emergence of modern Arab nationalism had undermined the religious foundations of Islamic societies and compromised the will of Muslims to defend their faith and honor. Most Arabs saw 1948–1949 as a crushing setback for the Arab nation as a whole; the brotherhood saw in it a possibility for Islamic renewal. It was time to trumpet Islamic universalism over ill-founded and narrowly defined national loyalties. Modern nationalism, an alien concept brought from the West, introduced sensibilities that were antithetical to genuine Islam. Brothers asked, if somewhat rhetorically, what Arab nationalists gained when they joined the British in overthrowing the Ottoman Empire? What resulted from Arab complicity in the demise of a legitimate Islamic regime? The answer: (Christian) rule over Islamic lands and the Balfour Declaration, a document in which His Majesty's government pledged itself to help create a Jewish national home in Palestine, thus paving the way for the Zionists to usurp Muslim territory.

As a result the Jews—the most accursed of all God's people—defile sacred Muslim land, including Jerusalem, the city from which the Prophet Muhammad ascended to the heavens. The brotherhood held that no one has the right to concede even a part of Palestine to unbelievers. Islamic tradition and law are clear; territory within the "The Abode (*Dar*) of Islam" is not negotiable; when lost to foreign invaders, there is a religious duty to reclaim it—all the more so when the land embraces Islam's third-holiest city. In sum, the brotherhood argued that there can be no Jewish state of any sort on Muslim soil, least of all in historic Palestine.

The brotherhood's strategy for dealing with Zionism was much the same as that of all Arabs immediately following the "catastrophe." In no way would they recognize even the fact of Israel's existence. They would use any means possible to isolate the fledgling Jewish state from the world community until it collapsed under pressure or was overcome by reinvigorated Arab armies on the field of battle. The tactics for destroying the Zionist state— whose very existence they chose not to recognize—were, however, quite different from those of the Arab nationalist camp. Unlike the leaders of Arab states who continuously talked of military triumph in the not-too-distant future, the Islamists saw the redemption of Palestine as a long-range project. In that sense, they subscribed to the quietist agenda of Islamic revival. They were unburdened by time. There was no prepared schedule for the inevitable redemption of Palestinian and Arab honor. Recognizing that Arab leaders preferred talking of action rather than acting, brotherhood theoreticians declared that there could be no success against the Jews if Arabs were to do business as usual. An Islamic solution was required. The restoration of Arab honor and dignity depended first and foremost on Islamic revival everywhere in the Near East. From that perspective the Palestinian cause, however important, was a mere sideshow to a broader Islamic agenda. Only when Islamic states replaced the secular polities of the moment, and only when the stateless Palestinians transformed their own society to conform to Islamic law and tradition, could a jihad to liberate the Holy Land have the desired consequences. In such fashion, the brotherhood recognized the emotive force of Palestinian nationalism but harnessed it to a larger pan-Islamic project: the ultimate restoration of a universal Islamic community. Only such a community as existed in the days of the Prophet and the powerful caliphs could successfully fend off the challenge of the West and make Islam triumphant once again.

In the end, the brotherhood was prepared to offer only spiritual guidance and sage political advice. However much they decried the secular nation-states and their ruling authority, the brothers tended to eschew any direct call to arms against fellow Arabs. The Egyptian society, which generally served to inspire the other branches, was not anxious to confront the government—not in Egypt or anywhere else. Given the repressive forces of the nation-state, the brotherhood reasoned that a direct confrontation with established government was an exercise in futility. Periodic challenges to state authority always met with failure. The Palestinian brothers adapted a similar line in Gaza and the West Bank when those areas were ruled by the Egyptians and Jordanians, respectively. After a brief honeymoon, the Egyptian authorities in Gaza stifled the brotherhood as it had in Egypt. The Islamists of Gaza then fostered a more or less clandestine movement. In the West Bank, ruled by the Jordanians, the brothers were given greater latitude, and so they organized more openly while establishing contacts with fellow movements throughout the Arab world. In neither case did the brothers and their like-minded supporters raise a challenge to the ruling authorities. After the Israeli conquest of 1967, they followed a similar course under the new administration. There was no shame in that. In choosing a long-range strategy rather than engage in premature armed conflict, the Palestinian brotherhood could and did rely on precedents ultimately derived from the life of the Prophet. The earliest converts to Islam were only obliged to declare belief in Allah and the broad moral principles reflected in the so-called "Pledge of the Women" (*bay'at al-nisa'*). Only later, when Muhammad had raised sufficient military forces to take the field with confidence against his enemies, did converts to Islam pledge to unsheathe their weapons in the "Pledge of War" (*bay'at al-harb*).

The accommodating attitude of the Palestinian brothers was noted by the Israel administration in the occupied territories. In order to set up an effective counterweight to the secularist PLO, they allowed funds to be channeled to the Islamists, assuming that the latter were more interested in Islamic education than waging war. That held true not only of the brotherhood, but also of government-appointed religious authorities that the brothers had begun to undermine. Israel's planners were led to believe that educational projects promoting Islamic values would encourage inward reflection and religious piety rather than political activism. In the end, propping up the Islamists instead of the PLO proved to be a grievous error as Islamic revival became increasingly more militant everywhere in the region. In 1967, there were seventy-seven mosques, mostly controlled by officials responsible to the governing authority. By the outbreak of the intifada, some twenty years later, there were two hundred, most of them controlled by the Palestinian Brotherhood and other Islamist organizations.

As the occupation wore on, the brotherhood's agenda for delayed gratification became a problem. Among Arabs, the Palestinians remained the only people without a polity of their own. Given the complicated agenda set forth by the Islamist theoreticians, there seemed to be no end in sight to this injustice. By 1979, some thirty-odd years had elapsed since the catastrophic loss of Palestine, and no Islamic state had been established in any of the countries that were direct parties to the Arab-Israel dispute. If Palestinians had to wait for the Islamist scenario to play itself out, generations might pass without their achieving statehood. A dozen years after the Six Day War, Israel still retained absolute control over all Palestine. It was one thing for Palestinians to live under Arab/Muslim rule in Gaza and the West Bank before 1967; they could accept that, however bitter the taste. It was another matter altogether to live under a Jewish occupation that shamed them and dishonored both Islam and their Arab identity. Facing that reality, Palestinian Islamists formed new groups espousing active resistance against the occupiers, much as their Egyptian colleagues breaking with the brotherhood turned increasingly violent in attempts to Islamize their own country.

ISLAMIC JIHAD

Most important of these new Palestinian groups was Islamic Jihad, founded in 1979 by the aforementioned Fathi al-Shiqaqi and 'Abd al-'Aziz 'Awdah, a fiery preacher trained in Islamic theology. The atmosphere was soon ripe for attracting hard-core believers. The ignominious retreat of the PLO from Lebanon following the Israeli invasion in 1982 caused dismay and then disaffection in mainstream nationalist ranks. The defeat in Lebanon and the

exile of the Palestinian leadership to a distant Tunisia reduced the PLO's capacity to take the fight directly to the Israeli enemy. Within the ranks, some
PLO figures even contemplated abandoning the concept of a secular–democratic Palestinian state in favor of a more modest two-state solution along
the lines of the old 1947 partition plan. Other members of the PLO who
had been associated with the brotherhood at one time or another embraced
militant Islam; still others who had been secularists now accepted religion
as the solution. Many Jihadists were recruited in Israel's prisons where Islamists proselytized actively among detainees who had grown lax in their
faith. The result was a generation of born-again Muslims ready to do combat with the Jews. Casting their net so widely, the new militants expressed
sympathy for Fatah, the largest group within the PLO. They took note that
many Fatah leaders had at one time been active Islamists, including Arafat
himself, and that despite its current misfortunes, Fatah's military wing had
been the first armed Palestinian group to actively engage the Israeli enemy.
That respect for the old warhorses also made for a degree of tactical flexibility; the Jihadists could and did seek cooperation with favored elements of
the secular mainstream when it suited their purposes. Fatah in turn recognized the value of militant fighters situated in the territories. Similar cooperation would mark relations between the mainstream nationalists and the
Islamist movements born during the general uprising that began in December of 1987.

Searching for shock troops to fill the rank and file, the Islamist movement seemed particularly appealing to younger men of modest social
means, those stagnating in the refugee camps, persons left jobless or at best
employed performing menial tasks, people without a meaningful future,
and, most important, people without major family responsibilities. Such a
profile suited Islamic Jihad, as it would Hamas (see below). As the leadership organized tight clandestine cells (*usrah*), it needed operatives who could
move about freely, innocuous people whose activities would attract little attention and whose deaths, however mourned, would not destroy the fabric
of their larger families' lives. Young men, their very manhood emasculated
by their circumstances, thrilled to the danger and violence that was to become the movement's mode of operation. Some violent acts were well
planned; others were seemingly inspired by events of the moment; still others were random occurrences. Jihadists would later play a prominent role in
the suicide bombings that began in 1993. Because Islamic law and tradition
forbids suicide, such operations had to be redefined in Islamic terms. For
the religious authorities who countenanced such actions—many did not—
the suicide bomber was understood to be a martyr (*shahid*), the equivalent

of a brave soul who volunteers for a military mission against the unbelievers with full knowledge that he is not likely to return. Such an individual is automatically promised the pleasures of Paradise, which according to Muslim belief are considerable.

Aside from the clandestine warriors who were given to tight discipline in small cells, the movement could be described as a political amoeba. Its ranks divided and subdivided into splinter groups, only to reform and rejoin at a moment of convenience. To be sure, the overarching views of Islamic Jihad were well known and approved by many if not most Palestinians. However they defined themselves, the Jihadists never sought a complete break with either the nationalist or Islamist past, and so their appeal was broadly based. They issued a general call for resolute action to destroy the Zionist entity and in its stead establish an Islamic state in all of mandated Palestine. To that end, Palestinians were encouraged to draw inspiration from traditional Islamic sources. But these sentiments were not fashioned into a discrete ideological platform. Unlike the brotherhood, the PLO, and Hamas, the Islamic Jihad movement, which would take root in 1988, did not give formal expression to its ideology. The organization was without an official charter; it had no learned jurists who composed lengthy Islamic tracts, nor did it establish and circulate official publications that elicited a steady stream of religiously informed commentary. Rather, Islamic Jihad made its positions known through articles in two foreign monthlies broadly sympathetic to the militant line. Only after the 1987 intifada did the movement put out its own publication, a bulletin printed in Lebanon. There were also leaflets, flyers, and wall posters, as well as the sermons of the Jihadist imams. Extrapolating the movement's views from these diverse sources leads one to believe that its political vision was, from the outset, highly derivative, a mixing and matching of old and new Islamist opinion from Egypt to Iran.

The new Islamic militants continued to draw inspiration from the teachings of the brotherhood, but, having taken a proactive stance against Israel and Zionism, they inclined to the views of the martyred Egyptian brother Sayyid Qutb, an outspoken critic of Nasser's regime, who was subsequently executed by the state. Unlike other leaders of the society who looked to cooperate with the authorities, Qutb called openly for decisive action. His views electrified militant Islamists; they continued his call for resistance a decade and more after his death in 1966. According to Qutb, the Arab world was beset by a new age of ignorance (*jahiliyah*) comparable to that which existed before the Prophet's mission and the onset of Islam. This new jahiliyah undermined traditional belief and observance and left the faithful without religious guidance to deal with the unbelievers and the influence of their godless culture. As Arab governments were complicit in repressing the true Muslims, they would have to be replaced immediately and by any means necessary. In this Manichaean battle that pits good against evil and religion against heresy, there can be no giving ground. One must seek an immediate return to the Islam of Muhammad and the early Islamic community. The sovereignty of God must replace the rule of man.

The leaders of Islamic Jihad were also attracted to the writings of the Ayatollah Khomeini, whose followers overthrew Iran's secular regime and established in its stead a true Islamic state, an event that was to mark a major watershed in the history of modern Islamic revival. Palestinian militants were particularly admiring of the way the Iranians embraced the Palestinian cause as their own. Special praise was heaped upon Hezbollah, the Iranian-sponsored Shiite party that fought the Israelis and their Christian proxies in South Lebanon. Indeed, the Palestinians established contact with the Hezbollah and received their indirect support in mounting operations against the Israeli occupation. When Israel withdrew completely from Lebanon in 1999, the Palestinians celebrated the move as a stunning defeat for the Israel Defense Forces (IDF) and saw Hezbollah as providing them with the necessary strategy to defeat a better-armed foe. The success of Hezbollah demonstrated to Palestinians that Israelis, however powerful, lacked the endurance to withstand the constant pressure of small operations that would bleed them and destroy their resolve. If only from a tactical point of view, there was no need to compromise with the Zionist enemy. Quite the opposite; some militants believed that the time had come to fully integrate Iran and the Shiites into the larger Arab-Sunnite Islamic fold.

At first glance, close cooperation with the Shiites might seem rather odd. Virtually all Palestinian Muslims are Sunnites. Relations between these rival branches of Islam have a long history going back to the formative period of Islamic civilization (seventh and eighth centuries C.E.) often marked by mutual antagonism that has given rise at times to open conflict. From the outset, each group has claimed that its leaders inherited the mantle of the Prophet and thus possess the authority to command the universal Islamic community. As the Shiites were a distinct minority often lacking the resources to challenge established rule, they generally practiced taqiyah, or "dissimilation," a tactic in which they did not actively oppose the Sunnite authorities but waited instead for some ill-defined messianic moment in which to press their claims. Theirs was the quintessential politics of accommodation. A minority strand within Shiism tended, however, to seek a more active role, giving rise thereby to periodic rebellions that most often ended badly. At best, Orthodox Islam—taking license to use that expression—tolerated the Shiites and treated them and their beliefs with suspicion. At times, militant Shiites were derisively referred to as "Jews" (*Yahud*) because their heterodox and seemingly dangerous views were allegedly introduced to Muslims by 'Abdallah ibn Saba, a legendary figure said to have been an early Jewish convert to Islam. Among the Wahhabis of Saudi Arabia and their followers, the Shiites were long considered unbelievers. But unlike the Sunnites of Iraq, the Gulf States, Saudi Arabia, and Lebanon—polities where the Shiites are numerous and seen by the Sunnites as threatening their rule—the Palestinian Sunnites have taken a more accommodating attitude toward their long-term religious rivals. They see them as potential allies against the common enemy, the Jewish state. From the perspective of Palestine's Sunnite Muslims, Israel is backed by the immense power of the Jewish world and firmly supported by the imperialist West. Given that, there is need to overcome long- and well-established antagonisms in the Muslim camp. The time has come for all Muslims to join ranks in support of the Palestinian cause. Even Shiite Iran, a non-Arab state that had been at war with Iraq's Sunnite rulers (1980–1988) and that continues to be viewed by its other Sunnite Arab neighbors as a threat, was and is still seen by Palestinian Islamists as a welcome ally.

The idea of eliciting Iranian support was particularly appealing to the religious nationalists of Islamic Jihad and other like-minded champions of Islamic revival. Whereas the Shah's Iran had close relations with Israel, the Islamic Republic fully embraced the Palestinian cause and declared the reconquest of the Holy Land and its holiest city, Jerusalem, a prime objective of their own Islamic revolution. Above all, the Islamists were inspired by the way the Ayatollahs had transformed Iran into a genuine Islamic state. There was admiration for the clarity of the Iranian Revolution. Khomeini's vision of Islamic revival was correctly understood as a titanic struggle of "us" against "them." The West, particularly the United States, represented a satanic (*shaytaniyah*) force that endangered Islam itself. In that struggle, Islam would emerge triumphant, not only in Palestine and throughout the region, but everywhere else as well. Duly impressed, Palestinian Islamists turned against Arab Iraq and proclaimed support for Shiite Iran in the lengthy war between the neighboring states.

The mutual sympathy between Iran's Ayatollahs and the Palestinian revivalists would lead to direct links between the militant groups. When in 1992 a shortsighted Israel government banished some four hundred activists to neighboring Lebanon, they were welcomed by Hezbollah. They were fed, housed, and given technical training that would allow them to combat the occupation with methods that were more sophisticated. When the exiles returned to the West Bank and Gaza after the 1993 Oslo Accords, they were given a hero's welcome, and then they laid the groundwork for further resistance. The Palestinian–Iranian–Hezbollah connection continues until this very day.

As for Islamic Jihad, despite its high profile, it made only marginal inroads in building up its following. It is estimated that at the time of the first intifada, the Jihadists numbered between two and four thousand, not a staggering figure. In the Palestinian universities, the movement failed to dent the traditional support for the PLO and the Muslim Brotherhood. Even at the Islamic University in Gaza, the most traditional of the Palestinian institutions of higher learning, the adherents of Islamic Jihad could only muster the backing of some 5 percent of the student body. But that did not mean that the accommodationists of the Palestinian Brotherhood had won out, and the struggle for a Palestinian state would not turn extremely violent.

With the outbreak of the first intifada, a spontaneous popular uprising against the occupation, the leading brotherhood figures decided to abandon their traditional policy of accommodation and ride the waves of current sentiment by embracing the rebellion. The decision to break with the past and engage the Israelis openly made the long-established and exceedingly well-organized brotherhood the movement of choice, not only for Islamic nationalists, but also for many who had previously favored the secular orientation of the PLO. With that decision, the model of a secular-democratic state—officially advanced by the mainstream nationalists but clearly out of favor with many of them for years—was increasingly challenged by another model, that of a Palestinian state ruled by Islamic law.

HAMAS: THE PALESTINIAN BROTHERHOOD CALLS FOR MILITANT OPPOSITION

The most powerful Islamist group to emerge after the intifada was the Islamic Resistance Movement, an offshoot of the Palestinian brotherhood better known by its acronym, Hamas. As do all Islamists, its followers turn to the past for inspiration. The very name they adopted for themselves suggests an age far removed in place and time. Hamas is not simply an acronym derived from the Arabic for Islamic Resistance Movement (*[h]arakat [a]-l [m]uqawamah [a]-l I[s]lamiyah*); it conjures up memories of hums, a practice going back to the lifetime of the Prophet (if not earlier), when it signified the observance of rigorous religious behavior, and by extension,

dedicated warriors. As a noun, hamas has long meant ardor, zeal, even fa-
naticism. A mutahammis is an ardent follower, or someone of absolute resolve. The movement thus invokes a sense of total dedication closely linked
to religious sensibilities and armed combat. Those sensibilities are best ex-
emplified by its founder and longtime spiritual leader, the martyred Sheikh
Ahmad Yassin. The sheikh's humble lifestyle was in stark contrast to the
high flyers of the PLO. Confined to a wheelchair for most of his life and
in extremely frail health, Ahmad Yassin projected the image of a saintly
Muslim dedicated to God and the Palestinian cause. Neither time in prison
nor all of Israel's military might could deter him from openly promoting an
Islamic state in all of Palestine and through all means, including violence.
For his followers, the assassination of the sheikh in 2004 only served to un-
derscore the impotence of Israel to combat the force of his rhetoric and,
beyond that, the ideals of the movement he led. In the end, the occupiers
of Palestine required an attack helicopter to still a barely audible voice that
issued forth from a physically disabled body.

When Hamas was founded in 1988, shortly after the outbreak of the
first intifada, Israeli officers, monitoring events, concluded that its overall
views, leadership, and many of its initial supporters were drawn from the
ranks of other Islamist movements. Their intelligence proved quite accurate.
Sheikh Yassin, its spiritual leader, had ties to the Palestinian branch of the
Muslim Brotherhood, as did all the founding members. The same was true
of Mahmoud Zahar, and 'Abd al-'Aziz al-Rantisi, two leading figures of the
political wing. In theory, the brotherhood maintained its organizational
structure, with Hamas a separate branch. In fact, the two were and continue
to be intertwined. Indeed, one could argue that Hamas is the Palestinian
Muslim Brotherhood reconstituted to forcefully oppose Israel and its occupation. What distinguished the new movement from the old Muslim Brotherhood was its willingness to take up arms against the Zionist enemy in pursuit of a nationalist and Islamic agenda. What distinguished Hamas from
Islamic Jihad and similar militant groups was the manner in which its tightly
organized political wing played an extraordinarily active role in Islamic education and the social and economic life of Palestinians living in the West
Bank and especially in Gaza. Like Islamic Jihad, Hamas had strong appeal in
rural areas and refugee camps, thus paving the way for new Palestinian leaders not identified with urban elites, as had traditionally been the case.

As the brotherhood did prior to the intifada, Hamas persuasively enforced religious standards and behavior and adjudicated disputes among
Palestinians riven by clan and tribal rivalries that carried forward from generations past. In effect, Hamas created a government of sorts within a gov-

ernment (first under the occupation authorities and then under the ruling Palestinian Authority). Most importantly, no Palestinian movement has been able to match Hamas in its remarkable ability to both inspire and mobilize the all-important Arab public, especially in the teeming refugee camps that dot the Gaza Strip. It is no small wonder that Hamas has attracted many followers from other Islamist groups and the Arab population at large. Some Christian Arabs even found Hamas appealing.

The ideology of the movement was first detailed in its charter (*mithaq*), a document circulated in August of 1988 six months after the first uprising in Gaza. The aims of Hamas have also been articulated in wall posters, pamphlets, an "official" publication titled Muslim Palestine (*Filastin al-Muslimah*), and various articles that have appeared in the Arabic press. In disseminating its positions, Hamas is not limited to the written word; their spokesmen also appear on the Arabic satellite television that now blankets the Near East. The movement's views, which rapidly emerged and bear much in common with those of Islamic Jihad, have remained much the same over time. While Arabs addressing Western audiences or Westerners sympathetic to the Palestinian cause are apt to declare that Hamas has shown or is about to show signs of flexibility in its stance toward the Jewish state—or, in any event, that it is prepared to be flexible in the interests of the Palestinian nation—in truth, the leadership of Hamas has been remarkably consistent in its declared aims, at least judged by its public pronouncements and its calls to action. The charter, first issued some sixteen years ago, remains the quintessential expression of the movement's tactics and strategy and its overall vision of the future. Any government formed by Hamas in the wake of their recent victory in the 2006 parliamentary elections will be guided by, or at least have to consider, this broad-ranging document.

The document is all inclusive in that it not only speaks to the goal of liberating Palestine and creating an Islamic state, but also establishes guidelines for dealing with a wide variety of issues, social and political. As with many of Hamas's pronouncements, the language of the charter is laced with references to early Islamic history and traditional religious sources, beginning with the Qur'an. Palestine is declared an Islamic trust (*waqf*) given to all Muslims until the Day of Resurrection. That is, when the Arabs overran Palestine (in the seventh century C.E.), they requested guidance concerning the fruits of their conquest. Rather than give ownership of the land to the Arabian tribesman as the spoil of war, the caliph 'Umar ibn al-Khattab is said to have decided that Palestine should be consecrated as a trust for all Muslims in generations to come. If the historicity of this story is dubious, the point is nevertheless clear. No part of Palestine can be surrendered.

No single Arab regime or number of regimes acting together has the right to break this trust and give up any of this land, not even the Palestinians themselves. Abandoning claims to any part of Palestine is therefore considered nothing less than apostasy (*kufr*); reconquering the land is considered a solemn religious duty.

Because the (non-Muslim) enemy occupies land held in trust for the faithful, each and every Muslim has a personal obligation (*fard 'ayn*) to enlist in a holy cause (*jihad*) to retake it. This reading of Islamic jurisprudence, which Hamas shares with Islamic Jihad, stretches the law pronounced by mainstream Muslim legal experts. Personal obligations are usually restricted to such matters as prayer and fasting or vowing to go on minor pilgrimages or religious retreats. Jihad, often translated simply as "holy war," is generally regarded as a collective (*fard kifayah*) and not individual responsibility. The burden of this second responsibility is thus borne by the entire Muslim community. Hence, some Muslims may be legally excused when the struggle is engaged. By declaring the jihad to reclaim Palestine a fard 'ayn, the spiritual leaders of Hamas assert that no adult Muslim can avoid his or her duty; regardless of circumstances. In theory, slaves—if there were still slaves among the Palestinians—could engage the enemy without consulting their masters. Likewise, women can join the battle, even without their husbands' permission. Because boys legally reach their majority in early pubescence, even children are obligated to enter the struggle.

By invoking Islamic history and legal precedent in this way, Hamas allows no compromise in which the State of Israel will exist in perpetuity. In that regard, there is complete agreement with Islamic Jihad and other Islamist groups. The final borders of the Jewish state, much debated over time, are an artificial issue. No Jewish polity—or indeed any foreign polity—can take dominion over this sacred Arab/Muslim land. Initiatives toward genuine peace with the Zionist enemy are therefore in contradiction with the declared aims of Hamas and the religious foundations upon which its Islamist ideology is based. That is not to say that all attempts at negotiation are invalid or condemnable. Muslims have long negotiated the surrender of territory to them as dictated by Islamic law—a precedent reportedly established when their armies first crossed into the lands beyond the Arabian Peninsula.

We should be clear as to the nature of such negotiations. Talks leading to capitulation are not arranged in order to arrive at a compromise with which two warring parties can live. Rather, they represent the formal and final ratification of an objective reality that both sides clearly perceive. Both the language and body language of the negotiators may make the path to

capitulation less humiliating for the defeated party, but victor and van-
quished alike are well aware of what has transpired and will play the game
out according to the defined rules of the treaty. Following historic precedent, the Islamists could be somewhat gracious in victory but without con-
ceding anything of substance to their foes. There is no indication, however,
that Israelis are prepared to capitulate and give up their territorial enclave,
as did the Jewish tribes of Arabia in submitting to Muhammad.

Muslims can also declare an armistice (*hudnah*), when conditions for
prolonged struggle are unfavorable; the Prophet himself did that with the
polytheists of Quraysh. The practice of declaring an armistice was not limited to the Prophet's lifetime. Over the course of some eight hundred years
of struggle with the Byzantine Empire, active warfare along the frontier,
usually conducted during the summer months when the weather made
fighting less onerous, was often interrupted by periods of relative calm, mutually agreed upon by both warring parties. Nevertheless, a cessation of
hostilities, defined as a hudnah, is always of limited duration. On this notion, all Muslim jurists are agreed. Although such an arrangement may last
for years, the battle must be resumed when the calculus of power favors the
faithful—in 2004, Hamas did indeed declare that it was prepared to accept
a very limited hudnah if in return Israel would halt its targeted assassinations
of Islamist operatives. The hudnah, though never formally agreed to by
both parties, remains more or less in effect. More recently, Palestinians have
referred to a less formal tahdiyah, or "lull" in fighting.

Despite their ideological fervor, some Hamas leaders display a pragmatic outlook. The idea of an extended hudnah has surfaced from time to
time, most recently in the wake of the Palestinian elections in 2006 when
Mahmoud Zahar went so far as to raise the possibility of negotiations with
the Zionists, albeit negotiations that would not require formal contact with
representatives of the Jewish polity. Similarly, leaders of Hamas have declared a willingness to accept the fruits of any Israeli concessions obtained
through any (indirect) talks with the Zionist enemy, including a Palestinian
state that would be limited to Gaza and the West Bank. There is, however,
always a caveat to what might seem at first a serious attempt to moderate
the current struggle. The Islamists declare they will accept what Israel con-
cedes, provided they do not have to formally acknowledge the existence of
the Jewish entity or abandon the struggle to liberate all of Palestine and establish a proper Islamic state on its holy soil.

While admitting there are precedents that allow negotiations, even
with the Zionists and their friends, Hamas has been inclined in the past to
view these precedents as pointless. The charter addresses this matter directly.

It asks how one can seriously believe Jews and their Christian allies will accept Muslim demands given their long record of deceit, and why Muslims should trust them even if they do sign a formal agreement. Can Muslims rely on the offspring of Muhammad's enemies and those of the hated Crusaders? To be sure, any concessions by the enemy that ask nothing in return would be welcome, but peace initiatives and international conferences are at most likely to be a sideshow without a last act. What then is the strategy for Palestinians seeking justice for their cause? For Hamas and other Muslim militants, the answer is clear: There is no solution to the Palestine question except an all-embracing religious struggle that will result in an Arab state governed not by codes imported from the West, but by traditional Islamic law. In such a state, some Jews may be allowed to live, but they will be subject to the traditional rules that set Muslims and non-Muslims apart. In Islamic lands, Jews and Christians cannot aspire to be more than a protected minority (*ahl al-dhimmah*), subject to (discriminatory) legislation outlined in classical Muslim jurisprudence.

Jews or even Arab Christians would hardly welcome the prospect of living under Islamic law, and yet the leaders of Hamas are confident that Jews will ultimately accept minority status in an Islamic Palestine as life within the Jewish state becomes increasingly intolerable. In the end the Zionists, lacking legitimacy and proper roots in the region, will be beaten down by the declining quality of their life and succumb to the "Islamic solution." The conventional wisdom among Islamists is that the enemy cannot withstand a relentless war of attrition waged by the Palestinians and their supporters. Thus, from an ideological and tactical perspective, there is no call for major compromise. To the contrary, Hamas seeks to mobilize the broadest possible support for the ongoing struggle against the enemy, whatever level of intensity that struggle demands at the moment.

Because Palestinian nationalism is linked to the creation of an Islamic state governed by religious law, the Palestinians should enlist the Arab Muslims of neighboring countries, or so the Hamas charter declares. Indeed, the crisis in Palestine will become the order of business for the entire Islamic world. Even a cursory reading of the Islamic past indicates that Palestine is very special for the entire community of the faithful. Drawing on well-known traditions, Hamas reminds all Muslims that they originally prayed in the direction of Jerusalem, and they have long venerated Jerusalem's Aqsa mosque as one of the three holiest in Islam. And so the liberation of sacred Palestine is binding, not only on the Palestinians and their Arab brothers, but on the entire Islamic world. Reclaiming the Holy Land from the Zionists is as much a cause today as it was for all Muslims in the time of the Crusades.

The terms used to refer to the enemy are revealing. Speaking of Israelis, Palestinians sometimes refer to Zionists (*ṣāhyun*), a political assignation, seemingly limited to the current Arab-Israel conflict and the Palestine Problem from which that conflict derives, but often as not, they simply refer to "the Jews," (*al-Yahud*), a generic label that has had pejorative connotations since early Islamic times. Among Islamists, Israelis are also called "unbelievers" (*kafirun*), a Qur'anic term originally reserved for polytheists that was soon applied to all non–Muslims and eventually Muslims who were found lacking. The identification of Jews as kafirun and opponents of the Prophet is already noted in early Qur'an commentary. In modern Islamist writings, "unbeliever" often appears with "Crusader," the former meaning Israeli, the latter Westerners who colonize and otherwise intervene directly in the affairs of the Arab/Muslim world. In such fashion, Jews and Christians are seen as having entered into an unholy alliance against God's faithful. What does it mean to call Israelis unbelievers? Drawing on traditional Muslim sources, the Islamists conflate the citizens of the modern Jewish state with their ancestors to prove Israelis are unworthy and deserving of God's wrath. Regarding that assertion, they cite biblical history where a self-critical Jewish tradition records time and again the faulty behavior of the ancient Israelites. What then can one expect of a people who so often betrayed their own prophets and then rejected their own scripture by denying that it predicted the coming of Muhammad, the most sublime prophet of all? A familiar litany of Qur'anic invective against the Jews is thus invoked repeatedly in the writings of Hamas.

An anti-Jewish tone is set by the preamble to the Hamas covenant, a quote from the Surah or segment of Muslim scripture known as "The Family of 'Imran," that is, Amram the father of Moses. The followers of Hamas (or all Palestinians, or indeed all Muslims) are reminded that "You are the best community ever brought forth for humankind. . . . Had the people of the book believed [in Muhammad's mission, which is foretold in their scripture] it surely would have been better for them. Some of them [converts to Islam] are believers; most of them are transgressors. They will not injure you, save for a trivial slight. Should they [decide to] do battle with you, they will flee [literally "show you their backs"]; they will receive no support [from their erstwhile allies]. Wherever they might be, they are stamped with [signs of] humiliation, unless protected by bonds to Allah, or men. They are laden with God's wrath. They are stamped with this misfortune because they did not believe the Lord's signs and killed [their own] prophets unjustly, that is, [they are punished] for rebelling and transgressing" (Qur'an 3:110–2).

The classically trained religious leaders of Hamas who helped frame the movement's covenant or charter were well aware of the major commentaries and exegetical works that give broad meaning to Muslim scripture. No doubt, they chose these verses most carefully as indeed they do all references to traditional sources. As regards the "best community," they surely understood that the commentary is ambiguous. Some scholars say the reference refers to a specific group of Muslims among Muhammad's companions, others that it means the all-embracing ummah, the universal community of believers, regardless of place and time. Given these two readings, the covenant may be understood as referring to Hamas, the larger Palestinian community, and/or the still larger universal Islamic community whose support Hamas wishes to attract. Similarly, the "people of the book," those who do not believe in Muhammad's mission, would ordinarily be understood as both Christians and Jews. But as regards this passage, the sum of Qur'an commentary throughout the ages clearly reveals the Jews alone are intended. More particularly, the reference is to those Jews who denied the Prophet's legitimacy as distinct from 'Abdallah ibn Sallam and his circle who converted to Islam ("some of them are believers") because they, unlike most Jews, acknowledged what all Jews knew in their hearts, namely, that proof of Muhammad's coming was found in their own scripture. Worse yet, some Jews resisted the Prophet politically, even to the point of taking up arms against him, albeit without success. With these verses pressed into their consciousness, the people of Hamas are led to believe that in the end the Zionists will not be able to defeat them in battle. That being so, they will flee in the face of the Muslims as did their ancestors, the Jewish tribes of Arabia referred to, however obliquely, in Qur'an 3:111.

The original context of verses 111 and 112—"They will not injure you . . . should they do battle with you, they will flee . . . wherever they might be, they are stamped [with signs of] humiliation," and so forth— seemingly refers to Muhammad's ultimatum to the Qaynuqa', one of the Jewish tribes of Medina. Rather than accept the Prophet's challenge to engage the Muslims in combat (over what began as a trivial prank), the Jews, abandoned by their most prominent ally and supporter, a hypocrite among the Muslims, turned over their armor and lands to Muhammad and the faithful. Many Muslim commentators extend this verse to apply to all the Jewish tribes of Arabia who resisted the Prophet and were then humbled by him and his forces. That being so, history will repeat itself. The Zionists will turn heel and flee or be defeated just like their Arabian ancestors, including the defenders of the last Jewish stronghold, the oasis of Khaybar. Following their defeat at Khaybar, the Jews were never again a factor in Islamic politics until the rise of modern Zionism. When the youth of the first intifada took to the streets against the Israeli occupation, their battle cry was, "Khaybar! Khaybar! Oh Jews. The armies of Muhammad are destined to return"—an expectation that the wheel of history will turn back to better times. Similar references to classical Muslim sources and early moments of Islamic history are sprinkled throughout the Hamas covenant, always with the same message of Jewish perfidy and the inevitable Muslim triumph.

In all likelihood, this pungent message of the covenant was both familiar and well received by those acquainted with the Hamas text. The anti-Jewish polemic of the Qur'an is not dry theological meandering about competition for sacred space. Because it originates in scripture, and scripture is always present in a Muslim's life, regardless of place and time, the anti-Jewish material has been commented on in every generation. Moreover, unlike historical and literary works, which tend not to be revised and therefore disappear or lose meaning in time, the sum and substance of early Qur'an commentary tends to be quoted repeatedly by later authors. There is then an uninterrupted polemic against the Jews that extends from the time of the Prophet until today. The invective against the Jews has also been the standard fare of popular preachers and sermons in mosques. Anti-Jewish elements have thus seeped into every level of society, among the educated and uneducated alike, and form the conventional Muslim wisdom about Jews and Judaism. Hamas taps into these sentiments that are often learned from childhood.

For Hamas, as indeed for all Islamists, the struggle with contemporary Israel is not simply the consequence of the modern Zionist project, that agenda to reconstitute the Jewish people in their ancient homeland that had been a Muslim polity for the better part of fourteen centuries. The struggle is more than a battle of conflicting national aims. Islamists, indeed all traditional Muslims, see the current struggle against the Zionist entity as nothing less than a continuation of Muhammad's battles with the Jews of Arabia, events that took place in the seventh century C.E. In this respect, Hamas's charter has an entirely different resonance from that of the PLO in the 1960s.

CONFIGURING THE ENEMY

Not surprisingly, Hamas regards the "false" State of Israel as a religious polity, not unlike the true Islamic state they hope to establish in historic Palestine. This rather skewed conception of the Zionist project leads to a somewhat bizarre description of modern Israeli society. Conceived, largely built, and ruled from the outset by Jews embracing or leaning toward secularism, Israel is transformed by Hamas into a full-blown theocracy. This portrayal of modern Israel, gleaned from a reading of the state's more recent history, contains some elements of truth, but overall it amounts to a gross if revealing distortion. For example, contrary to the claims of Hamas, the IDF does not consult the Hebrew Bible for rules to engage in war. One would be hard-pressed to think of a single senior officer who was devoutly religious when serving on the General Staff. Positions in the IDF's highest-ranking body have gone most often to those with relatively secular backgrounds, such as soldiers who grew up on agricultural cooperatives (*moshav* or *moshavah*) and collective farms (*kibbutz*; pl. *kibbutzim*). In all likelihood, this profile of the General Staff will change as observant Jews in the ranks have volunteered in disproportionate numbers for elite fighting units. Still, it is hard to imagine the future IDF being held captive to a religious ideology, although individual officers in the ranks may well face a choice between their religious convictions and the orders of the day. Conscription is universal for Jewish men and women in Israel, and the army is obliged to accommodate the religious needs of all, such as making sure that base and field kitchens operate in accordance with Jewish dietary laws. But women claiming to be observant and fearing for their modesty can easily be excused from having to serve. Similarly, tens of thousands of ultra-Orthodox men can and do avoid the draft by opting to become rabbinical students, much to the distaste of a majority of those who serve in the IDF.

Nor is Hamas correct in claiming that children are deposited in collective farms so they may be properly reared in the faith. In fact, the vast majority of kibbutzim are thoroughly secular. At the extreme left, some even may be described as demonstrably antireligious. While it is true that there are regulations prohibiting public transportation on the Sabbath and religious holidays, as the Islamists claim, these regluations are not universally applied. Most business establishments, other than restaurants, close for the Sabbath and festival days, but to the chagrin of the rabbis, many have found ways to remain open. Similarly, while religious authorities certify most kosher restaurants, countless establishments do not conform to Jewish dietary laws.

Competition between religious and secular forces is also evident in Israel's government, which has always depended on tentative alliances. After a brief period in the limelight, during which it crudely attempted to stem the advance of secularism, Shas, the largest of the religious parties, was ousted from the ruling coalition. To add insult to injury, a party led by militant secularists replaced them. Polls projecting the results of the elections to be held in Israel in March of 2006 seemed to indicate that the religious parties would remain marginal. If the Labor party joined forces with Kadimah, a recently formed centrist party dedicated to territorial concessions and a two-state solution, the influence of settler rabbis on government policy will be lower than ever before. To leaders of Hamas, it makes little difference who rules Israel; the Zionists are all the same. The Islamists do not seem to appreciate the fine differences among Israel's many political factions, even within the religious bloc. The rabbis who inspire Shas and Agudat Yisrael, the largest and most influential religious parties, have been more concerned with preserving the nation's Jewish soul than getting their followers to settle the occupied territories and/defend them by force of arms.

All evidence to the contrary, Hamas persists in regarding Israel as a religious polity, the mirror image, so to speak, of what they desire to create: an Islamic state in Palestine. The Islamists have never been able to grasp that most modern Jews can embrace a secular outlook without abandoning Jewish history, tradition, and love for a land the Jewish people have cherished for the better part of three thousand years. Perhaps that is because secularism, so appealing to Jews, is a modern European conception thoroughly alien to Islam and traditional Islamic society (see chapter 10). The insistence of Hamas on defining the Zionist polity in religious terms has curious implications. The theocratic nature of the Jewish state is regarded by the Islamists as a sign of strength, not weakness. There is a grudging admiration for the way in which Israel has melded religion and modern technology. Linked by a common faith, the Zionists are said to have used the mass media and public education to develop an esprit de corps that is lacking in the contentious Arab camp. Muslims seeking to end the Zionist regime and create in its stead an Islamic state in Palestine are advised to emulate the foe, at least in that respect.

In order to defeat a Zionist polity founded on religion, Arab governments must throw off the shackles of secularism imported from the West. Choosing the path of Islam, they should take as their model the idealized Islamic community of the Prophet's time. Only then will Muslims have the wherewithal to deal with the theocratic "Zionist entity" (*al-kiyan al-sahyuni*), the international Jewish network that supports it, and the imperialists who are drawn into world Jewry's wide web of deceit. That will not be easy as the enemy is formidable and operates on a global scale. As do most Arabs, the Islamists believe that Jews control the Western media, university faculties, and international monetary institutions. Jewish plotters bear responsibility for the French and Russian revolutions. On a grander scale, they manipulated the world into fighting the Great War of 1914–1918 and the even greater conflict that followed some twenty years later. As they have done throughout their history, including the time of the Prophet, Jews continue to practice deceit. Preserving the rights of Palestinians and the Islamic heritage will therefore require a massive struggle in which all Palestinians and their Muslim allies join hands and deploy forces.

In formulating their views and call to action, the leaders of Hamas were well aware that words come cheaply in the Arab world. So many conferences had been held to uphold Arab solidarity over the years, but so little positive action followed. Nor could one say that the old Palestinian leadership did much to alleviate the distress of their people. Hamas pledged to remake Palestinian society and shore up its religious foundation. From the outset, the great strength of the movement has been its ability to improve the welfare and self-esteem of a humiliated Palestinian community. At the same time, the movement, true to its name, established a separate armed wing named after the martyred 'Izz al-Din al-Qassam, a leader of the Arab uprising against British authority in the 1930s. The jihad called by Hamas thus works on two levels: It creates the social infrastructure for an Islamic state of Palestine waiting to be born, and by arming clandestine militant brigades, it takes the fight to the Zionist enemy.

THE HOME FRONT: HAMAS AND THE COMMUNITY

Hamas has established a wide network of agencies that provide social services. These include medical and drug rehabilitation clinics, nurseries, kindergartens, social clubs, sporting events, libraries, and a vast array of programs geared to Islamic education because Islam is the only solution (*al-hall*) to what ails the Arab body politic. The old brotherhood's Islamic Center (*al-mujamma'ah*) became the launch pad for establishing elements of a state infrastructure in the absence of a state. In Gaza, the Islamic University quickly became the movement's stronghold. Not only did Hamas clerics control the faculty of theology, but Mahmoud Zahar—who would assume local leadership of the movement following the assassinations of Sheikh Yassin and al-Rantisi—served as dean of Natural Sciences. As news of Hamas successes spread, particularly its armed struggle, the movement's influence extended to the universities of the West Bank. In election after election, the Hamas slate captured more student votes than any other single party, including Fatah, which had long been entrenched on the campus scene. These elections were a harbinger of events to come. All that activity went a long way in promoting among Palestinians a sense of national consciousness that is directly and unequivocally linked to Islam.

In theory, the creation of an Islamic state in all of Palestine, the dream of many Palestinian nationalists, must mark the beginning of the end of their discrete sense of nationhood. From an Islamist perspective, that is the ultimate irony; for the very existence of the nation-state is incongruous with the hallowed concept of the ummah, the universal Islamic community that recognizes no autonomous communities and recognizes no differences rooted in geography, ethnicity, or language. The Palestinians, having established a model Islamic state, will thus become the vanguard of a larger Islamist movement that will embrace all Muslims, who will eventually shed their respective nationalist convictions and restore the universal Islamic polity and the glories of the past.

The strength of Hamas is not only its vision of a distant future but its ability to indirectly influence the lives of current Palestinians. Numerous Arabs, humiliated by the Israeli occupation and seriously diminished economic opportunities, have found relief in the services provided by Hamas and solace in their message. What counted and still counts for these Palestinians is not outward manifestations of wealth but the inward satisfaction that comes with being an observant Muslim. This is within everyone's reach, regardless of their station in life. Hamas has not made the poor affluent, nor will it in the future. Its programs, however effective, do not substitute for the work of a real state. But the movement has certainly alleviated the sense of frustration that many Palestinians felt and continue to feel, particularly in the overcrowded refugee camps. More than that, it has provided a sense of dignity for the poor and those otherwise distressed by the general malaise that has gripped their world.

Above all, it was Hamas's refusal to compromise with the Zionist enemy that won them adherents and the instant recognition of the Arab public. Other Palestinian groups had preached and carried out violence before, but none succeeded like Hamas in mobilizing the Palestinian community to engage in organized protests, strikes, and demonstrations of all sorts. More than any other nationalist group, they became the symbol of active resistance to a demeaning—indeed a humiliating—Israeli occupation. The first intifada had released pent-up feelings that would not be capped easily, if at all. The vastly overpopulated Gaza Strip and the high level of unemployment produced idleness, then aimlessness, and eventually depression that gave way to rage. In a world hitherto ruled by patriarchs, fathers lost the respect of their children, uncles of their nephews and nieces.

There were also deeply rooted cultural factors that led to despair, particularly among single males. Palestinian society, like all Muslim societies, is highly traditional. For Palestinians, the opportunities to express manhood are rare, especially to middle-born males in large families dominated by elder siblings. Massive unemployment led to idleness and despair as young Palestinians reached midadolescence and then early manhood. Violence directed at an appropriate target thus became the tonic for a deep malaise. There was a real enemy that had to be confronted; the manifest destiny of Palestinians was to achieve what all other Arabs had before them: an independent state of their own. Nothing less than honor and justice were at stake. There was an occupation to get rid of, a political community to be created, and revenge to be exacted. Hamas—imbued with religious ideals, demanding religious discipline, and, most important, a leadership that demonstrated dedication and self-sacrifice—became the ideal engine to power a national movement of the disaffected and disenfranchised. And so, Hamas mobilized for war in early 1988.

Although they had stockpiled arms earlier in anticipation of such an event, the current leaders of Hamas, then all members of the brotherhood, did not give any hint of engaging the enemy. When the occupation authorities discovered the cache of weapons, Ahmad Yassin, the spiritual head of the movement, explained that they were necessary to protect the Islamists from their secular rivals. The explanation did not wash, and Sheikh Yassin was imprisoned. Weapons or no weapons, the brotherhood had no specific plan for rebellion even as the intifada erupted spontaneously late in 1987. Like the PLO, they had been caught unawares as the first days of rioting quickly evolved into wide disobedience and then a full-fledged insurgency. It was not enough to try to co-opt the grassroots rebellion that would not subside. It became necessary for both the Islamists within the occupied territories and the mainline nationalists in exile to claim that they had planned and initiated the intifada. As did the Abbasid revolutionary leadership 1,200 years earlier, the leaders of Hamas felt the need to reshape a history that was into a history that should have been. Like the Abbasids, who remained underground while others openly risked their lives to overthrow the then current order, the leaders of Hamas retroactively fitted their role in combating the Israelis into an earlier history. Muslims looking to the past for legitimacy and templates of contemporary behavior have long rewritten the present to make it consonant with earlier realities. In this instance, as in the case of the Abbasids, the past was revised so that it might conform to contemporary events. Among other claims, Hamas contended that their charter, a call to arms, was formulated before the events in December and certainly long before it was made public months after the outbreak of violence. In any case, Hamas became the vanguard of active Palestinian resistance and was directly responsible for shaping an evolving Palestinian national consciousness firmly rooted in Islam.

At the base of Palestinian resistance were preschoolers and students in the lowest grades. Too young to engage the occupiers directly, they played games of war with toys, biding their time until they could participate more actively. Above them were prepubescent youth and teenagers, ready to skip classes to take to the streets to throw stones at the Israeli army and otherwise taunt them. This game of war was more dangerous and therefore more rewarding than ordinary child's play. And yet, if we consider each foray the equivalent of a military sortie, the actual chances of being seriously injured—let alone killed—in these rites of passage are extremely slight. The youth that took to the streets did not think it would be their last encounter with the enemy. Much like Western adolescents who risk death driving recklessly, young Palestinians thought they knew enough to hold back when the odds might turn against them. They would go so far and then retreat to safety. For the unleashed young Palestinians of the West Bank and Gaza, danger was intoxicating. A mere surface wound was enough to establish a reputation among peers. But the Israelis did not always oblige, and accidents also happen. One can be caught in the wrong place at the wrong time, as were many innocent bystanders. The enemy, against standing orders, might use live ammunition instead of rubber bullets. Even rubber bullets can sometimes kill; they often maim. Tear gas can be deadly for asthmatics and others with respiratory problems. And so, adventurous youth engaging in a ritual theater that simulated serious combat became martyrs to the Palestinian cause. Officially, many were celebrated; their names and faces appeared on wall posters; their funerals were attended by large throngs shouting revenge and firing celebratory rounds into the air. How grieving parents might have felt in their private moments is more difficult to gauge. As the rebellion turned increasingly more violent, the most celebrated of all the Hamas affiliates were the men of the 'Izz al-Din al-Qassam brigades, a clandestine network of fighters that planned and carried out armed operations against Israeli military and civilian targets. It should be clear that Hamas has not been alone in resisting the occupation. There have been (among others) Islamic Jihad; the hard-to-control militants known as the Tanzim, including the Fatah Hawks, a young group of loose cannons associated with Arafat's wing of the PLO; and, after the second intifada in 2000, the al-Aqsa Martyrs Brigades, also loosely linked with Fatah. From time to time, hitherto unknown groups suddenly appeared to take credit for particular operations against the enemy and then fade into the woodwork. Smaller factions subdivided and then reformed as new entities; similarly, their leaders shifted allegiance back and forth. It was also not unusual for different militant groups to simultaneously lay claim to a successful operation. There was (and still is) much to be gained in the Arab street by displaying a high profile in the active war against Israel.

By 1990, it seemed that the Arab rebellion, which broke out three years earlier, could not be sustained at an intense level. The intifada appeared to be running out of steam. The daily ritual of the stone throwers went on and on, like the last act of a play without end. The supply of both stones and youth may have been inexhaustible, but there were no real gains. The IDF had taken stock of the situation and adjusted its tactics to narrow the odds in its favor. Army roadblocks prohibiting free movement became ubiquitous. Along with that, the number of Arabs permitted to work in Israel was reduced, often dramatically. That caused extreme hardship among families of men who depended on this work for a livelihood. Then Arabs willing to risk their lives against Israelis ran short of weapons. A kitchen knife was not a proper substitute for a pistol; homemade explosives were far less effective than the real thing. There seemed to be less leverage that might move the Israeli authorities to back down, if they were ever so inclined.

6

HAUNTED BY THE PAST

The Islamists and the Peace Process

As the first intifada lost steam, Hamas's dream of an Islamic state in all of mandatory Palestine was further undercut by Arab nations that championed the Palestinian cause. The Arab world, at first enchanted by Palestinian resistance, was eventually drawn into peace initiatives with the Jewish state, a path unimagined but a short time earlier. The last and most significant of these events was initiated by the Palestinian leadership in exile. With the successful conclusion of clandestine negotiations held in Oslo, the unthinkable happened. In 1993, the Palestine Liberation Organization (PLO), the implacable enemy of Israel, was prepared to recognize a two-state solution. If all went according to a plan still to be defined, there would be mutual recognition between an Arab state of Palestine forged out of the West Bank and Gaza and a Jewish state of Israel in what remained of mandatory Palestine. A declaration of principles, sealed with a handshake on the White House lawn, signaled the impending return of the PLO leadership from exile. Shortly thereafter, the old PLO warriors led by Arafat arrived in the territories with a mandate to set up a fledgling Palestinian Authority (PA). Established in areas ceded to the Palestinians by Israel, the PA was to become, in effect, a forerunner to the government of an expected Palestinian state. Much to the alarm of the Islamists, who could not and would not recognize a Jewish state on sacred Muslim soil, the fallout from Oslo proved exceedingly popular with Palestinians suffering under the occupation. Here was an opportunity to rid Gaza and the West Bank of the Israeli occupiers and at the same time establish the infrastructure of a legitimate Palestinian state about to be born.

The hopes for a vibrant Palestinian society soared. Wealthy Palestinians returning from abroad bought property with which to establish residence. Some sunk fortunes into various entrepreneurial schemes. A

157

Palestinian stock market was created for potential investors, and perhaps most bizarre of all, a gaming establishment was opened in Jericho. The city that Joshua had conquered to begin the Israelite conquest of Canaan was now home to a casino that catered to inveterate Israeli gamblers. Muslims are prohibited by religious law from games of chance, but raising revenues from Jews given to a deplorable habit was an idea whose time had come.

It all seemed so promising at first, but old ways were hard to break—fortunately for the Islamists. Leaders of the PLO who knew only revolution found the practice of responsible government difficult. Nascent Palestinian rule was overly centralized. The security apparatus was made up of numerous branches controlled by Arafat, who cleverly played one against the other. Various government agencies became the personal fiefs of their bureaucrat overseers. Once ensconced in Gaza and pockets of the West Bank, officials of the PA indulged in massive corruption; there was no one and no institution to restrain them.

Palestinians who had borne the brunt of the Israeli occupation and whose quality of life had diminished considerably during the first intifada were appalled at the license of the official bureaucracy. One had only to compare the modest dwelling and lifestyle of Ahmad Yassin with the magnificent villas of high-flying PA officials. As schoolteachers and other civil servants went unpaid for lack of funds and the Palestinian economy ground to a halt and then went into reverse, PA bureaucrats, even those at middle level, were seen chauffeured about in luxurious automobiles. Worst of all, the public treasury, a sacred trust of the Palestinian people, had become the personal fund of President Arafat. Tens if not hundreds of millions of dollars donated for the welfare of the Palestinians went unaccounted for. No effort was made to keep orderly books; quite the opposite, the leader of his people seemingly maintained numerous accounts in numerous locations under various names. No single public official had the code to unlock all these transactions. Rumor had it that Arafat had amassed a fortune of some two billion dollars in the secret bank accounts; some estimates put it at six billion. Arafat himself did not live a life of personal luxury. His absolute control of finances was rather a lever with which to exercise influence. But the public extravagance of his wife, including many shopping trips to Paris, did not sit well with Palestinians barely making do. When she then took up residence in the French capital, she lived in a grand style that cost the Palestinians well over ten million dollars in one year. The rampant corruption and profligacy combined with the failure to sustain proper services were repugnant to Palestinians who had long endured the Israeli occupation and dared to hope for positive change and a life of dignity. The Islamists, Hamas in particular, were able to exploit the underlying dissatisfaction with the PA and what turned out to be a decided lack of movement toward the creation of an independent Palestinian state.

Heralded by most of the world as an unprecedented breakthrough in Israel–Arab relations, the Oslo Agreement was viewed from the outset as a sacrilege in Islamist circles. Given the dictates of Islamic law and custom, no part of historic Palestine could be formally abandoned to the Zionist enemy. No Islamic state could be established on a truncated homeland. In sum, the agreement with Israel was as false (*batil*) as the Zionist entity itself. If formal recognition of Israel were not enough to disturb the Islamist camp, the enthusiasm the Oslo Accords generated among Palestinians threatened to erode the influence Hamas had carefully cultivated with all segments of Arab society, both in Palestine and beyond. The triumphant return of Arafat and other PLO leaders from their places of exile signaled that a well-financed Palestinian Authority, a state apparatus of a state in waiting, would successfully compete with or—worse—take over Hamas's charitable agencies. The extent to which the PA would make a mess of running the areas under their control was unfathomable for most Palestinians at the time. More apparent was the danger that the militiamen who challenged the brutal Israeli occupation would be replaced by a Palestinian defense force certain to be controlled by Arafat's hand-picked officers. There was the danger that the new security services would spend more time protecting the interests of the recently installed PA and less combating an enemy with whom the PA was now pledged to make peace.

The rejectionists were not without cards to dramatically change the nature of the game. Above all, they could resort to violence that could beget further violence, thereby destabilizing delicate talks toward a final settlement. When a Jewish fanatic opposed to the peace process assassinated Yitzhak Rabin, Israel's popular and trusted prime minister, he set into motion a series of developments that dramatically altered the euphoric mood that greeted Oslo. There was no Rabin to calm passions when the Islamists initiated massive suicide bombings in the Israeli heartland. The scale of the carnage moved a furious Israeli electorate to the right. However narrowly, they voted for a new government that showed absolutely no enthusiasm for pursuing the peace process then in existence. The PA responded with petulant symbolic gestures that Israel's new government took as excuses to freeze peace talks, while at the same time they intensified Jewish settlement in Judea and Samaria. The failure to move forward with peace and the further expansion of Jewish settlement in the West Bank set the ground for further violence. Although the PA condemned suicide bombings and other subsequent incidents, it did nothing to control the perpetrators. Quite the opposite, needing the support of the street it had long neglected and the backing of prominent religious luminaries, the leaders of the PA established a fragile coexistence with the Islamic militants. The PA could allow alternative views and even behavior if there was no direct threat to its authority. When the PA felt it necessary to crack down on the Islamists through detentions, the closing of institutions, and the like, the measures were always short lived. With the game played according to these loose rules, the rejectionists had license to oppose Israel directly without fear from the Palestinian authorities.

And so, the routine shootings and stabbings of the past were now augmented by young men, and in a few instances women, who strapped on belts of explosives and detonated themselves in crowded locations within the heart of Israel. Their martyrdom would lead to the deaths of many Israelis and the maiming of many more. It was one thing to take on the Israel Defense Forces (IDF) in an ambush, or kill Israelis in a drive-by shooting on an isolated West Bank road, or even filter into settlements with murder in mind; killing a dozen and wounding dozens more in the heart of Tel Aviv or Jerusalem was quite another matter. The number of Israelis seriously wounded in any given incident was likely to be higher than monthly, if not quarterly, totals in the past. Muslims had finally found an effective way to compete with the IDF's vaunted high-tech weaponry. A single Muslim youth willing to give his life to enjoy the immeasurable pleasures of Paradise and thus win fame for himself and his kin could spread terror into the hearts of a haughty enemy.

For Jews who lived in Tel Aviv, the all-too-familiar daily stone throwing, the Molotov cocktails, and the occasional shootings and knifings of the first intifada had been somewhat removed from daily life. To be sure, that was not so for the regular army and reservists who participated in the confrontations. But with the advent of the suicide bomber, all Israelis faced unexpected danger. In short order, they became more wary of visiting public places or taking public transportation. Mothers were constantly on the cell phone checking the whereabouts of their children. Tourists were reluctant to visit. Restaurants closed, and hotels lacked clients at a time when the economy, reacting to a global slump, turned downward. The world, including past friends of the Jewish state, took notice, indeed celebrated the victimization of the Palestinians, a people without a land, humiliated by an "illegal" occupation, but yet brave enough to confront the military might of the occupiers with the meager weapons they possessed, including the suicide bomber.

Throughout the Near East, the Arab street was wildly enthusiastic. It was not simply the militant that took delight in television footage of dead and maimed Israelis. In the West Bank, students at a leading Palestinian university set up an exhibit that vividly depicted the dismembered victims as a way of glorifying the bombing of a crowded Jerusalem pizza parlor. Arabs who were genuinely horrified at such indiscriminate killings and quick to condemn them found it necessary to add a caveat in public: The Palestinians had simply exhausted every other avenue to ending the occupation. The rejectionists had succeeded beyond expectations. There was an enormous sense of satisfaction in watching Israel bury its dead. No celebrations of martyrdom were scheduled for Israelis caught in the wrong place at the wrong time: grandparents and their grandchildren out to lunch at a pizzeria; a father discussing a forthcoming wedding with his daughter at a Jerusalem coffeehouse; an Israeli Arab restaurant owner greeting Jewish guests in an integrated Haifa neighborhood, and the like. In effect, the rejectionist bloc led by Hamas had brought the newborn peace process to a standstill.

Neither a new Israeli government—hardened by developments but generally sympathetic to negotiations—nor an American initiative to bring Israelis and Palestinians together—first at Camp David and later in Taba—moved the quest for peace forward. The complete story of the failed negotiations has yet to be revealed. There can be little doubt, however, that in 1999–2000, Arafat failed to seize the historic moment and risk a dramatic change of direction in Arab-Israel relations. Ehud Barak, then Israel's prime minister, would have been no easy partner on the road to peace, but the proposals he put forth to the Palestinians, hard as they may have been to accept, were likely the best they could hope for for some time to come. There was also much left to negotiate. The Israeli position was not hardened in stone; the final borders were yet to be determined, along with other issues pertaining to sovereignty. No Israeli head of state had gone so far in recognizing Palestinian yearnings for a land of their own. Barak was even willing to accept partial responsibility for the flight of the refugees, albeit in oblique language that referred to the consequences of war. Faced with a truncated polity that would be considerably smaller than Israel and a Jewish state that would fully retain its Jewish character—that is, a Jewish state that would not admit, as a matter of principle, that the exiled Palestinians of 1948–1949 had a right to return—Arafat held out for absolute justice. Unlike Zionist leaders who in 1948 seized the historic possibilities inherent in a flawed partition plan and created the first Jewish commonwealth in some two thousand years, Arafat rejected a compromise that would have enabled him to lead his people on the inevitable path to statehood.

The stage was thus set for a second Palestinian rebellion, the so-called Aqsa intifada. This time it was the PLO that seemingly called the tune. With Arafat's compliance—some claim his initial direction—the second broad assault against Israel ratcheted up the level of violence. Israel responded in kind, indeed many times over. An ineffective and certainly impolitic Labor prime minister, Ehud Barak, was turned out of office, and replaced by Ariel Sharon, a former general committed to Jewish settlement in all of historic Palestine. Sharon was wary of any arrangement with Arafat, whom he considered a congenital liar and unreliable partner. Beyond that, he was on record as being against creating a viable Palestinian state, preferring instead some sort of rump autonomous region that was totally unacceptable to all Palestinian nationalists. Known as the "bulldozer," Sharon threw the IDF into the fray against the rioters and armed rebels and with devastating results. In four and a half years following the outbreak of the Aqsa intifada, more than three thousand Palestinians lost their lives, and ten times that number were wounded, some very badly. Blocks and whole neighborhoods of Palestinian cities, towns, and villages were demolished in the interests of Israeli security. Many leaders of the rejectionist bloc were hunted down and eliminated—not only leaders of the military wings, but also political figures like Sheikh Yassin and al-Rantisi. Others were forced into hiding and/or kept constantly on the move. An army of Palestinian informants supplied the Israel authorities with accurate and up-to-date information, making long-range planning difficult and in certain instances impossible for the rebels. The suicide bombers appeared to have been hastily trained and lacking proper psychological preparation. They were not nearly as effective as their predecessors. The boast that there was absolutely no shortage of volunteers for martyrdom was perhaps belied by a different truth. With the already excruciating pressure on Palestinian society mounting, and with leaders of Hamas and other Islamist groups targeted for assassination, some leaders of the rejectionist camp reportedly sent their children abroad to keep them out of harm's way. In 2004, Hamas signaled that it would no longer dispatch suicide bombers to Israel if Israel would refrain from targeting its leaders. An uneasy and informal truce has prevailed. Other rejectionists have sought to continue the struggle; their efforts have been sporadic and ineffective.

The most salient victim of the PA's failure to curb violence and Sharon's harsh retaliation has been the Palestinian economy. Whereas it struggled during the first intifada and the early years of the PA, it has now become a basket case. Fully one-third of the PA's budget consists of donations from abroad. The level of assistance per capita to keep the PA's ship afloat—some three hundred dollars for every Arab in the West Bank and Gaza—exceeds that of any recipient nation since World War II. The future looks even bleaker. Arab labor, once preferred by Israeli businessman and contractors, has been replaced by hundreds of thousands of guest workers from Europe, Africa, and Asia. Many of these foreign laborers have managed to stay on long after their visas expired and are now more or less part of a permanent workforce. At one time well over a hundred thousand Arabs made their way to Israel every day. Their loss in earnings has had and will continue to have a devastating effect on the welfare of so many families in Gaza and the West Bank. Unemployment in Gaza is currently put at around 70 percent. In many cases, savings are completely depleted. There is even talk of malnutrition among certain destitute families.

Another weapon deployed by Sharon was much talked about in Israel, even before he came to power. Unable and unwilling to negotiate with an Arafat-led PA, the current Israel government chose the path of unilateral disengagement. In a dramatic move that earned some criticism in Israel and more abroad, Sharon began building a massive physical barrier to separate the two peoples and keep Palestinian assailants from reaching their targets in Israel's heartland. The fence, which extends in many sectors beyond the "green line" that separated Israel from the West Bank before 1967, has created extreme hardship for those Palestinians caught within its path. Where Israelis see a fence guaranteeing greater security, Arabs see a wall to cut a potential Palestinian state into a series of Bantustans. At Gaza, there is no need for such a fence, for one already exists, and so a different form of disengagement is planned for the strip. It would appear that the West Bank fence has already had some effect. At the time of this writing, suicide bombing, once a regular occurrence, has become a sporadic event, although this is clearly due in part to the Hamas unofficial truce with Israel. It is too early to tell, but like the first intifada, the second may be winding down without any appreciable gains for the Palestinians.

Disengagement did not end with the plan to create a fence all along a temporary (or permanent, if necessary) border between Jews and Arabs. In 2004, the Sharon government formally announced its intention to evacuate the Jewish settlements of Gaza, a move intended to remove several thousand Jewish settlers who had settled amid a million and more Arabs, thus requiring the heavy presence of the IDF to protect them. Evacuating the settlers from Gaza would render the IDF less ubiquitous in the lives of Palestinians residing there, thus reducing if not eliminating most of the daily clashes. Despite verbal and less passive resistance by the settler movement, the painful evacuation of Gaza, which was conducted with remarkable efficiency in 2005, was interpreted by many in Israel as a sea change in Israel's policy. The same Ariel Sharon who had declared one of the Gaza settlements to be the gateway to Tel Aviv was now determined to alter the landscape of Jewish settlement, not only in Gaza but also in various areas of the West Bank. The old warhorse had been convinced that it was not in Israel's interest to rule the millions of Arabs in the West Bank and Gaza and that it was time for all of Israel to endorse a two-state solution. That prospect seemed more attractive following the death of Arafat in November of 2004.

POST-ARAFAT: THE FUTURE COURSE OF PALESTINIAN NATIONALISM AND THE PROSPECTS OF STATEHOOD

During the height of the violence, the Israelis demolished most of Arafat's Ramallah headquarters and confined him to a truncated living space within. He remained there until his final illness like a caged bird, his every move restricted by the Israeli government. Repudiated by the United States, considered redundant by Israel, and distrusted by many Europeans, the aging revolutionary offered no realistic vision of a Palestinian future even at the very end of his long career. There could be no peace with him, but it seems there can also be none without him. As the iconic figure of the Palestinian struggle for statehood, he alone had the charisma and the political capital to forge new directions of policy, but he lacked the capacity to transcend his revolutionary origins and become a statesman with a sense of the future.

With the "father of his people" gone, the victim of a mysterious illness, Palestinians and Israelis expected significant change, perhaps sooner than later. More and more, young Turks within Arafat's own faction were calling for reforms to limit the kind of influence he wielded in so personal a fashion. More and more, there was popular support for reform and responsible leadership in all segments of Palestinian society. One thing seemed reasonably clear: With a multitude of would-be contenders and conflicting interests, no future Palestinian leader would be able to concentrate as much power in his hands as Arafat did for the better part of forty years. Even before Arafat's death, there were signs that changes might be imminent. In the last year of his life, some Palestinians went so far as to openly protest their president's high-handedness, thus confirming sentiments expressed in polls taken in 2000, before the Aqsa intifada froze political change. The overwhelming majority of Palestinians surveyed in May of 2000 favored sweeping reforms, including unifying the twenty-odd security forces that Arafat played against each other, holding elections, and adopting a basic law by which the PA would govern. Perhaps more than anything, the populace desired the sacking of public officials given to corruption and mismanagement, the very same sentiments that gave rise to much hope of better times following Arafat's death. Respecting the man as a symbol of Palestinian nationhood, many reformers were prepared to have Arafat live in Palestinian memory as a blessed figure whose visage graces the walls of home and shops, but they hoped no successor of his would be able to manipulate Palestinian politics as directly as he did. Accepting the mandate to forge the new politics was a founding father of the PLO, a veteran of the exiles in Beirut and Tunisia, a longtime associate of Arafat, and ultimately, the person to succeed him.

The new president of the PA, Mahmoud Abbas, although forged on the same crucible as Arafat and the other revolutionary leaders dominating the PLO, was in every respect a different cup of tea from his predecessor. Whereas Arafat wore a combat jacket and sported a traditional Arab headdress, symbols of Palestinian resistance, Abbas was impeccably dressed in suit and tie; where Arafat was flamboyant, highly secretive, and kept to a bizarre schedule in order to keep his associates and rivals off balance, Abbas was the quintessential soft-spoken technocrat; and where Arafat was highly manipulative of his aides and all the Palestinan factions, Abbas sought to develop a consensus. These were taken as positive signs; Abbas was seen by the Israelis and their friends in the West as a possible partner in a serious talk of peace. But to the Palestinians, Abbas's performance seemed exceedingly drab; his desire for consensus had compromised much-needed reform and had robbed the ruling authority of its capacity to act decisively in stabilizing an increasingly lawless Palestinian society. Nor could he stanch the corruption or effect dramatic change in the economy. There was a reluctance to jettison old comrades, even those beyond redemption. Where decisive action was called for, Abbas always seemed to waffle. In sum, he was perceived by his people as being weak. In time, the Israelis and their friends drew a similar conclusion. Above all, the new president was regarded by them as incapable of reining in the Islamic militants. When Israel demanded he disarm all the freewheeling militias, Abbas attempted instead to co-opt them into a burgeoning and unwieldy security force, a decision that has yet to bear fruit. And so, the Sharon government did not look to Abbas, preferring instead to go the course of unilateral disengagement. Failing to achieve concessions from Israel and from elements within Palestinian society, Abbas, although admired for his forthrightness, lost credibility as a political leader.

Hamas's decision to run a full slate of candidates in the election for Palestinian parliament scheduled for January of 2006 had the potential to change the landscape, and it did. Contrary to all expectations, its candidates achieved a spectacular success, bringing to power a party dedicated to Islamic government and opposed in principle to any peace with Israel. This unexpected turn of events raises a number of questions: Where are the Palestinians now headed? What Palestinian nation is likely to emerge in the wake of the most recent events, and what will be the touchstone of its national consciousness given the chaotic state of the present body politic, and the state of the economy, and a bargaining position seemingly hardened in stone?

Catastrophe would be a proper label to describe the current state of the Palestinians. No matter what positive gloss Palestinians and their supporters would like to place on their resistance to Israel's presence in the West Bank and Gaza, the lives and livelihood of Palestinians are at greater risk than at any time since the Six Day War. Everywhere public services have broken down—in some areas the PA is a government in name only. Because Sharon emasculated the security services by systematically destroying the symbols of their authority, order is often maintained by neighborhood thugs who formed armed militias loosely linked to militant factions. How is this continuing situation going to lead to the nation-state envisioned by Palestinians and those who wish them goodwill? Will it be the Islamic state championed by the Islamists, the secular-democratic state originally trumpeted by the PLO, or an Arab Palestine sharing the area of the former British mandate with a more inclusive State of Israel—that is, a sort of binational polity that accommodates Israel's Christian and Muslim Arabs, as if Jewish sensibilities did not reflect the core of the state's existence? Having failed to dislodge the fledgling State of Israel by open warfare (1947–1949), cross-border incursions (1949–1967), the hijacking of airliners and attacks on Jews and Jewish institutions in Israel and abroad (post-1967), or more recent suicide bombings, the Arabs of Palestine might conclude in their more reflective moments that, for the foreseeable future, Israel will be here to stay.

No thoughtful Arab can seriously believe that Israelis will voluntarily abandon the concept of a Jewish state in their historic homeland for a so-called secular-democratic state that most Palestinians now reject, at least according to data amassed by Arab pollsters. For Palestinians, the ultimate objective remains an Arab state in all of Palestine. This is not to say a binational state has no enthusiasts these days. Having been put to rest at Oslo, the notion that Israelis and Palestinian Arabs can somehow share a single polity in what had been the Palestine Mandate has seemingly risen in flight like a phoenix from the ashes, but truth be told, it has not flown very far. A few Western and Israeli (or former Israeli) intellectuals stubbornly cling to the notion of a binational state in historic Palestine—especially the cosmopolitan talking heads who dismiss all forms of nationalism and mono-culturalism as vestigial appendages in a rapidly shrinking globe. Embraced by neither the majority of Arabs nor Israelis, the shared state solution remains as always a dead issue.

An Islamic state in all of Palestine, the dream envisioned by Hamas and other Islamists, is also unattainable. The Islamists have not the wherewithal to impose such an outcome. On the other hand, Israel will hardly dissolve itself to allow for a Muslim state in which Jews live as a protected minority, subject to discriminatory legislation mandated by Islamic law. To think otherwise is to indulge a fantasy. And so, looking realistically at the near future, one could argue the only conceivable way out of the present morass is to return to the concept proposed and accepted by the negotiators at Oslo. There will have to be two states in historic Palestine: a Jewish Israel and an Arab Palestinian state whose borders and character are yet to be determined. If and when such a compromise is worked out, it will weigh heavily on all Muslim Arabs, regardless of their current political affiliations and religious sensibilities. If the abortive Oslo Accord is any indication of the future, many if not most Palestinians may greet a newly formed state of their own with sighs of relief and considerable fanfare, but ultimately they will look back with resignation and regret, if not bitterness. From their perspective, any compromise that denies Arabs full sovereignty in all of Palestine is an injustice. Were that not enough, for some Arabs it is also a gross betrayal of Islamic belief and tradition. Neither the mainstream nationalists nor the Islamists currently in power will feel easy about any permanent settlement that allows the enemy a separate and legally recognized place in the land the Palestinians trumpet as their own.

A concession of that magnitude will be not be easy for the Palestinians to negotiate, and once negotiated, it may prove difficult to sustain in ensuing years. If the proposed two-state solution did not succeed after Oslo and active American intervention, what guarantee is there that it will become the linchpin of successful peace negotiations, especially as Hamas is currently the leading Palestinian faction? On the Israeli side, it remains to be seen whether the government can return to the Camp David and Taba talks as starting points for serious deliberations as long as the Islamists are committed to a policy that does not and will not recognize the legitimacy of the Jewish state and its right to exist in perpetuity. Arafat's intransigence, coupled with his apparent lack of any feasible plan or vision for the future, may well remain an enduring legacy. Are there any signs that there are indeed Palestinians ready to move toward a solution to the long-standing Arab–Israel problem, or what is more likely, a long-term accommodation that will allow Jews and Arabs alike a lengthy respite from conflict? If such Palestinians materialize, will they have partners in Israel?

Many Palestinians who participated in earlier peace talks are respected by Israeli negotiators. The reverse is also true. There are now any number of Palestinians with firsthand knowledge of Israel and considerable familiarity with its society and institutions. The ranks of the PA include youngish functionaries who speak Hebrew that they acquired serving time in Israeli prisons. Having entered prison as bitter youths without any real understanding of the Zionist enemy, a number have left appreciating the vibrancy of the Jewish state. Above all, they have come to value how Israeli society tolerates—indeed encourages—widely divergent views, including those that are outwardly critical of Israel's leading politicians.

One veteran of Israeli prisons is Salah al-Din Musa, the city manager of Jenin, a troubled urban center of forty-five thousand whose old quarter was leveled by the IDF in response to a wave of suicide bombings. According to Israeli authorities, 38 percent of all suicide bombers originated or reached Israel by way of Jenin since the outbreak of the second intifada. Today, Jenin stands virtually isolated, surrounded by the security fence that cuts it off from not only Israel, but also its Arab neighbors in the West Bank. Order is maintained by armed youths led by the leader of the local al-Aqsa Matryrs Brigades, himself a veteran of Israeli jails. The public officials of Jenin run their city but they do not rule it. Arafat did not intervene; even when allowed beyond his compound by the Israelis, he kept his distance. The city manager left prison dreaming to be an attorney and did in fact obtain a law degree in Sweden. When interviewed by James Bennet of the *New York Times* (July 14, 2004), he contended that Arafat and the leadership of the PLO were left with two options. The first: They could dissolve the PA and declare open war against Israel, an act of bravado that he did not espouse. Jenin has already witnessed the destructive power of the IDF acting in a relatively restrained fashion. Musa is no doubt aware of what would happen to his city in an all-out conflict with Israel's powerful army. Instead he opts for the second option, however bitter. As he put it to *The Times*: "The Palestinian Authority should stand in front of the people and say, 'We are defeated but this is not the end of the world. This is a new stage of our life.' And then you say to the world, 'Please help us,'" a seeming endorsement of a two-state solution.

One of the most powerful figures associated with the PA is Muhammad Dahlan, a refugee from the Gaza camps who served as director of preventive security. Opinionated and fearless, he had been at odds with Arafat on a number of occasions. Dahlan, a veteran of Israeli prisons who reads Hebrew and speaks it fluently, is considered by his former captors to be a realist with whom one can do business. That he challenged Arafat from time to time only solidifies their good opinion of him. His demand—never met—that Arafat relinquish personal control over the PA's many security services and that they be brought under one roof and employed, when necessary, to bring freewheeling gunmen under control, spoke volumes to Israel's vision of a proper Palestinian partner in the quest for peace. Addressing a conference in June 2004, Dahlan entertained questions about the envisioned Israeli withdrawal from Gaza. He reportedly said that in the wake of Israel's unilateral evacuation of settlements and the withdrawal of military forces assigned to guard them, the Palestinians would have an opportunity to build a model society. The alternative was to embrace chaos and destruction. He went on to say that the Palestinians had previously embarked on a path of self-deception. By all accounts they had failed, in that they neither made peace with Israel nor successfully waged war against it. The time had come to choose. Either there would be war or there would be peace. If it were to be war, he would be the first to take up arms. Lest one believe that Dahlan was seriously contemplating all-out war with Israel rather than calling for a realistic peace, an interview that he gave to a *New York Times* reporter a month later (July 15, 2004) makes his position clear. Sitting in his office, he spoke of the PLO's indecision (meaning Arafat's failure to embrace a decisive course of action). He noted that the old guard was at the same time for and against the intifada and for and against terror. It was time to choose. Either the Palestinians would achieve their independence or become "a Somalia" (meaning a country without a proper government ruled by self-serving warlords). While Dahlan did not explicitly prefer peace over war, there is every reason to believe that is what he meant when he concluded, "Enough is enough." He seemed to imply the pragmatic view that half a loaf—even a stale loaf—offered by an Israeli government would be enough to sustain a fledgling Palestinian polity and allow it to take hold. Would others, particularly the Islamists now in power, assess the situation in so stark and realistic a fashion?

According to polls taken by Khalil Shikaki (Shiqaqi) during the height of the Aqsa intifada, most Palestinians preferred an Arab state in all of Palestine, a nonstarter for any new peace initiative. And yet, according to Shikaki, the highly respected pollster of Palestinian opinion, the overall data seemed to reflect a certain sense of weariness that might be massaged into supporting a reinvigorated peace process, provided that the Palestinians felt they were being treated fairly and with dignity. A June 2003 survey disclosed that nearly three-quarters of the Palestinians polled supported a year-long hudnah, a voluntary cessation of violence against Israel. A full 80 percent favored a joint cease-fire of continuous duration. There is every reason to believe these sentiments persist. A two-state solution may be at odds with ultimate Arab expectations and deep-rooted Muslim tradition, but under the present circumstances, it is all the Palestinians can expect to achieve. Beaten but certainly not bowed by the horror of recent years, most Palestinians may be willing to consider a compromise that calls for living with a Jewish state for a finite but undetermined period of time. The triumph of Hamas at the polls in 2006 was less an endorsement of their hard position vis-à-vis peace with Israel than a rejection of the ineffectual and corrupt leadership of the PA. The vote for Hamas was a vote for a return to some semblance of normalcy and not the endorsement of endless war.

The rejectionist movement, having swept aside the opposition in the recent election, is faced with an obvious and perhaps unforeseen dilemma. The PA that they are about to control is seemingly bound by the Oslo agreement and a two-state solution. Hamas can of course declare the agreement null and void, but that would create an unwanted stir among the Americans and Europeans who have much invested in the peace process and who also underwrite much of the PA's budget. Were the West to withhold its contribution, and were the Israelis to refuse to return the taxes it collects for the PA as they have done in the past, the damage to the already devastated Palestinian economy could pass the point of no return. Nor are conservative Arab states likely to support in full a new PA that threatens to destabilize a volatile region and thus endanger their own regimes.

Hamas will soon discover that it is one thing to supply soccer balls to restless youth, establish drug programs, run medical clinics, and support a wide range of much needed social services and educational initiatives, all with great transparency, but it is quite another to tackle the monster of the Palestinian economy, which is a shambles, particularly in Gaza. The future economic picture is anything but clear. Hamas has inherited a situation that is not about to improve dramatically, even over an extended period of time, even if all the usual sources of funding were guaranteed. It is quite a stretch to imagine Gaza as a future Singapore, the Asian commercial center with which it was compared in past grandiose assessments. It will take an enormous infusion of foreign investment merely to improve the lot of the average Gazan to where it had been before the first intifada.

It is not merely the economy that should trouble the new government. Dominating the politics of Gaza and the West Bank, the Islamists will be held responsible for governance well beyond the social services they presently coordinate. There is, first and foremost, the matter of internal security, especially the pervasive sense of lawlessness. As the senior partner if not sole authority in any government that is formed, the movement's leaders will have to rein in local thugs and overzealous militants while keeping their own armed brigades quiescent. Thus far, Hamas has been able to impose discipline within its own ranks—since August of 2004 they have for the most part maintained a self-declared hudnah, prohibiting attacks on Israel and keeping a lid on inter-Arab confrontations. But now the Islamist movement will also have to account for the well-armed loose cannons associated with Fatah. Many supporters of Fatah are situated within the PA's security forces and will not give up their positions easily, if at all. Immediately after the election, the younger generation of Fatah took to the streets, and while their rage was directed at their elders in the movement, it could easily turn against the new government.

There is also Islamic Jihad to consider. The latter continuously attacked Israeli targets in Gaza and beyond, and following the evacuation of the settlements, have maintained their operations against targets in Israel itself. Despite the declared hudnah, the Israelis can be expected to respond promptly and decisively to any provocations as before. The IDF will not stand for random mortar rounds that continue to be fired into Israel proper. With that, the Islamists in charge of the government will be held responsible for the unstable conditions, as was Mahmoud Abbas. To achieve calm in the Palestinian sector and guarantee continued funding, Hamas will have to persuade all the Palestinians to sheath their swords in Gaza and the West Bank, at least for the time being, and find a means of dealing with Israel without somehow acknowledging its right to exist. At no time should we expect them to go against the grain of all that they believe and accept a permanent Jewish state or thoroughly secular Arab state in Palestine. Retaining ideological purity in the real world is no small problem for the Islamists, now that they have gained power.

In the West Bank there will be no complete evacuation of settlements, let alone the Jewish communities that ring the city of Jerusalem. The formal disposition of that area will only be resolved by serious and direct negotiations in which the Arabs will be faced with major concessions. Short of a formal agreement with the Palestinians, the Israelis will continue to build the fence that will define their security border, if not a permanent border between themselves and the Arabs beyond. In any serious negotiations with the reconstituted PA, Israel will demand recognition of Israel's sovereignty and the legality of a Jewish state whose final borders will be fixed. No Israeli government will settle for anything less than a genuine peace and recognition that is de jure as well as de facto. If and when peace is made with the Palestinians and the Arab nations that remain formally at war with the Jewish state, there will have to be diplomatic relations and some promise or hint of commercial arrangements and cultural exchanges. The Israelis are not likely to accept less than they have managed to obtain from Egypt and Jordan, two nations with which they have signed peace treaties. The militants might be prepared to partake in running a quiet and peaceful Gaza, because it need not compromise their basic position, which denies Israel's right to exist. It is another thing to accept a comprehensive settlement that leads to what Islamic law and tradition prohibit, namely, a Jewish polity on Muslim soil. Bear in mind they will be under continuing pressure from both the West and the Arab world to declare an end to violence and find a way to negotiate directly with representatives of the Israel government. They will also be asked to somehow disavow their proclaimed intention of replacing the Jewish state with an Islamic polity in all of Palestine.

The Islamists thus find themselves in a difficult situation. But they have been there before. As early as 1992, a year before Oslo, the momentum for peace presented the militants with a dilemma: Should they participate in elections to representative institutions in the West Bank and Gaza under Israeli occupation, particularly if any such elections might be linked to (future) concessions to Israel in the form of a two-state solution? With the drift of official Arab thinking running against their maximalist position at the time, the leadership of Hamas undertook a detailed review of its options. That assessment is found in a secret document that circulated through the leadership and rank and file. The document addressed what seemed at the time a very real possibility, namely, that negotiations would inevitably lead to an interim agreement establishing Palestinian self-rule in the occupied territories. In such an arrangement, the Israel occupation would remain in place, but the Palestinians would be allowed to govern themselves until a final agreement creates a viable Palestinian state along with the Jewish State of Israel—hence the need of elections.

Were the movement to stress ideological purity and reject all participation in a governmental process before the creation of a Palestinian state (and presumably the dissolution of Israel), it would not be able to secure important levers of power in a transitional Palestinian authority. And so, Hamas accepted the principle of participation provided that the elections would be fair and under international and not Israeli supervision. The document presented a number of scenarios including possible outcomes of the electoral process. It is plain that Hamas was fully aware of the realities on the ground and was willing to embark on a pragmatic course provided that it did not have to compromise on fundamental principles. Above all, the movement did not want to create a situation that would lead to civil war within the broad nationalist camp. Likewise, the PLO was anxious to avoid an outbreak of significant violence within Palestinian society. The result was an uneasy truce that was to paralyze any real movement toward a final settlement with the Jews even after the promising start at Oslo.

A dozen years after Oslo, the militants remain adamantly opposed to any permanent settlement, except on their own terms, but they—along with all the other Palestinian factions—are terrified of the prospect of civil war. They are also aware that as expectations for normalcy rise, there may well be serious slippage of support for maximalist positions, particularly if those positions interfere with the flow of funds necessary to improve the daily condition of Palestinians on the West Bank and in Gaza. How then can Hamas reconcile its firm commitment to past and present principle while juggling the politics of the moment? The Islamists will most likely look to the past for some precedent that would allow them an opportunity to square the circle; that is, they will seek an Islamic solution.

There are indeed many instances when Islamic polities exchanged ambassadors and conducted negotiations with nonbelievers who occupied territory within the Abode of Islam. The most noteworthy examples are the Christian kingdoms in the Iberian Peninsula; the Byzantines who on occasion occupied part of the border regions separating what is today southern Turkey from northern Syria; and the most pungent example of all, various forms of cooperation between the Crusaders and their Muslim rivals. Hamas could very well cite these precedents, especially the last two, as in the end, the Muslims triumphed over the invading Franks and the Christians of Asia Minor. Better still, they could draw instruction from the Prophet who negotiated a truce with the pagan oligarchs of Mecca and then entered the city in triumph a year later—the agreement, known as the Truce of Hudaybiyah, was in fact cited by Arafat in justifying the Oslo Accord.

Directing the Muslim faithful to various declarations attributed to the Prophet, the spiritual leaders of Hamas could reinforce the notion of biding time until a more propitious moment compels them to act. There is no shortage of religious texts and legal opinions upon which to establish formal relations with unbelievers bordering or occupying Muslim lands. In return for these arrangements, Hamas would no doubt insist on the creation of a genuine rather than rump Palestinian state on the West Bank and in Gaza, with borders that conform with the pre-1967 lines (if not the partition plan of 1947) and a capital situated in East Jerusalem. In addition, they will surely demand a just solution to the plight of the Arab refugees, which would signify for Hamas the right to return to their homes in Israel proper. This kind of solution to the Arab-Israel problem was previously advanced by the PA at the Camp David talks and also by the Saudis in a Beirut conference of the Arab League in 2002. Neither reestablishing the pre-1967 borders, nor granting Arab refugees the right of return, will satisfy Israel, regardless of which government Israelis elect. But were Hamas to agree to direct talks without preconditions and guarantee a long-range hudnah that called for normalization of relations with the Jewish state, albeit without formally recognizing its legitimacy, Israelis would be hard-pressed to brush aside such an offer to enter into talks, because in such circumstances Israel's friends would press them hard. As a long-range objective, Hamas could continue to expect the dissolution of the Jewish state and the creation of an Islamic polity in all of the Holy Land, but that need not prevent the Islamists from shaping their policies to accord with political realities. When asked about relations with Israel shortly after the parliamentary elections, Hamas leaders spoke of the immediate need for a Palestinian state along the lines mentioned above and conceded the possibility of a long truce with Israel. The final resolution of the problem—that is, the creation of an Islamic state in all of Palestine—would be left to a future generation.

As we write shortly after the historic parliamentary election, Hamas has yet to crystallize even the outlines of a projected plan of rule. And so questions remain: How can the new PA led by Islamists negotiate with a Zionist entity whose very legitimacy it cannot and will not recognize? How will it respond to the United States, Europe, and various international bodies who regard Hamas as a terrorist organization bent on the destruction of a member of the community of nations? How will Hamas deal with the myriad problems in Gaza and the West Bank? The initial response to the economic squeeze threatened by Israel and the West (if Hamas did not disavow its maximalist stance and armed struggle) was defiance. Rather than abandon its cherished principles, the movement declared Palestinian needs would be met by alternative sources of funding from wealthy Arab states. Although these states did pledge to provide help for current problems, it is unlikely they will meet the expansive needs of the new PA, estimated at 1.5 billion dollars a year simply to meet the government payroll. Regarding not negotiating with Israel, there were pressing issues that required immediate attention, for example, the movement of trade through checkpoints and arrangements for Palestinians to work at their jobs in Israel, situations ordinarily dealt with by officials at border crossings. Having to deal directly with a polity they did not recognize, the leaders of Hamas spoke of conducting "indirect talks," presumably through other Arab states and/or seasoned negotiators of the PA working with Mahmoud Abbas, whose post as president was not affected by the election.

The Islamists appear to have been as surprised as their opponents at the outcome of the vote. The preliminary and exit polls all revealed that Fatah would emerge the winner, though without a clear majority. That being the likely result, there was speculation as to whether the mainline nationalist movement would ask Hamas to join the government and/or seek alliances with other groups within the PLO. In a stunning reversal of expectations— all the more so as exit polls indicated them winning slightly less than 40 percent of the vote—Hamas and the independents it supported won 76 of the 132 seats, forming thereby an absolute majority in the newly elected parliament. Under the circumstances, Mahmoud Abbas would be forced to ask the leadership of Hamas to form a new government. Should this come to pass, and the Islamists rule as the majority party with all others in opposition, they alone would be responsible for stabilizing the areas under their control, improving the economy, providing necessary social services, and attracting external funding to make all that necessary. It would be a tall task given their long-range ideological commitment to armed struggle and refusal to deal directly with Israel, positions that might compromise their sources of funding. Just recently, the Israel authorities closed the Karni Crossing, allegedly for reasons of security. As a result, Palestinian farmers lost half a million dollars a day as their fruits and vegetables rotted instead of being shipped to markets in the Jewish state. Similar incidents are bound to take place in the future and will require the direct intervention of representatives on both sides of the divide. As did the first PA, a Hamas-led government will be forced into constant contact with the authorities in Israel.

There is a touch of genuine irony to Hamas's triumph. Had they lost the election but gathered 40 percent of the vote as predicted, they might have had the option of taking part in some government decisions. If asked to serve in a government led by Fatah and other factions of the PLO, the Islamists could have insisted on controlling the ministries that address their direct concerns and influence the hearts and minds of the Palestinians— health, welfare, religious affairs, and education—and they would be sure to promote Islamic values and demand proper Islamic behavior. Given their track record in providing social services and the like, there is every reason to believe they would have earned the public's admiration for a job well done. At the same time, the mainline organizations would have been mired in the usual muck, paying the price for ineffective government and any concessions made to Israel during negotiations. In a sense, the Islamists could have eaten their cake and kept it, too.

Having triumphed, and with a sufficient number of seats to rule without a coalition, Hamas's initial reaction was to act is if it had lost, or won ever so narrowly. No doubt, they were well aware that by ruling alone they might have to compromise their ideological purity and tactical flexibility. Their first inclination was to seek partners from the old regime. The idea of a coalition with Fatah was floated, as was an offer to integrate Hamas's militant brigades into the Palestinian security forces. They also sounded out a prominent PA figure with considerable negotiating experience, asking him if he as willing to intervene with the Israelis (as the Islamists were not about to acknowledge the legitimacy of the Jewish state by entering into direct talks with its appointed representatives). The initial response of Fatah was negative, angry, and in certain instances violent, although the violence was largely directed by the younger generation of Fatah at their elders in the movement. The initial consensus among the defeated was to let Hamas take full responsibility for running the PA. As one Fatah official put it: "Let them worry about the garbage." Clearly, those who negotiated with Israel in the past will be reluctant to do so again if they did not have the full backing of the new government. Why should they bear the responsibility and the brunt of criticism that is sure to follow if and when compromises are brokered?"

It remains to be seen whether Fatah and the other mainstream nationalists will close ranks and remain in the opposition. Should that be the case, Hamas could turn to independents elected with their support, earmarking them for appointments that the Islamists do not covet. One can imagine a figure such as Ziad Abu-Amr being offered an important ministry. A respected political scientist and independent legislator with flawless English and wide contacts abroad—including Israel—and more important, carrying no political baggage from the past, Abu-Amr would seem an ideal person to run the foreign ministry. In similar fashion, Sallam al-Fayyad, the able minister of finance who resigned his post with the previous government over issues of transparency, could well be asked to take the reins once again. Such an appointment would go a long way in reassuring those nations and institutions that shore up the Palestinian economy that their contributions will genuinely improve living conditions in the lands administered by the PA. As we write in February of 2006, the situation is quite unsettled; the next months, if not weeks, may reveal the trend of things to come.

The most critical task facing the Islamist movement will be putting an end to lawlessness within Palestinian society and keeping the self-declared hudnah in effect, among not only their own fighters but also all the other armed militias and organized bands of thugs. Some groups will certainly resort to violence for self-serving purposes unrelated to the Arab-Israel conflict. Others, for example Islamic Jihad, will be inclined to continue the armed struggle in an effort to undermine any long-term arrangement with Israel, should the new Palestinian government move in that direction. Were these challenges to materialize, would the new PA do what David Ben Gurion, Israel's first prime minister, did after the Jewish state was created? At a critical moment during Israel's War of Independence, he ordered the regular army to spill Jewish blood by firing on an independent militia. Following the war, he boldly disbanded all the militias, including an elite force that had truly distinguished itself during the fighting. Put somewhat differently, would any Palestinian leader order the security forces to disarm and otherwise deactivate militant brigades and armed thugs acting or threatening to act outside government authority? More important, would the forces of a nascent Palestinian state made up of these brigades be willing and able to carry out such a command. If the answer is no on either count, the future of the Palestinians will be bleak indeed, as will that of Israel and the entire region.

As regards the future viability of any Palestinian state, much will depend on how firmly national consciousness is rooted among the Palestinians themselves. This might seem at first a rather curious comment. Why should one question their identity as a discrete Arab nation when their quest for a state has captured the attention of the entire world and stirred its moral conscience? Even those critical of Palestinian methods can understand how tragic circumstances have forged among them a sense of common identity. Here is a people either stateless in their own homeland or living in exile amid their Arab brothers, in most cases without rights of citizenship. Nevertheless, they remain hopeful. Why should anyone doubt the motivating power of their nationalism when they have taken to the streets against the IDF, the most powerful army in the region? But what will happen if the Zionist enemy, having withdrawn from Gaza, also withdraws from enough of the West Bank to allow for a viable Palestinian state? How will the national consciousness of the Palestinians shape their destiny? Although attention remains largely riveted on the quest for statehood, it is neither premature nor inappropriate to contemplate the future Palestine.

Time and again we have noted that nationalism is a recent development in the Arab world. Because the very concepts of nation and nation-state do not run deep, there have been problems in uniting disparate peoples of the Arab Near East in common polity. In one Arab country after another, allegiances to the motherland are diluted by competing loyalties based on powerful and long-established ethnic, religious, linguistic, local, and clan affiliations. A Western author writing about the Arab states chose for the title of his book *Tribes with Flags*. The descriptive label, however marked by whimsy, is not altogether devoid of truth. Arab states often seem like large tribal configurations made up of numerous kinship groups and their clients and retainers. We should note that such tribal societies tend to be unstable over the long run as the center rarely withstands the pull of anarchic behavior. It would appear that strong states emerge among the Arabs only when the ruling authority can act unburdened by democratic restraints and the conflicting needs and desires of its heterogeneous population. In the absence of a shared sense of polity, states such as Saddam's Iraq and the elder Assad's Syria relied on oppressive security forces that knew no restraint when brutality was deemed necessary for the circumstances. The Iraqi poison gas campaign against the Kurds and the Syrian massacre of Islamists in Hama are illustrative examples. An orderly society may also take root when competing groups within a newly formed nation-state, each without the wherewithal to overcome its rivals, are delicately balanced in a symbiotic relationship (Lebanon before the civil wars and Syrian domination is an example). It may also occur when enormous wealth spread large buys compliance at home and cooperation abroad (consider the oil rich states), or when a cohesive and disciplined ruling establishment, conscious of its limited power but wizened in the ways of Arab political culture, affects policies that balance competing interests without relinquishing state control (the case of the Hashemite Kingdom of Jordan). There has also been a history of weak states unable to withstand the centrifugal forces that threaten to tear them apart (current-day Algeria and Lebanon during its lengthy civil war).

What would one anticipate of a future Palestinian state? Which of the above models would it likely resemble? The aftermath of Saddam's fall underscores how fragmented and fragile Iraqi society is in the absence of effective centralized government. But unlike Iraq, where Sunnite Arabs in the center have long been in conflict with ethnic Kurds in the North and Shiites in the South; unlike Lebanon, with its mosaic of armed religious communities composed of Shiite and Sunnite Muslims, various denominations of Christians, and a large Druze community; and unlike Syria, with its Shiite and Sunnite Arabs, Alawites, Druze, Kurds, and others; the Arabs of

Palestine seem to be fairly homogeneous. Christians, well educated and worldly, once played an important role in Palestinian Arab society, but they have been reduced to no more than 5 percent of the total population. With the current revival of Islam, they have been completely marginalized. Nor does the Palestinian tent accommodate significant numbers of minority Muslims. Virtually all the Palestinians are Sunnites. Granting all that, uniting the Arabs of Palestine in common polity will not be easy. If the past is our guide, the founding fathers of the future Palestinian state are likely to encounter serious internal divisions.

Looking back at the modern history of the Holy Land, one encounters numerous rivalries among beduin tribes and conflict between the beduins and Arabs of the settled areas. There are also rivalries between peoples of neighboring towns and villages and between extended clans (*hamulah*) distributed widely throughout the country. For the more distinguished and urban-centered families, rivalry was, more often than not, restricted to matters of business and political maneuvering. But from time to time, particularly in rural areas, rivalries led to bloodshed and then retaliation that occasioned the further spilling of blood. The Ottoman Turks, themselves Muslims, barely controlled a lawless countryside for much of the nineteenth century. The British in turn were forced to harsh measures in putting down the Arab rebellion in 1936–1939, and yet, at that time, Arabs killed more Arabs in clashes between rival clans than did the British authorities in their attempt to establish public order. The memories of this strife and the allegiances from which it stemmed have not disappeared; they have been swept under the rug and can only emerge once an Arab Palestine takes shape and the spoils of rule are up for grabs. To be sure, Palestinian society has also changed, perhaps more dramatically than meets the eye. The old land-owning rural elites, once enormously powerful in Palestinian politics, have had to share power with new elites situated in burgeoning towns and cities. Many of the new leaders, mostly younger men in their thirties and forties, are from families of rural and modest origins. They will not return to the past quietly, if at all.

The increasing lawlessness of the current situation, somewhat reminiscent of the 1930s, may well continue after Palestinian statehood. Even if the security forces are prepared to act decisively, it will not be easy to cap the violence. A generation of children who have grown up in games of war and lack parental control will not easily adjust to a well-mannered and law-abiding society. Should the fledgling regime be challenged, there might very well be civil conflict, perhaps worse than that which existed some seventy years ago. If the Palestinians themselves were incapable of producing order, would any Arab state intervene? And were they willing to intervene, would the Palestinians accept their presence? Would Israel stand by idly or see any such intervention as a threat to its own security? It is of course possible that the transition to statehood would go smoothly, and despite potential problems, Palestine will emerge as a model polity, thereby fulfilling the fervent hopes of Muhammad Dahlan and others. Only time will tell.

There is also the question of governance. It is difficult to imagine an Islamic state governed by traditional Islamic law or even a sort of Iranian-style government in which the religious authorities have veto power over the civil administration. There are already murmurings among Christian Arabs and some secularists about the future course plotted by Hamas. For their part, the leaders of Hamas have remained low key about any major changes that would reflect Islamic sensibilities. How would the more militant Islamists react to an extended hudnah when a Palestinian state occupies only part of the sacred land set aside in trust for Muslims alone? The ultimate triumph for Hamas and its supporters is the melding of Palestinian nationalism with Islamic tradition—in short, the creation of a future state properly governed by Islamic law in all of historic Palestine. At the moment, the leaders of Hamas seem to recognize that that glorious future may take some time. As long as Israel remains strong, the hudnah may have to be declared again, perhaps repeatedly. After all, it took several generations for Muslims to finally rid the Holy Land of the Crusaders. Given Israel's dynamic society, its military prowess, and the general support that it receives in the Western world, particularly the United States, even Arabs who make a virtue of patience are likely to be tested.

Whether the Arabs will accept the reality of the moment and moments to come or resort to violence in pursuit of what they perceive as absolute justice is yet to be determined.

DEMOCRACY AND THE PROSPECTS FOR AN ARAB-ISRAEL SETTLEMENT

Palestinians across the political spectrum have long demanded their government respond to the people's needs. The corruption and high-handed ways of the PA eventually gave rise to increasingly vocal calls for transparency—calls that generally went unheeded by the oligarchs of the PLO. Related to those demands for a more responsible government, Palestinians spoke of the need for democratic change beginning with honest elections. The result of the most recent vote was proof positive that these sentiments for greater democracy and honest government reverberated throughout Palestinian society. But what do Palestinians envision when they refer to democracy, and what is the likelihood that such a vision can become reality? And if some form of democracy were to evolve among the Palestinians, how might that affect a possible settlement with the Jewish state?

The American effort to establish a Western-style democracy in Iraq is an indication of how difficult it is for foreign forms of governance to take root in the Arab Near East. Not sufficiently—if at all—appreciative of cultural difference, not sufficiently aware of the complex structure of Iraqi society, and (if those were not enough) blissfully ignorant of Iraq's long history, American policy makers would appear to have made a muck of things—at least to date. Lest we be overly critical of the Bush administration for a rather loose game plan to stabilize Iraq and bring it into the democratic fold, we should be aware that well-meaning Iraqis, including those who returned from exile, were only too aware of the fractious nature of Iraqi society and the historical circumstances that shaped long-standing conflicts within it. But they, too, have been stymied, not for lack of good intentions or doing their homework—the overwhelming majority of those Iraqis who plan their country's future are well meaning rather than self-serving. Having taken on the responsibility of building a new Iraq, they have examined numerous forms of democratic governance in seeking to establish a model that might suit the particular and exceedingly difficult needs of the Iraqi people. It is still too early to write off these efforts and declare the democratic experiment a catastrophic failure, but the short-term prognosis is anything but encouraging. One thing is certain: Should democratic institutions be introduced, the Iraqi versions will reflect the local and regional political culture and will thus be different than those of the West. The same is likely to be true of the Palestinians when they look for templates with which to create a state of their own.

Oddly enough, some Western critics who accuse the Bush regime of arrogance and cultural myopia have themselves been guilty of not understanding the deep structures of Islamic civilization and the residual effects of a cultural and political heritage that goes back at least fourteen hundred years. Western analysts and Arab secularists holding Western values believe that emergent democracy will be accompanied by a more even distribution of wealth and by broad participation in governmental processes. Some social scientists have argued that civil society will eventually take root in the region because the Arab nation-states will need to tax their populations more heavily, encouraging thereby a popular involvement with the process of governance. Others have argued that the demands of the emergent global economy will require a vast bureaucracy of skilled technicians, a kind of informed citizenry more given to democratic sentiments than the military cliques or tribal families that currently rule. To be fair, these brief comments reduce complex arguments to rather simple if not simplistic propositions, but they are an accurate rendering of scenarios envisioned by more than a few observers.

To be sure, much of the optimism about the inevitable triumph of democracy in the Arab world was expressed before America set out to "free Iraq." If the events in that country have taught us anything at all, it is to exercise great caution in predicting the future, particularly as regards the possibilities of Western-style democracy in the Arab world. The notion that increased taxation and/or the demands of the global economy will erode authoritarian forms of governance dramatically understates the capacity of autocratic regimes to adjust to the realities of the marketplace and, even barring that, to enforce compliance on their constituents—even by brutal means if necessary. Islamic history is filled with accounts of rulers who ignored rational economic policies and long-term planning for short-lived gains and personal aggrandizement.

Some Palestinian exponents of Islamic revival are also confident about a democratic future. As do other Islamists, they foresee a time when the *mukhabarat* states of the moment—that is, governments with highly invasive security forces—will be replaced by Islamic polities more responsive to the needs of the faithful. But the revivalist hopes for the future are not linked to any social science models developed in the West. They do not see democracy as being akin to the revolt of taxpayers in Orange County, California. For Hamas and other revivalists, democracy is not a radical departure occasioned by changes in the collection and allocation of resources but a return to traditional Muslim values and forms of rule. Their claim is that democracy and free elections played a role in the formation of Muslim society some fourteen centuries ago. As proof of that, they point to the time of the Prophet and his successors, the four *rashidun*, or so-called righteous caliphs. The revivalists consider this time to be a period of pristine Islam, a sort of primitive democracy that was unfortunately sullied by the political and moral corruption of persons and parties who preferred the temporal world to that of religion. For Palestinian reformers, this version of the past is the accepted basis for evaluating current experience and the means of anticipating what should take place in the future. Their embrace of that idealized early Islamic community is shared by all revivalists in the Arab world.

Aside from how democracy in Islam was and is to be defined, linking an anticipated democratic future to the early Islamic community should leave most historians uneasy. The expectation of democratic change suggested by the Islamists is no less problematic than that Western vision in which Islamic states change course dramatically to form hitherto unknown civil societies with fully developed democratic institutions. A minor and (to our knowledge) unreported event reveals the nature of the problem. Shortly after the outbreak of the first intifada, two American scholars met in Gaza with Mahmoud Zahar, then the reputed leader of Hamas's political wing. Pressed about democracy in a future Palestinian state, Zahar noted wryly that the Western press, so critical of Muslim governments for their lack of democratic forms and behavior, was quick to support the Algerian authorities when they nullified the results of the first popular and truly democratic election to be held in a modern Arab state, an election in which the Algerian Islamists scored a dramatic victory that would have eventually paved their way to power. Following that, he asked why Muslims should look to the West for examples of democracy and popular election; these were characteristic forms of true Islamic government. According to Dr. Zahar, the democratic process is rooted in the experiences of the early Islamic community and was part of its religious and political structure.

When informed that the current term for elections in Arabic (*intikhabat*) is a nineteenth-century creation, stimulated no less by Near Easterners looking to Europe, and that *dimuqratiyah* is, in any case, not a word of Arabic origin, Zahar mentioned the ancient tradition of *shura*, meaning "consultative assembly." In response, the American professors noted that shura does not signify universal suffrage but a privilege that allows a few tribal elders to concentrate decision making in their own hands. As to the early caliphs and democracy, they pointed out, of four righteous caliphs, three were assassinated and the other's succession was imposed on the community by less than a handful of individuals. In point of fact, Shiites and Sunnites still contest that succession more than thirteen hundred years later. This brief episode in Gaza underscores how differently realities are perceived when one is truly sensitive to language and categories of definition.

Revivalists like Zahar are certainly aware of the distinctions between Western democratic forms and behavior and the world of early Islam. Moreover, they are not embarrassed by liberal—or if one prefers progressive—friends into giving lip service to Western ideals. Democracy, while highly valued, represents for them a rather different concept than "the rights of man" or the "bill of rights." There are, to be sure, more secular-minded Muslims who still look to Europe and the United States. There are a number of them in the ranks of the Palestinian intelligentsia. It would be foolish and shortsighted to dismiss summarily Muslims who have been directly exposed to Western democracy and, having embraced the concept, are prepared to make it part of their own native governance. That said, in traditional Arab/Muslim societies, the overwhelming majority of believers are inclined to look to their own distant past when searching for legitimate forms of political institutions and behavior.

It is a moot point whether the current Muslim interest in democracy, however that interest is expressed and however democracy is conceptualized, will stand the test of time. It is still too early to tell whether the encroachment of modernity forged in the West will have as dramatic an effect on the political thinking of Muslims as it has had on their material life. Perhaps something labeled by them as democracy, and maybe even resembling Western democracy, will emerge as an indigenous development with claims on the Muslim past. Two hundred years and more have passed since Napoleon invaded Egypt, confident of the superiority of his civilization and filled with presumption about civilizing others. History has yet to sort out what the West has done to the peoples of the Near East. We cannot imagine any responsible scholar wanting to go on record predicting what is likely to happen in the next decade, let alone in the next century.

We can be fairly certain of one thing, however: Democracy, as it is understood in the West, will not take root in the Arab world by fine-tooling local and regional economies and reallocating wealth more justly. The key to change in the Islamic societies of the region is the ever-more-difficult task of changing historical consciousness, that is, of changing the manner in which Muslims use the past to create paradigms of present and future behavior. That change cannot be mandated, nor will it come as did revelation to the Prophet Muhammad, "like the crack of dawn." Shifts in historical consciousness are occasioned by experiences that tend to unfold over long periods of time accentuated by dramatic moments that jar and then uproot conventional wisdom and cherished conceptions. Since the encroachment of the West some three hundred years ago, much has occurred to disturb Muslim sensibilities and shake the self-confidence of Arab leaders and states—not the least being the establishment of a Jewish polity in the Arab Muslim heartland. Nevertheless, the historical consciousness of Arab Muslims remains firmly rooted in a history and tradition that calls for strong resistance to structural change.

Still, for the sake of argument let us assume that the Palestinians are able to establish a truly democratic state in part of mandated Palestine. Let us assume still further that the other confrontation states in the Arab–Israel dispute follow their lead. Can such transformative changes in the political life of the Arabs lead to real accommodation with the Jewish polity in their midst? Put somewhat differently, can democracy in the Arab world overcome the prejudices against Jews and more recently against Zionism that are part and parcel of an inherited and revered Islamic past? One can also reverse the question and ask whether true democracy can take root in the Arab world without first settling, or at least greatly alleviating, the pernicious conflict between Jews and Muslims that so exacerbates tensions of all sorts in the region. At present, the conflict represents a match ready for striking in a room filled with flammable substances.

For visionaries, the flame of peace is eternally lit. No statesmen has been more active in the quest for a solution to the Arab-Israel conflict than Shimon Peres, recipient of the Nobel Peace Prize and the driving force, if not the architect, of the Oslo Agreement. In numerous interviews, public appearances, and published works, Peres has trumpeted a vision of an idyllic Near Eastern future. The distinguished former prime minister of Israel foresees a time of economic prosperity and social justice made possible by democratic states pledged to act in harmony with each other. This view of progress and a world to come sees the Jewish State of Israel as a full partner in the Near Eastern equivalent of the European Economic Union. He is certainly right in stating that Israel has much to offer its Arab neighbors. His country is a real democracy, rich in human resources, and in the forefront of modern science and technology. Peres's vision is certainly uplifting for those who have the interests of all Near Eastern peoples in mind. There is, however, a sense of déjà vu to Peres's grand scheme. A century ago, Theodore Herzl (d. 1904), the founder of modern Zionism, laid out his own vision of the future. In his utopian novel *Altneuland*, he writes of a future Jewish state in the historic Land of Israel. Guided by modern science and technology, the Jews will reclaim their ancient homeland and establish within it a society marked by equality, tolerance, and respect for all, including the Arabs. It is hard to imagine that Herzl's bold vision had any appeal for contemporaneous Arabs; Peres's views, though not meant to be condescending, are looked at with great suspicion by Arabs today. There is the fear that Israel's westernized culture and economic strength will overwhelm its Arab neighbors.

In the West, it is often thought that intellectuals champion a progressive future. One might think therefore that the intellectuals of the Arab confrontation states would be the first to seek a dialogue with Israelis and would in like fashion give vocal support to any efforts at establishing a just peace. The opposite seems to be the case. After Arafat, Rabin, and Peres shook hands on the White House lawn in 1993, a dramatic moment that seemed to herald the beginning of the end of more than fifty years of conflict between Israel and its Arab neighbors, doors were opened to discuss joint economic ventures. There was a flurry of activity between executives on both sides of the previous divide. Preliminary agreements were reached, and grand projects contemplated, none grander than a major airport that Israel was to have built for the Jordanians at the Dead Sea. All that was put on the shelf as the peace process ground to a halt, a victim of spiraling violence, Arafat's political machinations, and the reluctance of Israel's Likud party to offer any serious initiatives. In spite of occasional efforts to revive the peace process, grand schemes for economic cooperation remain dormant. Nevertheless, there is reason to believe that interest could be rekindled should there be substantive progress toward a meaningful peace agreement. Economic cooperation on a grand scale still entices Jewish and Arab entrepreneurs. In contrast, Arab intellectuals, with a few notable exceptions, have been far more negative about establishing contact with their opposite numbers in Israel.

Following the peace treaty with Egypt, Israel moved quickly to establish a research center in Cairo. As a result, numerous Israeli scholars and scientists have visited Egypt along with a host of Israeli tourists. The same is true of Israel and Jordan, and Israel and Morocco. For the most part, the traffic flows one way. With some notable exceptions, Arab intellectuals are the most vociferous critics of Israel and its policies and have been throughout the many attempts at achieving normalized relations with the Jewish state. During the 1990s, the crown prince of Jordan invited a large number of Jordanian intellectuals and professionals to meet with him in his palace. Although obliquely framed, the agenda was to discuss the possibility of greater contacts between the Jordanians and their Israeli colleagues. The invited guests expressed considerable resistance to the idea. When pressed as to why they were so reluctant to meet with Israelis, they spoke of the dangers of "judaizing Arab culture" (*tahwid al-thaqafat al-'arabiyah*).

However important it may be to the future of Muslim Arab society, the democracy that so many Arab intellectuals champion may not result in a more tolerant attitude to Jews and the Zionist project. One might even argue that the ultimate litmus test for democracy's prospects in the Near East may well be whether Arab/Muslim states accept non-Arabs and non-Muslims living in the region as truly legitimate players in the larger game of public life. That would hold true for the "Saturday people" and the "Sunday people," that is, Jews and Christians. Regarding that, the conversation with Dr. Zahar in Gaza was not encouraging. When asked of his vision for the future, Zahar spoke of the need for Islamic states, including an Islamic state in all of mandated Palestine. When asked about non-Muslims, he referred to the traditional role of *dhimmis*, communities protected by the Muslim authorities as mandated in the Qur'an but subject to discrimination suggested in scripture and elaborated on in Islamic law and political theory—hardly a situation that speaks to a solution of the current impasse between Israel and its Arab neighbors. Nevertheless, Zahar was convinced that the non-Muslim monotheists would welcome Muslim hegemony as they allegedly did in the so-called Golden Age in Spain, when, as he put it, "The houses of Muslims were open to all Jews and Christians." There is a remarkable irony in this comment. The very notion of a golden age under Islamic rule was, by and large, the idealized invention of nineteenth-century Jewry tasting the early fruits of emancipation in the Christian West. Given the actual condition of Jews (and Christians) under Islamic rule, a vision of the past that affords them no more than the status of dhimmis would seem to leave little room for a democratic future. If a Jewish state is to be accepted as a legitimate partner in the Arab world, the Muslims, who number well over 90 percent of the region's people, will have to realize, however grudgingly, that memories of the past can be harmful as well as edifying. They will also have to recognize more fully that Jews are guided by a past of their own.

Part II

THE MODERN STATE OF ISRAEL

Integrating Pasts Real and Imagined

7

A LEXICON OF NEAR
EASTERN IDENTITIES

The Jewish People by Various Names
and Foundational Narratives

An ancient people who have continuously graced the stage of history, Jews have been known by different names, all of which date back several millennia. There is, for one, the biblical "Hebrews" (*'Ivrim*), an enigmatic term used to distinguish the families of Abraham's progeny from the Egyptians, oppressors in whose land the Hebrews reportedly dwelt for some four hundred years. More widespread are the references to "Israelites" (*b'nei Yisrael*), literally "the progeny of Israel," Abraham's grandson; and similarly, "the House of Jacob" (*beit Ya 'aqov*), after the name originally given to Israel by his father, the patriarch Isaac. The term "Jews" (*Yehudim*), the most widely used descriptive label of our times, first appears in the postexilic period. It is derived from Judah/Judea (*Yehudah*), the territorial enclave of the tribe of Judah, a region of the Palestinian highlands that became the spiritual and political center of the Davidic dynasty (ca. 1010–586 B.C.E.), and subsequent to the return of the exiles from captivity in Babylon (ca. 515 B.C.E.), the home of the Second Hebrew Commonwealth. Following the Roman wars and the end to Jewish sovereignty in the Land of Judea or Israel (66–70 and 132–135 C.E., respectively), the label of choice, although hardly the exclusive label among Jews themselves, seems to have been "the people of Israel" (*'am Yisrael*) or simply "Israel" (*Yisrael*). This is distinct from the modern "Israelis" (*Yisraelim*), which refers specifically to citizens of the State of Israel (*Medinat Yisrael*), regardless of their religion or ethnic identity. One is obliged to ask what specific associations link the bearers of these distinctive labels in different eras and geographical locations.

191

WHO ARE THE JEWS?

Before modernity produced significant change in the nature of Jewish societies, the questions of who a Jew is and what the relationship is of those
calling themselves Jews to biblical Israel—or, more broadly, to ancient Israel—would have sparked little curiosity, let alone controversy within the
evolving Jewish communities of Europe and the Near East. A Jew was defined by Jewish law (*halakhah*) as a person born to a Jewish mother or converted to the faith in accordance with well-established religious procedures.
Ever since the rabbis attempted to sort out the muddle of Jewish identity
inherited from biblical and Graeco-Roman times (ca. 200 C.E.), matrilineal
descent or proper conversion have been the only bona fide credentials for
those claiming to be Jewish. For well over a millennium, this formula defining Jewishness applied, regardless of where Jews were situated. It even held
true for Jews who denied their heritage, or, beyond that, abandoned altogether the community of the faithful. To be Jewish was not a matter of
choice or self-definition, as it had been for some Jews in Hellenistic and in
Roman times; it was a matter of law. That law, initiated by rabbinical authorities some eighteen hundred years ago, was an innovation that eventually displaced well-worn customs, including practices attested in Hebrew
scripture.

In biblical times, identity in the Israelite community was tied by
blood to the father, or by affiliation with the father's extended household.
Comprising clients and servant families, as well as concubines and wives
and their offspring, the father's household often represented individuals of
different ethnic and religious origins. In such circumstances, questions of
identity could become ambiguous. Despite an expressed preference for
preserving lines of kinship among Israelites and later legal directives to
marry within the group, biblical Israel, even as portrayed in the Bible, was
a more heterogeneous society than we sometimes imagine, particularly
among the elites. Ruth, reportedly the ancestor of King David, was linked
by family ties to the Moabites, descendants of Abraham's nephew Lot.
David, in turn, had offspring by way of a Canaanite princess taken captive
in battle, and his son Solomon is said to have consorted with a thousand
wives and concubines, many of them foreign born and retaining polytheist beliefs and practices. The much-reviled King Ahab took as his queen
the Tyrian Jezebel, described by the biblical author as the éminence grise
behind the throne. Her brutal sister (or daughter) Athaliah actually ruled
the Kingdom of Israel for six years, the only female monarch in the history of that ancient state.

Later Jewish tradition, biblical as well as rabbinic, did not look kindly at liaisons with foreigners, and so various non-Israelites entering Israelite households were castigated for political meddling and, worse yet, for causing religious backsliding among the Lord's elected. Solomon's foreign women were said to have introduced their native Gods to Israelite society, and Jezebel reportedly undermined traditional Israelite values of governance, so much so that her husband, Ahab, who by all appearances was a formidable ruler, is reduced by biblical tradition to a foil for his wife's ambition. As a result, the house of Omri, the dynasty that gave rise to Ahab, comes to an end following his death and the savage murder of his wife. Similarly, Solomon's powerful kingdom is rent after he was laid to rest because, under the influence of his foreign-born women, Solomon ceased to walk in the way of the Lord. Eventually, the biblical guardians of monotheism regulated marriage; women from among the various groups of Canaanites were prohibited to Israelite men, no doubt a sign that such unions were frequent.

Despite the intermingling between Israelites and others, one detects a common thread that binds the biblical community as well as successive communities of Jews. Regardless of time and place, Israelites and Jews alike have claimed links—either direct blood ties or other means of affiliation—to ancient ancestors, thus allowing them to embrace the faith of forefathers, actual or adopted. That embrace of that past produces the desired image of an unbroken chain beginning with Abraham, the progenitor of the ancient Israelites, and by extension the spiritual ancestor of all Jews in all times.

JEWISH IDENTIFICATION IN MODERN TIMES

The circumstances of modern life, particularly among European and North American Jewry, have made Jewish identification ambiguous once again. Much to the concern of traditional rabbis, doubts are now raised about the efficacy of halakhah in determining who should or should not be considered a Jew. The less-demanding process of nonorthodox conversions and the increasing acceptance of paternal as well as maternal lineage as a legitimate marker of Jewish identity have become a matter of great controversy, especially among American Jews, most of whom identify with conservative or reform Judaism, the more lenient (or, if you prefer, the more liberal) streams of the faith. In the state of Israel, the rabbinical courts, which control family law, reject paternal lineage as a legal basis for Jewish identity, and recognize only conversions sanctioned by the long-standing traditions of halakhah. The rabbinical courts determine who is and is not legally Jewish. At stake is the right to marry Jewish partners without formal conversion; the status of children born to mixed marriages, including marriages between individuals who fully identify as Jews but whose Judaism lacks halakhic authority; eligibility regarding the Law of Return, which allows all Jews Israeli citizenship; and a host of other matters that depend on how one legally defines Jewish identity.

The current ambiguity concerning who is and is not a Jew and the controversy to which nonorthodox conversion has given rise can be directly linked to the rapidly changing condition of modern Jewry and to a shift in demographic trends that seemed so favorable to Jewish continuity before World War II and so devastating thereafter. The population of world Jewry at the outbreak of World War II had been estimated at roughly seventeen million, a six-fold increase in a mere three hundred years. Of these, some five million Jews were in the United States; eleven million or so lived in Europe, most of them concentrated in the Soviet Union, Poland, Germany, and countries that were at one time part of the Austro-Hungarian Empire. Another half million had come to settle in mandatory Palestine, the area out of which the future State of Israel would be carved. The rest, mostly in the Islamic Near East, were distributed in smaller communities, many of them dating back to pre-Christian times. At the war's conclusion, world Jewry had been reduced by approximately a third, European Jewry by some six million. Losses were particularly heavy in Central and Eastern Europe. In Poland alone, a prewar community of more than three million souls, fewer than thirty thousand Jews remained; the rest were displaced or decimated by the Holocaust. The most recent estimates of Jewish demography indicate a world population somewhat in excess of thirteen million. That being the case, the decline occasioned by the horrors of the war has not been made up over the ensuing half century.

If anything, demographic trends indicate that the Jews will be hard-pressed to hold their current numbers given widespread intermarriage, assimilation, and a declining birth rate in the industrialized societies of the West. The numbers may look somewhat more encouraging if one adds to the accepted figure of some thirteen million those individuals who are not Jews legally speaking, that is, persons not born to a Jewish mother or not properly converted to the faith but who, nevertheless, consider themselves in some fashion to be Jewish or "part Jewish." As examples, one could cite children who are non-Jews according to traditional Jewish law, but who are with some sense of Jewish identification, and unconverted spouses who are willing to oblige their partners in sharing a measure of Jewish observance and/or otherwise being sensitive to and identifying with Jewish communal concerns. Reform Jewish congregations have long encouraged such individuals and families to become part of their communities and have made the process of conversion less of an obstacle, some might say less of an ordeal. When one includes in the demographic mix of "non-halakhic Jews"—those who are legally Jewish but thoroughly nonaffiliated or are even converts to other faiths—the disputed estimates of "Jewishly connected" Americans increase from roughly 4.5 or 5.5 million to 8.7 or even 13.3 million. The same would be true in some measure for other highly assimilated Jewish communities. On the other hand, the long-term Jewish identity of these nonaffiliated individuals and families is problematic. All the data seem to indicate that over time, their offspring will be less inclined to acknowledge their Jewish roots and less likely to participate in Jewish communal activities.

THE STATE OF ISRAEL AND WORLD JEWRY

The perceived threat to Jewish continuity in the Diaspora underscores the significance of more encouraging demographic trends in the Land of Israel. Regarded since ancient times as the spiritual heartland of the Jewish people, the Land of Israel is currently emerging as home to the largest Jewish community in the world. One of the more important demographic patterns since the end of war and the destruction of European Jewry has been large-scale immigration to the Jewish state. Most recently, the new arrivals have included a large number of non-Jews from the former territories of the Soviet Union, individuals and family clusters who have immigrated to Israel along with their Jewish relatives. All in all, the Russian arrivals in Israel since the 1970s number about a million. Regardless of their religious origins, these immigrants will all acquire a Jewish identity of sorts if they remain permanently. Their children and children's children will certainly be integrated into Israel's society, which is distinctively Jewish, even for Jews who claim to be secular or consciously antireligious. For Jews often identify as a people even when they reject inherited religious beliefs and practices. Even those Christian relatives of Russian Jewish immigrants will have a real connection and sense of identity with Israeli culture. Additional immigration to Israel, from whatever source and for whatever reason, is likely to preserve and even strengthen Jewish/Israeli identity. With or without another massive wave of immigrants, the Jewish community of Israel, which is not threatened by assimilation, is destined to be larger than that of the

United States, currently the largest of the Diaspora communities by far. Moreover, the Jewish birth rate in Israel exceeds that of Jewish communities in the industrialized West, thus projecting, as long as that trend holds, a still larger Jewish community in Israel relative to the rest of world Jewry. Given the inroads of intermarriage and the concomitant loss of Jewish identity that is so prevalent in most of Europe and the Americas, within decades, the Jews of Israel may well outnumber the rest of world Jewry combined.

For those concerned about Jewish continuity, there is a mixed message in this anticipated state of affairs. Lacking substantive Jewish education, as most do today, Diaspora Jews may find themselves denied direct entry into the bank of memories that has forged the self-awareness of individual Jews and the collective identity of the Jewish people since ancient times. The inability to read and analyze Jewish sources, especially in the languages in which they were composed, is thus likely to create a serious rupture between the present Diaspora and that rich and long-lived Jewish past. There is the danger that historic memories representing the cumulative experience of thousands of years will fade to the point of insignificance in the more-assimilated communities. Echoes of a past that Jews have traditionally fashioned into templates for survival will become increasingly dim in successive generations. Should that occur, there may be a decisive break in what has been for each generation of Jews a historical link going back to biblical times. Many reflective Jews fear, with good reason, that such a break will compromise any real sense of Jewish continuity, thus putting Diaspora Jews and their Judaism at risk.

In contrast, truly literate Israeli Jews, regardless of religious outlook and observance, have been able to use the full record of the Jewish people as building blocks with which to create a vibrant Jewish present and envision a meaningful Jewish future. With the vast majority of Israelis expressing a broad interest in the larger world, the Jewish state has become the venue of a highly diverse and modern Hebraic culture and society. Perhaps the most remarkable achievement of the Zionist agenda has been the rebirth of Hebrew as a living language, one suited for scientific as well as religious discourse—for everyday life, as well as life confined in and by religious institutions. One should not be misled by a sacred tongue serving a wide variety of temporal purposes. Despite the old quip that Israelis tend to be "Hebrew-speaking gentiles," (*goyim dovrei 'Ivrit*), Israel is and will remain, in almost every respect, a Jewish state, the majority of whose Jewish citizens relate to the long history of the Jewish people, beginning with the world of the Bible and continuing to present times. Given that Israel has become the fulcrum of this evolving Hebraic culture, and given the signif-icance of that culture to Jewish continuity within the Jewish state and be-yond, the current Arab-Israel problem turns out to be more than a struggle between competing polities, each wishing to occupy the same sacred turf. At stake for Israelis and Jews everywhere is not only the survival of the Jew-ish state, but also the preservation of a vibrant Judaism in the modern age.

Considering the long and checkered history of the Jewish people, there is a sense of déjà vu when encountering present circumstances in Is-rael and the Diaspora. Those who embrace a larger view of Jewish history can point out that Jews have often experienced assimilation and declining numbers and, more often than not, they have been without an independent or even autonomous polity of their own. Nevertheless they have managed to survive, a distinctive people bearing a distinctive culture. Against all ex-pectations the story of the Jews has remained, contra the acclaimed twentieth-century philosopher/historian Arnold Toynbee, an instructive saga of marvelous adaptation in challenging circumstances. Toynbee may have considered Judaism the fossilized relic of a remote past, but of all peo-ples forged in the crucible of the ancient Near East, the Jews alone survive with their linguistic and cultural identities intact.

For a historian who viewed the growth of civilization in terms of challenge and response, Toynbee's assessment of Judaism seems a bit odd, if also churlish. True enough, Toynbee was trained as a classical scholar and not a Hebraist, but we do not think Toynbee's lack of familiarity with Jew-ish sources completely clouded his critical judgment. By referring to Ju-daism as a fossilized relic, Toynbee seemingly reflects residual anti-Jewish sentiments that were conventional wisdom well into the twentieth century. As did Christian clergy who wrote histories of Judaism, Toynbee declared the Jews as mired in what he considered the unchanging and ill-adapted world of a rabbinic Judaism that first evolved in the Graeco-Roman Near East. Indeed, histories of Judaism written or influenced by men of the cloth often ended with the rise of Christianity; at the latest, they ended with the rabbis of the Talmud, which extended the story until roughly the sixth cen-tury C.E. What followed these rabbis was thought of as mere imitation. That is, Jews using a familiar rabbinic template in all ages and in wide geograph-ical settings reproduced again and again versions of essentially the same be-liefs, practices, and communal life. Ironically, this view of Judaism, un-changed in essence over the past two thousand years or so, is mirrored in the outlook of the more insular Jewish religious communities of today.

Any view that proclaims Judaism is ossified, regardless of time and place, misreads both the ancient rabbis and their successors throughout the ages. Like Muslims, Jews have always been wedded to the past. But unlike the Muslims who, given their enormous successes, generally embraced a triumphal view of history, Jews, given their small numbers and facing disproportionate realities of power, most often balanced tradition and historical expectations with the contingencies of the moment. Therein lay the paradox of Jewish survival, which depends on continuity, but also requires change. Jewish civilization has never been static despite an enormous reverence for the past. The rabbis of the Graeco-Roman period, those communal leaders who shaped an evolving Judaism based on biblical precedent, understood very well the need to embrace the past when confronting the difficulties of the present and facing the uncertainties of the future. That unbroken link between the Jewish past and present is at the root of strategies for continuity and survival. Understandably, it has been emphasized repeatedly in generation after generation of widely dispersed Jewish communities.

As with subsequent periods of Jewish history, Graeco-Roman times (ca. fourth century B.C.E. to seventh century C.E.) suggest an age of flux, a richly textured series of moments that are in many respects reminiscent of the Jewish condition in the modern age. According to learned demographers, some four to six million Jews inhabited the provinces of the Roman Empire during the heyday of Jewish growth, a formidable figure that must have encouraged Jews to be confident of both their present and future. Put somewhat differently, one in every eight citizens of the East Roman Empire allegedly maintained affiliation with some form of the many varieties of Judaism then practiced. In terms of modern demography, this ratio would translate into roughly thirty-five million Jews inhabiting the Near East and North Africa. If these numbers are at all accurate, never before and never thereafter did Jews enjoy so favorable a demographic balance. The covenant that God made with the biblical patriarchs, promising them offspring "as numerous as the stars in the sky" (Gen. 15:5), is yet to be realized—witness the current demographic imbalance between Jews and Arabs in the Near East and the implications of that imbalance for the future of the modern State of Israel. There are at present some three hundred million Arabs and some five million Jews in the region. Even as regards the Graeco-Roman world, a word of caution is in order. The high estimates of Jewish population in the East Roman Empire are based on exceedingly thin data, often linked to an almost arbitrary use of multipliers, for example, the number of paschal lambs reportedly consumed during pilgrimages to the Temple in Jerusalem. Such attempts at determining population should be regarded with considerable skepticism. Nevertheless the indicators, such as they are, point to significant and highly diverse Jewish communities spread throughout the Near East, North Africa, and Asia Minor, as well as nascent Jewish settlements along the northern Mediterranean and the trade routes of the Roman Europe.

Lacking sources that describe many Jewish communities in detail, especially those communities situated well beyond the leading and better-known centers of Jewish life in the Fertile Crescent and Egypt, we are at a loss to reconstruct ancient Judaism in all its richness. But based on materials acquired from wide-ranging archeological digs and new literary materials from peripheral areas of Jewish settlement, it is safe to say that the picture of Jews and ancient Judaism that has been transmitted through classical Jewish texts does not represent the sum and substance of all Jewish experience in Graeco-Roman times. The revered sources that have become the normative rabbinic tradition reflect only a small part of a more complexly illustrated canvas, a polychrome picture that has faded with each passing age. The Judaism inherited by medieval and modern Jews from the Graeco-Roman age, or, if you will, from the age of the rabbis, is the evolving culture of a truncated religious society, determined to preserve its identity and sense of community in challenging times.

Despite the many permutations made necessary by changing circumstance and new environs, that evolving religious culture has always reverberated to a Jewish past, a history that extends backward into a distant and ancient Near East. Be it in good times or bad, the past—whether real, embellished, or even invented for whatever reason—became, until recent assimilatory trends in Europe and America, an indelible part of Jewish historical consciousness, a model for action as well as a source of much needed consolation. There is, however, another side to Jewish uses of history. Being wedded to the past has never paralyzed Jews in dealing with the exigencies of the moment or anticipating the vagaries of the future. Throughout their long and troubled history, the people called Israel have not allowed received narratives or statutes of contemporaneous religious law to rob them of flexible responses in a changing world. By reshaping the most appealing and beneficial aspects of foreign cultures to fit a specifically Jewish mold—that is, to borrow from others without compromising Jewish sensibilities or values—and by reformulating their own customs and observances to accord to new realities, based in each case on the authority of religious law, Jews took out a patent on survival. Of all the civilizations that emerged in the remote history of the Near East—many blessed with enormous wealth and state power—only the civilization that evolved out of ancient Israel can be traced through a continuum that extends to this very day. The flexibility to adjust to new circumstances without compromising the essential core of Jewish identity and values explains why the history of the Jews and of Judaism, as a living people and a living civilization, continues despite all odds to find its place in the larger narrative of humankind.

Much like modern Jewry, the faithful of the Graeco-Roman world experienced the challenges of assimilation and catastrophic events that threatened the continuity of Jews and Judaism alike. Such challenges, beginning with the Roman Wars of the first century C.E., demanded effective responses from a much-beleaguered community. As a result, the condition of the Jews and the nature of Jewish institutions were not allowed to remain moribund during the early evolution of rabbinic Judaism. Rather than give rise to an overly legalistic and frozen faith, that which detractors of the Jews have labeled "Pharasaism," the ancient rabbis shaped their Judaism to surmount immediate challenges as well as adapt to future environments and circumstances. In effect, the rabbis created a vision of community and, beyond that, a communal infrastructure with which future generations of Jews could overcome catastrophe in their own times, just as the rabbis and their followers survived the destruction of the Second Temple in the first century C.E. The end of the Second Temple marked the depletion of the immense sacred capital invested in Judaism's holiest shrine: namely, pilgrimage and all the other ceremonials acts linked to temple ritual. Were that traumatic disruption of national religious life not sufficient to cause deep concerns about the very survival of the Jewish people and their faith, there was the concomitant loss of sovereignty over Judea, that is, the Land of Israel. The Roman War of 66–70 C.E. brought about the end of the Second Hebrew Commonwealth, the polity that had succeeded the fallen House of David some five hundred years earlier. The failed Bar Kochba rebellion in 132–135 C.E. marked the last serious attempt to restore Jewish rule until the emergence of modern Zionism almost two thousand years later. Following the destruction of the temple and the loss of Jewish sovereignty, Jerusalem was refashioned into a Roman city and renamed Aelia Capitolina, thus ending a thousand years of historic association. In effect, the victorious Romans declared an end to what had been the political and spiritual epicenter of the Israelites and their successors ever since King David proclaimed Jerusalem his capital and David's son Solomon reportedly built the great shrine to Yahweh on what is called the Temple Mount.

With these calamities in Roman times, Jews, whatever the nature of their communities, went from a relatively secure if not favored position to one of anxiety. At stake was their meaningful survival as a distinct people claiming a unique relationship to their ancestor's God. Various Jewish communities in the Diaspora seemingly disappeared; in any case, we hear little from them and in many instances nothing at all. No doubt, some communities lingered only to disappear thereafter. Certainly, there was a decline in absolute numbers as loosely defined Jewish groups, weakened by political misfortune, eventually joined the victors, be they pagan or later Christian. The precise picture of these developments is not clear. Despite recent advances in scholarship, we still know little about the far-flung Jewish settlements beyond the mainstream of normative Jewish life. A general observation is, nevertheless, in order. What bound the surviving Jewish communities and secured for them a present and future as distinctively Jewish communities was the ability to refashion old institutions to suit changing circumstances without ever abandoning memories of the past. With the loss of the Second Temple, the synagogue, already a prominent institution, particularly in the Diaspora, became the linchpin of Jewish communal life in the Land of Israel as well. Synagogue worship substituted for a temple ritual, which it often recalled, even when the temple stood. Schools of rabbis displaced completely a priestly class made redundant by the loss of the national shrine and, as guardians of the faith, the rabbis promulgated new laws to accommodate the realities of the moment. Above all, pragmatic approaches to Jewish law expounded by the rabbinical authorities in successive ages brought coherence and accountability to Jewish life wherever Jews settled, whether in small groups or in significant communities.

The survival of the Jews and Judaism as a distinct people and civilization also depended on retaining foundational myths, stories originating in biblical narratives that were imaginatively reshaped by subsequent generations of exegetes and commentators. The foundational myths, together with the law and accounts of Jews in the postbiblical period, comprise a didactic version of Jewish experiences throughout the ages. That master narrative of Jewish life might be described as metahistory because it transcends the bare particulars of fact and fiction to provide a rationale and blueprint for a people's survival. The evolving story of the Jews, as conceived by Jews, is thus truer than history itself might have been. Nor were the lessons derived from the master narrative limited to the exigencies of the here and now. These privileged accounts of the past not only contained prescriptions for survival, but also gave rise to the hope, indeed the expectation, of future redemption. Based on contemporaneous readings of biblical prophecy and other sacred literary artifacts, the people of Israel—the descriptive label most frequently used by Jews to refer to their collective being—yearned continuously for a rebuilt temple and the restoration of Jewish sovereignty over the land of their biblical ancestors. The residual strength of ancient accounts linking Israel the people and Israel the land to each other and to the one and only God of Israel has given every generation of Jews a sense of common identity and purpose. These even include proud secular Jews of modern times who are skeptical of God's intervention in human affairs, if not the very existence of an almighty being.

THE FOUNDATIONAL NARRATIVE OF THE JEWISH PEOPLE: BIBLICAL TEXT AND TRADITIONAL COMMENTARY

The Hebrew Bible, which represents the core of Jewish belief, begins with creation itself. But for all intents and purposes, the story of the Jews as a people starts with Abraham, the first among humans to believe in the one and only God. The accounts of Israel's origins, the foundations of the master narrative representing the lengthy and circuitous history of the Jewish people, takes us from the beginnings of monotheism to the formation of the Israelite community. It then goes on to the conquest of Canaan, the rise and fall of the Kingdoms of Judah and Israel, the building and destruction of the first temple in Jerusalem, and ultimately the return of the exiles from the Babylonian captivity and the restoration of national life in the homeland designated for Israel by God. All in all, the events depicted in scripture and the commentary to scripture represent a time span covering the better part of two thousand years from early second millennium B.C.E. (the patriarchal period) through much of the Hellenistic era (beginning in 323 C.E.). The choice of works to be included in Jewish scripture was already determined by the first and second century C.E. The various ancient books stitched together in the final text have been enfolded into the evolving tale of the Jewish people throughout the ages.

Believing Jews maintain that the Hebrew Bible, a text pored over for the better part of two millennia, reproduces holy writ exactly as God intended, a canonical text that could be read without contradictory messages. Despite seeming discrepancies of content and style, the agreed-upon text could be understood as it was meant to be by those skilled in the traditional hermeneutics of scripture. Recovering true meaning from these sacred texts was no mere intellectual pursuit. The study of the biblical world gave rise to models of behavior for far-flung Jewish communities in subsequent ages and changing circumstances.

One has always to gauge the emotive power of transcendental myths. It is one thing for a people to identify themselves by the master narratives

of their history. It is another for the same people to be moved by that narrative into concerted and sustained action, a kind of response to historical
contingencies that calls for determination and sacrifice when causes are
considered critical and just and, more generally, when the welfare of the
community is at stake. The Jewish master narrative makes real demands on
Jews. It has stirred Jewish consciousness, even during the modern age and
the onset of extensive assimilation. Proudly identified Jews who fully accept
modernity may have adopted values and patterns of behavior from the non-
Jewish world, but the core of their outlook and their responses to history
as they thought it was and as they see it unfold still reflect received versions
of the Jewish past. A sense of tribal or even national solidarity still charac-
terizes the Jewish people long after the disappearance of the original Israelites. In that respect, modern Israelis share much in common with their
biblical and postbiblical ancestors.

The manner in which Jews draw together in response to extraordinary
crises are cases in point—witness the overwhelming support for the fledgling State of Israel among virtually all Jews in the aftermath of the Second
World War; the relentless effort to resettle Holocaust survivors; the absorption within Jewish communities of subsequent refugees and political exiles,
regardless of cost; and, in particular, the role of the Jewish state as a safe
haven for Jews in distress. All these extraordinary responses to critical moments in recent Jewish history reflect a very real engagement with an imagined Jewish past. As the pithy expression goes: "All Jews are [at all times] responsible for one another." That support for the modern State of Israel and,
more generally, for all of world Jewry, begins with the purported origins of
the Israelites in biblical times, an ancient story of a chosen people and a
promised land.

LINKS TO THE PROMISED LAND: THE ORIGINS
OF THE ISRAELITES AND THEIR CIVILIZATION

The story of Israel's election and its links to the promised land begins with
the patriarch Abraham, the first among humans to recognize the one and
only God. According to Genesis 11, Abraham (then called Abram) was
born in Ur of the Chaldeans (southern Mesopotamia) and then came to
settle in Harran (far to the North), having been brought there together with
all his family by his father, Terah. The unfolding story of Abram/Abraham,
as related in Jewish scripture, will not take place in Mesopotamia, the land
of the patriarch's origins. Nor will it take place in the household of his

polytheist father in Harran. In the very next chapter of Genesis (12:1–3), God commands Abraham: "Go forth from your native land and from your father's house to a land that I will show you. I will make you [the progenitor of] a great nation, bless you, and make your name great, that it may be a blessing. I will bless those who bless you and curse those who curse you; all the communities on earth shall bless themselves through you."

And so, Abraham went to Canaan, first to the area of Shechem (present-day Nablus) and then to the hill country east of Bethel (then called Luz). At both places, he pitched his tent and erected an altar to his God, Yahweh. It was at Shechem that God first promised Abraham that his progeny would inherit the land then inhabited by the Canaanites, a promise that would be repeated several times over throughout the patriarchal narratives. Following that, Abraham journeyed by stages to the Negev, and after a stay in Egypt occasioned by famine in Canaan, he came back to the land vouchsafed by Yahweh for his descendants. Having returned to Canaan, Abraham retraced his earlier movements before setting up his tent at Hebron. Abraham's odyssey thus took him to major locations of the hill country and the south, places that would later serve, in accordance with God's blessing, as designated settlements for Abraham's progeny, the future tribes of Israel. When his beloved wife, Sarah, died in Kiriath-Arba (the original name of ancient Hebron), Abraham purchased a burial site nearby, the so-called Cave of Machpelah. In a manner of speaking, the spiritual gift of a promised land was given worldly legitimacy when the patriarch obtained clear title to the enclave at Hebron from the local Canaanite owners (Gen. 23). There at Kiriath-Arba/Hebron, the patriarch buried his wife and was himself later buried, along with his son and grandson, Isaac and Jacob, and their wives, the matriarchs Rebecca and Leah. Rachel, Jacob's second wife, was buried in Bethlehem nearby. As a result, Hebron and its environs have long been considered the second-holiest of all Jewish sites in the Land of Israel. It is surpassed only by Jerusalem.

Inspired by Abraham's decision to inter his family in Hebron, pious Jews throughout the ages have sought burial in the sacred soil of the promised land, even if their remains had to be brought from distant places, as were the bones of Joseph, which were carried from Egypt and interred by Joshua at Shechem after the Israelite conquest of Canaan. History is filled, however, with ironic turns. The place of the burial crypts in Hebron, one of the holiest sites of Judaism, has been taken over by others. For many generations, the alleged graves of the patriarchs and matriarchs have been encased by a magnificent mosque, a tribute to Islam's embrace of Abraham and a thousand years and more of Muslim sovereignty over the Holy Land.

It is thus no surprise that like Jerusalem, the eternal city claimed by Arabs and Israelis alike, Hebron and its modern Jewish suburb, named Kiriath Arba by ultranationalist settlers, are sources of great tension between Israelis and Arabs today. Similarly, during the Aqsa intifada, the tomb of Joseph in Nablus, which had been converted by settlers into a Jewish house of study, was retaken by the Muslims and initially declared a Muslim place of worship. All this contentiousness has its roots in a drama from a distant past, when God blessed his faithful servant Abraham, promising him both numerous offspring and hegemony over the land of Canaan.

As with the purchase of the Cave of Machpelah, the fulfillment of God's broad promise to Abraham is contingent on some form of contractual arrangement (Gen. 15). Abraham is enjoined, therefore, to sacrifice a number of different animals and birds. The acceptance of these offerings by God leads to a formal covenant between the Lord and his mortal servant. That is, reciprocating for the various sacrifices, God promises the yet childless Abraham offspring as numerous as the stars in the sky and then declares: "To your offspring I give this land, from the River of Egypt [i.e., the Wadi al-Arish, which separates the Sinai Peninsula from the Negev desert] to the Great River, the Euphrates" (Gen. 15.18). For the true believers, this declaration of a remote past, which is repeated time and again (albeit with shifting borders), remains central to Jewish claims of sovereignty over the land of their forefathers. As long as the people of Israel recognize their God, the legal transaction between Yahweh and Abraham is inalienable.

But there are as yet no offspring to settle the land promised to Abraham by God. Much to Abraham's dismay, his beloved wife Sarah (then called Sarai) is seemingly barren. To comfort her husband and provide him an heir of his own issue, Sarah offers Abraham her Egyptian servant, Hagar, who gives birth to Ishmael, the son born to Abraham at age eighty-six. When Ishmael reaches his presumed age of majority (thirteen), God reaffirms the covenant made earlier to Abraham and stipulates that this covenant will apply as well "for your offspring to follow, through the ages, as an everlasting pact." In such fashion, the Almighty will be the (personal) God of Abraham's family for all times. As before, Abraham, hitherto called Abram, is designated the progenitor of a host of unnamed kings and nations. A critical proviso in this revisited covenant is that God promises to Abraham and his offspring the entire land of Canaan as "an everlasting possession." To mark the eternal relationship that will exist between the patriarch's folk and Yahweh, Abraham is instructed that he and all of his family, now and in future times, are obliged to circumcise their male households, including all slaves (Gen. 17:1–14). Removing the foreskin eight days after birth has thus become the ceremony by which male Jews officially become members of the community called Israel.

At this point of the biblical narrative, there is no direct line leading to the people of Israel, God's chosen future settlers of Canaan. There is only Ishmael. To be sure, Hagar's son is also circumcised in this collective ceremony and is a figure much beloved to Abraham (who, according to the rabbis, dotes on his only son despite Ishmael's immoral behavior, a rather elastic reading of the biblical text). As it were, Ishmael's future is not in Canaan, but in lands nearby. There is, however, no need for concern. God is well aware of the grand design He has concocted for Abraham's (as yet unborn) progeny, the gift of Canaan. Abraham's God will not renege on His part of the agreement. There will be more for Abraham to savor; the first Jew will soon have a legitimate heir (Gen. 17:15–22). Beloved Sarah will finally give birth at the age of ninety, a joyful occasion for an old man who had abandoned all hope of a child from his beloved wife. Nevertheless, the unexpected gift is not without concern.

Abraham, now a hundred years of age, is quick to realize the implications of having a younger son born to a wife while there is an older child born to her servant. There is the problem of patrimony and potential competition among the sons. While the Hebrew Bible does not address this problem directly, at least not in this setting, the question of inheritance is implied in Abraham's subsequent pleading on behalf of Ishmael. Having heard of the impending birth of Isaac (who we are to assume will receive Abraham's inheritance though the younger of the brothers), Abraham asks God "to let Ishmael thrive," and God responds affirmatively, promising to make Ishmael's line exceedingly fertile and a great nation (Gen. 17:20). (In both Jewish and Muslim tradition, Ishmael will be the progenitor of twelve powerful Arab tribes.) But lest Abraham and the reader be misled, God lets it be known that the covenant between God and the patriarch will be maintained, not with Ishmael, but with Isaac, the son soon to be born to Sarah. (Muslim tradition, though laudatory of Isaac, favors the elder son, the forefather of the northern Arabs and alleged ancestor of the Prophet Muhammad). The biblical tradition is, however, clear. With God's unequivocal promise to Abraham, Isaac's progeny, the descendants of his son Jacob (later renamed Israel) will inherit the promised land of Canaan (the very land contested by Arabs and Israelis, the modern analogs to the Ishmaelites and Israelites of an ancient past). Given Abraham's plea to "let Ishmael thrive," God will not forsake entirely the elder son and his progeny. But as does Ishmael the father, the twelve sons he sires and their descendants will have to content themselves not with Canaan, a so-called land of milk and honey, but northern Sinai and Arabia, a vast wilderness, parts of which they will share with the children of Keturah, the woman whom Abraham will take after Sarah's death. These non-Israelite descendants of the patriarch will form the core of mighty Arab tribes that will leave a deep imprint on the later history of the Near East.

Having promised Abraham that Sarah's progeny will have a glorious future, God reaffirms his original covenant, this time with Isaac. He will increase Isaac's offspring as promised (earlier to Abraham) and will give them the entire land of Canaan. As if to foreshadow the later conquest of Canaan (and also the sojourn in Egypt), the narrative switches immediately to tense moments between Isaac and the indigenous Canaanite inhabitants of Gerar (later Beersheba), a place in the promised land where Isaac herded his ever-increasing flocks and grew wealthy and more powerful to the chagrin of the natives (Gen. 26). A similar promise is made to Isaac's son Jacob (Ya'aqov) even though he, like Isaac, is a younger brother, having emerged from his mother's womb grasping the ankle (*'aqev*) of his twin, Esau. But Esau favors polytheist Canaanite women and not the women of his father's and grand-father's extended households. And so, a scheme is concocted to fool Isaac into giving his patrimony to Jacob. With that, the die is cast; God will speak to Jacob in a dream: "The ground on which you are lying [Canaan] I will give to you and your offspring Your descendants shall be [as numerous] as the dust of the earth" (Gen. 28:13–5). Like Ishmael, Esau will be denied the right of the first born, and like Esau he will be compensated. As was Ishmael, Esau is destined to father a great nation of twelve future rulers. As was Ishmael, his offspring will preside over a wasteland, in Esau's case, the inhospitable preserve of the Jordan rift and the barren hills that overlook it in Transjordan. This is the region called Edom, or "Red Land" after the color of its sandstone hills, a name that also suggests a link to the ruddy (*admoni*) Esau. Jacob, soon to be renamed Israel (Yisrael) for having wrestled (*yisra*) with a heavenly being (*el[ohim]*), will also give rise to a nation of twelve rulers, the sons whose offspring will be known as "the Sons of Israel," that is, the ancient Israelites.

For believers who read the biblical account, the patriarchal narrative helps to explain the evolving map of the ancient Near East, particularly in those regions denoting the settlement of Abraham's extended family. In Sinai and Arabia (including what is today the desert region of southwest Jordan) were Arab tribesmen: the Ishmaelites and the descendants of Keturah, the wife of Abraham's final years. In southeast Transjordan were the Edomites, the alleged progeny of Esau, a wild people who take up a life of warfare and brigandage. Moving northward in Transjordan are the

Ammonites and Moabites, the issue of Abraham's nephew Lot, peoples of lesser status than the Israelites but clearly preferred to the sons of Ishmael and Esau, let alone the indigenous polytheists of Canaan. Following the Israelite conquest of Canaan, the Israelite tribes of Reuben, Gad, and half of Manasseh will also settle in on the east side of the Jordan. Dan will in turn inhabit lands east of the Sea of Galilee. The choicest domains are, however, in Canaan, which will be conquered and settled by the rest of Jacob/Israel's descendants from the local peoples, who, according to varied biblical lists, include Canaan(ites), Heth (Hittites), Jebusites, Amorites, Girgashites, Perizzites, and Hivites. There is also the coastal plain inhabited by the Philistines, invaders from the Aegean Sea who became part of the larger ethnic mix of the land of Canaan. All these groups, the inhabitants of Canaan as well as Abraham's non-Israelite progeny, are pictured in the larger biblical narrative as debased rivals to God's chosen people. In the grand scheme that slowly unfolds, the Israelites are seen as destined to prevail. How else could it be, given God's covenant first made with Abraham and then Isaac and Jacob, and repeated time and again to their successors?

Having been elected by God from among all peoples, the ancient Israelites and the Jews to follow always defined themselves as different from their neighbors, certainly regarding faith and religious behavior. That sense of exclusiveness, based on claims of a unique relationship with the Almighty, has become a burden as well as a privilege for Jews throughout their lengthy and event-filled history. According to Hebrew scripture, there will be a day when all the nations will recognize the Lord, and all the people of Israel will be vindicated and thrive in the land chosen specifically for them. But until that day, God's chosen are reconciled to being a chosen few, and subject to the vicissitudes of an often-unfriendly history, the promises of Yahweh to Abraham and the other patriarchs notwithstanding. So it has been from the very beginning of recorded Jewish history.

EGYPT AND THE FORMATION OF THE ISRAELITE POLITY

With famine once again ravaging Canaan, Jacob's issue, some seventy persons in all, are forced to seek shelter in Egypt. As they had during the famine of Abraham's time, they went to the granary of the Fertile Crescent to ride out the storm. But all does not go well for Abraham's descendants. One of Jacob's sons, Joseph, had risen to a high post in the court of the Pharaoh and served him well. But after that generation of Abraham's offspring died off, a new Pharaoh came to power, a ruler who "knew not of Joseph." The seventy members of the extended kinship group, called here Hebrews, had grown by then into a much larger, more powerful society, thus occasioning Egyptian fears they might "join [Egypt's] enemies in fighting against [the host country]." As a result, the Hebrews are subjected to forced labor, and their first-born males were put to death, so as to keep their numbers down and reduce the threat of rebellion. Thus begins the infamous sojourn of Israel in Egypt, a plight that reportedly lasted more than four hundred years, just as Abraham had foreseen in a terrible vision reported earlier (Gen. 15:13–14).

In the end, the God of the Israelites knows his obligation, the sum and substance of his covenant with Abraham. He will send Moses to lead a fledgling nation out of Egypt and into the wilderness of Sinai. This will mark the beginning of a forty-year trek that will ultimately end with the conquest of Canaan, partially fulfilling God's previous promises to Abraham and the patriarchs Isaac and Jacob. The Egyptians will be forced to allow the exodus of their captives because God has unleashed terrible plagues on them, the last of which is the smiting of the first born, a punishment that seemingly mirrors the willful killing of Hebrew children mentioned earlier. The Israelites will be spared because they will slaughter a lamb on the eve of the event and smear the blood of the animal on their lintel and doorposts, so as to alert the angel of death that the household within is protected. No foreigners or non-Israelite laborers were permitted to partake of the paschal lamb unless they were circumcised, an act that would spare them death because it admitted them into the larger Israelite polity then being formed. The same was true of the household slaves of the Israelites. Circumcision, the ritual act through which Abraham created the first monotheist community out of his own household, was now repeated many times over in the extended households of his progeny. Only seventy souls when they entered the land, the nascent Israelite people leaving Egypt was reportedly six hundred thousand strong. That number did not include the women and children, or the "mixed multitude," a heterogeneous population that attached itself to the Israelites leaving the country. Until the Exodus, the reported history of the Israelites is that of an extended group of kinsmen. Henceforth, it will be one of a diverse and great people brought to common purpose and fulfilling a destiny carved out for them by no less than the Lord of Hosts.

For those who had recently attached themselves to this emerging polity, there could be no doubt that the Exodus was a defining moment, for both them and Abraham's descendants. The God of Israel himself reportedly took charge of the event. As Jewish tradition states: "And Yahweh brought us out of Egypt, not by the hands of an angel, or heavenly being [*saraf*] or messenger. It was rather the Blessed Be He in His own glory and Being." The manner in which God personally intervened at a critical moment in the formation of his people is a tale that continues to resonate among the faithful. Over countless generations, the story of the Exodus has been commemorated during the Passover meal (*seder*), perhaps the most observed of all Jewish rituals. It is said that the more one repeats the story, the more praiseworthy he or she will be.

The oft-cited account of the Exodus is no idle tale designed to amuse and delight receptive audiences. There has always has been a sense of immediacy to reiterating this connection with the past. On the night of the holiday (two nights in the Diaspora), Jews are enjoined to retell the story of the departure from Egypt as if they themselves were experiencing the moment. Some Yemenite Jews actually act out elements of the Exodus. Nor is Passover eve reserved for telling the story of the Exodus alone. The ritual text (*haggadah*) now read in traditional households folds the account of Israel's sojourn in Egypt within a larger and highly checkered picture of Jewish existence. This longer view of Jewish history begins with accounts of the patriarchs and ends with the spirited singing of "Had Gadya." A popular ballad about a goat, "Had Gadya" is said to refer to the inevitable disasters that befell all those oppressing Jews throughout the ages. According to this view, the last refrain of the ballad—a verse in which God slays the Angel of Death—refers, however obliquely, to what will be the final redemption of the chosen people. At that moment, God's promise to Abraham and his progeny will be fulfilled. Indeed, the very last pronouncement of the Passover ritual—"Next year in Jerusalem"—speaks to the dream embraced by Jews throughout their extended exile, namely the restoration of a sovereign Jewish polity in the land of their forefathers. There is logic to ending the seder with such a dramatic statement. By declaring, "Next year in Jerusalem," participants in the Passover ritual link God's promise to the patriarchs and his embrace of the Israelite polity with Jewish claims to the land promised them by their Lord. Not coincidentally, some modern haggadahs published in the West end with "Hatikvah" ("The Hope"), the nineteenth-century hymn composed by the Hebrew poet Naftali Herz Imber. Set to the haunting music of a Moldavian folk song, Imber's stirring verses, which express Jewish longing for a fully restored ancestral homeland, have become the national anthem of the State of Israel and, more generally, of Jews everywhere. And so, these modern haggadahs, already rich with traditional allusions to Jewish redemption, have become powerful statements of Zionist fulfillment.

We read in the Passover haggadah: "Blessed be He who keeps His promise to Israel." No moment in Jewish history spoke so dramatically of God's concern with and responsibility for his people than the day he forced Pharaoh's hand. With that action, more than six hundred thousand souls made their way from Egypt into the desert. At the core of the emergent Israelite polity were the twelve tribes representing Jacob's offspring. Included in the larger assembly departing from Egypt were those who had become attached to these twelve kinship groups. What was still lacking was a formal legal arrangement that bound the expanded Israelite polity to God, as did the earlier covenant between God and Abraham and his pledges to the patriarchs Isaac and Jacob. The evolving narrative of the people of Israel would soon turn to that.

According to traditions venerated by Jews, Christians, and Muslims alike, that missing legal contract was later established at Sinai when the Israelites received the Ten Commandments, a series of pronouncements binding Yahweh and his expanded flock to one another. The nature of this latest covenant has been much debated by modern scholars. Some see it as a treaty between ruler and vassal, an arrangement modeled after suzerainty treaties from the ancient Near East. In any case, Jewish tradition understood the law received at Sinai and also in subsequent revelations as a contractual arrangement binding Israel to God and, beyond that, as a paradigm for Israel's behavior, both spiritual and temporal. The rabbis of Graeco-Roman times, seeking religious authority for their legal innovations, maintained that both the oral (rabbinic) and written (biblical) law were revealed at Sinai and that both laws were then transmitted over subsequent generations by the recognized authorities of the moment: Moses to Joshua, Joshua to the tribal elders, the elders to the judges, the judges to the prophets, and the prophets Haggai, Zechariah, and Malachi to the men of the Great Assembly, that is, to the progenitors of rabbinic Judaism. In time, the oral law was also committed to writing and, together with the Hebrew Bible, it governed every aspect of Jewish life. The vast compendium of legal materials found in the Torah and Talmud gave rise in turn to a steady stream of commentary and supracommentary, a legal and intellectual enterprise that continues until this very day. If the Exodus created the Israelite polity that evolved into the Jewish people we now know, Sinai began the process that binds all Jews and distinguishes them from the other nations of the world.

It is one thing to have God's law; it is another to obey it in full. According to Jewish sources, the generation that entered the wilderness of

Sinai was unworthy of taking control of Canaan, the land of milk and honey promised by Yahweh, first to Abraham and then in successive moments to his descendants and the emerging Israelite polity. This collective punishment, visited upon an entire generation, underscores a remarkable feature of the regnant Jewish tradition. From the very outset, Jews have always been made to feel unworthy of God's beneficence. No one is spared: not David, the greatest of Israel's kings; not Solomon, the wisest; not even Moses, God's quintessential servant and arguably the most perfect of all Jews, regardless of place and time. The prophet who led his people out of Egypt and delivered unto them the Ten Commandments would not enter Cisjordan where his forefathers raised their flocks. Instead, he would be buried at an undisclosed site in Transjordan overlooking the promised land below—so close and yet so far from the final destination of his followers. Not he, but his protégé, Joshua, son of Nun, would be the one to undertake the long-awaited conquest of Canaan, fulfilling thereby God's oft-stated promise to Abraham and his progeny.

THE PROMISED LAND

At God's command and with his full blessing, Joshua and a new generation of Israelites would conquer the land before them. As he did during the Exodus from Egypt, the God of Israel personally intervened on behalf of his people. It is no coincidence that the conquest of Canaan began only after a new generation born in the desert was circumcised and celebrated the Passover offering (the indication of a people reborn, a covenant reaffirmed, and a plea for God's direct support in the ensuing campaign). As it had been during the Exodus, the Israelites would emerge victorious because of a series of miracles, beginning with the creation of a dry path through the waters of the Jordan, a route that enabled Joshua's army to traverse a natural barrier, just as Moses and his followers passed earlier through the Sea of Reeds. God, who had extended his "mighty hand" on behalf of Moses and the newly formed Israelite people, would do so once again, this time on behalf of Moses' appointed successor and the next generation of the faithful.

Much of the biblical book of Joshua is devoted to a detailed account of the conquest of lands occupied by Canaanites, Hittites, Hivites, Amorites, Girgashites, and Jebusites. There are reports of stirring victories. One after another, towns and regions of the promised land fall to the invading hosts. Time and again, the enemy is routed and the victorious army of God rolls relentlessly forward. The offensive continues following the death of

Joshua, but the land is not fully secured, as God had initially promised. Certain regions continue to be occupied by the indigenous peoples of Canaan. There is then the danger of polytheist recidivism, a situation reportedly foreseen by Joshua before his death.

In characteristic fashion, the Hebrew Bible—recognizing political realities in retrospect—prepares the reader for a dramatic turn of events that has already taken place. The failure to fully cleanse Canaan of the polytheists is made part of God's larger design. A snare is put before the new generation of Israelites to see whether they truly merit the land promised Abraham and his progeny. The Israelites, unable to resist the temptations of exotic local cultures, are unfaithful to their Lord. And so, the remaining indigenous inhabitants are given license by Yahweh to subjugate his people, a reminder that the Israelites have not fulfilled their part of the covenant that binds them to their God and God of their fathers. On occasion, charismatic leaders based within individual tribes, so-called judges, rise to defend the interests of the Israelites and steer them onto the right path, but never in a manner that leads to lasting virtue and, with that, final triumph over the enemy. The people continue to be seduced by polytheist culture and, as a result, must pay for their indiscretions. That is God's decision.

This picture of the past, obtained from the Hebrew Bible, is the teleology of a subsequent generation of biblical theologians. Its purpose: to explain why Israel, a people chosen by God, is nevertheless subjugated by the more powerful political actors in the region. But the Hebrew chroniclers also have a keen insight into the dynamics of social and political history. The period of the judges, as they envision it, reflects the weakness of a loose confederation of tribes, sharing a larger identity and common purpose but wracked by internal political wrangling, and thus unable to coalesce in moments of crisis. In effect, the Israelite tribes are victims of not only their sins, but also their tribal sensibilities. The final passages of the Book of Judges sum it up very well: "Thereupon, the Israelites dispersed, each to his own tribe and clan; everyone departed to his own territorial enclave. In those days, there was no king in Israel; everyone did as he pleased" (Judg. 21:24–5).

These last verses of Judges are a segue to Samuel I and the subsequent histories of the Bible that follow. A new concept of governance will be embraced by the Israelite tribes, that of monarchy. There are, nevertheless, ambivalent feelings about the centralization of power in the hands of a single ruler, particularly by the biblical theologians who later sat in judgment over the monarchs of the realm. It is their view, which is projected backwards into the alleged events of an earlier age. Responding to demands of the populace for a king, the prophet Samuel is seen as presenting the Israelites with a rather unpleasant scenario of their future under centralized rule. A catalogue of abuses is laid out before the people. The prophet foresees that monarchy will result in the concentration of power, heavy taxes, the loss of individual freedoms, and a loosening of the bonds of solidarity fostered within tribal networks. Having heard all that, the Israelites insist on having their way so that "they can be like all other nations" (Sam. I 8:10–20), inverting the concept of the chosen people, whose one true ruler is the God of Israel.

Indeed, the first experiment at monarchy ends in calamity; routed by the Philistines, King Saul falls upon his own sword. But a young successor, David, son of Jesse, already anointed in Saul's lifetime, will forge a powerful kingdom, and that kingdom will be consolidated by his extraordinary son, Solomon. The conquest of the land begun by Joshua will be completed by the house of David. David will earn the praise of the biblical theologians because he is said to have walked in the ways of his Lord. A closer look at the biblical text speaks less kindly of the most perfect of Israel's kings. The monarch from whose loins a dynasty of some five hundred years was established, and whose progeny will give rise to the Messiah, is not without human failings. A current Bible scholar with a fondness for hyperbole has described David as a thug and serial killer, a picture that takes considerable license with scripture. That distorted picture of the king is, however, not entirely a modern invention. Even those ancient chroniclers who promoted the interests of the Davidic dynasty could not resist a critical glance at the father of the house or all the more so at his tarnished successors.

The cost of a strong monarchy is a fascination with alien ways and compromised social justice. A price will have to be paid for all these indiscretions. The Israelites will once again be dominated by more powerful polities: Egyptians, Assyrians, and Babylonians, among others. Eventually, both the northern (722 B.C.E.) and southern kingdoms shattered (586 B.C.E.); some of their peoples were sent off into exile, their rulers never to rise again. While the people of Israel managed to forge another autonomous polity after the return of the exiles (ca. 515 B.C.E.), one that also lasted upwards of half a millennium, this new commonwealth, the successor to the Davidic monarchy, suffered a fate similar to that of the Israelite kingdom. Such was the tragic cost of rebelling against imperial Rome. Numerous generations after the patriarchal period, God's promise to Abraham was yet to be fulfilled. The Jews of the second Hebrew Commonwealth, successors to their ancient Israelite forebears, were dispersed throughout the world, without a land of their own until the emergence of the modern state of Israel some two thousand years later.

For those who compiled the historical narrative of Jewish experience, this was a troubling state of affairs. How can it be that a people specifically chosen by God and destined for such greatness from the outset, was not able to sustain the fruits of the Almighty's beneficence? From the perspective of a venerable Jewish tradition, they were not worthy. Contemporaneous Jewish communities suffered the fate of the first Jewish community: the followers of Moses who wandered about the desert for forty years and were ultimately denied the promised land. In such fashion, actual states of the past, which most often left the Israelites and their successors a small and beleaguered society, were transmuted by the Jewish metanarrative into a story of moral failing.

Shaping their own versions of the long and checkered history of the Jewish people, Zionists both secular and religious have turned, time and again, to biblical Israel. A detailed discussion of modern Zionist narratives and the power they exercise over current Jewish consciousness is found in chapter 9. All that needs to be said here is that the Zionists inherited two visions from a deeply rooted past. On the one hand, there was a somber and lachrymose view of Jewish experience explained by the unworthy actions of God's chosen people, a fate to be accepted by keeping a low profile and performing acts of penitence in the hope of winning God's favor once again. That model was linked largely but not exclusively to Israel's experience in the Diaspora. On the other, there was the model of proud behavior rooted in memories of the conquest of Canaan and the formation of a viable Jewish polity in the promised land. Because Zionists clearly favored an activist course for the Jewish people, the story of biblical Israel, albeit with a Zionist gloss, has become, *mutatis mutandis*, part and parcel of modern debates between Zionists, between Zionist and non-Zionist Jews, and between the Zionists and their Arab adversaries. Those debates are in need of much discussion, especially as they are often juxtaposed with modern research on the world of the Hebrew Bible and because of the effect of that research on the master narrative of the Jewish people.

8

JEWS, ARABS, AND MODERN
BIBLICAL SCHOLARSHIP

*Academic Politics and the Politics
of National Consciousness*

Long before the biblical canon was fixed—at the latest in the first or second century C.E.—segments of Hebrew scripture had already achieved
sublime status among God's chosen people. The patriarchal narratives, the
exodus from Egypt, the wandering in the wilderness of Sinai, the conquest
of Canaan, and the rise and fall of the monarchy, were all part of recorded
"Jewish" experience generations before there was a universally recognized
Bible. Together with later rabbinical commentary, these early and imaginative renderings of biblical Israel remained firmly imprinted on the historical imagination of Jews, both Jews who studied the textual tradition or acquired knowledge of it through the telling and retelling of familiar tales. In
effect, the received story of the biblical Israelites became the foundation of
an evolving Jewish master narrative for some two and a half thousand years.

The emergence of modern biblical studies in the nineteenth century,
particularly the branch of scholarship that became known as higher biblical
criticism, challenged orthodox views. The extended narrative whose didactic message shaped the very core of Jewish thinking and behavior could
no longer be accepted as it had been, at least not by Jews fully embracing
the modern world. The claim that the ancient editors recovered all of God's
revelation and produced a biblical text whose individual segments were
seamless strained credulity. In light of philological and stylistic analyses
made possible by the recovery of long-lost Near Eastern languages and lit-
eratures, a much-revered Hebrew scripture came to be viewed as a pastiche
of different traditions, each the literary creation of its own time and place.
Jews familiar with modern European historiography also became aware that
the biblical authors did not represent history as it was, but, more likely, as
it should have been. Reflective Jews, including many who remained devout, concluded that the biblical text can and indeed should be interpreted

217

outside its literal meaning and the religiously driven interpretations to which it gave rise. Those who considered themselves intellectually sophisticated were inclined to situate the Hebrew Bible within a broad Near Eastern setting and see it as a composite work of great literary inventiveness, linguistic complexity, and editorial ingenuity. Only the most reverent and tradition-bound among the faithful denied altogether the hermeneutic value of modern biblical scholarship.

Still, the Hebrew Bible remained the supreme monument of Jewish civilization and the fulcrum of Jewish identity. In that respect, at least, little changed with the advent of higher biblical criticism. For proud Jews, modern scholarship has not compromised the emotive power of Israel's foundational lore. Readers drawn by the transcendent force of the biblical story and its postbiblical permutations include Jews of secular outlook. The State of Israel's first prime minister, David Ben Gurion, whose lifestyle was thoroughly secular, read the Hebrew Bible with reverence. For Ben Gurion and many of the secular founding fathers of the modern Jewish state, the Bible was an inspiration for proud Jewish behavior and a guide to reawakened national consciousness. Similar views are shared by religious Zionists deeply steeped in the traditional interpretation of scripture. Succinctly put, the Hebrew Bible and its commentaries have had too long a shelf life to be easily cast aside just because modern academics dissect its structure and doubt the historicity of its more imaginative accounts.

Enlightened Jews, resonating to the familiar biblical text, have not found the methods of modern Bible scholars a necessary threat to their Jewish identity. Nor has greater biblical criticism dampened modern Jewry's enthusiasm for the very core of the Jewish literary tradition. Recovering the literary strata of Hebrew scripture is not seen as compromising the broader narrative of biblical history. If anything, it has opened the most revered of Jewish texts to new modes of interpretation and, with that, new intellectual delights. At first, most Jews were wary of modern scholarship, as it was rooted in Protestant faculties of theology. But over time, they came to embrace every aspect of biblical studies: philological and linguistic analyses; comparative religion; and archeology, the practice of recovering and interpreting material remains from the ancient Near East. Overcoming prejudices that in the past barred them from posts at leading universities, Jews became professors of Bible and ancient Near Eastern studies. Many have achieved great prominence. From their hard-won academic pulpits, Jewish scholars have staked out new ground with which to confront the conventional wisdom of earlier times, not only the exegesis and Bible commentary of long-standing religious traditions—as one would have expected—

but also the documentary hypothesis outlined by the first wave of higher biblical critics.

A growing consensus has developed among biblicists, Jews and non-Jews alike. Many are now agreed that the biblical critics of the nineteenth century had taken a good idea too far. The documentary hypothesis that dissected the biblical text into its component parts did not explain all that was intended of it. Confident of their methodological bearings, the higher critics set about producing the rainbow—or polychrome—bible, in which the Hebrew text was color-coded to represent the different strands that together compose the sum of its parts. Fragments of passages and even of words were torn out of context and highlighted in bright pastel shades to indicate discrete literary-historical traditions, each assembled at different moments in time and reflecting the different concerns of that moment. In the end, the never-completed rainbow bible proved to be a triumph more of graphic illustration than scientific achievement, not because the conceptual foundations of the documentary hypothesis were unsound, but because the hypothesis itself failed the ultimate test when applied to particular passages and even larger segments of more inclusive texts. The precise dating and provenance of specific literary sites remains a subject of heated debate.

For Jews clinging to old ways, all this scholarly debate was much ado about nothing. The dissection of the Hebrew Bible, which was said to reflect four (now nine) literary-historical traditions, was treated with disdain by those who continued to read scripture as a perfectly revealed text. Their faith in God's revelation remained unshaken, as always. Nor were more worldly Jews disturbed by academic theories that the Torah was composed of disparate literary sources. What mattered most, particularly to Zionists, was not the higher critics assault on the unity of the biblical text, but any claims that might undermine the far-reaching power of the biblical narrative. Discerning readers of the Hebrew Bible, having been introduced to the study of folklore, were well aware that the mythic character of the patriarchal narratives, the story of the Exodus, and the account of the Israelites in the wilderness might well have masked any kernels of historic truth contained therein. They might even have suspected that the charismatic leaders portrayed in the book of Judges were stock figures drawn larger than any real past. What they were less prepared to compromise were the declared links between their forefathers and the promised land. Even secular Zionists who rejected all theology and most formal religious observance found in the Hebrew Bible, particularly the description of the monarchy under David and Solomon, a template for reconstituting an ancient nation in its ancient homeland. Secular Zionists linked the Hebrew

Bible to their claims, not because of any essential truths it contained but because the text spoke to them of an ongoing history created by an eternal bond between a people and its land. Any theories that might undermine or deny altogether the reported links between that land, the ancient Israelites, and later Jewish communities might be seen as challenging the right of Jews to their own identity and place in history. It is then clear that for reflective Jews, both in Israel and the Diaspora, the modern debate over the Israelite past has become a matter of considerable importance. It has also taken on meaning for Palestinians as they seek to define their own national identity and assert their links to a contested land held sacred by Jews and Christians since ancient times.

THE PROMISED LAND AND THE CLAIMS
OF MODERN BIBLICAL SCHOLARSHIP

The challenge of modern scholarship to received versions of Israel's origins represents an ironic turn unforeseen by the early higher critics. If anything, these critics imagined that reading the Bible in a wider context would confirm the basic truths of the text they revered. Nineteenth-century biblicists who followed the discovery and decipherment of previously unknown Near Eastern languages anticipated, quite rightly, that recovering the literary output of Israel's ancient neighbors would help situate the biblical narrative in a broader setting. As a result, biblical scholars thought they would be able to reconstruct a richer and more detailed history of the Hebrew text and of Israelite society and culture. The evolution of biblical archeology created comparable expectations for recovering the material world of the ancient Israelites and the peoples in whose midst they dwelt. Altogether, it was expected that the newly uncovered materials would flesh out and confirm many elements of the familiar biblical tradition. Deciphering and commenting on ancient Near Eastern texts and excavating ancient Near Eastern sites would thus provide tangible evidence of Israel's origins and the formation of the Israelite polity in the promised land.

Scouring these literary sources, early scholars of the ancient Near East looked for and found analogies to the Hebrew narrative, whether or not newly uncovered ancient texts made for tight linkages with the world portrayed in the Bible. Over time, their successors lost interest in unsupported claims of cultural transference and in specious arguments defending would-be historical connections. Having begun with an outlook that was rooted in illuminating scripture, learned philologists eventually decoupled the study of ancient Israel from that of surrounding Near Eastern cultures. With that, they laid the foundations for the current study of the ancient Near East, a complex and demanding discipline with many subfields, the study of the Hebrew Bible and biblical history being just one among them.

Scholars examining newly published ancient sources and poring over material provided by burgeoning archeological activity found reason to be suspicious of major segments of the biblical account, including seemingly straightforward historical narratives. The result was a powerful impulse to revise history as we know it. Virtually every generation of modern scholars has transformed our understanding of the biblical text and the history and material culture of the biblical world. As in the past, most of today's revisionists remain part of mainstream biblical scholarship. The issues that divide them from their colleagues are matters of honest debate in which text scholars and archeologists agree to disagree in interpreting different types of evidence, much of it ambiguous. One of the central issues in the current debate is the strength of the early Israelite monarchy. Were the kingdoms of David, and more particularly Solomon, powerful and highly centralized states as we have been led to believe by the Bible and an earlier reading of the archeological record? Or are current revisionists correct in calling for a lower political profile for the early monarchy, based largely on their interpretation of the most recent archeological data? As in the past, today's revisionists remain part of traditional Bible scholarship. Despite occasionally frayed tempers, the discourse of mainstream biblical scholarship remains reasoned; the purpose of scholars is to recover elements of the shadowy Israelite past.

The same cannot be said for the so-called biblical minimalists, a handful of scholars who have broken from the mainstream and deny altogether the historical framework of the biblical chroniclers. Rather than accept the possibility of any discernible truth in the biblical account, they declare the well-known stories of Israel's origins and the kingdoms that followed literary artifices woven almost completely out of new cloth. As they interpret the biblical canvas, the depiction of Israel's origins, the conquest of Canaan, and the establishment of the monarchy and its early history are, in virtually all instances, total fabrications composed hundreds and hundreds of years after the alleged historic moment. If there is any residual truth to be found in scripture, the minimalists believe we are in no position to recognize let alone recover that truth. Fuller details of the minimalist brief are discussed later in this chapter. Suffice it to say, learned biblicists fully capable of interrogating the textual and archeological evidence are less dismissive of the biblical narrative. While they also doubt the historicity of particular biblical accounts and call for a revised history of early Israel, they are not prepared to throw out the baby with the bath water.

Taken as a whole, the current state of biblical studies is extremely lively—some might say too lively, particularly when one factors in the shrill voices of the minimalist school. At times, we have the impression of it being an intellectual free-for-all with few if any restrictions, more like an old-time dispute between hardened religious authorities than the reasoned discourse of the modern academy. Most of the spirited discussion reflects detailed and highly technical debates between mainstream text scholars, even more so between scholars whose research is largely based on written sources and archeologists drawing on evidence acquired in the field. Everyone wants to recover the broad outlines of the past, but too often they are at odds over how best to achieve that. More than ever, there is tension between those who dig into written sources and those who dig in the ground.

Much like textual scholars, archeologists were first driven to recapture the world of the Bible but through the study of material remains. Their lens on the past was focused on what could actually be seen or imaginatively reconstructed from snippets of evidence. At present, archeologists employ highly sophisticated techniques that allow them to recover and assess ancient technologies, patterns of subsistence, diet, socio-economic structure, and the like. Having absorbed recent social science, archeologists are also familiar with theoretical models of early state formation, our very concern here; all that is very different from the origins of the discipline.

The archeology of the Holy Land started modestly enough, with explorers puttering around sacred sites in the 1840s. In time, these investigations of existing buildings and their environs gave way to widespread exploration. Then, in the last decade of the century, archeologists began massive excavations of sites identified with locations in the Hebrew Bible. Having assumed that these mounds were in fact ancient biblical sites because of similar-sounding Arabic place names, the excavators went about the task of stripping away the earth. Although aware of the need for chronological pointers with which to date individual layers and the artifacts found therein, the archeologists of that generation did not produce a proper basis for establishing chronology. It was only when Sir Flinders Petrie arrived in Palestine around the turn of the century, and more particularly when W. F. Albright began excavating after World War I, that Palestinian archeology became more scientific and led to a complex and more extended historical analyses.

As director of the American School of Oriental Research in Jerusalem, Albright and his disciples systematically excavated a broad Palestinian landscape. In that effort, the archeologists sought to link the histories of diverse locations by establishing reliable guides for dating individual sites. This was achieved mostly by advances in recording and classifying ceramic ware that was found at each dig. With the Albrightian enterprise, archeology moved from random exploration, treasure hunting, and excavations of individual mounds to strategic digging that might reveal not only the history of particular sites, but also the social and economic profile of an entire region. Results obtained from many soundings initiated between the wars proved nothing less than a watershed in understanding the complex history of ancient Palestine and its environs.

The quest to recover the historic past by digging up the Holy Land also served the interests of believers for whom the Bible represented essential truths. The circle that gathered around Albright in mandatory Palestine and at the Johns Hopkins University, where he directed the prestigious Oriental Seminary, drew heavily from the ranks of Christian clergy, or in any case graduates of theological schools, like Albright himself. Many if not most of Albright's students taught at Christian seminaries or church-affiliated colleges and universities. That is not to say they could be rightly accused of being fundamentalists in their approach to textual problems or driven by naïve belief in their understanding of complex historical processes—far from that. But given their religious sensibilities, the Hebrew Bible was always with them, in a manner of speaking. That held true whether they sat at their desks or excavated in the field.

There was also the Palestine Oriental Society, which drew scholars from a wide variety of countries and cultural and religious backgrounds, as well as the British School of Archeology that at one time shared quarters with its American counterpart. Over time, a number of groups representing different European countries and church denominations established institutes of their own. The presence of these biblical scholars in the Holy Land was ubiquitous. Christians of all denominations, some church-linked and some not, peppered the landscape of mandatory Palestine.

To be sure, not all the archeologists active during the period of the British Mandate were churchmen, or former churchmen, or Christians cut more or less from that same mold. The Department of Antiquities, created by the British mandatory administration, employed both Jewish and Arab archeologists, however few in number. For Jews interested in the historic landscape of the Holy Land, there were institutions of their own making. The Palestine Exploration Society was founded in 1914, even before the onset of the British mandate. Later, in 1925, the Hebrew University in Jerusalem established as part of its original faculties an institute that trained an interwar generation of Jewish archeologists and sponsored fieldwork covering the length and breadth of the country. As regards field methods, the archeologists of Palestine's Jewish community (*Yishuv*) were influenced for a long time by the towering presence of Albright. A man of commanding physical stature and astounding intellectual breadth, Albright seemed to loom larger than life. There was also a personal rapport between the great man and his Jewish colleagues. Unlike most foreign archeologists working in Palestine, Albright learned modern Hebrew, which he spoke with some fluency. He also showed enormous respect for the economic and cultural vitality of the Jewish pioneers who had come to build up the country in anticipation of establishing a new and thoroughly modern Jewish homeland. The doyen of Palestinian archeology came to see the Zionists much as they saw themselves, that is, as a force for revitalizing a land that had grown stagnant with centuries of presumed neglect. In sum, his vision corroborated the Zionist interpretation of the past and, no less importantly, validated their expectations of the future. Above all, he had high praise for the professional skill of his Jewish colleagues; they, in turn, revered and honored him.

As did so many Christians exploring and excavating in Palestine, Jewish archeologists began their endeavors with the all-too-familiar Hebrew Bible in hand. But their task was neither to affirm nor reverberate to eternal religious truths, nor was it to revel in a distant past out of mere antiquarian interest. For the archeologists of the Yishuv, the recovery of ancient Israel, highly valued in its own right, was also a useful tool with which to carve out a Zionist future. And so, they turned to the ancient homeland for examples of a vibrant and flourishing past, the kind of past that might serve as inspiration for a new age and new Jewish commonwealth. Archeology represented a true marriage of modern science to nation building, all made possible because of the continued and powerful resonance of the Jewish foundational narrative. The emergence of the Jewish state in 1948 and, more particularly, the Israeli conquest of the West Bank in 1967, brought much of the ancient Land of Israel under Jewish control. The restoration of Jewish sovereignty to almost all the land of their forefathers stimulated further archeological exploration and strengthened the already existing links between Israel's archeological enterprise and the growth of the modern state.

As new data mounted, beginning in the interwar years, there was a perceived need to reassess the master narrative of the Jewish people, particularly the accounts of Israel's origins and, following that, the history of the early Israelite kingdoms. The evidence, textual and archeological, tended to reveal that the biblical account of the Exodus and the Israelite conquest of

Canaan could not be fully if at all reconciled with the unfolding historical and archeological record. Then, beginning in the 1980s, the recorded history of the early Israelite monarchy came under intense scrutiny. David and Solomon, portrayed by biblical chroniclers as mighty kings ruling over highly centralized states that projected power within all Canaan and beyond, were downgraded along with their kingdoms by revisionist scholars—in the case of David, to a local chieftain of a tribal or tribe-like configuration. Jerusalem, reportedly their capital, was not yet a major city but at best a dull and inconsequential backwater settlement. Unlike their predecessors and most of their current colleagues, some archeologists, labeled revisionists, could find no discernable trace of monumental architecture for the period of the united monarchy. The absence of impressive monuments suggested to them a biblical record reshaped in later times and circumstances to magnify the importance of their ancestors, legitimizing thereby their own reigns and policies. At the same time, a small coterie of biblical minimalists working outside the mainstream of biblical scholarship pounced on the new theories and denied altogether the historicity of the Hebrew Bible and the most ancient provenance of that highly revered text.

All this archeological activity, going back some eighty-five years, has given rise to unanticipated debates linked to the politics of Jewish and Palestinian Arab nationalism. For Israelis, the archeological record was seen as confirming the broad outlines of their ancestors' experiences in the Land of Israel. For Palestinians, who identified with the indigenous inhabitants, the ancient peoples of Canaan, the same archeological record denied the authenticity of the biblical narrative, thus undercutting Zionist claims to the Holy Land.

BIBLICAL REVISIONISM AND THE PERIOD
OF THE UNITED MONARCHY

The reigns of David and Solomon, the quintessential icons of a powerful Jewish state controlling its own destiny, are currently debated among both serious scholars and those who would manipulate scholarship for narrowly defined political purposes. Claims downplaying the united monarchy have thus caused a stir among those who follow trends in biblical studies—nowhere more so than in the State of Israel. The revisionist impulse was particularly disturbing to Zionists who saw the kingdoms of David and Solomon as proper models for a Jewish people reclaiming their ancestral homeland and charting a course to independent nationhood in modern times.

In and of itself, the debate stirred up by these archeologists has no political valence. Some of the leading critics of the biblical account are in fact
Israeli scholars deeply committed to their country. However much the lay
public of Israel is agitated by the attempt to debunk long-revered tales, the
issue dividing biblical scholars is not really one of national politics but the
elusive search for a more accurate description of the ancient past. It also
highlights the different approaches of those biblical scholars who value
written texts as historical data, however tendentiously driven, and archeologists who favor the evidence of material culture. In both cases, the evidence tends to be ambiguous and in need of constant review.

Serious text scholars readily admit how difficult it is to tease history
from the biblical account. Literary-historical studies have given rise to sharp
exchanges between individuals and schools of thought. When pressed,
archeologists will also acknowledge both the complexity and uncertainty of
their craft. At times, one may wish to question whether a hillock bearing
an Arabic toponym is in fact the precise site of a similar-sounding place familiar to us from scripture. Moreover, archeologists are limited to what they
actually find and can date with confidence. Their entire enterprise is based
on establishing chronological pointers, usually through an analysis of ceramic ware, which is then compared with shards from corresponding sites
said to be of the same period. It all begins with the ability to date an individual site or, to be more precise, on archeologists arriving at a consensus
regarding chronology.

As with textual scholarship, the archeological wisdom of the moment
can give way to new interpretations. From time to time, established
chronologies are reviewed and rejected in light of later fieldwork. Archeologists currently donning the mantle of revisionism would be well served if
they exercised a measure of politeness as well as caution in trumpeting their
latest views, all the more so in demeaning the views of their predecessors.
Indeed, if the revisionists had packaged their findings in more circumspect
language, they would no doubt have ruffled fewer feathers among their professional peers and the myriad amateurs who follow trends in biblical studies. Still, the revisionists remain very much a part of mainstream biblical
scholarship. Their colleagues may often sharply disagree with them, but
however contentious the debate, all sides recognize, albeit sometimes grudgingly, the seriousness of purpose and technical skill of their opponents.

The present controversy on the rise of the Israelite monarchy takes us
back in time. It was only some forty years ago that an earlier generation of
archeologists in Israel discussed the monumental architecture of the
Solomonic era at Gezer, Hazor, and Megiddo, all sites of major cities, re-

portedly built or fortified by the Israelite monarch. Referring to Solomon's forced labor projects, the biblical chronicler notes: "[They were initiated] to build the House of the Lord, [Solomon's] own palace, the citadel [*millo*] and wall of Jerusalem, and Hazor, Megiddo, and Gezer" (I Kings 9:15). During the 1950s and 1960s, archeologists managed to uncover the monumental gates of the latter three cities and found them to be of the same design, suggesting thereby that the fortification walls are of a piece, in accordance with the thrust of the biblical text. They were thus seen as part of a concurrent undertaking that included the massive development of Solomon's Jerusalem, for which there was no archeological evidence. Nor, alas, has any come to light since, despite intensive digs in and around the Holy City.

Readers relying on the biblical text were given to understand that the detailed account of Solomon's building activities accentuated the greatness of his realm and the power he was able to wield from his capital in the hills of Judea. It all seemed perfectly clear. That is hardly the case today. Archeologists led by Israel Finkelstein and David Ussishkin have challenged the accepted view of Solomon's power. The biblical text notwithstanding, they have reviewed the archeological data and concluded that the monumental architecture of Hazor, Megiddo, and Gezer, indicators of a highly centralized and powerful regime, must be from the following century, that is, not from the tenth century B.C.E., but the ninth. Rewriting a long-received history, they argue that the first great Israelite kingdom was not that of David and Solomon in the south—that is, in Jerusalem and the surrounding Judean hillside—but the House of Omri, the kingdom situated to the north in Samaria, the present Arab city of Nablus and its environs.

This argument is by no means limited to giving alternative dates for the monumental architecture of three fortified cities. Reviewing a wide range of archeological sites discovered in recent years, the new breed of archeologists concluded that the settlements of the Judean hills were relatively poor during the tenth century, too impoverished in fact to reflect the imperial state described in the Hebrew Bible. Perhaps that is why, for all its rich detail, the biblical text describing Solomon's reign has no parallel in extrabiblical sources. In contrast, the northern kingdom of the following century is represented as a powerful actor in contemporaneous Near Eastern accounts. If the Assyrian annals are to be believed, the House of Omri, more particularly his son King Ahab, was a formidable threat to the most powerful empire of the time. Oddly enough, the biblical account of Ahab's reign omits any mention of his confrontation with the Assyrians. Had it been reported by the biblical chronicler, the wayward king's foreign success might have been interpreted as a sign of his greatness. Instead, the author of Kings turns to domestic concerns and condemns Ahab for breaking with the ways of his people and his Lord. So perfidious was the king's behavior that in postbiblical tradition, the sullied Ahab will be one of a select group of humans denied a place in the world to come. By condemning Ahab for religious backsliding instead of praising him for standing up to the mighty Assyrians, the biblical narrative would appear to have turned history upside down, or, if you prefer, turned it north to south.

How then should we regard the biblical stories of David and Solomon? What could have given rise to so detailed, so vivid, and according to the revisionists, so exaggerated a portrait of these two monarchs and the southern realm, including the description of a major building campaign in which Solomon fortified three cities that, the revisionists concede, all have similar protective gates? Surely, these matching gates are a very odd coincidence given that the account of Solomon's extensive building activities is otherwise considered an imaginative construction of a nonexistent past. If they are to convince text scholars, the revisionists cannot simply discount the biblical narrative based on their reading of archeological data. They are obliged to explain why the biblical chroniclers reported "events" as they did; but in doing that, they too enter the gossamer realm of imagined history.

Their argument can be succinctly stated. As archeologists have found no physical evidence of monumental architecture or the accumulation of great wealth in the south, they have concluded that the kingdom centered in the Judean hill country was relatively poor and of no great consequence. It was only two centuries later, when the Assyrians broke the back of the northern kingdom, that the Judean monarchs were able to establish a powerful polity, and with that, Jerusalem took on the features of a major city. A purer form of monotheism was now practiced by the ancient Israelites as the southern kingdom underwent a period of religious renewal under King Josiah (640–609 B.C.E.). In keeping with these changes, the Israelite theologians rewrote the past in order to give the south a more prominent place in the extended narrative of the people. David and Solomon, local chieftains, were thus transformed into mighty monarchs. The limited territory they actually ruled was retroactively described as a vast state that extended well beyond the borders of Canaan. Seen from this perspective, the preserved biblical narrative is the literary effort of southerners advancing their political and moral claims by inventing a past that was not actually theirs.

There is much in this reconstruction of events that is accepted by the majority of biblical scholars. Josiah undertook reforms; the Judean state prospered in the eighth and seventh centuries B.C.E., and it is believed that much of the biblical text we read today was first formulated during those centuries. Scholars also agree that the biblical theologians described the early monarchy to promote the interests of the Davidic line. All that being the case, why has a largely technical debate among academicians given way to so much public controversy, both in Israel and the world at large? Why should reflective Israelis be overly perturbed if, in fact, the revisionists are basically right?

There is nothing in the revisionist argument that compromises the links between Jews and the land they long considered part of their ancient heritage. Perhaps Jerusalem was a relatively unimportant site during the early monarchy, but it surely grew in status thereafter. Perhaps Solomon did not build a magnificent temple as reported in the book of Kings, but a temple was subsequently built. When all is considered, the gist of the revisionist argument, which is based almost entirely on archeological evidence, is that the emergence of a powerful Israelite polity took place a century or so after we are led to believe that it did, and contrary to the biblical account, it did so first in Samaria to the north rather than Jerusalem to the south. Nevertheless, the southern kingdom managed to find its place in the sun two centuries later.

What truly disturbs the sensibilities of Jews is not so much a tenth century devoid of a powerful and highly centralized Israelite kingdom but the scholarly and political excesses of the so-called Danish School. The reference is to a small group of biblical minimalists who have broken with the mainstream by denying the historicity of all Hebrew scripture and challenging the accepted dates for the various strands that compose the text. With that, the "Danes" have challenged the entire mainstream of biblical scholarship. There are significant political overtones to the minimalist position. Academic controversy, too often marked by sharply expressed views and less-than-gentlemanly behavior, has been channeled by the Danes into denying the entire foundation of modern Israel's national narrative. At the same time, some minimalists and their followers avidly promote the concept of a legitimate Palestinian identity rooted in the ancient Near East. An arcane debate about the history of ancient Israel and the formation of the biblical text has thus become part of a larger political controversy between the modern state of Israel and Palestinian Arabs struggling to forge a nation-state of their own. Who then are the Danes and what is their impact on the controversial politics of the Arab-Israel dispute?

BIBLICAL MINIMALISTS AND ARAB-ISRAEL POLITICS

The Danish School represents a relatively small group of scholars, originally centered in Copenhagen but now situated at various academic venues, particularly in Great Britain. Although referred to as a "school," these scholars form a society of diverse interests and talents. What draws them together is a minimalist approach to the Hebrew Bible. They go several steps beyond their revisionist colleagues and contend that the Israelites of Hebrew scripture, their monotheism, their material and literary culture, their reported ties to the land of Canaan, even the Hebrew language, all came into being long after their purported origins. In sum, the biblical record as we now have it is an invented myth written in a language first devised by scribes in the Persian period (fifth century B.C.E.). Minimalists admit there may be rare echoes of a real history in the current biblical text, but they also maintain that few if any traces of this past can be extracted from the mythological overlay that has shaped the Bible's meaning for many generations of readers.

Skeptical from the outset, the minimalists began their assault on scripture by attacking the patriarchal narratives. Here, they were more or less on safe ground. Other scholars had also grown wary of reported links between the stories of Israel's forefathers and the world of second-millennium Mesopotamia. Upon closer examination, the biblical account was found to contain many anachronisms that could only have dated from centuries later. The minimalists then questioned the narratives of Joshua's conquest, Israel's origins in the land of Canaan, and the scholarship of past generations on that subject. Here too they were on relatively safe ground and not all that far removed from the conventional wisdom of an evolving biblical scholarship. But then they went several steps further and boldly denied the subsequent accounts of the biblical narrative in a manner that was bound to upset scholars, regardless of whether these biblical scholars favored squeezing history from texts or, like archeologists, they were more apt to trust the evidence of material culture.

For the minimalists, it is not enough to contend that the united monarchy was not the highly centralized and powerful state described in the Hebrew Bible. In effect, their claim is that there was no united monarchy at all, no David, and no Solomon. Not even the subsequent Israelite kings of the south, rulers described in detail in the Bible, are considered truly historic figures. There were no Israelites, or to be more precise, there were no Israelites as represented in scripture. For the minimalists, the current Hebrew Bible is not merely a text that reshapes the past to conform to the ideological concerns of the present, a proposition with which all responsible Bible scholars have long agreed. The familiar biblical text was produced almost entirely from new cloth as late as the Hellenistic period. One of the leading Danes has even attempted to prove—or at least strongly suggest—that the Hebrew Bible, which has been invoked to recover the history of the ancient Near East and has served as a basis for Jewish behavior and group identity for more than two millennia, reflects the world of the Greeks as much as the Fertile Crescent. For example, the original King Ahab, a figure whose historicity is conceded—he is, after all, mentioned in the Assyrian annals—is not at all the Ahab of the Hebrew Bible. The scriptural manifestation of this ancient ruler is modeled instead after Antiochus IV, the Seleucid monarch of the Book of Maccabees (175–164 B.C.E.).

We are obliged to consider the more general proposition put forth by the minimalists, namely, that the Hebrew Bible was an elaborate literary artifice portraying a history spun almost entirely from the imagination of inventive Hebrew scribes. This view raises an obvious question. Who would have created a mythic biblical history and civilization where none existed and to what purpose? In his book *In Search of Ancient Israel* (1992), Philip Davies, one of the leading proponents of mythic Israel, lays out the minimalist position in a manner fully accessible to an audience of nonspecialists. Davies, reflecting the views of his minimalist colleagues, argues that the Bible was authored by a settler population, an alien society that had been transplanted in Jerusalem and the surrounding hill country during the Persian ascendancy of the fifth century B.C.E. In effect, the biblical books of Ezra and Nehemiah, which purportedly describe the return of exiles from Babylon, mask a rather different story. The real tale is not one of returning Israelites who had been forced from their homeland after the fall of Jerusalem in 586 B.C.E., but rather that of a nonindigenous people transplanted in Jerusalem after the Persian conquest of Palestine. Lacking a history in their new environs, and hence without any sense of legitimate ownership to the land they came to occupy, this group of recent settlers found themselves in need of a new identity that could link them to Canaan's past. Residual folklore of the region, which might have referred—if ever so vaguely—to a historic figure or event, was thus woven by scribes into the fabric of a newly created national myth. Searching for ways to authenticate their claims, the settlers forged a history going back to a remote age, an era in which a fictitious Abraham entered into a covenant with his god Yahweh. In that pact, God reportedly promised Abraham's progeny the land of Canaan. The myths of Israel's origins in the land and of Israel's subsequent history until the Babylonian exile allowed the settlers, who would evolve into the Jewish people, to preempt the claims of the original inhabitants. And so, for more than two millennia, the Hebrew Bible, revered by Jews and Christians alike, became the central text for understanding the history of a distant past inappropriately named "the biblical period." An indigenous population that had remained more or less the same since remote times was thus denied a history and identity of its own. The date of the recorded biblical text varies among the minimalists, but all are agreed that in its current form, it stems from a time no earlier than the Hellenistic period, which began in the fourth century B.C.E.

To their credit, the scholars of the Danish school tend to read widely. In building their arguments, some move back and forth across disciplines, referring to works ranging from general linguistics to social anthropology and cultural studies. Thomas L. Thompson's massive and densely written *Early History of the Israelite People from the Written and Archeological Sources* (1999) contains a bibliography of more than thirty pages, a sign of considerable learning. It is, however, one thing to read widely; it is another to have the tools with which to interrogate the written word. On the whole, neither philology nor archeology, the twin pillars of ancient Near Eastern scholarship, are the strong suits of the Danish school, even less so of their camp followers. The result is twofold: There is a tendency to misread both literary sources and the evidence of material culture. At times, the line of argumentation is exceedingly tortured, the equivalent of forcing square pegs into round holes, all made necessary because the concept of a mythic Israel dictates the evidence rather than the other way round.

Seeking support with which to buttress their conceptual framework, scholars of the Danish school read widely and employ anything that might conceivably bolster their argument. All such data is then privileged, regardless of its source or merit. It is ironic that when it serves their purpose the most skeptical of the Bible critics are willing to embrace without question scholarship that is highly speculative and/or simply in error. Nor are they inclined to correct their views, let alone abandon them, when faced with overwhelming evidence to the contrary.

Having embraced the concept of a mythic Israel invented in the Persian period and given final expression only during Hellenistic times, the minimalists are left with much to explain. How can we, or, to be more precise, how can they square their Israel of the Persian period with the Israel of the Egyptian Merneptah stele, a text dating from the thirteenth century B.C.E.? What might be a problem for many reflective biblicists does not trouble the scholars of the Danish school. They maintain that the stele, inscribed eight hundred years prior to the alleged invention of mythic Israel, may refer to a geographical place called Israel and not a people. Those properly trained in Egyptian understood very well that grammatically, the text of the stele admits to no meaning other than the *people* of Israel. Still, without other contemporaneous sources mentioning Israel by name, it is difficult to draw any hard conclusions about the people of Israel listed on the stele and how they might be related to the Israelites of the Hebrew Bible, if at all.

The epigraphic evidence of the ninth century B.C.E. is decidedly less ambiguous. An Aramaic inscription from Tel Dan and a new reading of the famed Mesha Stone written in Moabite, a language closely linked to biblical Hebrew, both refer to the "House of (*byt*) David (*dwd*)," a seeming indication that the Davidic dynasty was well known roughly half a millennium before the minimalists contend it was invented. And yet, there is no reason for the minimalists to be perturbed, let alone panic. They simply read the letters *dwd* to mean something other than "David [King of Israel]." Orthographically, that is possible, but no responsible scholar would give credence to such an unlikely reading of the inscription. Still, there is a fallback argument. The Israel Museum staff is accused of forging the inscription from Tel Dan. Another contemporaneous reference to Israelites in the Mesha Stone is explained away by a similar sleight of hand. All that dovetails nicely with the broad political claims of certain minimalists, for we are then led to believe that just as the ancient Hebrew scribes invented an Israelite past in order to usurp the lands of the historic inhabitants of ancient Palestine, modern Israelis forge evidence to deny the rights of today's Palestinian Arabs. The latter are held to be the alleged descendants of the ancient peoples of Canaan and, by implication, the legitimate owners of the land. Of such claims, more is said shortly.

There is still more to trouble the Danish school. Contrary to their deeply held beliefs, the traditional biblical narrative seemingly contains echoes of a real past. Granted, for so much of the biblical account there is little if any corroborating evidence from extrabiblical materials, but how can we be convinced that ancient Israel is almost entirely the invention of the postmonarchic Persian period when many of Israel's monarchs listed in the book of Kings also appear in Assyrian and Babylonian sources? To be sure, one could argue that Hebrew scribes of the Persian period had some folkloric material to inform their literary imagination, but there are enough instances where the account of the biblical chronicler seems to fit a history known from an earlier world of Mesopotamia and Egypt. That being the case, why not promote the likely historicity of certain events reported in the Hebrew Bible? Perhaps the most notable example of such an historic echo is the story of the Assyrian king Sennacherib's eighth-century campaign against King Hezekiah and the fortified towns of the southern Israelite monarchy, an account that has parallels in the Assyrian annals. To be sure, history is disguised in both sources. But both agree that Sennacherib sent detachments to attack Jerusalem, that the Assyrian army surrounded the city, and that they withdrew rather than launch a decisive assault to secure the Israelite capital. Some scholars have even suggested that the biblical account of Sennacherib's campaign may contain snippets of genuine archival material—all that is very different from a literary artifice woven from new cloth centuries later.

As for the claim that the redacted Hebrew Bible is the creation of the Hellenistic period, the minimalists must contend with the very language of scripture. Meticulous investigations of biblical Hebrew texts and inscriptions have revealed a real distinction between so-called preexilic and postexilic writings, that is, between sources before the reported Babylonian captivity of the sixth century B.C.E. and the onset of the Persian period thereafter. Faced with this evidence, the minimalists found themselves in a quandary. Were the language of scriptural works thought by mainstream scholars to be preexilic and postexilic indeed different, one would ordinarily conclude that various books of the Bible were created at very different moments in time. And as the earlier works would have been written before the collapse of the Babylonian Empire, before any nonindigenous group of settlers could have been transplanted by the victorious Persians in Jerusalem, there clearly must have been both an Israelite people and written versions of biblical works long before the Persian let alone Hellenistic period. With that, the entire edifice of the Danish school collapses, along with the moral and political lessons that some of its supporters wish to impart. For there is then no basis for maintaining that foreign settlers of the fifth century, the alien progenitors of the Jews, usurped the history and rights of a population rooted in its land since time immemorial, the progenitors of today's Palestinian Arabs.

The minimalists have found themselves hard-pressed for an answer to the impressive linguistic evidence arrayed against them. The linguistic basis of their argument, such as it is, is a highly speculative article, twelve pages in all, by E. A. Knauf. Knauf suggests that, unlike other Near Eastern languages that evolved over time, biblical Hebrew is artificial, the creation of an identifiable moment in human history. To be more specific, it was created by scribes of the Persian period. Truth be told, Knauf's views have not won him many supporters outside the minimalist camp. Nevertheless, if biblical Hebrew were indeed the artificial language claimed by representatives of the Danish school, why should various books of the biblical canon exhibit such marked differences in vocabulary, orthography, phrasing, and the like? More important, why should inscriptions of earlier and later times exhibit similar differences? Ever imaginative, but clearly groping for an answer, some minimalists conclude that the differences were consciously woven into the text in order to create a second Hebrew, a seemingly archaic language that would lend legitimacy to the recently invented myths of the settlers as they struggled to wrest the land away from its native inhabitants.

Of all the arguments in defense of mythic Israel, the response of the minimalists to the linguistic evidence is by far the least persuasive. To claim that foreign scribes could have created a literature in two languages simultaneously—one a current language to describe the recent condition of their people, and one an artificial archaic language to describe an invented past in a manner that would silence their doubters—seems far-fetched at best. To think that possible, we would have to believe that a modern dramatist such as Tom Stoppard, the ingenuous playwright who has used Shakespeare's plots, characters, and themes to suit his own creative dramaturgy, could actually write a play comparable to Hamlet and then successfully peddle the work as being that of the bard himself.

It comes as no great surprise that the minimalists have come under withering criticism from text scholars and archeologists alike. On more than one occasion, that criticism has been expressed in harsh, almost vituperative language. Perhaps it is the overtly pugnacious style of certain minimalists that rubs nerves raw. Perhaps it is the irritating disparity between audacious claims on the one hand and lack of technical skills on the other. The self-proclaimed guardians of academic standards can become unusually sensitive at times. We might also consider the tendency of some minimalists to embrace intellectual trends that their opponents regard as faddish and devoid of merit. Whatever the case, even the gentlest opponent of the Danish school comes down heavily against them. In "The Copenhagen School: The Historiographical Issues" (2003)—a short but very thoughtful survey of the minimalist position—Marc Brettler, a scholar long interested and well published in biblical historiography, bends over backwards to do justice to various claims of the Danish school and then calmly and thoroughly demolishes each and every one of them. His is a rhetorical style other academics would do well to emulate.

On the whole, the minimalists have made little if any headway in changing the views of professional biblicists. They remain few in number and confined largely to circles in Copenhagen and the United Kingdom, particularly at the University of Sheffield. By no means should we consider the minimalists a persecuted academic minority. Admittedly, the tone of some critics has been nasty, perhaps excessively so, but one can hardly say the Danes have been muted by a conspiracy of their peers. The minimalists have never had a problem in disseminating their views, neither in academic nor more public forums. The print media have paid considerable attention to recent developments in biblical studies. Such accounts are often marked by a racy style, interesting graphics, and suggestive story leads, all designed to draw the attention of the average reader. Reporters, themselves without expertise to render qualitative judgments, have given equal weight to all positions regardless of merit, thus allowing readers to choose indiscriminately from among proclaimed truths. From time to time, the various issues dividing biblicists are also taken up in the *Biblical Archeological Review* (*BAR*), a glossy popular journal widely read by both professional scholars and amateur enthusiasts. The major combatants in the Bible wars have all had their say in the *BAR*. As a result, the debate over biblical revisionism has become broadly accessible for readers lacking the technical skills to follow dense scholarly arguments. Although they may have, at best, a partial grasp of the issues, some of these readers have actually become involved in the larger discussion. A number of literary critics and anthropologists have sought to influence the burgeoning debate over biblical origins and allegedly silenced histories. That is particularly true for those who use the noisy but relatively benign politics of the academy to stoke the fires of the attention-grabbing Arab-Israel dispute. With that, various assumptions of the Danish school have been recycled to serve the claims of Palestinian nationalism. As a result, an arcane debate grounded in archeology and textual readings has been transmuted into one of modern nationhood.

Having been rejected by mainstream scholars of the ancient Near East, minimalists embracing the Palestinian cause declare their critics agents of a universal academic conspiracy in which professors of western universities deny those who would speak on behalf of the colonized "other." Such a view is openly proclaimed by Keith W. Whitelam in his widely quoted book, *The Invention of Ancient Israel: The Silencing of Palestinian History* (1996), a work whose pungent subtitle completely captures the drift of the author's thesis and its debt to the literary critic Edward Said. Said, the son of a naturalized American citizen of Palestinian birth, spent his formative years in Egypt (1935–1948), his father having migrated there to open a branch of the family stationery business after a decade's sojourn in the United States. During the turmoil that followed the emergence of the State of Israel, the family returned to America where young Edward, then in his early teens, attended a prestigious boarding school and later pursued his university studies. At the time of his death in 2003, he was the Parr Professor of Comparative Literature at Columbia and indefatigable and eloquent spokesman for the Palestinian cause. A cosmopolitan exposed to the worlds of both East and West, Said argued that a politically and intellectually arrogant West has denied the colonized "other" the means and opportunity to define its own history and interpret its own native culture. Or, as Whitelam puts it with regard to biblical studies and the Palestinian people,

> There exists, then, what we may term a discourse of biblical studies which is a powerful interlocking network of ideas and assertions believed by its practitioners to be the reasonable results of objective scholarship while masking the realities of an exercise of power. We are faced with the paradox of the invention of "ancient Israel" . . . an entity that has been given substance and power as a scholarly construct, while Palestinian history lacks substance or even existence in . . . our academic institutions. Attempts to challenge this powerful narrative [of ancient Israel] are likely to be dismissed as politically or ideologically motivated and therefore unreasonable. (1996)

Like many writers, Whitelam positions himself for his audience by offering tidbits of autobiographical information, a sort of apology for not having written the kind of book that readers might have expected of him and that he himself had originally contemplated. He indicates that he began his work as part of a "grandiose scheme . . . conceived [as] an antidote to the standard histories of ancient Israel which have dominated biblical studies since the nineteenth century" (1996). But over time, he realized that he lacked the learning required for so prodigious an undertaking. That alone might have dissuaded him from his original goal. But Whitelam also came to realize that to complete such a project, he would have had to confront and overcome the innate prejudice that informed the way biblical scholars formulated and organized their research and then went about practicing their craft. He is convinced that the history of ancient Palestine (and its indigenous inhabitants) was hijacked by authorities interested only in "an ancient Israel conceived and presented as the [Judeo-Christian taproot] of Western civilization." To counter that approach, Whitelam ultimately decided on a project that would undermine the orthodox wisdom dominating biblical studies today. The larger work that would have required immense learning was thus put aside in favor of a polemic against or, as Whitelam would no doubt claim, a corrective to the current state of scholarship on the Hebrew Bible.

At first glance, there is nothing innovative about Whitelam's attempt to correct scholarship that links biblical studies directly and almost exclusively to a Judeo-Christian heritage. Assyriologists have long decoupled the study of the Hebrew Bible from the other civilizations of the ancient Near East. Archeologists tend not to refer to biblical archeology these days, but speak instead of Syro-Palestinian archeology, a descriptive label that expands their discipline beyond the borders of Canaan and the purported period of the Israelite polity—however that polity might be defined. We might add by way of explanation that that shift in the way scholars now think about archeology was occasioned by William Dever, perhaps the most vociferous critic of the minimalist school. Finally, biblicists situated at the leading departments of Near Eastern studies, scholars who in earlier generations would have been able to get by with a basic knowledge of Hebrew and Greek, find themselves obliged to command a host of ancient languages in order to engage in comparative studies, be they historical, linguistic, or literary. One can hardly claim that biblical studies, as it is now practiced in the leading academic centers of the discipline, are so parochial as to exclude the longer history of Canaan and its peoples other than the Israelites.

The early interest in the ancient Near East was guided by the centrality of the Bible in Judeo-Christian civilization. That interest continues to resonate among a general public for whom the Bible is both a source of comfort and a guide to moral behavior. Everyone admits to that, including the critics of the Danish school. That is hardly the case, however, in secular institutions of higher learning, or even some denominational schools with a scholarly tradition in biblical studies. We might well ask, why then does the story of the ancient Israelites still dominate the histories of Canaan, for it surely does? The answer does not lie in any theological concerns, or in any alleged cultural biases of Western scholarship. It certainly does not stem from any desire to thwart the national aspirations of today's Palestinian Arabs. Truth be told, the Hebrew Bible holds center stage because it contains the only sustained historical narrative we possess from and about ancient Canaan. None of the indigenous peoples mentioned in the Bible—not the Canaanites, Hittites, Hivites, Jebusites, Amorites, Girgashites, and Perizzites, or the peoples who lived in Cisjordan, such as the Moabites, Ammonites, and various Edomites—leave any extensive written sources. Similarly, the powerful Philistines, a sea people from the Aegean who invaded the country and settled along its coast, are known to us only from the remains of their material culture and what others say about them.

Aside from the Hebrew Bible, the only extended descriptions of Canaan before the emergence of ancient Israel are found in a cache of

Egyptian letters from the fourteenth century B.C.E. The texts, uncovered in Tel el-Amarna, the site of the royal city founded by the Pharaoh Amenhotep IV, are mostly written in Akkadian, an east Semitic language that was then the international lingua franca. However much influenced by west Semitic, the linguistic label attached to most languages of Canaan, none of these letters was penned in what may be called a Canaanite dialect, nor do they seem to reflect directly the broad views of the local population. There is, however, much to glean from the Amarna texts. Unlike the biblical account, a well-crafted literary work that exhibits the biases of the Hebrew chroniclers, the Amarna letters are archival documents. As such, they can be more safely used to reconstruct political structures and the unfolding events of the time. Not surprisingly, these documents have been closely studied and with much profit by Assyriologists and well-trained biblical scholars. But all told, these documents cover less than thirty years, hardly the stuff from which to write an extensive history of ancient Canaan—certainly not a history that would satisfy the minimalists and their supporters.

There is, to be sure, an extensive literature written in Ugaritic, a northwest Semitic language bearing some similarities to Hebrew. Ugaritic texts have proved invaluable to our understanding of certain biblical passages and more generally of biblical civilization. But there are no historical texts to speak of from the Kingdom of Ugarit. That aside, the kingdom was situated in northern Syria and not in historic Canaan, whose northern border lay far to the south in today's Lebanese region surrounding Tyre and Sidon. Any claim that Ugarit and its civilization can stand for the peoples of Canaan and their civilization, let alone be considered an antecedent to modern Palestine and Arabic-speaking Palestinians, is a bit much. Such a view, suggested by Basem Ra'ad, an Arab scholar of American literature, is an indication of how far politically committed amateurs are prepared to wade in unfamiliar waters. Having imbibed the intoxicating spirits of politically motivated minimalists like Whitelam, even specialists in American studies can register their views on the ancient Near East and its relevance to the current state of affairs. What is most startling about Whitelam's work is not his expressed desire to recover the history of non-Israelite Canaan. That is a project that all scholars of the ancient Near East can and have indeed embraced, including Israelis who have long sought to trace the history of their land and its adjacent regions from the Stone Age through the Islamic period. Among Israelis, there is absolutely no opposition to focusing interest on the history of Canaan or the various peoples subsumed under the label Canaanite. It is rather Whitelam's arbitrary labeling of the inhabitants of ancient Canaan Palestinians and his attempt to link these Canaanites cum

Palestinians to today's Arab inhabitants of the country that elicits negative comment. We have already noted the ambiguities surrounding "geographical" Palestine and the equally ambiguous notion of a Palestinian identity in premodern times (see chapters 2 and 3). If we can speak of Palestine and Palestinians in the most ancient world, it is only in reference to the Philistines (the biblical *P'lishtim*), whose territorial domain (*P'leshet* or *Pa-la-sh-tu*) gave rise to Palestine, the long-standing descriptive label that first took root in the Graeco-Roman period. Lest we forget, the Philistines themselves were not native to Canaan. Like the Crusaders who penetrated the land some two and half millennia later, the Philistines spoke a language completely unrelated to that of the other peoples. Their material culture and political organization were similarly distinctive and partially explain their initial success against the land's native inhabitants. Only later did the sea people from the Aegean become more fully integrated into the local culture, a process that still begs for detailed explanation.

The very notion of an indigenous people in the land known as Canaan is itself highly problematic. A geographical expanse serving as a bridge between southwest Asia and Africa, Canaan—or however we might refer to the aforementioned territory—was penetrated by many peoples at diverse moments of history. Some, including tribesman from Arabia in the seventh century C.E., settled permanently in their newly acquired domains. Like all previous invaders, the seventh-century Arabians eventually intermingled with the local inhabitants. If one could actually trace the genealogies of to-day's Palestinians, one would likely find, among the larger mix, descendants of the ancient Philistines, as well as numerous other peoples that inhabited the land at one time or another, including the Christian crusaders. Israelis, those both of European stock and from Arab lands, can also be said to walk in the footsteps of time-honored ancestors.

What rights if any can be derived from such "historic" associations? Even before biblical revisionism became popular, Palestinian nationalists and their Arab supporters trumpeted the ancient Canaanites as their forebears. The connection was twofold: By originating in the Arabian Peninsula (see chapter 2), as modern Arabs claim (based in part on medieval Arabic genealogies), the Canaanites could all be considered Arabs. By eventually settling in the land now called Palestine, they could also be considered Palestinians. In contrast, the Zionist settlers from Europe are declared the descendants of the Khazars, Turkic peoples who converted to Judaism in the Middle Ages. These transplanted Europeans are clearly interlopers, a people without a history in the land they claim as that of their forefathers. Israelis from Arab lands may be native to the wider region, but they too lack

proper claims to Palestine, as they are descended from a nonindigenous people who usurped the land from its Palestinian owners, first during the Persian period and then again following the creation of the State of Israel in
1948. It comes as no surprise then that the minimalists have found favor
among Arabs in the West who have read or perused their current literature.
The same is true for more worldly audiences in the Arab world itself.
Thompson has been translated into Arabic; Whitelam and others are sure
to follow. It is only a matter of time before biblical minimalism becomes
the accepted currency of so many Arab intellectuals, Palestinians and non-
Palestinians alike.

At the seventh annual Jerusalem Day Symposium held in Amman in
1996, an event sponsored by Prince al-Hasan and devoted to "Western scholarship and the history of Palestine," Thompson, Whitelam, and the theolo-
gian Michael Prior all participated. Their contributions were "Hidden Histories and the Problem of Ethnicity in Palestine" (Thompson), "Western
Scholarship and the Silencing of Palestinian History" (Whitelam), and "The
Moral Problem of the Land Traditions of the Bible [the basis of Israelite/Jew-
ish claims to the Holy Land]" (Prior). Other presentations by scholars and political figures from the region included a talk in Arabic on "Canaanite *Arabs*,
the Builders of Jerusalem and other Cities of Palestine," (italics mine) by
Mahmud al-Zu'abi, a professor of history at Damascus University. One could
cite similar examples. For better or worse, the minimalist project has become
linked to a political debate in which Jews and Arabs match claims and counterclaims to regions and individual sites of the Holy Land.

What bearing does an alleged Western conspiracy to sever the historic
link between the indigenous peoples of Canaan and today's Palestinians
have on the politics of the region? Or to put the question somewhat differently, how would the political calculus of the Near East be changed if
the minimalist position gained ascendance in Western intellectual and political circles? If the revered narrative of ancient Israel is at best an account
of a world that "should" have been or, following the outspoken minimalists, nothing more than a concoction of Hellenistic times projected back
onto a more distant Canaanite past, why should anyone privilege that Jewish version of history over Palestinian versions of the past? Why should
well-meaning people of the West recognize Jewish claims to the Holy Land
when such claims are seemingly based on unreliable and biased texts? Why
not follow instead those minimalists and their supporters who completely
discredit the biblical account while supporting in full the cause of Palestinian nationalism? Needless to say, all these loaded queries and the answers
they demand are grist for the Arab mill.

Whether speaking of geopolitics or justice, Arabs have always held that Israel is based on myth and conceived in sin. Even Arabs prepared to live at peace with a Jewish state question its legitimacy. From their perspective, historic Palestine was Arab land, even in the most ancient times. And so, the United Nations Organization was wrongly motivated when it deliberated the future of mandatory Palestine in 1947. Both justice and history demanded that it should have remained Arab rather than partitioned into two proposed states: one Jewish, as in days of yore, and one Arab, to reflect some thirteen hundred years of Muslim rule in Palestine. If only the world had known and were guided by the real history of the land and its people.

The Arabs' perception that there has been an injustice continues to gnaw at their sensibilities. Palestinians are genuinely offended by what they declare a conscious denial of their history and the claims they derive from that imagined past. Reaching out to western audiences with arguments loosely based on idiosyncratic western scholarship, Arabs maintain that modern Israel, a polity that should never have come into being, justifies its expanded borders—indeed its validity as a Jewish state—by a deliberate misuse of fundamentally biased scholarship.

TRADITIONAL MUSLIM ATTITUDES TOWARD THE BIBLICAL PAST

However much Palestinians are inclined to invoke the minimalist position in laying out their case, the legacy of traditional Islam will always serve as a partial brake. That is certainly true for believing Muslims. The faithful, who represent the overwhelming majority of Palestinian Arab society, are obliged to recognize that the ancient Israelite past, as broadly outlined in the Hebrew Bible, is part of their own religious heritage. The Qur'an is laced with all sorts of references to biblical persons and events. Muhammad is presented in Muslim scripture and commentary as the last and most noble of a long line of prophets well known from the biblical record. His future coming and hence legitimacy was recognized in turn by all the prophets preceding him, beginning with Moses. And so, the first prophet of Jewish tradition and the Messenger of God who seals prophecy for the Muslims are bound to each other irrevocably. Nor is Muhammad the only Arab to be defined by a biblical past. According to Muslim tradition, all the northern Arabs, including the Quraysh and the Banu Hashim, Muhammad's tribe and clan, were the descendants of Ishmael, the eldest son of Abraham. Any claim that Moses and Abraham are mythic figures living in mythic times would be greeted as heresy among the Muslim faithful. Palestinians can well accept the minimalists when the latter link them to the ancient peoples of Canaan. They have claimed as much themselves. Indeed, they have gone further in arguing that the Canaanites originated in the Arabian Peninsula. The Arabs of Palestine can also subscribe to any theory that demeans western scholarship by seeing it to be inherently biased in favor of the Judeo-Christian tradition and, by extension, the historic claims of the Zionist movement. But they cannot in good faith jettison completely the versions of biblical persons and events that have long captivated them. Jews throughout the ages may have deliberately misread passages of their own scripture or falsified the text in an attempt to deny Muhammad's legitimacy, proof of which is contained therein, but God's earlier revelation to the Israelites cannot be denied as it was part of an ongoing prophetic saga. That saga was brought to fruition with the coming of God's last and most noble messenger, Muhammad ibn 'Abdallah from the Arab tribe of Quraysh.

Recognizing the importance of Israelite tales (*Isra'iliyat*) to their religious foundations, the early Muslims pursued an active interest in all sorts of Jewish memorabilia. They were no doubt titillated by accounts of the ancient Israelites and read the richly textured Arabic versions with much interest and profit. Intellectual curiosity alone does not account, however, for the extensive and sustained intellectual concern with ancient Israel. In pursuing the Jewish past, Muslim religious authorities were not interested in new and more broadly defined insights about the general nature of religious experience. The tales of the Israelites were not considered arcane legends, the sort of material that draws attention from modern folklorists or scholars of comparative religion. In outlook, the Muslim authorities resembled more closely the friars of the Christian West, learned men who saw themselves, first and foremost, as defenders of the true faith.

Muslims delved into the Jewish past because they thought it directly linked to the course of their own history and was important to their ideals, practices, and moral behavior. The Hebrew Bible, properly explicated, foretold the coming of the Prophet Muhammad. Similarly, postbiblical Jewish tradition predicted events taking place during the time of his successors, the Commanders of the Faithful. The manner in which the Israelites comported themselves was also an indication of how people with a revealed text can fail to comply with the ways of Allah. Seen through Islamic lenses, the Jewish "other" became a yardstick by which the Muslims measured themselves and measured their ummah against an older and less worthy monotheist community. Unlike the early Muslim polity, which represented a transcendent ideal for all generations of Muslims, the Banu Isra'il, or "people of Israel," were constantly rebelling against their God. They were truly a "stiff-necked" people, or as Muslims would have it a "thick-hearted" people. Proof of Israel's unworthiness, found often in a Jewish tradition that is intensely self-critical, was quoted liberally by Muslims. Such quotes continue to flavor Muslim polemics in their hostile engagement with Jews and the modern State of Israel. Thus, current Arab scholars who focus on the Hebrew Bible are inclined to demonstrate how particular passages are linked to Zionist ideology and behavior. Properly understood, Jewish scripture illuminates Israel's aggressive political aims and policies. For Muslims, to deny the biblical account as they understand it is to surrender both the underpinnings of their own beliefs and the material from which they fashioned and continue to fashion their images of Jews, Judaism, and more recently, the Zionist project.

Such as it is, Arab interest in the ancient Near East is linked everywhere to the modern nation state. Virtually all countries in the region sponsor their own excavations and license digs by foreign archeologists. These modern polities promote themselves as heirs to civilizations that graced their national domains prior to Islam. Even before a Palestinian state has been established, the current authority that rules in Gaza and areas of the West Bank has moved, however slowly, toward creating a full-fledged department of antiquities. Turning to the pre-Islamic world in search of nationhood and national symbols has an undeniable logic. How else would Iraqis, Jordanians, Lebanese, and now Palestinians, among others, create a deep-rooted and unifying sense of nationality where nations as we now know them never existed until recent times? Nevertheless, claiming ancient cultures that are foreign and distant as one's own, or even seeking to understand those cultures on their own terms, is a formidable undertaking. Islam defines the basic identity of the overwhelming majority of Arabs. As a rule, traditional Muslims have never related to a pagan pre-Islamic past, let alone claimed it for themselves. During the formative period of Islam, there was considerable curiosity about the world of the ancients, particularly that of the Greeks and the Israelites. The former provided Muslim thinkers with the so-called Greek sciences: philosophy, medicine, geography, astronomy, and mathematics, but they did not provide templates of moral or religious behavior. The Israelites provided Muslims with truth of the Prophet's mission, predictions of future events in the world of Islam, and an earlier monotheist history that bore studying, but all that was preparation for the quintessential Islam to follow.

Although many Arabs now express a renewed interest in the ancient world, that interest has not led to widespread and sustained scholarly enquiry such as exists in the universities and research institutes of the West Palestinian Intellectuals, stressing Arab links to Canaan's ancient people, may appreciate the significance of ruins and remote histories as political symbols, but they have yet to turn that appreciation into a serious engagement with the languages and cultures of the past. Arabs who trumpet the importance of their Canaanite forebears show little interest in text-critical scholarship. The study of ancient Canaan in the Western academy—which includes Israel's universities—ordinarily demands a knowledge of Hebrew, a command of several other Near Eastern languages, a familiarity with the literary legacy of the native peoples of Canaan, as well as training in comparative Semitic linguistics and grammar. None of these subjects is the strong suit of Arab universities. The few able Arab scholars who have made serious attempts to master these disciplines were mostly trained in foreign institutions.

At best, Arab primary and secondary schools pay lip service to the pre-Islamic history of the region. Unlike Israel's schoolchildren who are immersed in a biblical tradition that Jews have read and reread in the original language for well over two millennia, their Palestinian counterparts are not required to study, year in and year out, an ancient world they have only recently adopted as their own. The failure to focus more directly on Canaan and its history is not surprising. However much Muslim Palestinians embrace the Canaanite past, the history that has defined their identity for a thousand years and more is the rise of Islam and the Arab conquest of the seventh century. That all-powerful link between Arab Muslims and the Islamic past overshadows every other human experience.

9

THE EMERGENCE OF ZIONISM

A Secular and Humanist Narrative

> The Land of Israel was the birthplace of the Jewish people. Here their spiritual, religious and national identity was formed. Here they achieved independence and created a culture of national and universal significance. Here they wrote and gave the Bible to the world.

So begins Israel's Declaration of Independence, proclaimed on May 14, 1948, in a Tel Aviv auditorium by David Ben-Gurion, chairman of the Executive Committee of the Jewish Agency and soon to become the first prime minister of Israel. The thesis articulated here is a reflection of the fundamental core of Zionist thought and, as such, is one of the most revolutionary statements in the long history of the Jewish people.

As we observed earlier, for more than three millennia, Jews had understood themselves to be a people created in consequence of a divine promise, expressed in a covenant first established between Abraham and God. This covenant was reiterated and reaffirmed on numerous occasions in the biblical narrative of the history of the Jews. The episodes in this epic drama reflect the belief that God and Jews interact throughout history. Each has obligations toward the other. When Jews sin and fail to fulfill their responsibilities, they are punished. Exile was among the most severe and, certainly, the most long-lasting punishment, yet the Bible is replete with promises of return from exile and redemption. The path to national restoration was not through repentance alone. In the traditions elaborated by the rabbis over the centuries, even the mending of ways and contrition could not restore Jews to the promised land. God alone would determine when the time was ripe and the people were ready. Thus, national redemption was only partially in the hands of the Jewish people. Traditional Jews believed that divine intervention was the essential ingredient for undoing the travails of exile; that only through the agency of a Messiah would they be brought back to their ancient homeland. His coming, though, was inevitably a matter of speculation and ultimately beyond human control.

Israel's Declaration of Independence tells a different story. In this account of national redemption, there is no reference to God in the establishment of a Jewish state. Only the Jewish people are described as actors in their history. In the final sentence of the first paragraph, the declaration affirms that it is the Jewish people who "wrote and gave the Bible to the world." With this one sentence, the story of divine revelation at Mount Sinai is set aside. Further on and without reference to divine intervention—including none to the messianic age—the termination of exile is announced and Jews are invited to return home to build their homeland: "Our call goes out to the Jewish people all over the world to rally to our side in the task of immigration and development and to stand by us in the great struggle for the fulfillment of the dream of generations—the redemption of Israel." The only oblique allusion to God, aside from invoking the traditional religious concept of "redemption," is the invitation to "trust in the Rock of Israel," a metaphor that appears at the document's end, conveniently disguising, with deliberate poetic license, the relationship between Jews and the God with whom they had traditionally identified their fate. In July 1950, the State of Israel enacted the Law of Return that gave Jews everywhere the legal right to immigrate to the Jewish state, thereby transforming a messianic event into an act authorized by a democratically elected assembly and dependent on individual choice.

This deliberate rewriting of one of the longest extant traditions in world culture is a consequence of the experience of European Jews in the century before Israel's creation. For the Zionist framers of the Declaration of Independence, the State of Israel was created by a secular national liberation movement (albeit with roots in an ancient national culture), and so they announced it thusly to fellow Jews and to the world. As such, it is fundamentally and radically different from the contemporary Arab national movements that it confronts. As we shall suggest, over the past two centuries Jews and Judaism have been in the process of transforming themselves to accommodate the ideas put forward by a succession of movements including the Enlightenment, secularization, humanism, and modern nationalism. The differences with the Arab Muslim experience in the same period could not be sharper, and in this distinction, one can find much of the explanation for the difficulty in bridging the gulf between these two cultures in their contemporary confrontation.

RESPONSES TO MODERNITY

Zionism as a secular national movement is rooted in the response of Jews to the Enlightenment that promoted belief in reason and science as alternative or (at least) additional epistemologies to faith and received religion. As Europe organized into national states during the nineteenth century, Jews began to imagine themselves as belonging to the exclusive and distinctive community of faithful adherents to Judaism. Through the nineteenth century, increasing numbers of European Jews endeavored to become citizens of the emerging states and members of the civil societies they spawned. In sum, Zionism grew out of the experience of confronting both the opportunities and the dangers inherent in the changes that spread over Europe after the French Revolution.

The magnitude of change was unprecedented in Jewish history. By 1900, 80 percent of world Jewry lived in Europe and all had to confront the changes taking place on the continent. In a century of extraordinary political and intellectual turmoil, Jews were probably more affected by the currents sweeping through European society than other peoples. Prior to 1800, they had been segregated into particular areas; had a distinctive language, often wore special dress that marked them off as a separate group, were excluded from many occupations including agriculture and thereby forced to concentrate in others, and had even maintained their own legal system in cases affecting only Jews. They also organized time differently. Although they used the solar Christian calendars for everyday affairs, they also retained for communal and personal purposes a lunar calendar in which the day began at sunset. They numbered years from creation, as understood from the reading of Genesis, as opposed to the solar calendar that measured time from "the year of our Lord," that is, from the appearance of Jesus Christ.

The paths from the closed and discrete world of the ghetto into modern society were many and diverse. Through the middle of the nineteenth century, most Jews were intent on adapting Judaism to the culture of the potential host society. Reform Judaism and then conservative Judaism emerged by the mid-nineteenth century. In reaction, traditional Jews came to call themselves orthodox by the 1860s. Led by Samson Raphael Hirsch, the leader of the Frankfurt Jewish community, many orthodox Jews sought the adaptation of traditional Judaism to contemporary science and society while remaining faithful to rituals and to Jewish law as exposited from revelation and Holy Writ (*halakhah*). At the extreme end of this spectrum, uncompromising reactionaries objected to any alteration. By the early twentieth century another movement, ultraorthodoxy, organized in opposition to any deviation from traditional Judaism. Their strategy was based on resistance to change and the dangers of the modern world through insularity and inflexibility. Thus the reform, conservative, orthodox, and ultraorthodox streams offered different or contradictory responses to the challenges of the Enlightenment and the rise of the modern state.

The question that challenged all who wished to remain Jews rather than merely convert or assimilate, whatever version of Judaism they professed, was how to maintain a Jewish identity when greater interaction with the culture of gentiles was inevitable. The timing, pace, and magnitude of change differed across Europe, but the underlying forces were similar. Jews attempted to adjust to the actual or expected introduction of liberalism and modernization into the societies in which they lived. Change first took place in Western Europe, initially in France, and radical ideas spread with the march of French armies in the wake of the French Revolution. Among these ideas was the proposition that societies could be constituted based on civic equality and that individuals might become citizens of modern states. In a wide variety of permutations from England and Holland through the Austrian-Hungarian Empire to Poland and Russia, this notion engendered rampant speculation among Jews and gentiles over the status of Jews in a new European order.

The prospect of such a shift was as wrenching as it was radical. The discrete and insular Jewish society was rooted in religion and cultural values that derived their authority largely from an ancient world that had long served as a guide to the Jewish present and future. The past of the Jewish imagination lay in the remote antiquity of the biblical through Talmudic periods. It was bound to a tradition of holy texts that derived their authority from divine revelation. Every truth ultimately had to be anchored in divine word as articulated in sacred texts. This past was immanent in the present. Traditional epistemology was contrary to the new "truths." Truth was now based in human reason and could even be proclaimed "manifest" and "self-evident," as in the American Declaration of Independence.

Revelation also had a national aspect that was immediate and palpable. Christians regarded their tradition as inherited from peoples who had now disappeared or at least receded from the stage of human history. Jews, on the contrary, regarded themselves as directly descended from the ancient Hebrews. They were not merely passive heirs of the past but still active partners to the original and still-valid covenant. Moreover, unlike Christians, who could fix themselves in contemporary time and space by identifying with a specific locale, Jews decidedly did not fix themselves exclusively to the locale in which they lived. Residence was temporary. This was just as well since Jewish history was replete with expulsion from one country after another. Both Jews and Christians agreed that Jews were in perpetual exile. In effect, what was permanent in Jewish life was membership in a society fixed by ancient divine law. This explains, in part, the radical nature of the impact of modernity on Jewish life. It was not only a change in outlook where faith was supplanted or augmented by reason; Jews were expected to become citizens of states and accepting of the logic by which they were established. As such, they were to adopt the responsibilities, obligations, and modes of behavior of host societies and become loyal to them. Most believed this was possible and opted for one or another form of this arrangement. This was a novel kind of conversion—not necessarily of religious faith but of social and political loyalty wherein they could add new affiliations without severing old ones. They imagined themselves as French Jews, German Jews, and so on, rather than exclusively within the confines of a Jewish identity detached in time and space. There appeared to be much to gain and little to lose.

New identities rested on the assumption that the host societies were willing to accept Jews with their differences. This was never a smooth process. A century after the French revolution, Jews were shocked by the Dreyfus affair that aggravated France beginning in 1894. The widespread and even frenzied popularity of the false accusation leveled against a Jewish officer in the French army diminished the prospect of successful integration. The rise of fascism and the spread of anti-Semitic racism would later confirm the difficulty, if not impossibility, of successfully negotiating entry into modern Europe.

The Dreyfus affair stands midway between earlier disappointments and the rise of anti-Semitic, totalitarian movements of the Right and the Left. The Russian pogroms, the anti-Jewish riots of the 1880s, were on a far smaller scale than the catastrophe of the mid-twentieth century, but they nevertheless had a very profound effect. They inaugurated the massive movement of Jews fleeing Eastern Europe. This movement not only heralded geographic change, but it also questioned whether security and equality could ever be found in Europe. The result was the great migration of Jews to the United States, and for a small minority, the idea that only a return to the homeland could provide sanctuary. It is in this context of the turn toward Jewish territorial nationalism that Zionism originated.

Leo Pinsker (1820–1891) provided the intellectual framework for this departure with *Auto-Emancipation: An Appeal to His People by a Russian Jew* (1882). This essay was a clarion call that attracted a generation of the disaffected and that is still considered a classic text of Zionist thought. His fundamental insight was based on psychology. "The Jews," he wrote, "are not a living nation; they are everywhere aliens; therefore they are despised." Xenophobia, he argued, is a natural human condition. The civil and political emancipation of Jews was not enough to provide them with respect and safety. The concluding summary of *Auto-Emancipation* reflects his frustration, even despair, of accommodating Jews within the new states and societies of Europe. It not only analyzes the dangers, but also offers the beginnings of a program. The ultimate statement, drawn from an ancient text in the Mishnah, *Sayings of the Fathers*, is typical of the way Zionists adapted texts initially framed in a religious context for their contemporary political program: Jews must save themselves from destruction. It is characteristic, too, that Pinsker does not expect or ask for divine intervention. Jews will have to act on their own:

> The proper and the only remedy would be the creation of a Jewish nationality, of a people living upon its own soil, the auto-emancipation of the Jews; their emancipation as a nation among nations by the acquisition of a home of their own.
>
> We should not persuade ourselves that humanity and enlightenment will ever be radical remedies for the malady of our people.
>
> The lack of national self-respect and self-confidence, of political initiative and of unity, are the enemies of our national renaissance.
>
> In order that we may not be constrained to wander from one exile to another, we must have an extensive and productive place of refuge, a gathering place which is our own.
>
> The present moment is more favorable than any other for realizing the plan here unfolded.
>
> The international Jewish question must receive a national solution. Of course, our national regeneration can only proceed slowly. We must take the first step. Our *descendents* must follow us with a measured and unhurried pace.
>
> A way must be opened for the national regeneration of the Jews by a congress of Jewish notables.
>
> No sacrifice would be too great in order to reach the goal which will assure our people's future, everywhere endangered.
>
> The financial accomplishment of the undertaking can, in the nature of the situation, encounter no insuperable difficulties.
>
> Help yourselves, and God will help you!

Pinsker was one of a growing number of Jews who searched for a response to European culture beyond a transformed Judaism. Often already secularized, they sought their place within society both as individuals and as Jews. Whatever philosophical or political strategy they chose, they believed that integration was possible and desirable. Such optimism was expressed from the early nineteenth century by growing numbers of Jewish intellectuals who called themselves *maskilim,* which literally means "enlightened." They termed their movement *Haskalah* (enlightenment), the translation into Hebrew of the movement with which they identified and from which they drew inspiration.

The use of a Hebrew term was no accident. They were determined to revive Hebrew as a modern living language suitable for a modern people even as they drew upon traditional Judaism. In doing so, however, they privileged the Bible over the Talmud. They drew inspiration from the period of Jewish independence and sovereignty when prophets, judges, and kings led the nation, deemphasizing centuries of exile when rabbis served as spokesmen and arbiters of the national culture. Jews identified with the Enlightenment often vilified the narrowness of tradition-bound Jewish society and celebrated the vigor of a nation that functioned alongside other nations. In response, ultraorthodox Jews insisted on maintaining Hebrew for sacred purposes and using Yiddish in the other sectors of Jewish communal life. The haskalah and its use of Hebrew, then, became a significant indicator in Jewish secularity. It reimagined the Jewish people as a nation anchored in a secular tradition rather than what it had been for nearly two millennia—a national culture rooted in religion. Such were the nineteenth-century antecedents of the revolutionary opening paragraph of Israel's Declaration of Independence.

Pinsker's life is paradigmatic for the route from haskalah to Zionism. He grew up in a household that was ambitious to acquire European culture yet preserved Hebrew culture without strict adherence to religious practice. He studied medicine in a Russian university even as he developed as a writer on Jewish affairs. Through middle life, he promoted the possibilities of Jewish integration in an emancipated Europe. However, beginning in the 1870s he became alarmed at the realities of a growing anti-Semitism, both its spontaneous, popular expressions and government-inspired policies. For all the desire to become part of the new Europe, Pinsker retreated into a deep pessimism informed by the realities he witnessed. This pattern was repeated as successive generations of Jews, many in the vanguard of liberal, egalitarian, and revolutionary movements, became disillusioned. To paraphrase Arthur Koestler, an intellectual of the Left in the 1930s who came to embrace Zionism at one stage of his intellectual and personal journey, the European gods "had failed."

The crucial experience in Pinsker's life was the Russian pogroms that erupted in 1881. This event set off large-scale westward migration of Jews across Europe and particularly across the Atlantic to the United States. In the immediate aftermath of this violence, he traveled to Western Europe to urge Jewish leaders to accommodate Eastern European Jews within the western portion of the continent. In this he failed. Leaders of Western European Jewry advocated sending their Eastern European brethren out of Europe to America. In doing so, they in effect admitted that even Central and Western Europe might be problematic if too many Jews chose to live there. It was after this journey to the West that Pinsker published his seminal work *Auto-Emancipation*. He was unusual and prophetic in arguing that the proper escape route lay southward, across the Mediterranean to Palestine. Pinsker, the maskil, had lost faith in Europe and had become a Zionist.

Pinsker's contribution was not only his analysis of the power of an inherent xenophobia but in a call to practical action. Believing that Jewish survival required a return to a land that they could call their own, he joined the fledgling and spontaneous organization committed to supporting pioneering in Palestine that was sprouting up in Eastern Europe, Lovers of Zion (*Hovevei Zion*), and founded a branch in Odessa. By 1884, this autonomous association formulated a common program in Kattowitz (then Prussia, now Poland) with Pinsker as chairman. At the same time, between 1881 and 1884, the first Zionist colonies were established in Palestine. Zionism had taken the first steps from theory to practical realization.

This story was repeated time and again. By the mid-1890s, it was the turn of Theodor Herzl, an assimilated Viennese journalist who had reported on the Dreyfus trial. In *Judenstaat* ("Jewish State" 1896), he went far beyond Pinsker's pamphlet and laid out a practical political and settlement program that electrified European Jewry and set the stage for an international movement. Following on the tradition of Pinsker at Kattowitz, he called on European Jews to assemble in Basle to establish the Zionist Organization in 1897. A cross-section of European Jewry from Britain to Russia responded. Indeed, membership in the Zionist movement would rise and ebb in response to ever more disastrous events, from the chaos of Eastern Europe during and after World War I and the Russian Revolution through the upheavals in Central Europe with the rise to power of Nazism in the 1930s. After World War II, most of the remaining Jews in the world were at least sympathetic to Zionism, if not actually dues-paying members.

If not active Zionists, they identified themselves as "pro-Zionists." Opposition had moved to the margins of the Jewish community.

THE ETHOS OF SELF-HELP

As Zionism took root and spread, an essential element was amplified in a variety of intellectual as well as practical ways: the call to self-help with which Pinsker concludes *Auto-Emancipation*. A few examples of the diverse effect of this revolutionary idea should indicate its pervasive impact. In perhaps the most memorable line of the post-Dreyfus generation and in the immediate aftermath of the Kishinev pogram (1903), Hayyim Nachman Bialik (1873–1934), the popular Hebrew poet admired and quoted by Zionists, wrote in his epic poem, "The City of Slaughter," on the pogrom: "The acacia tree blossomed, the sun shone, and the slaughterer slaughtered." The meaning was clear to all. In a world that proceeded in apparent wondrous normality and even beauty, Jews were being killed and no one, not even God, intervened. Readers understood that they had to save themselves by taking their destiny in their own hands lest, as Bialik concluded the poem, they continue to "seek handouts as before." This poem was part of the cultural baggage that the second generation of Zionist pioneers (Second Aliyah 1904–1914) took with them as they departed for Palestine. Among its members were the founders of the State of Israel, including David Gruen, soon to become David Ben-Gurion.

Another popular Hebrew poet, Shaul Tschernichowsky (1875–1943), defied convention by using the sacred tongue to urge adoration of the Greeks and their Gods. In such poems as "In the Presence of the Statue of Apollo," Tschernichowsky urges fellow Jews to remove themselves from the ethos of the Talmudic study hall and embrace that of attention to physical beauty and prowess. It was a message to change values and norms. In the terminology of Max Nordau (1849–1923), yet another assimilated Jewish writer born in Budapest, Jews should become muscular Jews (*muskeljüden*). The adulation of the physical rather than merely the spiritual affirmed the need for action by the self-reliant. This idea is further discussed in chapter 10. Suffice here to note that Hebrew literature at the turn of the century and beyond valorizes youth as the typical hero. The message is that young Jews should choose their destiny; the future of the Jewish people as a whole is in their hands.

The history and literature of the Zionist movement is vast, and open to extensive analysis and categorization. The challenge of doing so has engaged many learned and sophisticated scholars. For our purposes, it may be more useful and effective to delineate where the extended discourse and disputation of Zionists inevitably led. That is, Zionism was at its core dedicated to transforming Jews through education and resettling them on the land of their ancestors. Both purposes were interrelated. A "new Jew" was necessary to meet the challenge of transferring Jews back to the homeland. Here we deal with aspects of educating the new Jew. In the subsequent chapter, we discuss the actual settlement experience.

EDUCATING NEW JEWS

For the past two centuries, Jews have been engaged in the challenge of fully embracing and integrating Western culture into their own civilization. Western ideals and governance are also at the core of the Zionist project, the creation of a Jewish state. The transformation of a religious culture is a phenomenon understood in the West, where Christianity underwent such a process over an extended period beginning with at least the Renaissance. There were bloody and extended wars of religion between parts of Europe and within states and polities. These conflicts were worked out by the eighteenth and certainly nineteenth century, when the Enlightenment continued with the process of transforming European civilization. Tensions with religion have remained, but the ground rules of interaction between the secular and modern with the religious and the traditional have been largely resolved. It is out of this tumultuous experience, although nonviolent in the Jewish case, that Zionism emerged. It was in this crucible that Zionism met the difficult and often contradictory challenge of reshaping the Jewish past to meet the present.

The movement toward a secular nationality found clear expression in the new Paideia or educational ideology invented by Zionism. The process began in Europe among those who shared in the Jewish enlightenment and had become convinced that a new type of Jew was necessary. In many ways, this was similar to the discussions found in many national movements and in new states. Idealized Germans, Americans, and Soviets have been part of the essential elements of building modern nationalities since Napoleon undertook to establish a national educational system at the beginning of the nineteenth century. In the case of Zionism, shaping the new Jew revealed fundamental tensions in fashioning a national secular culture rooted in actually living again in the homeland rather than maintaining a traditional, religious, national culture adapted for a people enduring in ever-changing dispersion.

From the outset, the central problem for secular Zionist educators has been how to provide Jewish children in a Jewish society with a Jewish education. They wanted Zionism's children, immigrants and native-born, both to be loyal citizens deeply rooted in their new country and at the same time to recognize and maintain ties with world Jewry and to a culture that they believed Jews throughout the world share. These distinct aims are in some ways difficult to reconcile and raised novel and unexpectedly difficult issues. They emerged with particularly great force after the establishment of Israel, when Zionist educators had full control over the state system and a significant budget to implement their ideas.

Zalman Aranne, Israel's minister of education for most of the crucial, formative, postindependence generation, succinctly articulated the dilemmas facing the Jewish state at a session of the Knesset (Israel's Parliament) in 1959 in what has become a classic formulation:

> The national school in this country has had to contend with a number of educational contradictions since its very beginning. How to educate youngsters here for loyalty to the Jewish people when the overwhelming majority of the Jews are in other places? How to implant in youngsters here a feeling of being part of Jewish history when half of that history took place outside the land of Israel? How to inculcate Jewish consciousness in Israeli youth when Israeli consciousness and the revolution it demanded denies the legitimacy of exile and dispersion? How to educate Israeli youth who receive their education in a non-religious school to appreciate the cultural heritage of the Jewish people which for most of its time has been suffused with religion? (1959)

Aranne was more successful in defining the problems than in gaining assent for proposed solutions. In this he was not alone, for all secularized Zionists had tried to square a by-then-familiar circle. How does one create a secular national culture for citizens of a modern state out of a religious national culture developed over centuries by a dispersed people? This challenge continues to vex reflective Israelis. Some issues and concerns are shared with Diaspora Jewry. They, too, contend with educating a modern people that is increasingly removed from a shared, religiously anchored culture and commited to non-Jewish, secular nationalisms. (See chapter 7.)

Zionism's relation to Europe is crucial to understanding the nature of the dilemma. At least until twenty years into the establishment of the state, nearly all who had authority in shaping Israel's schools were born and educated in Europe, and their traditional Jewish schooling as well as their secular learning were European. Both Ben-Zion Dinur and Zalman Aranne, the ministers of education who presided over and contributed most to charting education during Israel's first two decades, acquired their schooling in the yeshiva (the traditional Talmud-based academy) and their professional training in universities or technical schools.

They are representative of the generation that immigrated to Palestine primarily from Eastern Europe in the decades before and after World War I. They left Europe when they were in their twenties, steeped in ideologies highly critical of the traditional Jewish society in which they were raised and anxious to draw on the best of European culture. They became leaders and innovators in a new land where the traditional authorities such as parents, rabbis, and the community were absent or exercised far less control on thought and behavior. Unlike immigrants to other lands, they did not contend with the problems of assimilation to a host culture. The Arab Middle East had little to offer. Given their European orientation, Zionists found little in the Arab world that could serve as a basis for building a politically and economically progressive society. Moreover, Muslim society rejected Jews, relegating them to a separate and secondary status. In this circumstance, it was natural that in realizing the avowed purpose of creating a new and independent society, Zionists would imagine a revolutionary *Bildung* as fundamental to their program. Thus, by explicit declaration and actual practice, Zionism was an educational movement.

Yet in their deliberations and debates, the men and women responsible for planning a curriculum for the young citizens of the new society expressed an abiding sense that there could be no complete rejection of Jewish life in Europe. Something had to be retrieved from the culture they had known, something of value, which could and should be mixed with new elements in order to create the new individual and a new society. There was, as Aranne's statement indicates, a large measure of paradox and contradiction in their efforts. The chemistry in achieving the appropriate formula of revolt and preservation was complex and often experimental. Contemporary successors, more than half a century after the establishment of the state, are still racked by doubt and dissension in determining what can be maintained from Jewry's European past and how it can be refashioned in Israel's schools.

The experience in negotiating what to extract was extraordinarily rich. Unlike many other theories of what Jewish life could or should be in the modern age, Zionism was able to institutionalize ideas from its earliest years in Palestine. By the time of Israel's independence, there was a significant history in institution building. Next to settling the land and more than even defense, schooling accounted for the largest segment of the Jewish prestate settlement's expenditures, and it continued to attract a large part of Israel's budget. This investment commanded the attention of political and intellectual leaders as well as the powerful lobby of unions representing teachers and writers.

The locus of most extreme innovation was to be found in the liberal or bourgeois schools, in those schools sponsored by labor Zionism during the Yishuv, and in the amalgamation of these two streams after independence. From at least the 1920s through the present, these schools instructed no less than three-fourths of the children in Zionist society and have become in the course of this century the largest Jewish school system ever established. The divides described by Aranne in 1959 still plague Israelis today. There continue to be difficulties in devising a curriculum that will at the same time define and transmit an agreed Jewish character of Israel, engender loyalty to the state, and provide a firm basis for cohesion with world Jewry. These problems are inherent in the secularity of Israeli education and in the Zionist movement.

The substitution of a religious national tradition by a secular national one is manifest in curricula as a reinterpretation or suppression of traditional texts and the invention of new ones. The place of the central text of traditional Jewish life throughout the European Diaspora—the oral law as expressed in the Talmud and rabbinic literature—was diminished. Instead the Bible became the central text of modern secular Jewish culture, and it is read as a historical and ethical document with a humanistic rather than a theological orientation.

The introduction of Hebrew rather than Yiddish as the language of instruction throughout the entire curriculum changed the status of what had been a sacred language (*lashon hakodesh*), and the use of modern Hebrew literature and Jewish history as moral and political instruments reinforced the role of the people in shaping Jewish culture. Historicism similarly influenced the approach to the study of the Bible and the ancient periods of Jewish history through the present in a radical conception of human affairs. That is, the presence of God was removed from an active role in Jewish history even as he receded from Bible and other writings previously considered sacred. The direction was humanistic in the fundamental sense of that term. It centered on the individual Jew and the Jewish people united in polity.

In addition to obvious roots in European culture, Zionist humanism was the conscious response to a dangerous reality. In the face of rising hostility toward Jews on the continent and with no expectation of divine intervention on their behalf, Jewish passivity had to be brought to an end. Secular Zionists claimed that Jews had to reinsert themselves as actors in history by coping directly with their problems. Leaving Europe for Palestine was essential, and many did, particularly Russian Jews before WWI and the Russian Revolution, Polish Jews in the 1920s, and Central European Jews with the rise of the Nazis in the 1930s. This emigration was but a first step toward forging a new national character.

Several illustrations drawn from the Israeli national curriculum formulated during the first decade of independence under the rubric of "Jewish Consciousness" convey the Bildung Zionism imagined. Moreover, comparison of the curriculum for the secular public schools (*mamlachti*) with that of the religious public schools (*mamlachti dati*) indicates the character and direction of the Zionist educational program when free to develop on its own. Both offered courses in the sciences and modern languages. Both streams offered the same Jewish subjects—Talmud, Bible, Hebrew language and literature, and Jewish history—but in different proportions and emphases. The degree of radicalism in the secular Zionist approaches to past and the future is clearly revealed by its revolutionary treatment of subject matter that only superficially appears similar in both school systems. The implications of this discussion clearly extend far beyond the school and essentially define the intentions of the Zionist revolution.

NEW TEXTS FOR A USABLE PAST: TALMUD, BIBLE, LITERATURE, HISTORIES

The gulf between secular Zionist and religious Zionist education is striking in the treatment of the Talmud or oral law, the essential core of Jewish education for well over a millennium. The 1957 curriculum for Zionist religious high schools retained the traditional rationale that had been in place for generations of Jews. Official guidelines stated that it was to "deeply involve the student with the appreciation that the oral law is an integral part of the Torah which has been given by the Almighty so that the student may perceive it as a base for personal conduct and observance of rituals" (Ministry of Education, *Curriculum*, preface).

Moreover, students were enjoined to appreciate the role of the rabbis of the Talmud and their successors in understanding oral law "through the generations." Aside from civil jurisprudence, the Talmudic tractates selected deal with religious law, regulations, and ritual. That is, the focus was on holidays, prayers, and the conduct of family and daily life.

In the secular high schools, the Talmud was studied as a historical document. Here official guidelines enjoined presenting Talmud "in the context
of the continuity of original Jewish creativity by studying typical portions"
of the text (Ibid.). The materials chosen for secular high schools consisted
largely of segments relating to civil jurisprudence (*nezikin*), particularly laws
of liability and workers' rights. That is to say, the Talmud was seen as the
source of ethics that were accepted as universal by contemporary humanism, liberalism, and Labor Zionism. Moreover, the text was divorced from
divine revelation. In a tendentious display of practical theology, the ancient
rabbis had retroactively accorded the oral law status as a revealed text that
transcended time. In a radical departure from this tradition, the Talmud of
Israel's secular schools historicized the text and placed it in a specific and finite context. Students were directed to appreciate the cultural, economic,
political, and social experience of Jews who lived in Talmudic times. In this
way, the Talmud was disassociated from world of the elementary schools
and advanced Talmudic academies of the ghettos and hamlets (*shtetl*) of European Jewry. The Talmud was now to be viewed as the creation of proud
and autonomous communities in Babylonia rather than an elaboration of
God's word given at Sinai. There was still another argument for measured
doses of selected Talmudic texts in a secular curriculum. Reading the language of the rabbis could contribute to the revival of Hebrew. Knowledge
of the Talmud would enrich the vocabulary of Israeli youth with the language that had long been familiar to highly literate Jews.

Zionism's curriculum also jettisoned divine immanence from the
Bible. This new perspective had been enshrined in the opening paragraph
of the Israel's Declaration of Independence. The first sentence proclaims a
widely accepted understanding that "the Land of Israel was the birthplace
of the Jewish people"; the last sentence of the paragraph says, "Here they
wrote and gave the Bible to the world." As stated at the beginning of this
chapter, this revolutionary claim to human authorship dramatically and decisively overturns the principle, adhered to for more than three millennia,
that God gave the Torah to Moses and the Jewish people.

In the secular schools, students examined "the world of the Bible,"
delving into the economic, cultural, and social life of their predecessors, the
ancient Israelites. There was also a patent attempt to employ Bible study to
advance contemporary Zionist ideology. For example, the ancient Hebrew
kingdoms were referred to as "the state" (*ha-medinah*), even though the idea
of the state was not a construct that existed in the ancient past. Selected
texts also served as precedents validating contemporary events and policies

and even a guide for future action. Again, for example, the prominence accorded the Book of Joshua stems from casting the possession of the homeland in the twentieth century as a reenactment of an earlier generation reclaiming the promised land after the long sojourn in Egypt.

Other links of the ancient Israelite past to the present were intended to highlight the unique place of Israel among the nations; to enhance student knowledge of the Hebrew language; to acquaint Israeli children with the fauna, flora, and landscape of the country; and to induce a sense of rootedness in the old/new homeland. On the other hand, traditional study of rabbinic commentaries as aids to understanding the Bible was more or less excised from the secular curriculum. When quoted, it was to clarify the language of the Bible rather than valorize rabbinic legends about biblical persons or event.

As in the case of culling useful texts from the Talmud, the secular curriculum removed portions dealing with rituals and ceremonies associated with religious worship. Leviticus, a text that deals largely with the priestly code and rituals, was thereby nearly excised from the curriculum. Secular schools retained only those few sections that deal with celebrating the sabbatical and jubilee years and similar topics that could be interpreted, by modern Israelis, as ethical legislation protecting the rights of workers. The study of the Bible thereby corresponded to that of the Talmud in which similar sections from the tractate of civil jurisprudence were selected.

At the end of the 1950s, there was a heated and extensive discussion in the Knesset subcommittee on education over whether to include the Siddur or prayer book, perhaps the most universal and ubiquitous text in the history of the Jewish people aside from the Bible. Opinion was divided over whether it could be made a proper part of the literature curriculum. Some urged its incorporation for its aesthetic, linguistic, and historic value, arguing that it could be presented without theological reference and without imposing or even implying worship, the obvious purpose of a prayer book. Others rejected these claims, denying the possibility of making such distinctions. They found the book too closely associated with the traditions of the world they rejected. Apparently, they believed that while God's agency could be successfully removed from the study of the Bible, it could not be removed from the Siddur. Although it was often part of the curriculum in the prestate schools, it was no longer taught by the end of the first decade of independence. The result is that in Israel, generations of youth are educated in avowedly Jewish schools but without knowledge of the Siddur and synagogue rituals.

There was also debate over new topics that were not part of the traditional Jewish curriculum in Europe, namely Hebrew literature and history. In Europe, one became acquainted with these subjects outside a formal educational setting. Indeed, there was something subversive about delving into texts and narratives that were not strictly of religious significance. They offered European Jewish youth radically new options and were major sources of criticism of contemporaneous Jewish society. In the Yishuv and Israel, Zionist educators institutionalized Hebrew literature and Jewish history as central and essential components of the curriculum.

The guidelines for Hebrew literature typically began by indicating what the study of literature was not to include. It was not to engage in literary analysis or teach aesthetics and theory. The study of literature was to direct the students to the historical, social, and linguistic value of texts. It was, in effect, a complement to the study of history. Both history and Hebrew literature could be surveyed to analyze the shortcomings of Jewish life in Europe and the possibilities of new life in the Land of Israel. A national literature and a national history would be shaped by authors and professional historians and then transmitted by teachers in the schools. It was hoped, indeed assumed, that these texts and the narratives they promoted would imbue youth with both loyalty to the nation and an appreciation of its experiences and its goals. Above all, it would encourage them to become participants of the Jewish people in the homeland.

The literary curriculum composed a canon that was designed to realize these goals. Although it began with the Hebrew literature of the Middle Ages, it concentrated largely on the contemporary. It contained poetry, fiction, and essays including some by living authors such as Shmuel Agnon, the historian Ben-Zion Dinur, and even David Ben-Gurion. The line between art and politics was thin and permeable. Students also read translated texts from world literature, which actually meant Western literature. Classic works from the neighboring Islamic culture or more distant, non-European ones were not part of the curriculum. The list contains readings from Greek classics to Russian, French, and German literature of the past two centuries, much like familiar humanities courses taught in the United States before the advent of multiculturalism widened the choice of offerings. English classics were read in English. In sum, the curriculum was that of an enlightened European. This portion of the emigrants' European heritage was transferred intact. Throughout, there was a keen appreciation that literature served culture by reflecting its ideals, exposing its problems, and offering correctives. The study of non-Hebrew literature was intended to nurture social and political sensibilities. Finally, there was the manifest message that great literature, Hebrew and European, should express itself in the cultural experience of the nation.

The history curriculum had similar objectives. As many scholars have noted, history became the handmaiden of modern secular nationalisms during the nineteenth century. Zionist historiography emerged from this context. This is clearly attested in the introductions to texts and curricular guides. For example, in the guide for Jewish history produced by Aranne's ministry, the stated purpose for teaching history is "to instill in the heart of youth a national Jewish consciousness, to strengthen in them a sense for the common fate and destiny of all Jews, and to plant in their heart a love of the Jewish people in their land and throughout the world and make firm their bonds to Jews everywhere" (Ministry of Education, *History*, preface, 1957). In addition to this general commitment to Jews everywhere, students were enjoined to recognize the particular importance of the State of Israel "so that they may ensure its biological continuity and the continued historic existence of the Jewish people." The crucial objective was to instill "the feeling of personal responsibility for establishing the state and developing it." Some versions went so far as to suggest to the students that they be willing to sacrifice themselves for the state.

Religious Zionist educators could not accept this exclusive emphasis on the role of the people for shaping their own destiny. Guides to similar texts in religious Zionist schools pointed out that the object of the study of Jewish history was "to nurture the point of view that, at the root of human history and especially the history of the Jewish people, the hand of divine providence is at work and that the Almighty provides special guidance to the path of national life" (Ibid.). Moreover, they maintained that historical study must be suffused with a sense of God's involvement in human affairs.

Rejecting the notion that God would intervene on behalf of his people at a moment of his choosing, the secular curriculum criticized traditional Jewish passivity in the face of danger. The European Middle Ages, in which Jews suffered from widespread persecution, were subject to particularly negative attention. The same criticism was applied to recent Eastern European experience. The abject misery of Polish and Russian Jewry was vividly described in detail. Only the celebratory history of Zionist pioneering was given greater analysis and studied in more depth. In effect, secular Zionism created a sustained and comprehensive worldview in which its leaders and adherents were the central actors. In this context, they rejected "the world of their fathers," that is, the nostalgic European past that contemporary ex-European Jews were celebrating at the same time in America. They repudiated its formal religiosity; its understanding of itself and its place in history; and its language, rituals, and many of its values and customs. And they tried to replace all these by refocusing Jewish life in a secular national mode. Ultimately, there is a message of hope in this new narrative of Jewish experience. Jewish creativity did not end with writing the Bible. Through a revitalized national existence, possible only in the homeland, could a reconstituted Jewish people establish a culture that assimilates enlightened European values with a distinctive Jewish tradition and perspective. In sum, national cultural creativity was renewable.

INTERNAL TENSIONS IN THE ZIONIST BILDUNG

The irony and dilemma of secular Zionism is that it may have succeeded too well in disseminating criticism of Diaspora Jewry and their culture. The minutes of the meetings during Aranne's ministry are replete with criticism over what has been done and how to effect change. There is a deep sense that an unsuitable curriculum might have already engendered alienation and conscious separation from essential cultural resources and even attenuated identification with other parts of the nation. That was hardly the intention of Zionist educators. Nevertheless, they could not square the circle or admit reverence and authority for postbiblical texts that were no longer endowed with sacredness. They found it difficult to maintain lines between what was to be rejected and what should be maintained.

These difficulties were already foreseen among Zionist theoreticians in Europe. Ahad Ha'am (1856–1927), the leading proponent of a secular Jewish nationalism, sensed these problems a century ago. His 1898 essay, "The Transvaluation of Values" (*Umwertung aller Werte*), a study of the dangerous attractions of Nietzsche's philosophy to rebellious Jewish youth, is perhaps prophetic. In it, he urges youth not to abandon the moral traditions of the Jewish people and warns that a search for mastery over circumstances and an embrace of the unrestrained activism of the "Superman" (*Ubermensch*) would be disastrous. For example, the "call for the strong arm and the power and value of force . . . as opposed to the power of morality and righteousness" would result in emulating the "the fair beast" (*die blonde Bestie*). He exhorts against a flight from inherited culture, even as he advocates its transformation through secularization. This concern echoes in the writings of his disciples in prestate Israel. Inappropriate alien models could result in the corruption of Jewish youth. Indiscriminate change from known paths could produce unpredictable trajectories.

Using new methods to study familiar texts could also be dangerous. When he visited the new Herzliyah High School, the first modern secondary school established in the Yishuv in 1905, he realized that the new methodology for Bible instruction distorted the traditional reading of the text. Here and elsewhere, he expostulated on the need to secularize and modernize but, at the same time, to respect received texts. Once the authority of traditional methods and interpretations was questioned, there was no assurance that novel methods of interrogating the text would generate improved understandings and appreciation of common concerns.

Unease over unexpected and uncontrolled consequences became a constant undercurrent in a movement dedicated to radical change. According to the recent study by the anthropologist Tamar Katriel, beginning in the 1930s, the "sabra" or native-born youth are described as "speaking *dughri.*" That is, immigrant pioneers described the sabra as excessively direct, if not confrontational. These new Jews were unlike their Zionist fathers. Their discourse lacked niceties, refinements, and learning. Their actions were guided by pragmatism rather than realism. As far as leading secular educators were concerned, sabras had distanced themselves too far from the culture of their parents. The term *dughri* is borrowed from an Arabic word that means "straight" and "direct," as if to emphasize linguistically the distance between outlooks forged in tradition-bound Europe and those hammered on the anvil of settling the land in a changing Near East.

It is interesting to compare the emergence of the dughri sabra with the new American described in Emerson's famous essay, "The American Scholar." In both societies, the children of European colonists developed into a cultural type that was distinct from European origins. Both the new American and the new Jew had freed themselves from the culture of their ancestors and become authentically rooted in a new land while acquiring new national characteristics. A significant difference is that Emerson's forebears had been in America for nearly two centuries. Emerson himself was already an American, and it was perhaps natural for him to identify with and extol the local product of a new, national culture. For Emerson, Europe was a distant memory and foreign reality whose authority had undergone a long process of erosion. For Zionist theoreticians and educators, the European experience was still an integral part of their being. They were discomfited when they saw sabras dismiss as irrelevant a heritage they still believed contained a usable past.

Already in the generation prior to independence, the youthful "products" of Zionist education caused doubt, regret, and concern. Bialik, for

example, stood at the head of the Writers Association in 1932 in the presence of politicians, intellectuals, and hundreds of Tel Aviv's citizens in a
staged Trial of the Youth. It was an event that brought to public attention
the hopes and the shortcoming of Zionist education. Similar doubts aggravated educators during the 1950s. Israeli youth were only minimally connected to Diaspora Jewry and appeared indifferent to and ignorant of their
common cultural heritage. In the pungent dictum of Joseph Klausner, a
leading scholar of the old generation, they were "Hebrew-speaking gentiles." Reconnecting youth to their heritage thus became the centerpiece of
a national program designated "Jewish consciousness" and curricular reform
discussed earlier. This reform has also been questioned, producing in the
1990s a contemporary version of the postindependence reforms. It is already likely that this reform will also require correction. Zionist educators
apparently face an enduring dilemma in educating Jews for a Jewish state. It
has been very difficult to find a satisfying and successful formula for transforming Jews while retaining what is valuable in traditional culture. This
challenge, nevertheless, is fundamental to Zionist ideology. It is an inevitable and conscious choice that has little prospect of being resolved in
the future. Moreover, we know with the certainty of retrospect that to have
remained culturally and geographically immobilized would have had even
worse, actually disastrous, consequences.

NEW HEROES FOR NEW JEWS

The education of new Jews was carried beyond the classroom into the public square as Zionist society used interpretations of the past to create a new
future. The means employed were many as Zionist art and politics constructed public rituals, ceremonies, holidays, and monuments. In its use of
the public square, Jews emulated what they had witnessed in Europe. The
materials with which they worked were local, focusing on the Jewish experience in Eretz Israel, although there was one major exception: European
Jewry in the Holocaust. That is, they looked on and under the soil of the
homeland for indications from the Jewish past that could have relevance for
the present. In this investigation, the search for heroes was crucial. Some
were victors who had successfully proven themselves in the face of challenges to the Jewish people. Others had ostensibly failed but in their defeat
had demonstrated qualities of character that had merit and could inspire the
present.

The identification of heroes through reinterpretation of the past began in Europe during Zionism's first generation. Locating Jews who could
fight and take care of themselves was the prime area of focus. Such heroes
did not exist in the long history of the Diaspora, where Jews were notably
absent from the ranks of the military of the societies in which they had
lived. Jews could be found again in the ranks of armies of modern European states that included Jews as citizens. Therefore, it would be only toward the end of the nineteenth century and through World War I that significant numbers of Jews became soldiers across Europe. Ironically, Captain
Dreyfus of the French army was one of them. By the first decade of the
twentieth century, after a generation of pioneering, the first soldier-pio-
neers also emerged in the Yishuv as settlers who organized themselves in
the face of marauding beduins. By the 1920s, these early efforts at self-de-
fense produced the Haganah ("defense"), the militia that became the Israeli
army upon the establishment of the state.

Heroes were, of course, found in the Bible when Jews had sovereignty
and fought to preserve it. One interesting example is the changing image of
David. Were a child asked to draw a picture of David during the Middle
Ages, he probably would have produced a picture of a young man with a
lyre, representing the composer of Psalms who wrote songs of praise to the
Lord and his wondrous creation. In the twentieth century, a child of the
Yishuv and Israel might be more likely to produce the protagonist of Goliath and a successful guerrilla war leader who led his band to victory against
persecutors as he created his kingdom. There were also heroes after the biblical period, preeminently the Maccabees.

MACCABEES AND HANUKKAH

The idealization of the Maccabees began in Europe at the end of the nineteenth century with Zionists organizing into associations that bore that
name. *Maccabee* was initially the additional name given to Judah, the son of
the High Priest Mattathias, who was the leader of the revolt against the Syr-
ian-based Greek rulers of Eretz Israel in the second century B.C.E. The
name *Maccabee* was then extended to include the Hasmonean dynasty as a
whole. In Jewish religious tradition, the name was an acrostic whose letters
stood for, "Who is like You Lord among the gods." *Maccabee* could also
mean "hammer." It is this second meaning—the hero who strikes at the enemies of the nation—that captures the way in which the Maccabees came
to be appreciated by Zionists. Here, too, they preferred the historically useful to the theological.

An early and direct way in which this ideal was propagated was through youth movements. By the 1880s, Jewish youth in European universities, often excluded from student associations or fraternities because of ethnicity and religion, modeled their own associations on the closed fraternities. This included an interest in asserting virility through the practice of fencing and gymnastics. This movement spread beyond the university, where groups assumed names that spoke to the search for manliness and power. In addition to Maccabee, such groups called themselves "Ha-koah" (strength), "Bar-Kochba" (the heroic rabbi who lead a rebellion against the Romans in 132–135 C.E.), or "Betar" (the name of the fortress where Bar Kochba fell in 135 C.E. as well as the acronym for "Covenant of Trumpeldor," an early Zionist military figure who fell fighting Arabs). At the second Zionist Congress in 1898, Nordau gave voice to this movement in reminding the audience that "nature has endowed us with the spiritual qualities required for athletic achievements of an extraordinary quality. All we lack is muscle. . . . The more Jews achieve in the various branches of sport, the greater will be their self-confidence and self-respect."

The Hasmonean legacy was naturally appropriated in athletic competitions. In 1921, at the time of the twelfth Zionist Congress, the Maccabee World Union was formed. It was the successor umbrella organization to a host of sporting clubs organized throughout Europe since the end of the nineteenth century. Although ostensibly nonparty affiliated, it always maintained strong connections to the Zionist movement and formally joined it in the 1970s. The major purpose of the organization was the Maccabia, or the Jewish equivalent to the Olympics that brought Jewish youth to Palestine for a wide array of sporting events. The message was always clear. In the absence of a recognized conventional state, Jews could congregate in Palestine for national events including sporting competitions. The objective was not only demonstrating Jewish revival through the exhibition of modern "muscular Jews," it offered opportunities for social contact and advancing the national political agenda.

Invoking the Maccabees extended beyond the university into mainstream Zionist organizations as the Order of Ancient Maccabeans. First established in 1891 by members of Hovevei-Zion who emigrated to London from Eastern Europe, it soon attracted members from the elite of British Jewry including Israel Zangwill, Herbert Bentwich, and later Chaim Weizmann. Even before Herzl visited Palestine, it organized a "Maccabean pilgrimage," or what present-day Jews would call a "mission" to inspect the country and inquire what might be done to further its settlement. Subsequently, members collected funds to purchase land for Jewish colonization in the tradition of Hovevei-Zion and the Zionist Organization.

The invocation of the Maccabean experience was nowhere more evident than through the reimagination of the ancient festival of Hanukkah, which Zionists appropriated for a significant place within their public rituals. This eight-day "festival of lights" has its origins in the celebration of the purification of the temple in Jerusalem after contamination by Greek rulers who employed it for the worship of idols. Hanukkah means literally "dedication." Over the centuries, the focus for religious observance was in recalling the rededication of the temple by lighting a small amount of oil in the eight-stem candelabra that miraculously lasted for eight days. Zionism emphasized other aspects of those distant heroic events. It became the festival of the military miracle of "the few against the many," thereby emphasizing the courage of Jews in resisting the superior forces of Antiochus Epiphanes in the cause of national liberation in 164 B.C.E. This subsequent seventy years of the Hasmonean (Maccabean) dynasty came to be considered the most glorious since the first temple prior to its destruction in 586 B.C.E. and until the restoration of Jewish sovereignty in 1948.

From the first groups of pioneers in the 1880s, the example of the Maccabees was celebrated in song and public celebration. In Eretz Israel, these rituals, including relay races, often with torches, set out from Modi'in, the birthplace of the Maccabees. Throughout the rhetoric and rituals there was a significant new nuance that was captured by a song transferred by settlers to Palestine and usually sung as a round: "Who can speak [*mi yimalel*] of the heroic deeds of Israel; who can count them; for in each generation there shall arise the hero, the redeemer of the people." In fact, this was a corruption of verses from the Book of Pslams, chapter 102, verse 2, and from chapter 120. In the original, the "hero" is none other than the Almighty. It is in him that people are to place their trust, for it is through him that the Psalms promise that oppression and sufferings of the Jews will end. As we have repeatedly seen, from its very beginnings, Zionism replaced divine intervention with human heroes who would accomplish what previous generations believed required divine agency.

Many other popular songs conveyed this message directly and dramatically. For example, generations of Israeli youth learned in their kindergartens to march to "We carry torches" (*Anu nosim lapidim*): "We carry torches on dark nights / Lighting up the paths beneath our feet. . . . A miracle also happened to us / we did not find the canister of oil. . . . we went to the valley [of Jezreel, the site of pioneering farming settlements] and climbed the mountain where we found the wells of hidden light / A miracle did not happen to us, a canister of oil we did not find / We quarried in the rock till we bled, and there was light!" The miracle of light was to be found in the toil of the pioneers on the land rather than in the ritual lamps of the temple in Jerusalem.

Another example is "The Days of Hanukkah" (*Yemei ha-Hannukah*), a song that concludes with the phrase: "on the miracles and wondrous deeds that the Maccabees wrought." Again, it is people who make miracles, not an external force. The break with tradition was intentional, and the contrast could not be sharper. By contrast, the familiar Haggadah, or the book read at the Passover seder meal, celebrates only God as redeemer of his people from oppression in Egypt. There is no direct reference to his human agent, Moses. In Zionism's reconstituted Hanukkah, modern Hebrews imagine replicating the heroics of their Hasmonean ancestors without reference to divine intervention.

FALLEN HEROES: TRAGEDY AT MASADA

In the Zionist pantheon of ancient heroes, the perceived passivity of European Jews was so extreme that even those who took their own lives in failed but heroic defense were worthy of celebration. This was the final drama in the fall of Masada, a promontory in the area of the Dead Sea where Jews succumbed to a Roman siege in 74 C.E.

After the destruction of the Second Temple in 70 C.E., a group appropriately called the Zealots (*kanaiim*) continued to fight Rome. A surviving group of about one thousand retreated from Jerusalem to the fortress of Masada in a forbidding area near the Dead Sea where they held out against Rome's Tenth Legion for nearly three years. It took so long to overcome the Zealots because of their determination and the nature of the site. Masada, a complex of fortified walls, palaces, and other public buildings largely built by Herod, caps a formidable rock mountain that exposes the vulnerability of potential attackers. For three years, the Romans honed their weapons and built a ramp from surrounding sand and rock that lead up the mountain to overcome its sheer walls and enabled the use of weapons to break the defenses of the Zealots. The persistence of the Roman Empire in relentlessly pursuing a relatively insignificant number of Jews in such a remote area is almost as remarkable as the decision taken by the defenders to fight to the end in the face of certain defeat.

As reported by Flavius Josephus, a Jewish historian of that period, the Zealot leader, Elazar ben Yair, justified the decision for mass suicide in the following speech: "Since we long ago resolved never to be servants to the Romans, nor to any other than to God Himself . . . the time is now come that obliges us to make that resolution true in practice. . . . We were the very first that revolted [against Rome], and we are the last to fight against them; and I cannot but esteem it as a favor that God has granted us, that it is still in our power to die bravely, and in a state of freedom" (*The Jewish War*, bk. 7, ch. 8). After the oration, the men killed their wives and children, and then each other. They also destroyed their possessions except for food as testimony that "we were not subdued for want of necessities; but that, according to our original resolution, we have preferred death before slavery." With this, a rebellion that lasted nearly seventy years was terminated. Jewish independence was at an end, and Judea was to become Palestine as a punishment by the Romans who insisted on extirpating signs of the Jewish presence in the country.

This episode was long forgotten. Indeed, it was ignored by the rabbis and not mentioned in the Talmud. It is possible that the rabbis, after the destruction of the temple, wanted to demonstrate that Judaism could survive without land and sovereignty. They were engaged in reframing Judaism into a national religious culture that could survive until exile was terminated. They were apparently uninterested in glorifying Jews who were willing to die because they believed that national life without freedom and sovereignty was not worth living. This was the wrong kind of heroism. Out of the fall of Jerusalem, the rabbis emphasized the story of scholars who escaped the city through subterfuge to establish a Talmudic academy at Yavneh on the coastal plain. For the rabbis of the Talmud, the study of Torah guaranteed the future of the Jewish people. On the other hand, the story of Jewish resistance at Masada became for Zionism the source for one of the most prominent and oft-repeated refrains since the 1920s: "Never again shall Masada fall."

The emergence of Masada in the Zionist narrative began with the publication in 1927 of an epic poem by Yitzhak Lamdan. This work followed a 1923 translation into Hebrew of Flavius Josephus's *The Jewish War* that described the revolt against the Romans. Masada became within a few years an immediate part of the "usable past" that Zionists employed in constructing an explanation of themselves. In the face of the actual dangers of the Europe they left behind and the growing threats in the country to which they came, it was essential to strengthen the resolve of pioneers by appeals to ancestors who faced extreme dangers.

Lamdan's poem became a rallying point for expressing Jewish determination. He did not present an exact replication of the historical event. This was just as well, since in the course of the scientific analysis, both of Josephus's texts and of the archeological work undertaken by Yigal Yadin and others at the beginning of the 1960s, there would be considerable debate about what really happened at Masada and whether Yadin had consciously manipulated the account. Moreover, some would object to the celebration of suicide by fellow Jews, including Ben-Gurion. Yet there were elements in this story that have spoken to generations of Israelis.

Lamdan's Masada was immediately understood as more than a specific location. It was taken to be a metaphor for Zion, that is, all of Eretz Israel. For a still-modest community of settlers, Lamdan offered protest against the past and present: "Against the hostile Fate of generations / an antagonistic breast is bared with a roar / Enough! You or I / Here will the battle decide the final judgment!" (271). The poem ultimately does not advocate or celebrate suicide. Rather, it urges determination and courage in the face of situations that offer few if any alternatives. The maxim "never again" that was to be espoused after the Holocaust fit well within received Zionist ideology and current circumstances. For a people returning to their homeland the poem offered a rallying point in expressing their resolve to hold on to what they considered theirs and to reestablish continuity with their past: "Let us roar with a new and last roar of the beginning! Be strong, be strong, and we shall be strengthened!" Thus, rather than a paean to pessimism and despair, Masada could be understood as a message of determination and hope.

Since independence, the use of Masada has become entrenched and elaborated. After climbing up a difficult path to the mountain's top, soldiers have taken their oath of service as the dawn breaks over the Dead Sea with the refrain that "Masada shall not fall again." Youth groups hike across the desert to take the same path up the mountain to conduct their own ceremonies; tourists can now ascend via cable car to visit the site where they, too, are invited to reflect on Jewish heroism and Roman obstinacy in pursuing their victims. Over the years, Masada has become a site for pilgrimage even as pilgrimage to Jerusalem had been for the festivals of Tabernacles, Passover, and Pentecost. The transformation of Masada began in the 1930s with Hanukkah as a favorite season for the ascent. The fact that Hanukkah lasts for eight days has made it particularly useful for youth groups and even school excursions. In all these ways, Masada has served countless Israelis as a means for commemorating an ancient struggle for independence and identifying with the present conflict.

The mixing of sacred rites with secular rituals permeates Masada's contemporary usage. Foreign Jewish youth not only take part in the traditional climb and ceremonies but even perform bar mitzvah rites there. This kind of amalgamation may have been initiated by Yigael Yadin, the archeologist most associated with systematically studying the site. In the 1960s, he uncovered two ritual baths and a synagogue used by Masada's defenders as well as twenty-five skeletons of men, women, and children. In 1969, they were reburied in a religious ceremony with full military honors. His discovery, carried out amid widespread interest in his work, involved thousands of volunteers from Israel, including the military, as well as foreign professionals and amateurs who wished to be part of the extraordinary excavations that all agreed had something important to say about Jewish experience through the ages.

The Zionist narrative of Masada has come under severe attack within Zionism as well as by Palestinian apologists. For some, like the Palestinian anthropologist Nadia El-Haj, the version of Masada depicted here is part of a massive fabrication by Zionist archeologists to create a narrative validating Jewish claims to Palestine while stripping Palestinians of theirs. This criticism is tendentious but does touch upon the likelihood of Yigael Yadin's playing loose with the real facts uncovered in relation to extant ancient texts. There are, however, agreed-upon elements in any version of the story that make Masada a topic of dispute among those who attempt to make Masada relevant for the present.

Critics generally find that the Zionist use of Masada leads to exaggerating the sense of isolation and the assertion of "no alternative" in the face of an actively hostile Arab world. This reading of Masada can create problematic parallels: While contemporary Jews may view themselves as courageous descendants of the Zealots, the PLO and Arab states may be seen as successors to the Romans with their uncompromising determination to suppress Jewish independence. Resignation to the enemy's unremitting and absolute hostility gives pause to significant numbers of Israelis, for it places beyond possibility the attempt to find a way out of the current impasse. However genuine the threats to Israel, it has been argued that Israeli reluctance to search for alternatives could ultimately lead to another Masada or, at the minimum, unnecessary conflict with the Arab world. One proponent, Yehoshafat Harkaby, termed the potentially fatal tendency to retreat into a defiantly aggressive mode rather than seek compromise and accommodation as the "Masada complex."

Masada, then, is an example of how narratives of the ancient past are central to and even define Israeli politics. It has become a litmus test on the internal dispute of how Israelis should behave in the confrontation with Arabs. It has come to reflect differing assessments on the seriousness of the threats to Jewish independence and survival and the strategies that should be adopted in the face of these dangers. Most Israelis have shied away from an extreme interpretation, preferring compromise and pragmatism in the

Arab/Israeli conflict. It is significant that Ben-Gurion did not participate in the hagiography of the Zealots and their suicide. Mainstream Zionism accepted and celebrated the story but ultimately was not paralyzed by it. In fact, Israel has not adopted passivity with regard to an implacable enemy and despaired of finding accommodation. The catastrophe at the conclusion of the Masada of the ancient past has not been taken to mean that Israel's future is also one of collective catastrophe. The dominant tradition is the one that Lamdan actually first proposed. He did not celebrate suicide. Rather, he admired courage and endurance in the face of awful choices.

THE HOLOCAUST AS NARRATIVE AND POLITICS

A dilemma of difficult and even maddening choice lay at the core of how Zionism and Israelis dealt or, perhaps, should have dealt with the Holocaust, the greatest catastrophe in modern if not all Jewish history. This event in relation to Israel has played a very significant role in the Israeli historical imagination, in the country's internal politics, and in the attitude of its Arab neighbors.

The significance of the destruction of European Jews was articulated in the country's founding moment. The Declaration of Independence devotes to the Holocaust three of the opening ten paragraphs that justify the establishment of a Jewish state. The first of these begins with a historical justification. It asserts the Holocaust "proved anew the urgency of the reestablishment of the Jewish State" in view of the tragedy that "engulfed millions of Jews in Europe" and their inability to find shelter. This is an echo of the view first expressed by Pinsker's generation and validated repeatedly thereafter as successive waves of violence and pogroms culminated in the Shoah.

The next paragraph explains, "The survivors of the European catastrophe have a right to a life of dignity, freedom and labor" but were denied that right in their exclusion from entry into Palestine. Finally, "the Jewish people in Palestine made a full contribution in the struggle of the freedom-loving nations against the Nazi evil." Jews have thereby earned a place together with "the peoples who founded the United Nations." That is, fighting as a people in the war earned Zionism the right to benefits reserved for victors. This is the first time Zionism suggested that force of arms should play a role in acquiring title to a state. Yet even here it was not a right acquired through conquest of people resident in Palestine. Rather, it was joining an alliance against an external enemy.

The messages in this three-paragraph progression are that the aggression visited on the Jewish people in the immediate present requires a response. Jews still needed to protect themselves, they were willing and competent to do so effectively, and only a state would enable them to do so. This formulation seemed so manifestly accurate and appropriate that it has been surprising that discourse about the Holocaust has occasioned such discord in Israel.

There was no question about the horrors visited on Jews. Rather, the challenge came from those who questioned the behavior of Zionist leadership during and after the war. Critics initially came from the political Right. Their attack began during the Holocaust and reached a crescendo during the first decade of independence. They accused the Zionist leadership of passivity, ineptitude, and insensitivity toward fellow Jews. They charged that the Labor party, especially Ben-Gurion and those associated with him, did not react militantly enough, and thereby many Jews unnecessarily suffered and died. Moreover, when they did act, they tended to save their own, that is, the followers of Labor Zionism. The most notorious example, it was alleged, was what occurred in Hungary near the end of the war. The right charged that the Labor Zionist leader, Rudolf Kastzner, who served on the Committee for Aid and Rescue—a Zionist organization that provided assistance for the Jews in and streaming into the country—saved his family and friends at the expense of others in what was an overall failure to do more. Between 1954 and 1958, this accusation was at the center of court proceedings that resulted in Kastzner—and, by implication, his associates—being initially found culpable. The judge asserted that Kastzner, who had negotiated with Eichmann, "sold his soul to the devil." Kastzner subsequently committed suicide, only to be exonerated by an appeals court after his death. These events convulsed Israeli society and politics.

The accusation reverberated with other attacks on the Israeli leadership. Menachem Begin, the opposition leader from Herut, the predecessor party to the contemporary Likud, condemned Ben-Gurion's decision to accept reparations from the German government. These funds were considered contaminated, in fact "blood money" that desecrated the memory of the Holocaust's victims. One large-scale demonstration against the Labor-led government smacked of an attempted putsch when Begin led his followers on a violent protest against the Knesset. This was the most serious breach of public order in the new Israeli democracy.

The bitterness of the accusation and its polarization between the Right and Left had rhetorical and policy consequences that have left their mark on Israeli public life. The rightist rhetoric suggests that there are implacable enemies who would stop at nothing to destroy Israel. In response, Jews must be certain that "never again" should such a catastrophe occur. On the policy level, given the proclamations of Arab governments and media that the Jewish state be eliminated, Arabs replaced Nazis as targets of militant opposition. When added to the power of an aggressive nationalism that informed the ideology of the Zionist Right, this became a powerful concoction. Thus, the shadow of the Holocaust infused a significant segment of Israeli life with a combative attitude that became directed against anyone who actively opposed the legitimacy of the Jewish state and the sanctuary it provided. It was in this segment of Israeli society that critics of Israeli policy toward Arabs could find an explanation for supposed belligerence that was similarly derived from misinterpretation and overuse of the "myths" of Tel Hai, Masada, and other instances of Zionist heroism.

The tendency to militancy was not the exclusive domain of the Right. Much of the Left also sought to compensate for what was then perceived as the failure of European Jews to confront the Nazis and their allies. The sense of inadequacy was perhaps inherent in the structure of Zionist ideology that since its origins favored action and denigrated passivity in the face of attacks on Jews. As such, it extended beyond ideological boundaries. As is clearly explained in the recent biography of Aharon Appelfeld, one of Israel's leading writers on the Holocaust period, survivors also felt a measure of guilt. The privileging of action and even pro-action and initiative in the face of tormentors and enemies was institutionalized into the way Israel organized in public celebration the commemoration of the Holocaust. It was termed "Holocaust and Heroism Memorial Day" (*ha-Shoah ve-ha-gevurah*), since it was necessary to emphasize that Jews were not only victims but heroes, even during the Shoah, and that they had fought the enemy in the ghettoes and forests and through joining partisan groups. There was a widespread need to create distance from the impression that all Jews had gone to their deaths "like lambs to the slaughter." When, at the public trial of Adolf Eichmann in Jerusalem in 1961, Holocaust victims publicly bore testimony for the first time, there was an outburst of sympathy and understanding for what victims and survivors had undergone. Until then, Israelis gave priority to active heroism as a modern parallel to what had transpired at Masada nearly two millennia earlier.

Bravery, courage, militancy, and self-sacrifice were the ideals that publicly permeated Israeli society, and the official and public way in which the Holocaust was associated with them encouraged these principles. It is precisely this emphasis that a more recent generation of Israelis would find so problematic, particularly after the Israeli incursion into Lebanon in 1982. Largely from the Left, and perhaps best represented in Tom Segev's widely read (in Hebrew and English) *The Seventh Million*, the old charges of the Right that the Zionist leadership had done too little during the war was added to a new charge claiming that the Zionist leadership had become excessively aggressive after the war by drawing exaggerated and misleading conclusions from the Holocaust. The scholarship on which these conclusions are drawn has proven to be flawed. Nevertheless, they reflected a general willingness, even a need, to question received narratives of the past. Four and five decades after independence, the state was still embattled and much of the promised utopianism associated with Zionism still seemed distant, if not out of reach. This required an explanation to the point of revising what had been understood about the past.

In this revisionist narrative, the victims of aggression were not only Jews but also Arabs. Israel had become belligerent and insensitive. This led to an academic and public review of the entire Arab/Israeli conflict in which all violence was measured by the standards of "just" and "necessary" wars. According to the political Left, the most serious breach of these principles was the operation undertaken under the government led by Menachem Begin and Ariel Sharon in Lebanon in 1982. Begin's tendency to continue to invoke the Shoah and the clear immanence of that experience in his thought were seen as proof of how commemoration had gone awry. Sharon, the sabra born to battle and heroics, became the extreme incarnation of ill-conceived initiative and values. From there, it became a short step to review the entire relationship between Zionism and Arabs within Israel and beyond the borders as one in which Israel was no longer a passive victim but complicit in the hostility it excited, if not responsible for it. The abuse of the Holocaust thereby fit with the misuse of Masada.

Finally, there is irony in this revisionist account. While some Israelis claim exaggerated use is made of the Holocaust in shaping national culture and politics, the Arab world has become the most significant contemporary source of Holocaust denial. For many, the Shoah did not even happen. Criticism found in the revisionist narrative is carried to a bizarre and malicious extreme in Arab anti-Zionist media: The Holocaust is an invention conjured by Zionism in order to garner sympathy for an unjust cause.

CONFLICT AND CONSENSUS

The multiplicity of meaning that Israelis take from their past can be very bewildering and contradictory. In a very real sense, this is an inevitable consequence of the humanistic moment in Zionism. For religious Zionism for which there are sacred texts that express the divine word, there can be no controversy over the word itself. There can be, and often is, dispute over the interpretation of texts. As we have seen in the discussion over the response within Judaism to the modern world and to the plight of the Jews, divisions can be extreme and conflicting. Debate over the lessons of history and what they require of men may be even more intense in a secular and humanistic culture. For secular Zionism, man is the actor in history who relies on rationality for interpreting his world. He also has texts, but they are historical and open to interpretation even as are sacred texts. The consequence is that mainstream secular Zionism is open to constant internal debate. We shall have more to say about this condition and its consequences in the Arab-Israel dispute in a further chapter. For now, it is sufficient to observe that Zionism has succeeded in sustaining a democratically forged consensus despite often-vociferous internal dissension.

Achieving compromise and accord are rooted in a history and memory of shared spiritual and cultural experience. The power of this commonality has been sufficient to overcome the tensions arising from dissent. The fundamental bonding agent was the overriding commitment to peoplehood, the idea with which we begin this chapter in describing Zionism as a quintessential national movement, originating in the ancient world and transforming itself in the modern. It was this understanding that underlay the commitment to translate the ancient biblical promise of the return of the exiles into a temporal actuality. This was accomplished by the Law of Return, one of the first acts of the Knesset that defined the new state: "Every Jew has the right to come to this country as an *oleh* [immigrant]" (July 1950). It brought to the state people who Israelis view as belonging to the Jewish nation despite apparent differences in language, geography, color of skin, historical experience, political values, present-day culture, and the multitude of characteristics that normally divide people.

It was precisely this diversity that proved so powerful in mobilizing Israeli society. Differences required a constant reaffirmation of peoplehood that was accomplished by repeatedly invoking a shared historical experience in the face of manifest differences. The curriculum we examined earlier suggests one of the ways in which this was accomplished. It was in this spirit that a state, largely established by Ashkenazi or European Jews, energetically sought to incorporate Oriental or African and Asian Jews. At present, Israeli society is investing itself in attracting and integrating Jews as distinctively different as fair-skinned European and Asian immigrants from the former Soviet Union together with dark-skinned Jews from Ethiopia. Clearly, the power of belonging to the same people and the commitments that derive from this belief enable bridging wide gulfs. National solidarity has long been a key component of Zionist ideology and praxis.

Creating a functional polity out of diversity—the Zionist version of "e pluribus unum"—has required the skills of extraordinary political leadership dedicated and able to create a functional polity that can overcome potentially destructive disparities. The problem was well understood even before statehood. By the end of the 1930s, when Zionism was preparing for a partitioned state, Ben-Gurion began to explore how to ready a people inexperienced in sovereignty with responsibility for a modern democratic state. This required searching for the instruments for the integration of a diverse people.

Perhaps the most spectacular achievement in realizing inclusion was effecting the agreement of the ultraorthodox to accept the state and live under its authority. This was accomplished by the Status Quo Agreement, signed in June 1947 by Ben-Gurion as head of the Jewish Agency Executive, together with Rabbis Y. Fishman and Y. Greenbaum, as representatives of Agudat Israel, the anti-Zionist ultraorthodox party. It was widely expected they would testify against partition before the United Nations Special Committee on Palestine and thereby oppose a Jewish state. It will be remembered that they insisted Jews should await the Messiah. Rather than theological consistency, they accepted Ben-Gurion's promise that various items on their agenda would become national policy, such as the provision of kosher food in the army and public places, the promise that the Jewish Sabbath would become a national day of rest, recognition of rabbis as authorities in areas pertaining to traditional rites of passage, and so on. This was a price that Ben-Gurion, a dedicated secularist, thought should be paid so that all Jews, even Zionism's opponents, would become party to Israel's creation and future. In effect, a social contract was made between ultraorthodox Jews and secular Zionists despite the divide between the two groups.

It is clear that Agudat Israel ultimately would want a Jewish state to be subject to the authority of Jewish law rather than the legislation of a parliament. On the other hand, secular Zionists insist on democratic institutions rather than the authority of religious law. The Status Quo Agreement has been under continual review and reinterpretation as both sides have attempted to expand or diminish it in accordance with their own interests. Nevertheless, it has largely held. Both sides recognize that neither can gain total victory, and that both must compromise to share ground that is likely to be continually contested.

Inclusion and integration gained enormous momentum after independence. Prior to the state, political parties had their own institutions from schools and newspapers to neighborhoods and even a militia. The most dangerous to state authority were the militias that operated under contending ideologies and subject to separate authorities. While not successful in removing all such divisions—most notably separate educational systems—Ben-Gurion did succeed in creating one army under the sole authority of the state. More than persuasion was necessary. In one spectacular instance, the *Altalena*, a ship operated by the right-wing Herut party and carrying badly needed arms and nearly a thousand men prepared to engage in the battle for Jerusalem, was actually sunk in June 1948 by the Haganah, the armed force loyal to Ben-Gurion and the national institutions. In relatively short order, all independent military forces of the Right and Left were disbanded. The move to establish the authority of a central government was successful and carried out under a far-reaching national ideology Ben-Gurion termed "statism" or "étatism" (*mamlakhtiyut*).

The origin of the term reveals the essence of Zionism as an ideology and praxis. It is a modern Hebrew word whose three-letter root (m-l-kh) implies "to reign" and therefore is the basis for Hebrew words such as "king" (*melekh*), "queen" (*malkah*), and "kingdom" or "monarchy" (*mamlakhah*). Unlike all of these terms, mamlakhtiyut never appears in ancient Hebrew. It is a new construct that adapts the past to the needs of the present. In this, it is but another example of what other modern national movements have done. They attempt to leap across the proximate past to ancient sources in the service of the modern state.

In this particular case, Ben-Gurion probably also drew on what he witnessed of the transformations taking place in the latter days of the Czarist Russia and the early years of the Soviet Union. As his diary and writings indicate, he was aware of and used the Russian word *gosudarstvo*, which originally means "kingdom" and was then applied to refer to "state." Mamlakhtiyut is used by Ben-Gurion as a translation of gosudarstvo in its various permutations. Many describe the attempt of the Russian/Soviet government to unify the diverse masses of an immense empire and to create a unified political-cultural, metanational entity. The concept reflects the yearning for all-inclusiveness within the new state. Although Israel cannot be compared to the enormous expanse of the Soviet Union, certainly to Ben-Gurion and the founders of Israel there were distinct echoes of similarity in their attempt to weld into a new nation immigrants from about seventy countries and a multiplicity of ideological and theological worldviews. National solidarity, cohesion, and unity were prime challenges both in the lands from which many of Israel's founders had emigrated and in the new homeland.

The ground for mamlakhtiyut had been prepared in the political culture of the Zionist movement since its beginnings. Never had any one party, even Labor, gained a majority. A system of coalition building was established that required constructing majorities through the cooperation of competing ideological parties. Zionist politics required practical accommodation and compromise to achieve democratic majorities. This was accomplished despite splintering into relatively small factions that might be necessary for forming majorities. In this system, even small groups and those in the opposition were often able to receive rewards. This in itself contributed to sustaining a bewildering multiplicity of parties. In sum, the system encouraged compliance to the "general will" through cooperation among ideologically opposing groups.

Even Labor, often considered the hegemonic force in the Zionist movement, had to prioritize. Recent scholarship has charged that the primary commitment of Labor was to nationalism rather than to socialism. One severe critic on the Left has even provocatively labeled Labor Zionism a form of "national socialism." In this view, Labor reneged on its declared obligation to build a new social order based on economic and civil equality for all, including Jews and Arabs. On the other hand, critics on the Right fault Labor with being so intent on achieving Jewish sovereignty that it accepted the partition plans for Palestine in 1937 and 1947 without Jerusalem or significant other portions of the historic homeland. Zionism's leading party practiced pragmatism rather than ideological purity. There were Jews who needed the security that only a Jewish state in the homeland could provide. That was the common denominator out of which Zionism grew and around which Labor built a succession of coalitions.

It was for this reason that it was the leader of Labor, David Ben-Gurion, who had the responsibility for finalizing Israel's Declaration of Independence and read it out after obtaining the signatures of Zionist parties of the Right and the Left as well as the communists and the ultraorthodox. The irreducible minimum to which such a diverse collection would agree is quoted at the beginning of this chapter: Israel is the homeland of the Jewish people; for it was there that their national identity was initially shaped, and it was from there that they made a lasting impact on the world through the Bible. All could also agree that it was fitting and necessary that Jews return to build a new society, however differently they imagined it should be realized.

10

RETURN, RECLAIM, RECONSTITUTE

A popular Zionist folk song proclaimed the fundamental essentials of the relation between Zionist theory and praxis: "We have come to the land to build it and to be rebuilt by it." The focus in this chapter is on three interrelated topics that were understood as implicit in this song: How Jews understood returning to their homeland, how that was actually accomplished, and how Jews refashioned themselves in the process. In all instances, the "re" of re-turn, re-claim, and re-constitute is crucial. It points to how ideas of the past and their application in the present were central to the establishment of modern Israel and the shaping of its character.

RETURN: THE PEOPLE AND THE LAND

Jews, religious and secular, acknowledge the validity of the claim articulated in Israel's Declaration of Independence: "The Land of Israel was the birthplace of the Jewish people." Similarly, they understand themselves as belonging to a people whose origins are described in the Bible. It is in the chapters of Genesis that focus on the forefathers—Abraham, Isaac, and Jacob—that Jews encounter the narrative that describes and foretells the creation of a people that will persist throughout history. These founding stories are the roots of the nationhood Jews accept as a historical fact. The outlines of this Jewish historical narrative are also rooted in the fundamental texts that are part of the cultural heritage of Christian Europe where approximately 80 percent of world Jewry lived at the beginnings of the Zionist movement. Europeans shared a belief in the authenticity of the Bible even as they believed that the New Testament had supplanted the old. Nevertheless, the "Testament," in two senses of the word, both bore witness and provided evidence to the antiquity of Jews as a people and of their connection to the Land of Israel. The Judeo-Christian tradition supported the legitimacy of the Jewish historic claim to Palestine.

Zionists customarily called the land to which they returned "Eretz Israel," or the "Land of Israel," as it is termed in the Bible. In reclaiming ancient nomenclature and placing "the Land of Israel" before the world community, Zionism had the support of all Jews, however they stood on the issue of Zionism. Land of Israel was the familiar term deriving from holy texts, even when the more widespread Palestine came to be used in common parlance. Before the reality of a competing nationality became an issue, Zionists used Palestine and Land of Israel interchangeably in the titles of their organizations and in the letterheads of official stationery. From 1948, however, Palestine and Land of Israel were displaced in the Declaration of Independence with "the State of Israel." The Jewish polity required a name in accord with the customary usage of the twentieth-century political vocabulary. Outside the Arab Near East, "Israel" won nearly universal approval as a recognizable and appropriate name for the new Jewish state.

COVENANT AND NATION: THE SETTLEMENT ETHOS

Zionism understood the Land of Israel as a land belonging to a people, not individuals. A comparison with the American experience in settling the North American frontier with that of Jews in returning to the Middle East is instructive for understanding the difference. In both the American and Zionist frontier experience, ex-Europeans created societies to serve primarily the interests and needs of settler populations rather than those of the inhabitants they encountered. Both settler groups produced democratic societies, although with distinctive and even contrary characteristics. A crucial distinction is that Zionist colonization was a highly centralized and directed experience that supported socialist and communist as well as capitalist forms of settlement. Rather than promising individual self-betterment—the pursuit of individual happiness—which was the guiding ethos and purpose of the American pattern, the Zionist colonization encouraged individual and collective self-sacrifice. In the course of several centuries, the United States became a continental nation committed to individualism and to the furtherance and protection of personal rights. In contrast, during the past century, Zionism created about seven hundred urban and rural communities that were colonized, not by individuals but by groups of pioneers who were sent to locations chosen by settlement authorities to serve the interests of the Jewish people.

From the inauguration of Zionist colonization in the 1880s through the present, there has been almost no homesteading— the establishment of farms by private individuals. The family farm/ranch of Ariel Sharon is a notable exception. Israel has virtually not even any examples of "the little house on the prairie." Instead, there are various forms of village settlement of which the *moshav* (cooperative settlement of private landholders) and the *kibbutz* (collective settlement) are the best-known. Nor have towns or cities been organized and developed by "boosters," that is, individual entrepreneurs seeking personal profit. Urban colonies were founded either entirely by the national institutions or with their assistance. Rather than profit-seeking real estate promoters, associations of future middle-class burghers or working-class laborers established the country's major metropolis, Tel Aviv, as well as suburban estates and large-scale workers' housing estates in which most Israelis lived until well into the history of the state.

American and Zionist colonization were similar at the outset. Like the Puritan settlements in the New World, the first Zionist colonies in Palestine in the 1880s were "covenantal" communities established by modest groups of settlers who organized in Europe to emigrate to Palestine as pioneers, bent on fulfilling a national mission on behalf of the Jewish people. The language of the Zionist covenants resonates with references to national "redemption" as articulated particularly in the prophetic portions of the Bible, with Isaiah the favored text. Even when Zion's agricultural colonies were secularized, the dominant rhetoric referred to fulfilling historic national objectives. In the American experience, the cohesion and homogeneity of New England towns declined and common purposes were superseded by individual concerns.

Pioneering in the American and Zionist frontier experience has been idealized and stereotyped very differently. The equivalent of "pioneer" in Hebrew is derived from the biblical *halutz*, one who went before the people and was in their service. It derives from biblical passages describing how the Israelites overcame Jericho when they entered the promised land:

> And he [Joshua] said unto the people: "Pass on, and encircle the city, and let the *halutz* pass on before the ark of the Lord." And it was so, that when Joshua had spoken unto the people, the seven priests bearing the seven rams' horns before the Lord passed on, and blew the horns; and the ark of the covenant and the Lord followed them. And the *halutz* went before the priests that blew the horns. (Joshua 6:7–9)

While the root of the word *halutz* contains the meaning of "armed soldier," it also and more popularly came to mean one who goes before the people. The halutz is part of the avant garde. While halutz virtually disappeared from use in Hebrew for centuries, Zionist writers at the beginning of the twentieth century rediscovered the term and employed it extensively to describe pioneers (*halutzim*) and pioneering (*halutziyut*). Although the initial context was of one fulfilling a divine mission, secular Zionists readily appropriated the term and the concept in emphasizing the necessity for leadership that would act on behalf of a secular, national movement. Indeed, many of Israel's secular founders celebrated their own past in terms of halutziyut and were able to apply this term in a host of areas. Thus, one could also pioneer on the frontiers of the nation's commerce, education, literature, and so on.

What is common to all Zionist pioneering is that by definition it is never done by or on behalf of an individual and for self-interest. The idea of mission on behalf of the nation is the most common and strongest association with halutziyut. One may be an individualist in the sense of an eccentric, but peculiarities and individualism are placed in the service of the larger body from which one emanates and that one represents. In the United States, pioneers and pioneering have been traditionally viewed as sources of an individualism rooted in the realization of self-interest. Only since perhaps the 1990s can one identify a serious movement in Israel that views the land in more private, less collective ways that privilege the individual over the collective. Significantly, this phenomenon is often termed "Americanization."

The relationship between the nation or state to land and the policies that are deemed appropriate for its disposition are prime examples of the impact of the distinctive frontier experiences in both societies. Since the colonial period, the protection of private property has been connected with civil liberty and has become deeply-engrained in the politics and intellectual traditions of American society. External factors such as the abundance of land, the need to attract more settlers, the continuing erosion of powers of colonization companies, or other entities made the American version of liberty a real possibility for millions and contributed to the evolution of one of the most individualistic land systems anywhere. Indeed, an essential distinction between the two societies is that the State of Israel is defined in ethnic, national terms and was created as an instrument for fulfilling national Jewish purposes rather than the pursuit of happiness by individual Jews or anyone else. The prominence given the nation and its rights would have been unthinkable in the American context, where the state is not conceived as a particularistic polity created by and for a distinctive people or ethos.

The particular character of the Zionist commitment to peoplehood is illuminated by examining the linguistic value of the word *people* in Hebrew as opposed to its meaning in English. In one of the first translations of the American Declaration of Independence into Hebrew, the translator is at pains to explain that *people* in the American document refers to "members of society" (*b'nei hevra*). The Hebrew word for "people" is *'am* and it can have and often does have a more collective sense. *Merriam Webster's Collegiate Dictionary* gives the first meaning of "people" as "human beings making up a group or assembly or linked by a common interest." The implication is that the linkage is voluntary. Moreover, "persons" is offered as a synonym. A Hebrew equivalent, Reuben Alcalay's *The Complete Hebrew-English Dictionary* renders *'am* in the following order: "nation, folk, community, populace, inhabitants, tribe, crowd, multitude, mob." The sense of belonging to the collective, and not simply associating with other individuals, is paramount in the Hebrew.

This tendency is reflected in how the creation of the State of Israel is justified by the Declaration of Independence. Israel's founding document emphasizes collective or national rights rather than individual ones. The term "rights" appears seven times in Israel's Declaration and, in each instance, it is within a national context. For example: the document refers to the "right of the Jewish people and national renewal in its own land"; "the right of the survivors of the Holocaust for a life of dignity, liberty and honest labor in their nation's homeland"; the "natural right of the Jewish people to exist as all independent nations do in its own sovereign state"; "by the power of our natural and historical right." Moreover, the first set of paragraphs, fully one-half of the declaration, is devoted to reviewing Jewish history, which establishes the rights of the Jewish people to a state of their own in Palestine. Clearly, such an assertion of collective, national rights would have been premature and probably is still unthinkable in the American experience. Israel's declaration also claims that Israelis are endowed with individual rights, but this assertion comes only toward the end of the document in a section that echoes formulations of human rights promulgated by the United Nations, the international body that granted legitimacy to the Jewish state.

HOW HISTORICAL CONSCIOUSNESS SHAPED ZIONIST SETTLEMENT

This collective, national ethos found direct expression in the manner in which the country was settled. As we have noted, it was settled by groups usually acting within the age-old pattern of covenantal communities. The first and subsequent generations of pioneers organized and built villages in order to transform Jews into a Middle Eastern peasantry. In the process, they established hundreds of villages, about 250 from the 1880s until Independence and 400 more until the Six-Day War in 1967, when agricultural colonization largely ended. Thus, in less than a century, from 1882 to 1967, Zionist colonizers established more than 650 communities.

The first model for agricultural settlement was a colony of independent property-owners (*moshavah*). This was superseded by the cooperative farming village (moshav), and collective settlements (kvutzah or kibbutz). The early moshavah failed to achieve economic independence and did not develop quickly enough to enable large-scale colonization. Attempts at reform and experimentation lead to the design of the kibbutz or kvutzah and the moshav a few years prior to World War I. Whatever the particular economic basis for the village, socialist or capitalist, and whether secular or religious, the distinguishing feature of all of these villages was that they were based on a strong sense of community.

For all their ideological differences, capitalist and socialist Zionist colonists shared significant similarities with traditional Jews who remained in "holy cities" to await the Messiah. All sought to live within a communal framework, a common feature of Jewish life throughout the ages wherever Jews settled. Most founders of moshavah were traditional Jews, although they did not choose to live under an uncompromising regime supervised by religious authorities. Unlike their religious counterparts in cities, agricultural pioneers sought and anticipated ultimate economic independence even though they assumed they would require significant temporary financial support from sponsors abroad. Thus, Zionist villages were conceived as communities rooted in a common tradition and dependent on the support of fellow Jews who still lived abroad. The traditions of settlers extended beyond the Land of Israel to a world Jewish community that continued to transit history with a sense of mutual destiny and responsibility.

The source of this communitarian ethos has usually been traced to various streams of European cooperative, socialist, or communist ideologies. However, upon closer examination, the covenants of the moshavah suggest that Zionist communal thought was rooted in the religious experience, imaginations, and predilections of early planners and pioneers, and that their colonies re-created traditional patterns of bonding along national and/or religious lines. By World War I, the collective imperative was secularized and transcended regnant ideologies from socialism on the Left to free-enterprise capitalism. Still, it is noteworthy that Zionist colonizers from all ideological perspectives built village communities rather than latifundia, plantations, ranches, or homesteads as did other transplanted Europeans.

The communitarian and national orientation is expressed in the omnipresent founding documents of these settlements: their covenants and their regulations. These documents provide a clear statement of the intentions of the pioneers. One major collection of hundreds of covenants and regulations is contained in seven substantial volumes, a testament to the widespread appreciation for the roots and purpose of Jewish settlement. Together and individually, these statements reflect the aspirations and intentions of Jews from the small towns and cities of Eastern and Western Europe as well as those who emigrated from them to America.

The fundamental purposes put forward in these documents and the plans for their realization are remarkably similar. It is as if a recognized and agreed-upon archetype for community design had emerged without the deliberations and formal adoption of an international association. There was no single planner, group of planners, or planning authority in this initial stage of Zionist colonization. Not until 1897, when Theodor Herzl organized the first Zionist Congress and established the World Zionist Organization (WZO) did an international Zionist authority undertake to coordinate and implement a coherent policy of colonization. There were attempts that anticipate the work of the WZO, including regional conferences of the Lovers of Zion and the efforts of individuals, notably the Baron Edmund de Rothschild of France. But in the first generation, Zion was planned according to a common blueprint that reflected the aspirations of a multitude of Jews.

Often framed in Europe and transplanted with the pioneers, these documents affirmed social and religious bonds among the members. Social ties were paramount while economic distinctions were blurred, so that bylaws typically made no distinctions between poor and rich. The crucial marker was the differentiation of Jews on the basis of country of origin or religious practice. In the cities, for example, there were separate neighborhoods of Asian Jews from Bukhara or European Jews from Hungary where they followed the traditions of the Diaspora communities. Community members recognized the authority of a particular rabbi or religious movement such as a Hasidic sect. The regulations ensured that neighborhoods and housing estates would be societies of like-minded people dedicated to the agreed-upon purposes. A similar drive for homogeneity is evident among settlers of the countryside. Throughout Jewish Palestine, settlements were exclusive societies with democratic elements only for those permitted to join.

Zionists framed their compacts, covenants, and founding documents with biblical precedents and imagery as they returned to their promised land. Many explicitly use the word *covenant*, a term that appears frequently in the documents of colonizing societies in Eastern and Central Europe during the last two decades of the nineteenth century. Whether in the masthead, the opening statement, or a specific article identifying the purpose of the proposed society, covenants usually employ quotations from the Bible foretelling the time when Jews will take their destiny in their own hands and reclaim the land from which they have been exiled.

The Bible also provided founders of the moshavoth with a call for collective action. The organizers of Rehovoth (1890) begin their founding document, *The Book of the Covenant of Rest and Inheritance*, with a quotation from Isaiah (65:21–2):

> And they shall build houses, and inhabit them;
> And they shall plant vineyards, and eat the fruit of them.
> They shall not build, and another inhabit,
> They shall not plant, and another eat;
> For as the days of a tree shall be the days of My people.

Echoing Pinsker, the Lovers of Zion society of Warsaw in September 1883 rallied its members with a call for self-help, also from Isaiah (63:5):

> In the name of G-D who dwells in Zion!
> And I looked and there was none to help,
> And I beheld in astonishment, and there was none to uphold;
> Therefore, Mine own arm brought salvation unto Me.

This Warsaw constitution, framed in the aftermath of an outbreak of particularly violent pogroms, demands a solution to imminent national calamity. In the spirit of Pinsker's *Auto-Emancipation*, Jews are enjoined to save themselves by joining forces in rebuilding their national homeland and working the land in Zion. This urgent call to action, too, is cast in the language of ancient prophecy:

> Living in the city of Warsaw we have seen the signs of the present time, the burning sword of hatred, that is turning over today in human society. We have observed the plight of our people and its ruin. We are totally frustrated with the position of the nation . . . and we shall listen to the voice of God from the voices of the torches that are so powerfully calling the children of the scattered and separated people saying: "gather

together children of Jacob, understand the matter and understand what
you will."

Many covenants correctly refer to the intended colony as a "holy community." Adherents or inheritors of traditional religious culture could not
otherwise imagine life in the Holy Land, or perhaps anywhere. In Judaism,
there are commandments that can only be fulfilled and even prayers that
may only be uttered within communities. By tradition and religious law,
group worship offers greater possibilities than individual prayer. Moreover,
most institutions essential to the conduct of Jewish life require communities. It was therefore natural to envision themselves and their coreligionists
in Palestine as members of communities.

When secular pioneers infused with secular socialist ideologies came
during the Second Aliyah (wave of immigration from 1904 to 1913) and
the Third Aliyah (1919–1923), they also set out as members of groups, and
they, too, went to great lengths to work out and write down the arrangements of the communities they intended to create. While the pioneers of
the First Aliyah (1882–1904) anchored their beliefs and actions in religious
tradition, their successors based their communities on socialist conceptions
of brotherhood and on a commitment to national solidarity. What is striking, then, is that all Zionist villagers in this formative period of agricultural
colonization framed their communities in terms of national purposes and
imagined their preferences in terms of whatever social or economic ideology served those purposes best.

This commitment to community animated even avowedly secular pioneers. Perhaps the most famous group in the mythology of early Zionist
pioneering is the Biluim who took their name from the acrostic B-I-L-U,
or *Beit Ya'acov Lechu v'Nnelecha*—"O House of Jacob, Come ye and let us
go" (Isaiah 2:5). With a strong sense of the first person plural—"let *us*
go"—they constituted themselves into a community. Lacking financial resources and practical skills, this group of largely secular and socialistically inclined young people suffered great privation in an unsuccessful effort to
achieve a shared objective. Many left Palestine and only a handful actually
became farmers.

The founders of Rehovoth (1890) were far more successful and perhaps the least explicitly religious of the pioneers of the First Aliyah
moshavoth. Yet even their takanoth draw extensively on Jewish traditions.
Organized by largely middle-class pioneers who sought to further their
wealth within a communal framework, their regulations contain no mention of a rabbi, ritual bath, synagogue, and other religious functionary or

institutions. Nevertheless, such offices and officials were instituted in the new colony. In the spectrum of societies that the first generation of Zionists created, a recognizable similarity developed. The covenants of these colonies, then, reflected a common culture rooted in a shared tradition.

RECLAIMING THE LAND

Zionist settlers—whether rural or urban, religious or secular—viewed themselves as separate from the surrounding society and were so viewed by the Ottomans, who relegated them to the status of foreigners and members of non-Muslim religions. Jews were a separate community as were Christians and others. As in most cases where separation is enforced, it is rarely accompanied by equality. The British, who supplanted the Ottomans as Palestine's rulers after World War I, also viewed Jews and Arabs as members of separate communities. Typically, the British assembled statistics and published their censuses with people divided by religion: Muslims, Christians, and Jews. However, these distinctions were not strange or remarkable to Jewish immigrants, particularly from Eastern Europe. Jews who came from Russia, Poland, Romania, and the lands of the Austro-Hungarian Empire were accustomed to viewing themselves and others as members of distinct communities who enjoyed or endured differential status defined by law. This separateness was also expressed in the ways in which Jews acquired land, and how the land was defined upon acquisition and settlement. It became "Jewish" land, even as other territory was termed "Arab" or associated with any of the diverse groups that populated the country. Communal and territorial segregation lead to distinctive and conflicting claims to title over portions of the country, as well as the Land of Israel as a whole.

For more than three millennia, the Jewish claim to the Land of Israel was based on a divine promise recorded in Genesis (17:1, 7, 8):

> I will establish My covenant between Me and three and they seed after thee throughout the generations for an everlasting covenant to be a God unto three and they seed after thee. And I will give unto thee and to thy seed after thee, the land of their sojournings, all the lands of Canaan for an everlasting holding and I will be their God.

The underlying principle is that the earth belongs to the Lord. The claims nations or individuals may make to territory are legitimate only if validated by God. This conception, also found in Christianity and Islam, is based in Judaism on an interpretation of the first phrase in Genesis: "In the beginning God created the Heavens and the Earth." Rashi, the eleventh-century French-Jewish commentator, drew on an ancient and widely known rabbinical source of about a thousand years earlier in observing that were it not for this verse, "pirates"—that is, unlawful owners who would usurp divine intentions—might make claim to land. Rashi concludes that God has ultimate authority as the creator, and it is He who assigns title. In the case of the Jews, He made an everlasting covenant that connects them to the Land of Israel. When Jews deviated from that covenant, they were punished by exile.

Jewish title would be reasserted when God chose. This was an idea that continues to have validity among religious Jews and many Christians. For Zionists who drew upon Jewish religious traditions even as they secularized them, the Land of Israel remained the promised land, and actual possession could be restored. Suggestions that Jews might make claims as a nation on lands in Africa or elsewhere, even as a temporary asylum from the violence and dangers of Europe, caused a crisis among Zionists and were quickly rejected. The Land of Israel was the historic and future homeland.

For some religious Zionists, the right to the Land of Israel was absolute though subject to temporal compromise. The issue first arose in the debates generated by the 1937 proposals of the Peel Commission, the British body that investigated the impasse of Jewish and Arab claims to Palestine and the violence it produced. Some argued that the divine promise could not be contravened and that Jews could not accept partition of any part of the Holy Land. This group was in a minority until the 1967 war, when mainstream Mizrahi, the political party of religious Zionists, joined with a majority of the Labor Zionist movement in agreeing to partition. The minority viewpoint, later concentrated in the Block of the Faithful (*Gush Emunim*), remained but gained considerable strength after 1967 when Israel took control of the West Bank, the Golan, and Gaza. They agitated with increasing success from the mid-1970s to plant numerous settlements in the historic Land of Israel. This is the group that has been most active in opposing their dismantling and a large-scale withdrawal from Gaza and the West Bank. Demands for uncompromised title and control over all historic Palestine has clearly become a significant force within religious Zionism. It is still, however, a minority but an energetic and vociferous force within Israeli society as a whole.

Moderate elements within religious Zionism have not relinquished the belief that this claim would be ultimately realized. Their pragmatic approach is based on a theological principle: Even the most devout and righteous individual cannot know when God's promise will be realized, nor by whom. The issue of agency is particularly significant. There were those, like Rabbi Avraham Kook (1864–1935), the chief Ashkenazi rabbi of the Yishuv (Jewish settlement in Palestine), who believed that even secular Zionists were doing God's work. The State of Israel heralded the promised return to Zion. His followers accepted Rabbi Kook's endorsement of inserting into daily prayers a request that God bless the State of Israel as "the dawn of our Redemption" (reishit tz'michat ge'ulateynu). Still, they would not identify a particular political figure or political program as part of the divine plan to fulfill the divine promise.

On the other hand, Gush Emunim, a movement inspired by Rabbi Zvi Kook (1891–1982), the son of former Chief Rabbi Abraham Kook, maintains with certainty that their settlers and settlements are manifestations of the handiwork of God. Such a viewpoint cannot brook partition when the Land of Israel is in Jewish hands. The alternative Mizrahi perspective that does not claim to know divine intentions is more pragmatic and flexible regarding settlement programs. Most of the Mizrahi joined in supporting the British plan for dividing Palestine in 1937 and then endorsed the UN partition plan of 1947. Many continue to accept a Jewish state in the homeland together with an Arab one. This moderate position persists, notably in the Meimad movement, and accepts compromise with Palestinian Arabs for the sake of peace and the saving of Jewish lives. Clearly, religious Zionism can encompass multiple interpretations. Moderation and pragmatism as well as extremism and inflexibility can find sources of support in the interpretation of sacred texts.

POLITICAL THEOLOGY AND THEOLOGICAL POLITICS

Although attention to divine promises was found primarily in varieties of religious Zionism and anti-Zionism, it also echoed on the political Right of secular Zionism. It has been expressed in clear and popular form in what may be termed the "political theology" of Menachem Begin, the leader of revisionism from Vladimir Jabotinsky's death in 1940 until he resigned as prime minister in 1982.

Begin's political theology drew on an amalgam deriving from Jewish religious culture and contemporary secular ideas. The terms and tone of his rhetoric were replete with notions and nuances associated with religious discourse. He spoke of martyrs and redemption and frequently invoked references to the prophets and to the covenant between the Lord and the Jewish people. Nevertheless, he did not speak in the idiom of the rabbis and Jewish religious law. Instead, he espoused modern political discourse with concepts like the "inalienable historical right" of the Jewish people to return to their homeland. This claim is rooted in transcendent and timeless truths, and is therefore more binding than the decisions of temporal bodies, including the United Nations or legislation favored by a Labor-led Knesset. Moreover, rather than appeal to direct divine intervention he invoked "historical justice" when sanctioning acts of protest, including violence. Thus the 1947 United Nations plan for partition, as well as Labor Zionism's acceptance of this principle, was held to be invalid and justifying resistance. Nevertheless, expanding Israel's borders was but a theoretical issue reflected in the public discourse of the Right until 1967, when Israel conquered extensive territories in the heartland of the historic Land of Israel.

Begin's political theology began to have practical impact after he was invited to join the cabinet in an attempt to build national unity just prior to the outbreak of the 1967 war. This was the first occasion Begin sat at the center of Israeli power, having been successfully excluded by Labor for nearly half a century. Begin's voice joined with those of more hawkish Labor ministers, but his practical influence on government decisions remained marginal until a decade later, after the elections of 1977, when the Likud emerged as Zionism's leading party. It was only after this upheaval of 1977 that Israeli governments began to systematically lay claim to substantial portions of the West Bank and created the settlement map with which we are familiar today.

International as well as domestic politics did not permit Israel's outright annexation of territory except for Jerusalem, which was well within the national consensus. As is discussed below, even Ben-Gurion insisted on an enlarged Jerusalem as the capital of the Jewish state. International constraints forced Begin to adjust his tactics and rhetoric, although he remained faithful to fundamental principles. Thus, he could return captured territory to Egypt but not to the Palestinians. This was well within the bounds of right-wing ideology, since Sinai was outside the borders of historic Israel. It was but the land through which the Hebrews passed on their way to the promised land. Relinquishing this territory—with its strategic assets as well as cities such as Yamit on the Mediterranean and distant Sharm el-Sheikh and other resorts on the Gulf of Suez and the Red Sea—could be justified as useful for enhancing national security within Israel's proper borders. Withdrawal from these locations was but a tactical retreat enabling the maintenance of control over historic Judea and Samaria. This same logic has motivated many on the Right in their support for Ariel Sharon's decision for disengagement from Gaza in the summer of 2005.

Begin's policy toward the West Bank has been viewed through the prism of an "inalienable historical right." Throughout the negotiations with Anwar Sadat and Jimmy Carter at Camp David in 1978, Begin spoke of granting autonomy to the Arabs of Palestine since this did not impair Jewish sovereignty. "Autonomy" actually began as "cultural autonomy," evolved into "administrative autonomy," and finally became "full autonomy" in the context of a possible comprehensive peace. For Begin, however, no form of autonomy implied agreement to establish a Palestinian state. He consistently spoke of "Palestinians" but not the Palestinian people. That is, Palestinians may be recognized as individuals or as a group, but not as a people or nation entitled to a state. Begin's successor as prime minister, Yitzhak Shamir, was even more recalcitrant. At the 1991 international conference between Israel and the Arabs in Madrid, his government insisted on incorporating Palestinian representatives into the delegations of Arab states but would not recognize them as a discrete and independent body acting on their own behalf. This hard-line position changed only after the Rabin government joined the Palestinians in formulating the Oslo Accords in 1993.

The overwhelming victory in the Six Day War of June 1967 also opened the door in the center and left of the political spectrum for undercurrents that had been dormant or suppressed. Even Ben-Gurion, widely regarded as the exponent of realism and pragmatism, was swept up in the widespread public enthusiasm, if not ecstasy, released by the sudden and decisive victory. Accompanied by two generals in an army jeep and greeted by throngs of citizens, he made pilgrimage to Jerusalem the moment the Old City was captured and visited the Western Wall on the Temple Mount. He advocated retaining an enlarged Jerusalem, with its historic Jewish portions, as the historic capital of the Jewish state although he was willing to return much of the remainder of the captured territories in return for a peace treaty.

The turn of events of June 1967 is widely regarded as marking a watershed in Israeli life and Zionist thought. It was a moment many considered "miraculous," a sensibility sharpened by the widespread despair in the face of approaching doom, even a second Holocaust, that preceded the outbreak of hostilities. A return to the pre-1967 armistice lines seemed unnatural and wrong in that moment of national salvation. It was in this context of euphoria that the formula of "land for peace" took shape. It appeared to be fair and appropriate, although for most Israelis there have always been limits. Only very few were willing to return without exception the territories captured from Syria, Egypt, and Jordan. There were relative minimalists like Ben-Gurion. Others advanced strategic, historic, or religious arguments for maintaining control over particular territories. In the national debate that emerged and continues to the present, there has been a wide and changing range of opinion from those who remained closer to the initial formulas of restraint and adherence to partition, to those who insisted on expansion to fulfill Israel's historic mission and/or strategic needs for defensible borders. In the evolving debates, the movement for expansion reached a peak in the early 1980s.

Initially, Labor leaders such as Yigal Allon, one of Israel's leading military figures since the prestate period, repeatedly proposed only limited settlements in the West Bank as a means to enhance security. These included planting agricultural colonies in the Jordan valley as a means to establish a defensive line in the east against Jordan and possibly Iraq, and constructing suburbs around Jerusalem to enhance the city's defenses against possible attack. Allon advocated avoiding the rest of the West Bank including prominent biblical sites. In this way, Israel's governments signaled that they were leaving this territory for Arabs, preferably under Jordanian rule, within the proclaimed rubric of "land for peace." In this fashion, Labor Zionism maintained its commitment to partition, even if the area designated for Arab control had somewhat diminished. One can only speculate what might have happened if only three months after the war, the Arab League at Khartoum had not rejected not only negotiations, but peace with Israel and recognition of the Jewish state. With an accord apparently foreclosed, dreams of grandeur were no longer repressed.

The passions set free by the war are well illustrated by the case of Natan Alterman, the unofficial poet laureate of the Labor Zionist establishment and a close associate of Ben-Gurion. At the end of the war, he immediately joined the movement for a Greater Israel. Identified for over a generation with the pragmatic mainstream of the Labor Movement (Mapai), Alterman had now metamorphosed into the most vocal spokesman of a radical ideology distinctly allied to the Revisionist Right, although without Begin's language of "political theology." Together with other secular intellectuals and political leaders from across the political spectrum, Alterman lent respectability to a position that had previously been identified with the Zionist right-wing. As a consequence, Alterman contributed to a significant shift of the national consensus to the right. This swing had enormous impact on the Mizrahi, the party of religious Zionism that traditionally had been aligned with a pragmatic and relatively moderate Labor party.

The most visible and vocal consequence of this shift was the growing power of Gush Emunim, the activist group that incubated inside Mizrahi. By the mid-1970s they successfully pushed Mizrahi to the right and into a coalition with Begin's Likud. They claimed that it was they who were now the authentic instruments of Zionism's historic mission. Gush Emunim argued that the settler movement created by secular Zionism needed to be revived in order to address the challenge of the historic present when, after nearly two millennia, Jews were again in control over the whole of the Land of Israel. They pressed for expansion as they invested themselves in the mantle of heroic pioneers, a status that had been largely the preserve of the secular Left.

The spread of the "political theology" of the Zionist Right as well as the Greater Israel movement thereby paved the way for a religiously rooted irredentist movement that sought to regain the ancient or historic borders of the Land of Israel. Still, they were held in check until the 1973 Yom Kippur War by more traditional and conservative elements as reflected in Allon's conception of limited settlement based largely on strategic considerations.

The turning point came in 1974, when the followers of the younger Rabbi Kook successfully initiated a series of patently illegal actions. They were alarmed by what they perceived as a weakening of national resolve in the aftermath of the trauma of the 1973 Yom Kippur War. They were also concerned by the beginnings of a protest movement within the military establishment calling for a reassessment of government policies. In response, they developed an activist strategy for thwarting any move toward compromise. The first steps were the establishment of outposts on the West Bank at Sebastia and Ophrah against the wishes of the Rabin government, but with at least the tacit assent of Shimon Peres, the minister of defense who then identified with a hawkish outlook. Further settlements were few until the victory of Begin and the Likud in 1977, but each was accompanied by much fanfare. After the 1977 elections, the Likud embarked on an aggressively expansionist policy with Gush Emunim in the forefront. By the early 1980s, the government published plans for a massive campaign to construct settlements with an infrastructure of extensive roads and communications. The announced goal was to achieve throughout the West Bank a population of at least one million settlers. Although the actual number is still under a quarter of a million, a substantial infrastructure has been built and the political map of the West Bank has become enormously complicated.

The assessment of Gush Emunim was correct. Although Israeli public life moved to the right, an increasingly important countermovement developed. Beginning with the protest against the failure of the Labor government in the 1973 war, officers within the Israeli army began to question the wisdom and competence of the political leadership. The leaders of this movement inaugurated a series of actions that ultimately led to the Officer's

Letter of 1978 that marked the founding of Peace Now. They called for recognition of the Palestinians as a people and a nation, and for a more vigorous exploration of the possibility for a compromise that would necessarily result in a Palestinian state alongside Israel. The growth of this perspective, particularly after what many felt to be a disastrous incursion into Lebanon in 1982, let to a precarious balance in Israeli politics in which "national unity" governments encompassing Left and Right have been frequent electoral outcomes. The prospect of a stalemate or an eventual return to dominance of the pragmatic, secular position has always hovered over Gush Emunim. It has informed their demands for immediate implementation of settlement projects and encouraged preemptive and even illegal action when governments were slow to respond.

It is unclear where the contradictory pressures in Israeli society will lead. While a total disengagement from Gaza took place in the summer of 2005, only a few illegal settlements were removed from the West Bank. Although there is widespread understanding in Israel that a total disengagement may now be impossible, there is considerable pressure to work for an agreement that includes partition. The next chapter considers a fuller assessment of these internal conflicts and their prospects. It is more appropriate now to return to the analysis of how other branches of Zionism have worked out their claims to the country.

A RANGE OF ALTERNATIVE RELIGIOUS RESPONSES

Gush Emunim reflects a radical and activist course adopted by religious Jews. Other branches of traditional Judaism have followed a range of paths in articulating their understanding of the divine plan for Jews in the promised land. Ultraorthodoxy insists that the Land of Israel has been promised, but title will not be given until God is disposed to inaugurate the ingathering of the exiles through the intervention of the Messiah. For this reason, the ultraorthodox reject Zionism as an illegitimate attempt to hasten the messianic mission. The extreme Neturei Karta sect not only rejects Zionism but even the existence of Israel, preferring a Palestine Liberation Organization (PLO) state over the entire country until the Messiah sets things right. Other ultraorthodox go so far as to blame Zionism for the Holocaust, viewing that catastrophe as punishment for the sin of challenging God's orderly plan for Jewish redemption.

Less extreme and more numerous, other ultraorthodox groups, despite a theological rejection of Zionism, have adapted to the Jewish state even as they would to any other temporal government under which they might live. They seek government funding and participate in elections, even sending members to the Knesset or to serve in governments. Yet, their children do not serve in the army, nor do they participate in Independence Day celebrations or otherwise acknowledge the legitimacy of the state. This does not impede their efforts to use state powers to enforce adherence to Jewish law, as with their insistence that the Sabbath and dietary laws be observed publicly. Still, it is interesting that within ultraorthodoxy there are divergent responses to contemporary claims to the land. There are those who vote for right-wing parties that uphold Jewish rights to all of the Land of Israel. Others accept compromise since they view temporal claims to territory as secondary to saving Jewish lives through a peace accord. The exclusive right over the land and the return of Jews still await the messianic moment. The sanctity of life and the value of peace outweigh the attempt—even through the instrument of a Jewish state—to advance God's ultimate agenda.

Brith Shalom (the covenant of peace) is yet another movement of religious Jews, one that understands Judaism as properly searching for accommodation with Arabs. The movement believed in the covenant and Jewish title to the land but did not insist on Jewish sovereignty over the whole. Its leader, Martin Buber (1878–1965), was a religious Jew who did not identify with orthodoxy. A leading scholar of Hasidic Judaism, he developed a philosophy that emphasized the direct and ethical relationship between individuals, popularly known as the I-Thou relationship. His beliefs deemphasized ritual and Jewish law in favor of a focus on ethics. However, his commitment to Jewish peoplehood remained a central aspect of his religious understanding, as was the centrality of the Land of Israel and the need to establish a Jewish community there. Indeed, he left his native Germany for Palestine and, together with largely like-minded émigrés from Central Europe, founded the movement known as Brith Shalom. They were small in number but exercised a powerful influence particularly on secular Zionists.

Key to Brith Shalom was the commitment to create a moral society rooted in Jewish ethics. Unlike secular Zionists who viewed "historic" rights as crucial, Buber framed the legitimacy of Jewish settlement in terms of the religious obligation to establish a just society that would impact fellow Jews in the Land of Israel and beyond. In this romantic evocation of the Jewish mission to the world—"a light unto the nations"—the just society would serve as a center for Jews everywhere, whatever the actual size of the community in the Land of Israel; it would benefit the Arabs of the country; and it would restore the land, depleted from the neglect of centuries, and make it bloom again. On this last item, we have more to say later. Suffice it to note here that reclaiming the land and making it productive was viewed by Brith Shalom, secular Zionists, and much of the world as the basis for title to land anywhere and a fundamental ethical bond between a people—any people—and the Lord's creation. Buber often referred to his position as "Hebrew humanism." As with secular Zionism, Buber's humanism demanded action and saw the failure to fulfill any part of the covenant, including returning to the land and cultivating it, as inadmissible.

As violence erupted in Palestine in the 1920s, Brith Shalom advocated a binational state in which both Jews and Arabs had rights. As pacifists, they opposed conflict and the use of force for any reason. One member of the group, Judah Magnes, the founding president of the Hebrew University in Jerusalem, journeyed to New York in 1947 to argue unsuccessfully before the United Nations that partition into two states was wrong and that Brith Shalom's commitment to binationalism was the optimal solution. Magnes died while on the mission, and the idea was set aside. For both parties to the Arab/Israeli conflict, partition—not binationalism—has appeared to be the more feasible solution.

Whatever Brith Shalom's objections to partition, they celebrated Zionist pioneering. For Buber, the kibbutz was "the experiment that did not fail." Writing in the aftermath of the Second World War, when fascism and communism—movements with utopian aspirations on the Right and the Left—collided with devastating consequences, he found in the small, idealistic communities of Zionist pioneers the best model of utopianism in the contemporary world. Their secular but just societies illustrated how individuals could act in developing a bountiful and beautiful countryside. The mutually sympathetic bonds between Buber and halutzim were rooted in a shared humanism that held individuals responsible for creating just and productive societies.

A SECULAR FRAMEWORK FOR CLAIMING THE LAND: HISTORIC RIGHTS

Elements in Buber's religiously based thinking appealed greatly to secular Zionists. They, too, believed that settling the land with communities of Jews was a profoundly moral act. Nevertheless, secular Zionists required a point of origin outside Buber's theological framework. This was found in the historic right of Jews to the Land of Israel rather than in fulfilling religious obligations. Appeals to history were common to European national movements. They made extensive use of them in claiming territory and the right, indeed the obligation, to create modern states on ancient homelands. Jews incorporated and formulated the ideology of European nationalism in their own millennia-old beliefs regarding Jewish rights to the Land of Israel. Such historic claims were claimed by all the different and competing groups who formed the large majority of the Zionist movement.

These claims to a historic right emerge at the beginnings of Zionism in the 1880s. They were taken to be self-evident and did not require elaboration. Moreover, they could be taken for granted in a context where there were not yet competing claims. The country had been ruled for centuries by Muslim Turks who felt no need to publicly assert the validity of their title. Herzl's assertion at the second Zionist Congress in 1898 is typical of the ways in which Zionists articulated Jewish rights. He simply declared: "If there is such a thing as a legitimate claim to a portion of the earth's surface, all peoples who believe in the Bible must recognize the right of the Jews." In this he was apparently correct. Twenty Arab states were products of the disintegration of the Ottoman Empire and its reorganization by European powers in the aftermath of World War I. As part of this process of reassigning Ottoman lands to national groupings, Jews also obtained the promise from Great Britain through the Balfour Declaration in 1917 that Palestine would become a Jewish national homeland. It was only subsequent to this event and the rise of Arab nationalism that conflicting historic claims to Palestine begin to emerge.

VIRGIN LAND, WILDERNESS OR DESERT

A long-standing and crucial issue in the debate over Jewish claims to the Land of Israel is whether Palestine was *terra nullius*. To use the phrase that became widespread by the time of the Balfour Declaration, Palestine was "a land without a people, for a people without a land." Such a statement now appears to be inaccurate and offensive. Clearly, there were not only Arabs in Palestine prior to the earliest Zionist colonies, but they were the majority of the country's inhabitants until the State of Israel organized successive waves of massive immigration. It has been argued that demographic change in Palestine came only through force and over the opposition of the natives. The creation of the State of Israel, in this view, is just another instance of imperialism and should be condemned as a travesty of the civil and human rights of indigenous people. Such a view, which has been perpetrated by a host of contemporary authors from the framers of the PLO covenant to

Edward Said, as well as Revisionist Israelis and foreign historians, is a misleading oversimplification. In a common distortion, Said and his followers perhaps malevolently shorten the phrase "a land without a people" to "a land without people." Zionism never imagined the land was unpopulated.

The argument that Palestine was not *terra nullius*, and therefore belonged to the people already resident there, raises the important question of why the international community not only condoned but encouraged the establishment of a Jewish state. Such was the determination of non-Muslim members of the international community and its institutions beginning with the Balfour Declaration through the decisions of the League of Nations and the United Nations. The accusation that Zionism is but another instance of imperialism and colonialism reduces and obscures the analysis of an important historical phenomenon. Since *terra nullius* has been misrepresented with regard to Palestine and subjected to the distortions of political correctness, we must ask what such an apparently outrageous statement—"a land without a people, for a people without land"—once meant and how it served to legitimate Zionist claims.

Here, too, the invocation of history is crucial and is a phenomenon that extends well beyond particularistic Jewish thought. Indeed, the arguments of secular Zionism derive from the way other peoples, especially but not only Europeans, have claimed distant lands during the past three centuries. It is quite understandable why such contentions have been consistently rejected by Arabs as well as other non-European peoples. As we have seen in earlier chapters, Islam has asserted claims that are rooted in Islamic tradition and history. In effect, Jewish and Muslim discourses never really address one another. Arabs cannot or are unwilling to view the return of Jews to the country in terms other than another instance of Western colonialism.

Nevertheless, in 1917, at the time of the Balfour Declaration, Palestine was a sparsely settled and economically underdeveloped country from the perspective of Western observers who compared it both with other countries and with Palestine's own distant past. For example, a century ago, in 1900, the population of what today composes the Palestinian Authority and the State of Israel included less than one-sixteenth of the current population of more than eight million. There were no great cities, and the population was largely settled in villages and towns. There was no electricity grid until the 1920s when the Zionist engineer and entrepreneur Pinhas Rutenberg organized a company to produce and distribute it. The transportation system was primitive, with no paved road along the coast from Jaffa to Haifa until the British built one in the 1920s. The largest industries in the Arab sector were actually workshops or manufacturing establishments with no more than a handful of employees. Large-scale firms employing hundreds of workers such as Lodzia textiles, Palestine Potash, or Nesher cement were created during the British Mandate by Zionist entrepreneurs. The only exports were agriculturally related and of small extent, except for people—largely Palestine's Christians and disappointed Jewish pioneers—who could not find adequate opportunities in the country. Finally, extensive areas in Palestine were barren and uncultivated, devoid of trees and yet containing regions with numerous swamps. Palestine yielded but a modest produce that barely sustained a relatively small population.

This version of the sorry state of the country was captured in literally hundreds of travelers' accounts, numerous scientific reports, libraries of books, pamphlets, reminiscences, newspaper and journal articles, as well as photographs and even on film. In one memorable passage in Mark Twain's *Innocents Abroad* (1871), he comments on his disappointment in encountering a land that was so desolate. Examining the few, wrinkled grapes he found in a vineyard, Twain calls them poor imitations of the "Sunday School" grapes he associated with the country. Twain was overwhelmed by the disparity between the reality of a poor and underdeveloped country and the expectation, so carefully and deeply nurtured in the Holy Writ, that was at the core of Western culture. This was equally true of many Jews. They naturally believed that Palestine could be a land "flowing with milk and honey." It had once been a land of kings and palaces; successful farmers brought their bounty to Jerusalem three times a year and enjoyed a flourishing commerce that reached from Ethiopia to the provinces of present-day Turkey and across the Mediterranean to Spain.

Within this setting, it was possible for Zionist colonizers to imagine massive Jewish settlement. Suffice to recall here that by the 1930s, archeologists testified that during the Byzantine period, Palestine had around three million inhabitants or about three times more than in the country at that time. Statements of the country's potential were provided by geologists, geographers, and experts in semiarid zones with experience from the American Southwest to the Gobi desert in China, the dry regions of Australia, and regions of Africa. The data were crucial in calculating the "economic absorptive capacity of Palestine," that is, the number of people the land could support. The Zionist position was always expansive, envisioning the successful integration of waves of immigrants by employing advanced farming methods imported from Europe and the United States and yet without the displacement of Arabs who would similarly benefit from sharing in these improvements. Nevertheless, Arabs and their supporters wanted to justify keeping Jews out, and blamed the country's sorry state on changes in climate or other natural causes. Zionists and Arabs were thus in contention, employing different versions of the country's past, in arguing over its future.

The validity of Zionism's maximalist position is now abundantly clear. At the time, that is, in the decades prior to the establishment of Israel over Arab resistance, observers could not rely on actual evidence. They searched for and created frames of reference from other arid areas or from the history of the country and of other places across time. In so doing, supporters of Zionism invested that *terra nullius* with an interpretation that has been lost by contemporary critics. At the end of the nineteenth and beginning of the twentieth centuries, *terra nullius* had a distinct meaning. It was the product of Western thought since the Enlightenment and had become an established principle in international law. A brief excursion into the Anglo-American experience can illustrate this. The term is also important to understand, since it generated perhaps the most significant litigation between native peoples and largely European settlers in countries from Canada to Australia, the United States, and even to the Indian Hindu Diaspora around the Indian Ocean and Fiji. Moreover, the practical consequences of *terra nullius* are evident in the British policy regarding Palestine's future.

The idea that Palestine was a wilderness or desert is directly related to the British experience in North America in the seventeenth century. The first English settlers in New England in the 1620s commented on the paucity of local population in relation to the abundant natural resources. They argued that it was "lawful now to take a land which none useth and make use of." Under the leadership of Massachusetts Governor Jonathan Winthrop in the 1630s, the theory of rightful settlement was articulated in terms that derived from a Christian interpretation of the Bible. Basing himself on Genesis 1, as did the Jews, this Puritan wrote: "The whole earth is the Lord's Garden and he has given it to the senses of men, with a general Condicion [*sic*]: Increase and multiply, replenish the earth and subdue it." And for the (Indian) Natives of New England: "They inclose noe land, neither have any settled habitation nor any tame cattle to improve the land by, and so have none other but a natural right to those countries. So as if we leave them [land] sufficient for their use wee may lawfully take the rest, there being more than enough for them and us [*sic*]" (74). This is, in effect, a Protestant version of Rashi's interpretation of the opening phrase of Genesis: "In the beginning God created the heaven and the earth." That is, the earth is the Lord's, and ownership by individuals and nations is inherently limited. Moreover, proof of ownership is by working the land to make it fertile and productive. Neglect leaves it open to possession by others.

This notion became a staple of American thought. Typically, President James Monroe would write in 1822: "The earth was given to mankind to support the greatest number of which it is capable, and not tribe or people have a right to withhold from the wants of others more than is necessary for their own support and comfort." In this manner, Americans were urged to spread across a continent to people and to cultivate it. America was *terra nullius*; it was not because there were no people, but because it had potential that was not being used by its contemporary population.

What is interesting in this American experience is that although rights over land could, in theory, be acquired legally by conquest, nearly all of the land obtained by European settlers was actually obtained by purchase or by treaty. In this process of acquisition, theory moved from truths rooted in revealed religion to the principles of natural law. If Winthrop justified settlement in terms of a biblical mandate in the seventeenth century, by the eighteenth century John Locke justified settlement by secular natural law. Drawing on a body of thought that included Thomas More, Grotius, and the French philosophers, Locke's *Second Treatise of Government* claimed that the right to property is vested in one who works the land and makes it productive. If labor rather than mere residence, whether occasional or long term, endows one with the right to property, then working the land produces ownership, and land that is uncultivated and unchanged is available.

The calls for the "conquest of labor" or the "redemption of the land" that resonated in Zionist writings in the half-century before Israel's independence drew on this same fund of ideas that had spread throughout Western thought. They were not merely Eastern European concepts, nor were they rooted in romanticism; and they were shared by the Zionist Right and by socialist Labor. To acquire territory meant redeeming the land through its proper use. The insistent progress of Jewish settlement provided an impressive vindication of this vision. Over the course of a single century, Palestine was transformed from an underdeveloped corner of the Ottoman empire with a poor and technologically backward population into an advanced industrial society. Moreover, the citizens of Israel enjoy a standard of living on average that is as high as that of several Western European countries.

The expectation that such industry should be rewarded was so ubiquitous in the Enlightenment that it found its way into the formulation of America's Declaration of Independence. The colonists, in a famous phrase, claimed the right "to pursue happiness." The original formulation was the "right to pursue property." Property and happiness were very nearly interchangeable. This Lockean version of the social contract was the principle behind Jefferson's yeoman ideal, and it was this concept that justified the expansion of the United States across the continent while becoming the base for a legal system grounded in the protection of civil rights.

Locke's and Jefferson's theories found their way into a series of court cases in the 1820s and 1830s that have become the most quoted precedents in more than a century and a half of litigation between settlers and natives throughout the world. The most-cited disputes involved the Cherokee Indians and white settlers in Georgia and land rights in Indiana and Illinois. All were adjudicated in the United States Supreme Court of Chief Justice John Marshall, perhaps the most important early theorist of American liberties and institutional arrangements. He authored a series of opinions that synthesized legal theory and practice as inherited from the Enlightenment and the British colonial system. Although he accepted the validity of the traditional concepts of "discovery" and "conquest" as legal bases for claiming territory, his larger contribution was in setting forth the validity of purchase and treaties and making proper use of land through improvement and cultivation, both as the bases for defining the rights of natives and of settlers.

What is pertinent here is that the terms of this legal tradition were applied to Palestine before Zionism organized as an international movement. Israel Zangwill, David Ben-Gurion, Yitzhak Ben-Zvi, and a host of other Zionist writers and leaders at the beginning of the twentieth century did not invent new ideas. Rather, a succession of European visitors to the Holy Land in the nineteenth century applied existing concepts to Palestine and often called upon Jews to redeem the land with settlers who would make the country fruitful again. While Jews believed they had ample arguments within their own national, historical, or religious culture to convince themselves that they might claim the land, their sense of rectitude and legitimacy was substantially buttressed by historic and legal principles developed in Western societies. Secular Zionism also based its claims to land on principles that were generally considered to be universal, although they were actually the product of European thought.

The perceived failure of Arabs to properly use and maintain the land achieved the status of a scientific "fact," with "expert" reports filed by successive expeditions of the British-sponsored Palestine Exploration Fund (PEF) beginning in the 1870s. Particularly noteworthy are the early PEF surveys carried out by Lieutenants Conder and Kitchener (later Lord Kitchener of Khartoum). Conder expressed this in his 1876 report to the PEF on *The Fertility of Ancient Palestine*: "The curse of the country is bad government and oppression. Justice and security of person and property once established, Palestine would become once more a land of corn, vines and olives, rivaling in fertility and in wealth its ancient condition, as deduced from careful study of such notices as remain to us in the Bible and in the later Jewish writings."

At the same time, Sir Charles Warren wrote in *The Land of Promise* (1875): "Give Palestine a good government and increase the commercial life of the people, and they may increase tenfold and yet there is room. [The land's] productiveness will increase in proportion to labour bestowed on the soil until a population of 15 million may be accommodated there." An ever-increasing body of opinion held to the view that the people were at fault. Palestine had been and could be again a "land flowing with milk and honey." Moreover, since there was apparently little to learn from the present local population, outside ideas, technologies, funds, and even people had to be imported if the land was to be changed and improved. The belief that their ancestors had previously cultivated the land successfully enhanced the appeal of Zionism and invested in it a romantic appeal that attracted many Jews and Christians.

On the other hand, Professor Ellsworth Huntington of Yale inquired in *Palestine and its Transformation* (1911) whether man or nature was responsible for the country's obvious decline. He argued that the climate had changed. Higher temperatures and less rain caused desert. Lower temperatures and more rain created an environment that could sustain a more substantial agriculture. Thus, in the Roman–Byzantine period when the climate was more favorable, the population had reached perhaps the greatest extent in its recorded history. Drought and heat, not people, caused the decline of civilizations. Rain is the missing element.

Two young Zionist leaders, David Ben-Gurion and Yitzhak Ben-Zvi, recognized the political implications of Huntington's analysis and responded with their best-selling book on the means for colonizing Palestine, *Eretz Israel in the Past and in the Present*, published in 1918 while they were living as exiles from Turkish Palestine in New York. The two spent much of their time at the New York Public Library reading assiduously everything they could find relevant to the country's past and potential. They concluded that a population of ten million could live in the historic Land of Israel or the Palestine of both sides of the Jordan River. They well understood the political and moral value of holding natives rather than climate responsible for the drastic decline in the condition of the Holy Land. They concluded the two volumes with the claim that the land could be redeemed by industrious Jews. The authority for this conclusion was rooted in a comprehensive review of history as well as contemporary science.

This assessment was appreciated even by Europeans anxious to advance Arab rights who were generally unsympathetic to Zionism, such as Lawrence of Arabia. King Feisal, who at the time was negotiating with the British and the Zionists about his place in the new Middle East, publicly welcomed the investment of Jewish expertise as well as capital in Palestine. At the same time, Zionists recognized that Palestine already had a population, and they gave attention to sources of livelihood and the civil and religious rights of the Arab inhabitants.

COLONIZATION VERSUS COLONIALISM

Zionists adamantly rejected the charge made first during the mandate that they were engaged in yet another instance of European colonialism. In the words of Avraham Granovsky, a leading Zionist settlement official: "Jews come to Palestine to execute not a colonial, but a colonization policy." First articulated in 1931 in response to Arab accusations brought before a British commission to investigate communal violence in 1929, his analysis is also relevant to the contemporary literature of anti-Zionists and revisionist scholars.

Zionist settlement was not the product of conquest. It was based on the purchase of land or its acquisition through agreement. However, unlike the United States, Zionists were not a sovereign that could engage in making treaties. Attempts to gain territorial concessions from the Ottomans and the British were a staple of Zionist diplomacy from Herzl through the end of the British Mandate in 1948. The UN partition plan, for the first time, granted Jewish sovereignty and access to unused land that was under governmental control. Neither the UN nor the Zionist leadership intended the transfer of land or even a portion of the Arab population out of the areas of Palestine designated for a Jewish state. It was only in the course of the bitter Arab-initiated civil war of 1948 that land was conquered, either as a consequence of Arab flight and abandonment or of their forced expulsion.

It is significant that Zionism sought agreement over the right to settle in particular locales. Whatever absolute right Zionists believed they had, they well understood the practicality of legally acquiring territory from the resident population. As earlier chapters show, there was no independent authority in Palestine with whom Zionists could engage in reaching a settlement.

Elsewhere, settler groups invented "nations," if only because Europeans believed that treaties for obtaining land could be made only between apparently equal entities. Thus, colonizing powers "invented"—to use the current concept—artificial nations out of diverse groupings or tribes. This was not done in the case of Palestine's Arabs. Rather, it was widely held that they were part of the larger Arab nation that occupied much of the Middle East from northern Africa to the Persian Gulf. Hence, Zionist leaders sought to reach agreements with the Ottomans, European powers, and King Feisal. There was nothing at the time to suggest more direct negotiations. As late as 1947, the United Nations Special Committee on Palestine (UNSCOP) noted that a discrete Palestinian national identity was but an emerging phenomenon. It claimed that a distinctive Palestinian consciousness did not appear until after the Balfour Declaration and the establishment of the mandate or only after Zionism gained recognition for Jewish claims and programs. Paragraph 166 provided a succinct summary: "The desire of the Arab people of Palestine to safeguard their national existence is a very natural desire. However, Palestinian nationalism, as distinct from Arab nationalism, is itself a relatively new phenomenon which appeared only after the division of the 'Arab rectangle' by settlement of the First World War."

Recent academic scholarship does not substantially challenge this perception. Even important Palestinian scholars like Rashid Khalidi place the "awakening," although not the full development of a discrete Palestinian identity, in the decade prior to World War I. However, since even he presents a situation wherein Palestine's peasants lacked political institutions and the common visible expressions of a distinctive modern polity, it is not surprising that Zionism viewed them as integral parts of the larger Arab nation. Indeed, there is ample testimony that that is how they viewed themselves. Widespread recognition of Palestinian Arabs as a separate nationality with concomitant political rights is a relatively recent phenomenon that matured after Israeli independence and gained international support only during the 1970s.

Whether or not they constituted a discrete national group, the place of Palestine's Arabs within a Jewish sovereignty required definition. What did not occur was a policy of expulsion or transfer. Even Benny Morris, the revisionist historian most closely associated with documenting Israeli responsibility for the forced expulsion of Arabs during the War of Independence, does not see this as a consequence of concerted policy. He finds scattered evidence among the records of some Zionist officials for the idea of "transfer" but denies "any overall expulsory policy decision was taken by the

Yishuv's executive bodies . . . in the course of the 1948 war" (quoted in Rogan and Shlaim, p. 9). Moreover, the earliest instances of suggestions for transfer occurred during the mid-1930s at the initiative of British officials involved in the Peel Commission. Extensive and exacting research uncovered few incriminating incidents. These cannot be overlooked, but neither can the fact that they occurred during exceptional circumstances.

On the other hand, the vast literature of Zionist thought, diplomacy, and praxis records numerous examples of the attention given to building a country that would contain both Jews and Arabs. The issue and the record are public and readily accessible. Weizmann, for example, made speeches before innumerable forums proclaiming that Jewish settlement would take place "without harm to the present population, Jews or Arabs, and without displacing anybody" (quoted in The Jewish Agency for Palestine, 16). He vigorously objected to the oft-quoted statement of Sydney Webb, later Lord Passfield, who summed up his objections to further Jewish immigration with the claim that "there is no room to swing a cat in Palestine. It is full" (36).

Less well remembered but also part of the public record are the practical proposals of Zionist settlement experts. From the early 1930s, they responded to British White Papers by demonstrating in concrete ways how Zionist settlement could benefit Arab neighbors. Here there were no claims to racial or cultural superiority. On the contrary, they argued that there was no inherent Jewish technological superiority. What Zionist agriculture had achieved could be readily transmitted to others. This is exactly what happened in later years, when Israeli experts exported their achievements to Africa, Asia, and Central America, leapfrogging an Arab world that disqualified Jewish experts because of their religion and association with a Jewish state.

Serving and benefiting the Arabs in Palestine and the Middle East was integral to Zionist thought. For example, Herzl's utopian novel, *Altneuland*, depicts Jewish and Arab harmony in a society in which both benefit from a cornucopia of material blessings and mutual social appreciation. Both the Jewish and Arab heroes, David Litwak and Rashid Bey, are engineers who work together in harmony and enjoy friendly relations. At one point, Rashid Bey comments on the "blessings of Jewish immigration." He observes that Jews have brought Arab "employment, better food . . . their children go to school. Nothing has been done to interfere with their customs or their faith—they have only gained in welfare." In brief, Herzl envisioned Arabs would be responsive to the Jews, who would bring prosperity to the country, and that all would share in it. Such sentiments echo throughout Zionist writings over the past century. Zionism did not assume the inherent and permanent superiority of Jews or Europeans. In line with enlightened humanistic thinkers, they assumed the basic equality of all.

During the mandate, Zionist settlement did insist on Jewish labor to ensure that there would be employment for immigrants, but this was hardly exceptional; Jews were not employed in the Arab sector. Never, though, did this separation of the workforce imply inherent inequalities based on race, culture, or religion. Rather, it reflected the reality that in the Ottoman Empire, identities as well as associations were on an ethnic, religious, or national basis. Zionism had no intention of transforming the Middle East into an as yet unrealized American-style "state of its citizens." Rather, it expected Jews and Arabs to reach the same standard of living and share in regional prosperity. This principle underlies the widely read tract by Shimon Peres, *A New Middle East* (1993), which emerged as a blueprint for Jewish-Arab cooperation in the aftermath of the Oslo Accords. Peres envisages a peaceful Middle East where Jewish industrial and technological advances would work to everyone's benefit, and he predicts a future of harmony and peace.

The Zionist intention to share the benefits of their settlement experience was born of political necessity. The Balfour Declaration and the League of Nations recognized that even as Jews had the right to reestablish a national homeland in Palestine, the Arabs' civil, religious, and economic rights required protection. This was widely accepted by Zionist leaders and thinkers from across the political spectrum. It is not surprising that this was the position on the Left as well as of the intellectuals of Brith Shalom who supported binationalism, but even Vladimir Jabotinsky, the theoretician and leader of right-wing or Revisionist Zionism, advocated recognition and protection of all the rights of Arabs in Palestine except for national ones.

JEWS AS NATIVES

Zionist settlement also differed from European colonization because Jews had a prior and continuing connection to the land. The notion of *terra nullius* was designed to regulate the contact between foreigners and natives. Jews did not consider themselves strangers to the land. In Zionist theory and practice, reclaiming the land was an economic enterprise with a moral dimension. While the implications of *terra nullius* may have drawn on historical experience shared by many peoples at different periods and places the specific case of the Jews had a unique feature. They were returning home.

Unlike the experience of other European peoples in the "modern" period of European discovery after the voyages of Columbus, Zionist settlers did not come to master or despoil a rich foreign land flowing with oil, let alone milk and honey. Such a comparative perspective would lead us to consider whether Zionism was merely more or less just or benign than other forms of European colonialism. Zionist settlement may be more appropriately viewed from the perspective of more than three millennia of Jewish history and from the history of the country. This yields a far more generous view of Jewish settlement. It is this latter view that informed the world community in the period prior to the establishment of Israel.

It is for this reason that Arab apologists have gone to such great lengths to sever the historic connection between contemporary Jews and the historic Land of Israel. Denying this relationship makes it more plausible to view Zionism as but another form of European colonialism. Denial of these ties began to reach a wide public since at least the 1930s in the writings of Arab apologists such as George Antonius, the author of *The Arab Awakening* (1938). The trope developed in two directions. The first represents contemporary Jews as entirely distinct from the Hebrews of the Bible. The second claims that Jews do not constitute a nation or people but are merely adherents to a religion. These propositions dismiss beliefs Jews have held about themselves for millennia and reject the way peoples outside the Arab world have perceived Jews. Both denials—of the historic relationship to the land and to peoplehood—challenge the nature and enormity of the Zionist achievement at a time when the rights of nations are at the center of international discourse. This topic deserves separate treatment and is considered in the next chapter.

HISTORIC CONNECTION TO THE LAND

The discourse of claiming territory proceeds in two distinct directions. The first is internal and directed toward Jews themselves. The second is external and directed to non-Jews and the world community. The first contains elements about which Jews may differ but ultimately matter only to them. One such issue is the invocation of a divine promise and an interpretation of its meaning. The claim to a historic connection falls within the second category. In this instance, the argument may be based on scientific or generally observable proofs and may thereby resonate with the kinds of argumentation that other peoples make about themselves. The form of argumentation is often widespread, can be considered "universal," and has become part of the fabric of international law.

By the 1930s, there was a constant flow of literature detailing the relationship of Jews to Palestine. It appeared as academic scholarship with contributions by specialists in biblical history and archeology, the Hellenistic period and the Maccabees, and through Roman and Byzantine rule. This scholarship focused on the presence of vital Jewish societies for more than two millennia, from the Canaanites through well beyond the failed rebellions against Rome. Significantly, there were even Jewish communities in Palestine during most of the twelve centuries after the Muslim conquest. So even in the long period of exile when centers of Jewish life moved elsewhere in the Near East or to Western and Eastern Europe, there is testimony to a nearly unbroken Jewish presence that substantiates claims of continual residence in Palestine. As a last resort, Zionists could point to the small community of Peki'in in the mountains of the Galilee, not far from Safed, whose present-day residents could demonstrate that they were direct descendents of inhabitants of the village who had never gone into exile.

Although claims of connection and continuity could be made and sustained, it was nonetheless true that the Jewish community in Palestine was sparse at the inauguration of Zionist settlement. In a country with no regular governmental statistics, it is hard to establish firm numbers. As we have seen, at the eve of Zionist settlement in the 1880s, there were perhaps twenty-five thousand Jews in the country, most in the four holy cities of Jerusalem, Tiberias, Hebron, and Safed. More reliable statistics exist for 1900 indicating that one in ten, or fifty thousand out of a total population of five hundred thousand, were Jews. By the eve of World War II in 1939, one-third of the more than a million residents of Palestine were Jews. It was precisely this absolute and relative growth of the Yishuv that so aggravated tensions. Arabs saw this demographic change as endangering their position in the country. Zionists viewed it as a return to a historic situation that would benefit all. (See chapter 3.)

The internal discussion among religious Jews, and certainly sympathetic evangelicals but also many other Christians, could view the beginnings of large-scale Jewish immigration as a fulfillment of prophecy and thereby justified it. The discourse of international politics and law required another way of validating the same phenomenon. The discussion that originated among Zionists soon found its way into the international debates over Jewish immigration. One example of the evolution and presentation of this kind of argumentation is found in a tract published in the 1930s, first in Yiddish for American Jewish dailies and then in Hebrew for readers in the Yishuv, by Berl Locker, a leading Labor Zionist official resident in London as representative to the British government and to local Jewry. In *The Jews and Palestine: Historical Connection and Historic Right* (1938), Locker argues that Zionism is unique among movements that try to establish rights based on historic connection. He argues first that "the aim of Zionism is not to establish an alien rule over the population and the resources of the country for the benefit of an outside power, but to replant in its ancient home the people that was uprooted from it." He claims that Zionism was an exception among European settlement movements because it was engaged in the return of a people. The uniqueness of this phenomenon was given added force since they did not intend "to dominate and to exploit from without, but to come there to live and to work on the land, to build and develop it, to restore it. . . . Not to conquer a colony for a foreign motherland, but to build up a home and a fatherland for a homeless people." Thus, Zionism was colonization (settlement) and not colonization (an instrument of imperialism). People who return to a homeland engage in the former, not the latter.

Similar arguments were made by every Zionist leader, from David Ben-Gurion, Moshe Shertok (later Sharett), and Chaim Weizmann, to Vladimir Jabotinsky on countless occasions, including formal testimony before international commissions charged with examining counterclaims in the Arab/Jewish dispute. Their presentations were usually accompanied by the submission of extensive historical documentation as well as invocation of the significance of collective memory expressed in prayer and rituals and sustained in the national imagination. The widespread acceptance of their position was essential to the moral and legal legitimacy accorded Zionism and the State of Israel by Western-dominated international institutions.

"RECONSTITUTION" AND CULTURAL ACQUISITION: LANGUAGE AND NOMENCLATURE

The validity of the historic Jewish connection and its empowering qualities gained legitimacy in the international legal system when the British Mandate for Palestine in 1922 was established by the League of Nations. This body affirmed that Jews could "reconstitute" themselves in Palestine as a nation in their own land. "Reconstitute" had a clear and dramatic meaning. It signified recognition that the Jews were a nation like the other nations of the world. The mandate was intended to nurture and protect national development until independence as it did elsewhere in the system of mandates established at precisely the same time, notably for the Arab peoples of Syria and Iraq. Palestine was the locale designated for the Jewish people.

Reconstitution was at the core of the Zionist ideology. The use of the term in international law gave Zionist cultural, social, and political goals recognition and legitimacy. Terminology and declarations were not enough. Evidence of reconstitution was required to solidify the argument for the legitimacy of resettling the land. Together with making desert bloom and historical rights, "cultural acquisition" supported territorial claims. Perhaps the most visible sign of national reconstitution was the revival of Hebrew as a living language rather than merely a sacred one employed in ancient rituals and in the study of holy texts. Similarly, marking the landscape and the development of an indigenous culture with roots in the historic past was another facet of the same achievement. Both are examined in turn.

Language

New states that began as colonies outside Europe were often artificial or "imagined communities," and Europeans were crucial to their invention. The Zionist imagination created a society unlike European inventions. Jews explicitly distanced themselves in crucial ways from the European exile they left behind. They, of course, never imagined their polity tied to a European state. They always understood that the ultimate goal was independence. This was also largely true for the new society they intended to build. While in many ways they transplanted European culture, they consciously and overtly rejected it in yet other crucial areas. In particular, this involved a constant and deliberate attempt to endow the land with an explicitly Jewish character by recapturing and reshaping the traditional Jewish culture as practiced in the Diaspora to one applicable for the homeland. Perhaps the prime example is the singular success of restoring Hebrew as the language of the Land of Israel. It was through culture and the marking of the country with names that the imagination of Zionism consciously and clearly expressed its distinctiveness.

Although Hebrew was used continuously during the millennia of exile in the study of sacred texts and the conduct of learned discourse as well as in the liturgy, it was rarely a living language used to conduct personal affairs. Zionism, perhaps alone among contemporary national movements, succeeded in restoring an ancient language into a living one with vibrant popular literature, modern media, scientific scholarship, and the conduct of commerce and government. This remarkable phenomenon began with the conscious decision at the end of the nineteenth century to bring up children as Hebrew speakers. More than eight million people now speak Hebrew, more than six million—Jews and Arabs—in the State of Israel, more than a million in the Palestinian territories under Israeli control, and still others across the worldwide Jewish Diaspora. For a language that initially had no native speakers and a society composed of numerous immigrants who maintained their native languages even as they assimilated a new one, this has been an impressive instance of reconstitution.

The Hebrew renaissance indicates enormous cultural vitality and a product of a self-conscious and directed campaign. Its very success obscures the fact that other choices were possible. Zionists rejected two alternatives that may have appeared more likely and more natural. They could have transferred a European language to Palestine. In fact, Herzl was certain the language would be German, since he was unable to imagine conducting a modern society in an ancient tongue. He wondered, for example, how one could operate a train in Hebrew. When his followers insisted in 1911 that German become the language of instruction in the Technikum (later the Technion and the country's first institute for technology), a *kulturkampf*, or culture war erupted. Hebrew was victorious, though at that time it lacked even a basic vocabulary in the sciences and engineering. Words were invented from ancient Hebrew roots and modern terms were Hebraized. Interestingly, even major authors of the emerging national Hebrew literature grew up among European languages and spoke them in their own households well into the mandate. A generation of native Hebrew-speaking authors only emerged close to the establishment of the state and did not reach full bloom until the first decade of Independence. As Zionism enters its second century, there is no area of life in Israel that is not conducted in Hebrew, from nuclear physics to popular music, including a Hebrew version of rap.

The other possibility was Arabic. It is an unfortunate but understandable fact that proportionately, more Jews knew Arabic during the earlier periods of settlement, when Jews were a small minority living within a larger and established Arab population. As with minorities elsewhere, many acquired the language of the surrounding society. This was appreciated even in advance of large-scale settlement. Thus, when the Hebrew University was conceived in Europe, its founders planned that one of the initial faculties would be an Oriental Institute devoted to the languages and cultures of the Near East. With the growth of the Jewish population into a significant majority in Israel, knowledge of Arabic declined but remained extant most frequently among Jewish immigrants from Middle Eastern countries. Nevertheless, Arabic would not have overcome or supplanted the movement to reestablish Hebrew. Despite recognition of the need to know Arabic and Arab culture, Zionists found that Arab society was inadequate for supplying models of what Zionism required for constructing a modern Jewish society. There was little to learn from Arab experience in developing a modern economy, either in agriculture, industry, or technology. Similarly, while railway stations and factories might benefit in the use of arabesques as decoration, Arab architecture was unsuited to the requirements of modern buildings. The social, economic, and political systems, as well as the technologies expected in a reconstituted Jewish society, did not exist in the Arab Near East. Zionists borrowed and adapted European concepts and practices and even invented their own.

Nomenclature

A symbolic but crucial element in the search for an appropriate and authentic reconstituted culture is found in how Zionism set out to refashion the country's landscape. In this process, they consciously ignored and set aside many of the physical markers as well as the social and cultural ones of both the European past and of Arab neighbors. Secular Zionists, who controlled this process, recovered names found in traditional, sacred texts, particularly the Bible and Talmud. They also celebrated leaders who had helped the Jewish people persevere in the long exile and those who led them in the return home. Rules and principles for selecting names had existed informally since the 1880s and became institutionalized during the mandate. With independence, all obstacles to marking the landscape in Hebrew and Jewish history were removed.

Reconstitution thereby involved reestablishing the historic link between the Jewish people and the land through renaming Palestine. This process actually began in Europe in anticipation of colonization. Zionist societies across Europe since the 1880s not only imagined settlements, but also named them. Their covenants labeled the communities with names that manifested their intention to reshape the land in terms derived from Jewish texts, history, and traditions. For example, Rosh Pinah, one of the first settlements founded in 1882 at the base of the upper Galilee, means "cornerstone." The name derives from a verse from Psalms (118:22), which is frequently recited in prayers that metaphorically celebrate national salvation:

"The stone which the builders rejected has become the chief cornerstone,"
Similarly, Rishon le Zion, "a harbinger to Zion," was founded on the
coastal plain also in 1882. Its name, too, is based on a biblical verse: "The
things once predicted to Zion—Behold, here they are! And to Jerusalem a
messenger of good tidings" (Isaiah 41:27). Another, Ramat Rachel, "the
high place of Rachel," was founded as a kibbutz south of Jerusalem in 1926.
It overlooks the city of Bethlehem and the traditional burial site of the ma-
triarch Rachel.

Arabic place-names were treated as corruptions of Hebrew and were
replaced with what was taken to be the original. This practice was first established by generations of Christian biblical archeologists who, since at
least the 1840s, tried to recover Palestine's biblical (i.e., Hebrew) past that
they expected lay just beneath the ruins of a now desolate land. They
tended to view Arabs as primitive guardians of a country with a glorious
past. Discovery of the biblical place-names appeared to verify their understanding of their sacred and historical texts. Jews naturally continued the
process.

More contemporary materials drawn from the Zionist experience and
the struggle to establish a state also served as inspiration. For example, Sde
Eliyahu, a kibbutz in Beit She'an founded in 1939, was named for Rabbi
Eliahu Guttmacher, an early Zionist leader who lived in Germany in the
nineteenth century. Guttmacher stood against fellow orthodox rabbis in defending Zionism's position that Jews ought to take the initiative in solving
their problems rather than await the Messiah. Similarly, Zichron Ya'acov,
"Jacob's Memorial," was originally founded in 1882 on the slopes of the
Carmel by Romanian immigrants, who named it "Zamrim" after a nearby
deserted Arab village. Within two years, the settlement failed and was res-
cued by Baron Rothschild. The moshavah was then renamed in memory of
his father, Jacob (Ya'acov). Other settlements memorialized Zionist leaders
such as Haim Arlosoroff (Givat Haim 1932), Berl or Dov Beer Kaznelson
(Be'eri 1946), and the Hebrew writer Yosef Haim Brenner (Givat Brenner
1928). Also, Ha'Ogen, "the Anchor," a kibbutz on the coastal plain, was
founded in 1947 by Holocaust survivors who wished to indicate that after
their sufferings and wanderings they had come home and were anchored in
this land. Whether recalling people or historical events, Zionism set a Jewish imprint on the landscape to reflect national experience through the ages
in the homeland and Diaspora.

The hundreds of towns and villages placed across the map of Palestine
prior to the establishment of Israel were also given new or recovered Hebrew names. The landscape, too, was renamed with reference, whenever

possible, to the original biblical place-names. Thus, the Sea of Galilee again became the Kinneret, and a kibbutz of that name was established on its banks. Throughout, the new nomenclature was used to create a new reality. As Jews returned to the Land of Israel, they continued this process in an attempt to reclaim the grandeur of their own past. This, too, was unique among European-born colonizers. In Israel, there is no New Vilna, New Bialystock, New Warsaw, New Minsk, New Pinsk, nor New Plonsk, unlike in former European colonies that imagined a New England, New York, New Orleans, New Madrid, or Louisiana, Maryland, Oxford, Cambridge, Paris, Berlin, and so on. Instead, Zionists celebrated the return to history of biblical Rehovoth, Ashkelon, and Modi'in, the birthplace of the Maccabees. Jerusalem, of course, did not require a new name.

In addition to naming entire communities, Jews set their stamp on their interiors. Thousands of names were given to streets, public squares, and the landscape, with signs in Hebrew everywhere signaling the return of Jews to the Land of Israel. They also appeared on maps and in official documents, newspaper stories, literature, and song. When Israel was established, it set up its own committee for naming the landscape in its many particulars. Two of its members had served in a similar capacity as representatives of the Zionist authorities during the mandate and brought that experience to the new state. While the assignment of names had preceded the establishment of Israel, a sovereign Jewish state gave unprecedented latitude and authority. The committee named nearly eight hundred sites in the first fifty years of the state. The total effect invited residents and foreign observers to appreciate that the settlements were the concrete manifestation of national revival in the homeland.

The meaning of this large-scale enterprise of physical construction and spiritual renewal was also captured in music, art, and literature. Songs were perhaps the most popular and pervasive method for affirming the significance and meaning of settlement. Many of the melodies may have been European or contained echoes of Arab chords, but the words signified new meanings. Popular songs included "Mi yivneh ha-Galil?"—"Who will build the Galilee?"—and "Who will build a house in Tel Aviv?" Scores of songs were written to celebrate new settlements in every area of the country. Others celebrated the excitement of settling the hills and valleys of the Galilee and the Negev desert. The reconstitution of the Jewish people was translated from the language of political and legal documents to the lyrics and music of folk songs.

Although many songs were connected with rural, agricultural settlements, there was no less a repertoire connected with the building of Tel

Aviv. Poets and musicians in this center of nascent national culture celebrated what was taking place around them. They sang of hammers, crushing stones, whitewash, steel, and concrete. Some actually engaged in construction work and composed songs to imitate the rhythm of work in
paving roads or working on buildings. Another favorite theme was the
building of the port of Tel Aviv under the rubric of the "conquest of the
sea," even as land-based pioneers in the interior sang of the "conquest of labor" in the "redeeming of the land" or "making the desert bloom." Here,
too, there was a sense of collective rejuvenation through turning the sand
dunes into a thriving city and in mastering the proximate sea so that it
would serve the new Jewish city. One favorite captured the exultation of
the first day that the port of Tel Aviv opened. "Tel Aviv Shore" was first
sung as workers joined arms and danced in the water alongside the newly
opened pier: "With strength and song we are here, we are here; As we
turned sand into a city; We shall make the sea into a homeland!"

One could consider the collective work of modern Hebrew poets and
songwriters as a contemporary, secular version of the *Song of Songs*. This
book's very expressive and sensual language describes lovers amid the fauna
and flora of the Land of Israel. In Jewish tradition, it has been interpreted
as a metaphor for the love that exists between God and the children of Israel. God is symbolized as the bridegroom and his people are the bride. In
fact, verses and phrases from the *Song of Songs* have entered into the repertoire of contemporary secular Hebrew songs with the same intimate, lov-
ing relationship carried on by the people and the land. The intimacy of this
connection is reflected in the school texts of the Yishuv in a subject termed
"knowing the land" (*yediat ha'aretz*), where the biblical word for "knowing" refers to deep and intimate knowledge rather than mere information.

By 1949, nearly two hundred composers had produced more than four
thousand Hebrew folk songs, most of these since the 1920s. While some
composed melodies, others—including some of the most important Hebrew poets of the Yishuv—wrote the lyrics. The schools, the Jewish National Fund, the Histadrut, the kibbutz movement, other institutions, and
individuals provided a voracious market for what Eric Hobsbawn has
termed the "invented tradition."

This was clearly a paradox. Folk music and folk culture by definition
derive from the past, and their unknown authors spring from the people. In
this case, the songs were sung by immigrants seeking an authentic and deep-
rooted relationship with the homeland. Through ubiquitous choral groups,
records, radio broadcasts, and inexpensive sheet music, the repertoire became an instant common heritage. Again, some of the form—in terms of

melodies and harmonies—derived from Europe, particularly from Russia. Other songs derived from actual or imagined Yemenite traditions. These diverse sources blended to create a shared heritage that reflected love of the land and hope for regeneration by equally diverse groups of Jewish settlers who had committed to reconstituting themselves as a nation.

Recovery and invention of the Hebrew past is also manifest in other art forms. At the Bezalel School of Arts and Crafts in Jerusalem, the Bible played a central role in the motifs programmatically emphasized. Founded in 1906, the institution taught European techniques in the building and decorative arts but adapted them to Zionist purposes. Biblical motifs were favored as Bezalel artists dwelt on heroes, agriculture, and the celebration of festivals in the natural setting of the country. Although students studied current fashions in European painting from impressionism, futurism, and cubism, their work was consciously directed to the search for something new and nationally authentic. They struck roots in the landscape and developed a native vernacular related to but distinct from European models.

The rediscovery of the land, the rejection of Europe, and the creation of a new, modern Hebrew were captured in the term applied by the end of the 1930s to native-born Jewish youth: "sabra" (the fruit of a cactus). Ironically, the cactus and its fruit, also termed "prickly pear," was indigenous to America and arrived in Palestine around the seventeenth century, although it has been popularly considered native to Palestine. Different in culture and language from Diaspora ancestors, the sabra was the "new Jew" fostered by the Zionist movement. At one extreme, perceived and hoped-for differences led to a total rejection of Europe and the Diaspora experience, as in the Canaanite movement that appeared in the 1940s. More commonly, a process of more or less radical adaptation of European Jewish culture was advocated. Whatever the specific form or the result, Zionism challenged itself with the task of creating Hebrew-speaking individuals feeling completely at home in the old/new land and building a distinctive society that would be differentiated from the Diaspora and Europe. As we saw in the previous chapter, they may have succeeded too well. After the creation of the state, when the leaders of the Yishuv came to evaluate what they had achieved, they often lamented the culture of the sabra. The process of reconstitution could extend too far. Certainly by the 1950s, there were signs that sabras, the generation born and raised in Israel, had become too detached from the European roots of Zionist culture.

This theme of adaptation, transformation, and rejection of Europe reverberated throughout the intellectual and cultural reality of the Yishuv. It was patently clear that Zionism was not engaging in mere imitation or in direct transplantation. Rather, Zionists strove to imagine and renew a distinctive form of national life and to imbue the landscape and their culture with new meaning. It is abundantly clear that Zionists did not see themselves as foreigners or conquerors. For centuries, in the Diaspora they had been strangers. In the Land of Israel, they expended enormous creative energy to feel quickly and easily at home. The imaginings that animated the first generation of Zionists at the end of the nineteenth century found full expression in the Yishuv well before Independence. It was this rejuvenation that impressed a large portion of the world community with the vitality and reality of the Zionist entity. Two-thirds of the members of the United Nations voted for the partition of Palestine into independent Jewish and Arab states on November 29, 1947. Jews had successfully made the case that they were entitled to independence within that portion of the country they had so distinctively and successfully marked. The historic tragedy is that Arabs did not recognize the authenticity and legitimacy of what had been accomplished.

The search for recognition by Israelis continues. In the aftermath of the 1967 Six Day War, Arab states convening in Khartoum declared that there could be no negotiations, no recognition, and no peace with Israel. The first significant departure to this long-standing position came about a decade later, after another war and considerable negotiation, when Egypt's Anwar Sadat came to the Knesset in Jerusalem in 1978 to declare that there would be no more war and to directly recognize the existence and legitimacy of the Jewish state. Still later, in September 1993, the PLO signed accords with Israel in Washington that gave recognition to Israel, apparently transcending its charter that denied the legitimacy of Israel and enjoined all Arabs to use force to destroy it. King Hussein of Jordan signed a peace treaty with Israel a year later, in October 1994. Yet the extraordinary violence in the past decade, often in the form of terror attacks and suicide bombing, suggests how unstable these tentative steps to normalization and acceptance may be. For many Israelis, the possibility of overcoming Arab hostility is still an uncertain hope. Doubt is the consequence not merely of physical, political, and verbal violence from the Arab world, but also of the uncompromising rejection of any Jewish state, particularly among Islamic fundamentalists.

We now turn to a review of how Zionism and Israel have understood this rejection and how understandings of the past inform the approach to possible accommodation.

11

ACCOMMODATION WITH THE ARABS OF PALESTINE

Conflict and consensus have also marked Israel's attitude toward accommodation with the Arabs. Here, too, interpretations of the past contribute to how Jews assessed present and future relations. Prior to the outbreak of Arab violence after the Balfour Declaration and the issuance of the mandate, there was little sense among Zionists that there was to be a struggle with another national movement. For about the first forty years of Jewish settlement, Zionists attempted to convince fellow Jews as well as the world of the value and righteousness of their cause without reference to an Arab problem. The resolutions of the World Zionist Organization of this period contain no reference to actual or future conflict. In view of what has happened, scholars have tried to establish precisely when Zionists came to recognize that there was indeed a problem.

Many find the moment of discovery in an 1891 essay by a leading Russian Zionist intellectual, Ahad Ha'am (Asher Ginsburg), written after his first visit to Palestine. Titled "Truth from the Land of Israel," he devotes a total of all but two paragraphs to Arabs. While critical of the attitude of Jewish colonists toward them, his larger focus is on the mismanagement of colonization by Zionist officials and agencies. He never expresses doubt that Jewish settlement is a proper and justifiable project. In the brief reference to Arabs, he does suggest that tensions would quickly dissipate if they were treated better as individuals. Like others of his generation, he did not believe that Palestine's Arabs constituted a national entity that might challenge Jews. Moreover, in accord with his generation's understanding of *terra nullius*, he knew that the land had a limited population and was technically and economically backward. He expected that in the face of successful colonization, the locals would either welcome the benefits Jews would bring or eventually have no choice but to accept the reality of Jewish settlement when the number of Jews reached a decisive majority. Thus, Ahad Ha'am's minimal two-paragraph commentary, as one commentator has observed, "is the exception that proves the rule."

Yitzhak Epstein is probably the first Zionist who recognized in the local population a distinctive people with a potential for opposing Zionism. Epstein was a Russian-born pioneer who became a Hebrew teacher in the Galilee after immigrating in 1886. He expressed his forebodings in "A Hidden Question," an essay written in 1907 after twenty years of pioneering, in a relatively obscure Hebrew journal published in Palestine. Here, too, Epstein conforms to the regnant expectation that Arabs will accept Zionist society for all the benefits it could bring in economic prosperity, health care, and other services if, as Epstein cautioned, the Zionists treat the local population with consideration and wisdom. In this he followed Ahad Ha'am's advice. Epstein did not believe international diplomacy would be enough. He optimistically believed Jewish settlers could resolve differences with the local population over land, which he viewed as the primary source of conflict.

A wide and ever-increasing recognition of the potential conflict emerged only after the Balfour Declaration. Arab reaction soon followed in increasingly painful and violent forms. As early as 1920 or 1921, there were outbreaks of organized violence in rural areas and cities. The British response to Arab violence and political pressure resulted first in modifying the Balfour Declaration by detaching in 1922 the land east of the Jordan River, what is now the Kingdom of Jordan. They then progressively limited immigration and land purchases until 1939, when both were effectively halted. The bloody Arab Revolt of 1936 to 1939, as well as the approach of World War II, led the British to seek the support of the far larger Arab population in the Middle East, thereby bringing about the reversal in their policy toward Jews. In the face of these developments, Zionism sought to find an effective way to counter or at least mollify Arab opposition. As in so many other areas, there was considerable divergence on how to respond.

In an earlier chapter, we examined the views of Martin Buber and his colleagues in Brith Shalom. They drew on readings of the Bible that both promised the return of Jews and demanded they create a society rooted in Jewish ethics. Many were pacifists and thought that conflict had to be avoided at all costs. Judah Magnes, for example, left the premier pulpit of reform Judaism, Temple Emanuel in New York City, amid his opposition to American participation in World War I. Buber, Magnes, and their colleagues pressed for dialogue as the only means to resolve conflict. They never deviated from this position, despite growing pressure for transforming Palestine into a refuge for persecuted Jews. Their interpretation of Jewish tradition resulted in advocating a binational state, surrendering the idea that Jews would gain sole sovereignty over any portion of Palestine. Their memorandum to the United Nations on the eve of its decision to partition Palestine was an appeal for "an undivided binational Palestine composed of two nationalities, Jews and Arabs." They urged further that this state become a single "independent constitutional state."

This plan did not go anywhere since few outside a small core group of Jewish intellectuals and activists believed that either Jews or Arabs would compromise on their own nation-states. There were other impractical demands. Brith Shalom suggested limiting immigration in accordance with "the economic absorptive capacity of the country, the Jews being free to reach numerical parity with the Arabs." This antagonized Arabs who wanted fewer Jews. At the same time, it angered fellow Jews who demanded larger quotas in reaction to the growing menace of virulent European anti-Semitism. In sum, binationalism was a nonstarter. Brith Shalom and leftist intellectuals, particularly from the socialist Hashomer Ha-Tzair, were isolated voices overtaken by the vast majority that began to prepare for conflict. However attractive, pacifism and binationalism were largely perceived as exotic and eccentric in the face of a struggle for survival.

At the other end of the spectrum, Vladimir Jabotinsky, the leader of right-wing Revisionist Zionism, had long urged his followers that both Jewish history and what could be learned from comparable historical situations required the building of an impregnable defense to withstand long-term conflict. After having witnessed the first flare-ups of Arab violence, he wrote in "The Iron Wall," his 1923 seminal essay:

> It is impossible to dream, now and in the foreseeable future, of a voluntary agreement between Jews and the Palestinian Arabs. . . . Apart from those who were born blind, all moderate Zionists had understood that there can be no hope—not a glimmer of it—to obtain the consent of the Palestinian Arabs to the idea of turning "Palestine"' into a country with a Jewish majority.

His reading of history informed him that there is not one instance of a country where an indigenous population consented to their land being settled by newcomers: "And no such nation will willingly agree to new landlords or even to partners." He did not expect that Arabs would exchange economic and social advancement for giving up their homeland. "I totally reject," wrote Jabotinsky, "this explanation of the Arab character." In sum, he found no evidence that binationalism can work in Palestine or anywhere.

With the prospect of a long conflict with the Arabs of Palestine, patience, fortitude, and strength were the essential ingredients for ensuring success. Only if this were done could there be a successful and peaceful resolution. Jabotinsky notes, "I do not intend to state that no agreement with the Palestinian Arabs is possible. Only a voluntary agreement is impossible." He thought that so long as Arabs harbor "even a glimmer of hope that they could get rid of us, no promises or negotiations would bring them to change their minds." The creation of Jewish power and the willingness to use it are the only guarantees of success, which he defined as ensuring that within a Jewish state, "both people could live in peace like good neighbors." Until then, there could be no substitute for the "iron wall."

Jabotinsky's "iron wall," whether or not acknowledged, became the policy of Zionism for about the next half-century. Even Jabotinsky's opponents in Labor concluded that they required the requisite strength and willingness to use it in an inevitable struggle. Nevertheless, the Zionist Left and Right would repeatedly differ over significant issues: Precisely for how long will "the iron wall" be necessary? Are there actions or even gestures Israel can undertake to mollify Arab antagonism? How restrained or proactive should Israel be when confronted with violence? Can one discern signs of change on the Arab side? When does a militant reaction deepen hostility and even prolong it? These are the very difficult sets of calculations that all who accept Jabotinsky's analysis must consider. After all, even Jabotinsky posited eventual Arab acceptance of Israel. Assessing the attitudes and intentions of the enemy as well as interrogating one's own assumptions have become the underlying discourse within the Zionist movement, particularly among secular Jews. Religious Zionism will be treated in a separate discussion.

The building of strong defenses and the search for accommodation coexisted, even if the relative weight accorded to each changed. Ben-Gurion is the key individual through which to observe the process for a crucial forty-five years, from the Balfour Declaration through his retirement in 1963, when he served in nearly equal measure as the prime leader of the Histadrut, the chairman of the Jewish Agency Executive in Palestine, and Israel's founding prime minister and minister of defense.

TALKS BETWEEN JEWS AND ARABS

Ben-Gurion, who immigrated to Palestine from Eastern Europe in 1906, came to understand the depth of the Arab challenge only during the mandate. Although he recounts having contacts with Arabs soon after his arrival, these descriptions in his diary and other publications are personal and anecdotal, based on brief and infrequent contact since, typically, he lived within the confines of the society created by fellow pioneers. The need to establish official contact occurred only after he became chairman of the Jewish Agency Executive in 1933. It was then that he turned formally as well as privately to leaders of the Arab community in Palestine. The failure of these talks left him sensing the inevitability of conflict.

The search for interlocutors was difficult because of the imbalance between Jewish and Arab political organization. While the Yishuv had elected institutions that enjoyed recognition by the British, the League of Nations, and world Jewry, Palestine's Arabs had no comparable structure. They had, in Ben-Gurion's view, "no authorized spokesman and the leaders were divided in their views and attitudes" (1972). In this situation he chose to speak first with Musa Alami, who was serving as the attorney general in the Mandatory administration. He then turned to Anuni Abdul Hadi, the leader of the Istiqlal party in Palestine. Significantly, contacts were arranged through third parties, often by Judah Magnes of Brith Shalom. Direct communications were difficult because if they became public, the Arab side terminated them. Ben-Gurion, for example, once traveled to Geneva for talks, but this initiative ended when it was reported in the press. Reluctance to meet with Israelis has resulted in "track-two" or behind-the-scenes diplomacy from the 1930s through the meetings in Oslo and beyond. "Shuttle diplomacy," both public and private, has long been necessary. Third parties, whether the British, Americans, representatives of other countries, or international organizations, have often had to act as intermediaries. The underlying difficulty has been that Arabs have not acknowledged the legitimacy of Zionism and have been concerned that public meetings might appear to grant unwanted recognition. Abdallah and Hussein, the kings of Jordan who had extensive and ongoing contacts with Zionist leaders, usually succeeded in keeping them secret.

There are repetitive themes throughout these discussions. During the 1930s, Ben-Gurion insistently emphasized the benefits that Zionism would bring. In response, Musa Alami told Ben-Gurion in their first conversation that Palestine's Arabs would prefer the land to remain poor and desolate even for a century or until they themselves were capable of developing it properly. Even at the price of forgoing material benefits, Musa Alami and a long line of successors have consistently objected to Jews settling and exercising control over any portion of Palestine. Arabs correctly understood that Zionism would be consistently unyielding on the fundamental issues of sovereignty and the immigration that would make a Jewish state possible. Current Palestinian opposition to Israel's Law of Return may be couched in the guise of a democratic principle and human rights, but there has long been a demographic subtext: the struggle over the relative proportion of Arabs and Jews in the Holy Land.

Throughout his long career, Ben-Gurion elaborated on a vision of a renewed Arab Near East in which Jews would play a supporting but certainly not dominant role. The Jewish state would be integrated into the family of new nations that would emerge from the disintegration of the Ottoman Empire. Ben-Gurion maintained that the Arabs of Palestine "would remain where they were, their lot would improve, and even politically they would not be dependent on us, even after we came to constitute the vast majority of the population" (1972). He observed that they would continue to be part of the large Arab Middle East. In this, he argued, there was a basic difference between Jews and Arabs in Palestine: "For us, this Land was everything, *and there was nothing else* [Ben-Gurion's emphasis]. For the Arabs, Palestine was only a small portion of the large and numerous Arab countries." In this sense, the Arabs in Palestine would never actually be a minority, for their true patrimony extended from the Mediterranean coast to the Persian Gulf and from the Taurus Mountains to the Atlantic. It was beyond Ben-Gurion's ken and that of other Zionist leaders, then and thereafter, why the Arabs of Palestine would be unwilling to allow a Jewish majority in one modest corner of their vast world, and why this relatively small group, so able and willing to contribute to the larger Arab nation, was so completely and utterly rejected.

The relative small size of land required for a Jewish state was raised in a very different way and in far greater force to the non-Arab world. Jews needed Palestine more than Arabs. The appreciation for a Jewish state rested not only in history, ancient and modern, and on Arab neglect as opposed to the rights acquired through Jewish productive labor. The argument was also based on existential needs that endowed Zionism with "moral precedence." That is, while recognizing the rights of others to live in the same territory, moral precedence gave Jews priority because of the need to survive. Arabs had a vast estate and were not threatened with physical destruction. In making the argument this way, Zionist leaders invoked the "right of asylum" as a universal human right that warrants priority.

It is pertinent to recall that "moral precedence" was argued even prior to the Holocaust, when it took on even greater urgency. It was raised in a variety of forms ever since Pinsker and his generation sought a refuge for Jews after the outbreak of the anti-Jewish pogroms in 1881. In Palestine, this principle was invoked well before World War II. Both sides appealed to theology, history, and connection with the land in fact and in memory, but the right to asylum singularly marked Jewish claims. The argument for rescuing Jews was made with increasing urgency as the world became an ever more dangerous place for Jews in the interwar period. Ultimately, Ben-Gurion observed, if there was to be violence in Palestine, it was preferable to that which might occur in Europe: "If we had to choose between pogroms in Germany, Poland or some other Diaspora country and pogroms in Erez Israel, we would choose pogroms in this country" (1972). Zionism became so desperate for asylum that it was prepared to substantially reduce its claim to the historic and divinely promised homeland. Moral precedence thereby took priority even over historical claims and the divine promise for all of the Land of Israel. When Jews accepted partition, first at the suggestion of the British (1937) and then through the United Nations (1947), Arabs' obduracy became ever more frustrating and provocative.

Arab and Jewish positions had become well-rehearsed before Ben-Gurion conducted his final talks with an Arab leader in the spring of 1936. He then met with George Antonius, a leading Lebanese Christian who served under the British in Palestine and spent much time in London. The latter had a powerful influence with the British leadership through personal contacts and writings. While not an elected leader, he was widely recognized as an eloquent and influential Arab spokesman. Judah Magnes arranged the meetings for Ben-Gurion and participated in them.

The Ben-Gurion–Antonius meetings starkly reveal the terms of disagreement. In the course of three far-ranging discussions, they explored the history of the Jews and Arabs surveyed, as well as the contemporary situation. They also examined a variety of scenarios in which Jews might return from Europe and again become integrated in the Near East; Antonius suggested Syria, Iraq, and Transjordan as venues in addition to Palestine. Forms of governance were also discussed, including suggestions for a legislative council in Palestine and Jewish autonomy in cantons. What was clear from the beginning was a total unwillingness to consider that there might be parity in any legislative body in any canton or portion of the Arab world, including Palestine. Antonius insisted that Jews remain a minority everywhere. Over this fundamental issue, there was no compromise. The talks ended in April, and an Arab rebellion against the British ensued in Palestine and lasted for three years. Ben-Gurion never again met with an Arab leader before or after Independence.

Antonius's views were set forth in the period's most influential pro-Arab volume, *The Arab Awakening* (1938). It deeply affected British opinion, thereby contributing to the increasingly unsympathetic policy toward Zionism as expressed in the White Paper of 1939. That government policy statement effectively voided the Balfour Declaration by consigning Jews to the status of a permanent minority with severe controls limiting purchase of land and immigration. With this shift, the making of Palestine into yet another Arab state was apparently set in motion.

It is extraordinary that when Antonius and Ben-Gurion met, Antonius did not voice the views he was to popularize so soon thereafter. It gives one pause about the multiple levels at which Arab-Jewish encounters take place. Not everything is or, perhaps, can be voiced in direct encounters. Ben-Gurion did not feel challenged about the national character of Jews or their historic relationship to the land. He thought this was an obvious and uncontested fact. A little more than a decade after their meeting, Ben-Gurion would read out Israel's Declaration of Independence that contained the justifications for statehood based on the national and historic rights of the Jewish people. By then, the unexpressed opinion of Antonius had become a vital component in the Arab public position against a Jewish state.

The Arab Awakening argues that the Arabs of Palestine have deep roots and an unbroken connection with the land from the ancient, pre-Hebrew past. Conversely, it was the Hebrews whose connection was interrupted or lapsed. He would further claim that not only had the ancient Hebrews disappeared as a people, but also contemporary Jews are merely members of a religious confessional community. Judaism exists, but the Jewish people do not. This redefinition of Jews completely undermined the Zionist program. In the post–World War I world, "people" had the right to claim a state. Wilson's fourteen points, the creation of the League of Nations, and of the United Nations reflected the modern belief that the actors of history are necessarily nation-states. The origin of this idea is rooted in European thought after the French Revolution. Freedom and liberty could not just happen. They had to be implemented by political communities organized around distinct peoples. Hence, nationalism was considered a progressive ideal that would enhance the march of the Enlightenment's highest political ideals.

Ironically, at the moment Antonius was writing, Nazi Germany was carrying nationalism to such a brutal extreme that subsequent generations have sought to limit the abuses of the modern nation-state through appeals to "human rights." At present, many hold that national rights are necessarily secondary to human rights. However, this new concept was not yet invented or defined in the period when the crucial debates were taking place over the future of Palestine. The nation-state was the privileged form of polity in the absence of any other instrument to effectively extend and protect rights. To denationalize Jews therefore emasculated their claim to statehood and rendered them, at their peril, to the will of the gentile majority. This did not trouble Antonius. In his view, the Arabs of Palestine were the only people in Palestine, and only they had a right to a state.

This charge quickly spread, becoming a staple in Arab public documents and debates over the future of Palestine. It is still part of the anti-Israel discourse found throughout the Arab world. The Palestine Liberation Organization's National Charter of 1968 clearly reflects this view and has become the most potent instrument for disseminating and inculcating it throughout the Arab Near East and beyond. The echoes of Antonius are clearly found in the often cited paragraph 20:

> The Balfour Declaration, the Mandate Instrument, and all their consequences, are hereby declared null and void. The claim of historical or spiritual links between the Jews and Palestine is neither in conformity with historical fact nor does it satisfy the requirements for statehood. Judaism is a revealed religion; it is not a separate nationality, nor are all the Jews a single people with a separate identity; they are citizens of their respective countries.

With Jews stripped of their national identity, the way was cleared to claim Zionism was merely an extension of European imperialism. This, too, fits with Antonius's analysis of the behavior of the British and other Western powers after World War I. Thus, rather than enjoying the benefits and privileges of a "national liberation movement," Jews become colonialist oppressors to be opposed in a just war by an indigenous people. In the Hamas statements from the 1980s, opposition to Jews incorporates this analysis but moves beyond the secular political frame to a theological justification of the Muslim obligation for jihad. Stripping Jews of their nationality became integral to justify war to destroying the Jewish state.

THE IRON WALL AND THE SEARCH FOR COMPROMISE

Israel's war of independence concluded with armistice lines rather than normal relations and recognized borders. Suspension of war did not mean peace or recognition of Israel. There was no normalization of relations with open diplomatic relations and trade. Instead, there were constant terror attacks by fedayeen who crossed the armistice lines and attacked primarily civilians. These incidents and hostile declarations led to the expectation of a second round that occurred in the 1956 war with Egypt in the Sinai. There was yet to be another round in 1967. After yet another Israeli success on the battlefield, the 1968 Palestine Liberation Organization (PLO) National Charter pledged a continuation of struggle until Israel's destruction. It remains to be seen whether the post-Arafat era will bring yet another armistice in the form of a meaningful suspension of conflict or a fundamental change in Arab attitudes toward a Jewish state.

In the face of this reality, Israelis have supported a militarily strong state and have accepted the burdens this imposes. Consensus on these policies has not closed debate on critical security issues. Precisely how strong does Israel need to be and at what price? Even more difficult to ascertain, when is Israeli power and security sufficient to reach out and probe possibilities of change on the Arab side? Divergent assessments have increasingly aggravated Israeli society since the 1967 June War, when the Israeli victory over Egypt, Syria, and Jordan changed the political map of the Near East, particularly through Israeli control over the West Bank, then renamed Judea and Samaria.

CONTRASTING INTERPRETATIONS OF HISTORY: PERES AND NETANYAHU

There are two fundamental approaches among secular Zionists that provide differing answers, and each is rooted in a contrary interpretation of the Enlightenment view of human nature and history. They are best reflected today in the approaches taken by Shimon Peres, the disciple of Ben-Gurion, and by Benjamin Netanyahu, the disciple of Jabotinsky. Again, religious Zionism requires separate treatment.

Ben-Gurion tenaciously built up Israel's defenses. As noted earlier, he was the architect of *mamlachtiyut* (statism), a policy that resulted in a unified national army. His diaries reflect a continuous process of strengthening the military, acquiring arms, establishing defense industries, and otherwise engaging in security issues. Among the latter was an item that he carefully hid from public view. Despite the relatively small size of the country—still about only two million a decade after Independence—and a lack of economic as well as relevant material resources, he took Israel down the road of nuclear development. In so doing, he circumvented colleagues in Israel and defied the American presidents, Eisenhower and Kennedy. The political and financial costs were an enormous burden in a relatively new country straining under immigrant absorption, national development, and conventional defense.

Writing in the aftermath of Oslo Accords, Peres, who was charged by Ben-Gurion with obtaining arms for the 1948 war, explained that the difficulty of procuring arms and the sense of continuing threats convinced the Israeli leadership that the new state had to become as self-sufficient as possible for its own defense. The country was isolated in the Middle East and had no allies committed to acting in its defense. The great powers—the United States, Britain, and France—limited arms supplies to the region, a reality that worked to Israel's disadvantage. Since there was an expectation of additional "rounds," Ben-Gurion believed it was imperative that the country develop the strategic ability to deter the enemy. This was achieved largely due to the nuclear development program at Dimona, the Negev town proximate to an atomic reactor. During the Egyptian-Israeli peace talks in 1979 at Camp David, Peres reports that the Egyptians confessed the "decision to talk peace had definitely been influence by the Dimona project." Because of Dimona, Israel could not be destroyed, and peace became a logical option. The iron wall had worked with respect to Egypt. Peres believed the same held for the Palestinians, and this contributed to bringing them into the negotiations at Oslo.

With the prospect of a secure Israel, it became possible to invoke a deeply ingrained concept inherent in secular Zionism. That is, people and societies should and could be transformed. It follows from this that it is possible to design better societies with improved social relationships. According to an Enlightenment version of human nature, man is inherently good and any personal or social corruptions that afflict him could be transcended given an opportunity for personal and social reconstruction. It was this optimistic idea that motivated the intellectual and political activity of several generations of nineteenth- and early-twentieth-century reformers. Underlying this movement was the notion that people can be "re-formed." Indeed, reform became a key concept in Western political discourse and praxis from the early nineteenth century. Labor Zionism developed in this milieu. European Jews could and should be transformed, with Zionism as the instrument through which this would take place and with the kibbutz as the ideal agent for reconstruction. It was this form of utopian national reconstitution that shaped the thought of Ben-Gurion, Shimon Peres, and a host of other Zionists and it was for this reason they considered the kibbutz their spiritual if not their actual home.

If Jews may be transformed, Arabs may as well. In the previous chapter, we note that Zionist planners expected that the same kind of progress that Jews achieved in the development of Palestine could be replicated by Arabs. There was no racist view of the inherent superiority of Jews. For example, social as well as technological competence in agriculture was not the exclusive domain of anyone. Arabs, preserving their distinctiveness, might change and do so in such a way that would enable them to live peaceably with Jews. It was this optimistic attitude that motivated Peres, his lieutenant Yossi Beilin, and others involved in the negotiations at Oslo to support the accord with Palestinians.

Peres held out another idea that similarly derives from the Enlightenment. That is, people seek to be free to pursue their self-interest, a condition that is usually defined in material terms. On the one hand, he knows that Zionism was an irrational economic project. Western Europe, America, South Africa, Argentina, and Australia held out far more promise for material gain than emigration to Palestine. The decision to migrate to Palestine was an irrational economic choice in which personal gain was not the prime objective. In the same way, the attachment of Arabs to their lands is rooted in values and understanding beyond economic self-interest. Nevertheless, the pursuit of self-interest is a powerful motivation and can become a common denominator in bringing diverse people together to form all manner of political arrangements. Peace between Arabs and Jews was therefore considered possible despite differences between these peoples and their cultures. Rationality in the pursuit of material self-interest, a prime Enlightenment idea, might move people to privilege material self-interest over deeply held cultural values and beliefs. This idea is found as early as Herzl and has elaborated Zionist argumentation in subsequent decades. Peres and the current generation of Israeli leadership from Labor to Likud echo this conviction. It is for this reason that *Towards a New Middle East* deals extensively with plans for economic cooperation and invokes the experience of post–World War II Europe, when the American-initiated Marshall Plan stimulated reconstruction and the end of national hostilities. That experience had to be replicated in the Middle East.

There was one more item in Peres's battery of arguments. He called on Jews to make a conscious decision to ignore history: "But what is done, is done. We cannot change the past. When circumstances are propitious and so much is at stake, we must forget the past for the sake of the present." Even as history may inspire action, it may also inhibit it. Peres offered no universal principles as to when to remember and when to forget. In this instance, when he believed peace were possible, he counseled forgetfulness.

Netanyahu, on the other hand, insists on remembering out of concern that forgetting may lead to destructive self-delusion. His route to this perspective derives from an alternative Enlightenment version of human nature. Netanyahu is more sympathetic to the realistic or negative view expressed by Hobbes rather than Rousseau's optimism. Jabotinsky, Netanyahu's mentor, often quoted and popularized the Latin proverb employed by Hobbes: *Homo homini lupus est*—"Man is a wolf to man." Hobbes concluded that control of the animalistic side of human nature requires the construction of a social contract capable of enforcing restraint. For Jews, the past is replete with instances of the animus with which gentiles frequently held Jews and translated it into discrimination and violence. This, rather than divine punishment, is the explanation for the long history of Jewish suffering. This is the motif that informs Netanyahu's *A Place Among the Nations: Israel and the World* (1993), which like Peres's book was published in the immediate aftermath of Oslo.

Netanyahu's volume, far larger than Peres's slender opus of hope, details the long history of anti-Semitism in Christian Europe. The second portion examines in similar detail the history of mistreatment and prejudice in the Islamic world. Beyond this, he offers a chronology in which the central events in Zionist history are explained as responses to outrages against Jews in Europe and the Near East. He begins with the Russian pogroms in 1881 and Pinsker's Auto-Emancipation in 1882. The pattern is repetitive and explains the motivations behind Herzl and Jabotinsky's turn to Zionism. In more contemporary periods, he lists wars against Israel, terrorist attacks against Jews in Europe and the Near East, as well as anti-Israel resolutions in the United Nations. Moreover, he constructs a section of maps that visually illustrates the smallness of Israel in the hostile Arab Near East. Throughout, the vulnerability of Jews in the past and in the present is relentlessly drilled into the reader. Jews must be on guard against attacks by wolves in Europe and the Near East.

Netanyahu is also concerned by present-day realities. As Israel's representative in the United Nations, he witnessed Israel's growing isolation and the erosion of Israel's legitimacy in the international community. In the first half of the twentieth century, Jews gained the right to self-determination and the establishment of a Jewish state. This was consistent with the salience of nationalism as a central driving force in global affairs and contrary to the claim that Jews did not qualify as a people. Rather than improvement in Israel's situation, he is concerned with decline: "How is it that Zionism, which enjoyed such universal good will at the beginning of the century, is under such relentless attack at its close? . . . How is it that the very word *Zionist*, once proudly espoused by Christians and Jews alike, has acquired an odious or at least suspect connotation?" The Zionist Right demands more convincing proof than the Zionist Left before being willing to relax the logic of the iron wall.

Despite these differences, there is still considerable common ground between the secular Left and Right. Netanyahu observed: "Nevertheless, the differences that divide Israelis on political matters are dwarfed by the enormous areas of agreement that bind them together." The fact is that Peres and Netanyahu came to serve in a national unity government, and both held cabinet posts a decade later in 2004 under the rightist prime minister Ariel Sharon, whose government is dedicated to unilateral disengagement from many areas within the overall conception partition. Indeed, social survey research has shown that this is the position of approximately 70 percent of the Israeli public.

In the long view and with full recognition for the vehemence with which Right and Left have attacked one another, the historic record is that secular Zionism has accepted compromise at crucial moments in the Arab/Israeli conflict. This has long been the case with the Zionist Left. The side associated with Ben-Gurion has been consistently willing to do so since the end of the 1930s. The Likud came to support partition much later. Some observers mark their turn in the 1970s, when important elements on the Right began to view the Golan Heights and even portions of Judea and Samaria largely for their strategic importance rather than in mystical-historical and irredentist terms. By then, even Begin had desisted from invoking the traditional Revisionist mantra that Israel should include historic Gilad, or extend the eastern side of the Jordan. Once the shift from ideology occurred, it became increasingly possible to assess the advantages and disadvantages of holding onto contested ground where Jews are a decided minority. Even Netanyahu, as prime minister, declared in 1997 that historic Hebron, beyond a small Jewish enclave, would be a Palestinian city under Arab sovereignty, thereby acknowledging the reality that the whole of the Land of Israel, even some of its most historic and sacred portions, cannot remain under Jewish control. In 1998, at a meeting with Clinton and Arafat at Wye Plantation, Netanyahu offered to cede an additional 13 percent of Israeli-held territory as a step in negotiations with the PLO. In subsequent pronouncements Prime Minister Netanyahu held steadfastly to only two territorial restrictions. Israel would not return to the pre-1967 armistice lines, and the "unity of Jerusalem" must be maintained. In effect, the dream of a Greater Israel was no longer the Likud's ironclad policy. Instead, security arrangements rather than ideology alone would be factored into an instrumentalist or pragmatic approach to the politics of Israeli-Palestinian relations. Tensions between ideology and pragmatism, by their natures, induced instability and internal discord within the Right as they had earlier in parties in the Center and Left.

Internal negotiations among Israelis have come to increasingly focus on what is pragmatically possible to retain and yet ensure a Jewish state living in peace in an Arab world. At the time of this writing (2005), Ariel Sharon, perhaps more than any other public figure associated with militancy since the 1950s, may be leading the country in the direction of a secure Israel with a peaceful Arab state in Gaza and in Judea and Samaria. The uncompromising response to the intifada, the unilateral decision to build a wall of separation, and the plans for separation of a Jewish state from the balance of Palestine indicate to many that he can be trusted with the nation's security. That confidence has enabled him to apply his concept of the iron wall to contemporary circumstances.

CONTEMPORARY RELIGIOUS ZIONISM AND FUNDAMENTALISM

The path marked out by Sharon's government (and now his successors) is opposed by some of the secular Right among his own traditional supporters. Nevertheless, the greater and more vehement opposition comes from the religious Zionist camp. This brings us back to consider the significance of religion in shaping Jewish and Zionist politics. In discussing the response to the challenge of modernity and then Zionism in the two previous chapters, distinctions were made between secular and religious Jews. Within this dichotomy, there was yet a further division between ultraorthodoxy that defined itself as anti-Zionist and religious Zionists, usually associated with the Mizrahi party, who have been active within the Zionist movement from its beginnings.

Historic realities have brought ultraorthodoxy to moderate its behavior if not its ideological or theological position. While it continues to define itself as non-Zionist, many actually play an active role in the life of the state, taking part in elections and in the formation of governments. Some of its leaders have also served in the Israeli army. Ultraorthodoxy also maintains a generally rightist stand on the Arab/Israeli conflict, being unwilling to cede land settled or controlled by Jews. This position is based on an interpretation of Jewish religious law that derives from revelation. There is a relatively small segment of ultraorthodoxy that holds the contrary view. That is, saving lives through a peace agreement and even withdrawal has priority over ruling the divinely promised homeland. This pragmatic view is justified by an alternative interpretation of Jewish legal tradition. The position of the majority may also be partially explained by practical considerations. Since 1967 many ultraorthodox communities and educational institutions have been established in the Old City of Jerusalem, Judea, and Samaria. Divine law has been reinforced by practical considerations in shaping ultraorthodox politics.

However, the religious Zionists are particularly pertinent to this discussion. They have participated actively in the Zionist movement from its beginnings with important leadership roles in governing institutions prior to Israel's establishment and in nearly every cabinet thereafter. For most of this period, they were members of coalitions headed by Labor Zionism. Since 1977, when the Likud emerged as Israel's leading party, they have played significant roles in rightist governments. In both settings, they have contributed in significant ways to defining Israel's relationship toward Palestinians. While in Labor-led governments, they followed the moderate course adopted by Ben-Gurion and his successors. A majority accepted partition in 1937 and 1947. They also supported the proposition of "land for peace" as official policy in the aftermath of the 1967 June War. However, by 1977 they departed from the pragmatic and compromising tradition to join forces with secular nationalist elements who insisted that Israel retain control of the West Bank, Gaza, and the Golan Heights. The power of a belief in a divine promise to all the Land of *Israel* was no longer suppressed.

At present, religious Zionists constitute a principal opposition to Sharon's policy and the national consensus in support of disengagement and partition. The tensions between pragmatism and a religious nationalism that borders on messianism has splintered Mizrahi-producing radical parties whose members are threatening to dismantle settlements with force. There have even been calls to soldiers by rabbis to disobey orders if commanded to proceed with withdrawal. Extreme civil disobedience within religious Zionism is unprecedented. The privileging of clerical authority above civil government was explicit in ultraorthodoxy but long dormant in religious Zionism. Conflict between religious and civil authorities has been assiduously avoided. Members of religious kibbutzim and students of separate religious Zionist educational systems had learned that there does not need to be a contradiction between religious beliefs and responsible citizenship.

The roots of a pragmatic and moderate approach may be found in Europe, before Herzl founded the World Zionist Organization in 1897. Some orthodox rabbis, notably in the Frankfurt community, had been working for a synthesis of tradition and modernism since the last half of the nineteenth century. Many orthodox thought Zionism could be similarly synthesized with Judaism and therefore played a leading role in establishing colonies in the 1880s and 1890s. However, the growing secularism within Zionism challenged them into setting themselves apart within the movement. In 1902, leading religious Zionist leaders and rabbis met in Vilna to create the spiritual center (*merkaz ruhani*) or the Mizrahi party as a faction within the World Zionist Organization. The Mizrahi manifesto of 1902 pointed to the expectation of harmony between commitments to Judaism and Zionism.

When Israel completed control of the West Bank, latent tensions between religion and secular Zionist policies erupted with far-reaching consequences for the Arab/Palestinian conflict. Some continued with the pragmatism that characterized much of the Labor movement. They maintained the alliance with the Left and organized Meimad, a faction committed to accommodation with Arabs even at the price of partition. The majority have moved to the right. Gush Emunim (Block of the Faithful), the settler movement founded in 1974, generated great sympathy among religious Zionists and contributed to moving Mizrahi in this direction.

Even further to the right was a movement founded by Rabbi Meir Kahane that advocated transfer of Arabs outside of Israel and even supported the use of violence to accomplish this. The movement was so extreme that it was placed beyond the law and expelled from participation in Israeli elections and politics. Other groups have gone beyond the norms of civil society to create underground networks that have engaged in violence and terror. Out of such religiously rooted extremism came the killing of Peace Now activist Emile Greentzweig in 1983 and the assassination in 1994 of Prime Minister Yitzhak Rabin, after he signed the Oslo Accords, by Yigal Amir, a religious university student under the influence of extremist rabbis. There have also been sporadic attacks on Arabs as well as cells that have carried out actions against mayors of Arab towns on the West Bank. A group of militants even planned to blow up the Aqsa Mosque on the Temple Mount in Jerusalem. The common denominator of all these outrages is the belief that they were in accordance with Jewish law. Extremists viewed their Jewish victims as guilty of sin in consorting with enemies to transfer portions of the Holy Land to non-Jews. Violence against Arabs was also fed by religious rectitude and, in some cases, by the expectation that disruption of society would usher in the messianic era when Eretz Yisrael would be restored to Jews as predicted in apocalyptic texts of yore.

The departure from commitment to democratic civil society to radical religious fundamentalism can readily be viewed in the shift in authority from Rabbi Avraham Kook (1864–1935) to his son, Rabbi Zvi Kook (1891–1982). It was after the 1967 war that the teachings of the younger Rabbi Kook had an impact on Israeli public life through the activities of Gush Emunim. In the previous chapter, we note that the elder Rabbi Kook saw in the pragmatism and settlement program of Labor Zionism the instrument for advancing the divine plan. Settlement included the founding of religious kibbutzim on lands assigned by the Jewish Agency. Implicit in this activity was participating in a national movement that was directed by secular Jews in the framework of democratically organized institutions.

On the other hand, Gush Emunim, a movement inspired by Rabbi Zvi Kook, has maintained that their settlers and settlements are manifestations of the handiwork of God. From its beginnings, there is a record of confrontation between settlers with state authorities even though they presented themselves as following within the tradition of Zionist pioneering. While earlier generations had many points of friction with settlement authorities and the movements that sponsored them, they submitted to the authority of governing bodies. Gush Emunim has accorded higher authority to religious leaders outside the parliamentary system and civil institutions. This had been typical of the behavior of the ultraorthodox who view religious law as superior to legislation by secular civil bodies. This fundamentalist approach derived enormous energy from the belief that they were instruments in a divine plan to restore the Land of Israel to Jews in these first moments of the promised messianic age.

The younger Rabbi Kook taught that the 1967 victory was a miraculous event, evidenced by the passage to Jewish control of lands beyond the 1948–1967 borders. Divine providence should be abetted, not undone. The quickness and extent of the victory in a war that many feared would end in disaster led to a widespread sense of the miraculous, even among the secular. Among the followers of Rabbi Kook, there was the conviction that, at one stroke, God has placed the whole of the Land of Israel into the hands of his loyal servants. Indeed, Rabbi Kook predicted this result in a now famous sermon in the month preceding the war. His sermon gained immediate currency as a manifestation of prophecy. Disciples became missionaries in spreading the word and in recruiting settlers for biblical Judea, with the first contingent establishing themselves in a hotel in Hebron in the heart of an Arab city that before the Arab riots of 1929 had for centuries been home for pious Jews and a famous yeshiva.

The focus of settlement also moved north to Samaria to the heavily populated Arab areas. This was a direct challenge to what had been the policy of the Labor government that had purposefully avoided Arab population centers. Several settlements had been established in largely uninhabited areas along the Jordan River to indicate that that natural boundary was the security frontier, at least until regional peace was achieved. The only place that Labor encouraged significant settlement was in Jerusalem and its proximity, initially in areas Jews had inhabited prior to the 1948 war. Settling other areas could frustrate the possibility of trading "land for peace." It was against this intention that Gush Emunim acted. From its beginning in 1974, Gush Emunim was prepared to challenge legitimate and established authorities by illegally founding settlements in locales connected to historic sites with biblical associations.

After the Likud victory in 1977, the way was open to extensive settlement in the West Bank. The secular nationalism of the Right had long cherished reestablishing Jewish control over the whole of the Land of Israel. Nevertheless, the willingness of Prime Minister Begin to reach an accord with Egypt's Sadat raised alarms that even the Likud might compromise on its traditional position. During the 1970s, the secular Right began to weigh ideological commitments against strategic concerns. This resulted in withdrawal from the Sinai, including the Jewish settlements at Yamit and Sharm el-Sheikh, for the sake of a peace agreement. Most importantly, the Likud continued the Labor policy of not annexing the West Bank. The initial reason appeared to be the Likud's coalition agreements with Moshe Dayan, a former lieutenant of Ben-Gurion and a Labor Party leader, and with a party formed by Yigal Yadin, another general who had long been associated with Labor. The reluctance to annex proved to be permanent and was undoubtedly rooted in domestic and international opposition as well as doubts about the strategic necessity of control and the concern about governing a hostile population. Until today, the greatest part of the West Bank, nearly forty years after its capture and settlement, has not been formally integrated into Israel. Indeed, there are indications that even as some areas, particularly around Jerusalem, are being drawn to a more intimate connection with pre-1967 Israel, there is a loosening of the hold on much of the remainder of the West Bank.

The continuing ambiguity within the Likud aroused suspicion among fundamentalists. Their concern stimulated increasingly radical behavior.

Some activity was so extreme that it could only be carried out in an "underground" engaged in vigilante attacks on Arabs. A cluster of extreme rabbis centered in Kiryat Arba, the new Jewish settlement at Hebron, provided the rabbinical authority for such violence. This extraordinary and unprecedented behavior was a consequence of Gush Emunim's belief in its responsibility for the "redemption" of Judea and Samaria. While allowing settlements to expand, the Israeli government finally took vigorous action against the underground in 1984. One scholar then studying the movement argued that had the underground not been stopped at that time, it might have become the Israeli equivalent of the Irish Republican Army.

The largest of the extreme fundamentalist movements was inspired by Rabbi Meir Kahane, an American-born orthodox rabbi whose political debut took place in New York City, where he founded the Jewish Defense League in 1968. This vigilante movement was concerned with defending lower-middle–class Jews from street crime and black anti-Semitism in New York's neighborhoods. Their rhetoric was shaped by reaction to the Holocaust and promised that "never again" would Jews be victims. His success in mobilizing young people with a message of Jewish pride and militancy attracted the attention of right-wing activists in Israel who encouraged him to emigrate in 1971. Neither the Likud nor Gush Emunim could contain his energies. He struck out on his own, recruiting religious youth attracted to his message of unrestrained and illegal action against Arabs. The justification, he claimed, could be found in sacred texts that called for the cleansing of the country of their presence. He then advocated the physical transfer of Arabs by consent or force. This message brought him both support as well as opprobrium and censure. Nevertheless, this controversial figure won slightly more than 1 percent of the vote in the 1984 elections, enough to win a seat in the Knesset.

LIMITS TO FUNDAMENTALISM IN ZIONIST SOCIETY

The vast majority of Israeli society was appalled by the prospect of an avowed and aggressive racist entering the Knesset. Right and Left joined to outlaw Kahane, his party, and his ideas. Particularly significant is that the Right joined in. Kahane represented the disrespect for law, violence, and racism associated with fascism. Prime Minister Begin took the lead. He was joined by a host of leading figures who understood the challenge to Israel as a democratic state. Even a number of rabbis associated with Gush Emunim—found both in Kahane and in the Jewish underground phenomena—had to be uprooted. This was a searing episode that, in different form, echoes in Israeli society today, where the limits of a democratic society are tested by militant fundamentalists who urge disobedience by soldiers under orders to remove settlements.

Protest groups against settlement expansion, violence, and the stalemate in negotiations developed in parallel with the founding of Gush Emunim and fundamentalist groups. The most significant was Peace Now, an organization spawned by a protest movement inaugurated by the actions of Motti Ashkenazi, a reserve officer who protested the failure of civil and military leadership in the events leading to the 1973 Yom Kippur War. Protesters forced the creation of an official investigation that led to the resignation of political and military leaders. Doubt of the wisdom of the country's leadership became infectious and spread to other policy issues. By 1978, protest matured into the founding of Peace Now. This movement began with the Officers' Letter signed by hundreds of reservists who criticized Begin's government's hesitation in seeking territorial compromise during the negotiations with Egypt. From this beginning, the agenda spread to pressure for initiatives for peace agreements, the protest against the 1982 incursion into Lebanon, and the harsh response to the intifada that erupted in 1987. By 1988, Peace Now was called for recognition of the PLO and a return to negotiations on partition.

The breakthrough that was promised by the Oslo Accords in 1993 crossed party lines, winning support even among the Right. That support is still there as the second intifada that began in 2000 winds down. Every poll indicates that at least 70 percent of Israelis still support partition. The objections of the extreme religious Right have become regarded as obstacles to be overcome. The calls for civil disobedience by citizens and soldiers are widely regarded as repugnant. At the time of this writing, it is clear that the government headed by Ariel Sharon is mobilizing every institutional and moral force at its command to ensure the suppression of extremism. Through this suppression, the government successfully carried out the removal of about seven thousand settlers and thousands of additional supporters from Gaza in the disengagement process in the summer of 2005. In that, there is hope that the Israeli side will contribute to a successful resolution of the Arab/Israel, Muslim/Jewish conflict. Jewish fundamentalism has been contained, and its power is likely to continue to ebb. The secular and humanist tradition still charts the course of Zionist politics.

EPILOGUE

In this book, we have explored the Arab-Israel conflict by framing current issues in time-honored and conflicting narratives of Muslims and Jews. We framed the discussion this way because contemporary claims in the Near East are often based on historical understandings shaped over centuries, if not indeed millennia. Returning to the past thus gives us insight when examining the specific roles of recent individuals, groups, and historic processes. Turning to the immediate past and present, we examined the behavior of elites, especially during moments of crisis when decisions made by individuals and/or small coteries of leaders have dramatically altered events in the region. Balancing history from above with history from below, we considered as well the policy and behavior of more inclusive groups: political parties of all sorts and professional and religiously based organizations. Needless to say, the larger historical contexts also commanded our attention. We factored into our analysis the modern encroachment of the West, the trauma of the Holocaust and the sympathies it engendered for the Zionist cause, the emergence of the Cold War and its effect on the region, Arab nationalism and the competition among Arab states, the revival of Islam, and other stimuli of modern times that have furnished the means and occasions by which individuals and groups have acted and will continue to act on the stage of history. In sum, we found ourselves gauging the here and now vis-à-vis the lingering but still powerful cultural influences of an omnipresent past.

Culture can be an extraordinarily energizing and creative force; it can also be destabilizing. There are certainly many common elements on the ethical, moral, and theological levels that the Abrahamic communities share. But they also resonate to that which is provocative, if not incendiary. That was true in premodern times; it is especially true when the past informs

347

contemporary national politics. Theoretically, Arabs, as Muslims or Christians, and Israelis as Jews can find within their own traditions the means by which to live in harmony with the other if they were so inclined. The reality is that this has not yet happened, especially as regards Jews and Muslims (and also Muslims and Christians). The metaphor of the "warp and woof" may be helpful in understanding why. One can readily acknowledge that within venerable and highly developed cultures, there are many strands one may choose when weaving memory and tradition into founding myths and operative social values. For example, at different times and places, some have chosen to turn the other cheek and have elected for forgiveness and tolerance with all God's children. At other moments and locales, different people have acted with extreme cruelty to dissidents and strangers within their midst. In the Near East, Crusaders, jihadists, messianic Jewish nationalists and militant settlers, suicide bombers, and mere common soldiers have all drawn upon religious texts, oral traditions, and received histories to justify aggressively hostile actions. Peacemakers and diplomats may reinterpret many of the same traditions to suit their agendas or cite other traditional texts and shared experiences to advance what they would describe as concepts of social justice and compromise. As regards the latter, perhaps the outstanding example of our own time is to be found in the choices made by Nelson Mandela and his associates. He and fellow inmates emerged from twenty-seven years of brutal imprisonment on Robben Island with a commitment to truth and reconciliation rather than retribution. They explained that choice, which electrified the world community, in language that drew on both their African and Christian heritage. They could also have drawn on the same traditions for exacting punishment on those who so wickedly afflicted them. Instead, they found within their broad culture the resources for choosing otherwise.

The choices that confront Arabs and Jews today also require retrieving from their own traditions those elements that will enable each to imagine polities that can live side by side in harmony, or at least without engaging in debilitating conflict. There are many different historical strands from which Jews and Arabs may choose. How they weave the fabric of their histories and their futures, both independently and in dialogue with one another, is still open. Historical outcomes are in so many respects the consequence of choices that people make. So it is with the Arab/Muslim-Israel/Jewish conflict. While both peoples may be equally "haunted by pasts real and imagined," the decision to reach for an accommodation has not been evenly balanced. In appraising one another, Zionists and Arab nationalists weigh rather different perspectives.

The distinguishing characteristic of Zionism is that its secular narrative still predominates despite provocative challenges from a militant religious minority. This is because Zionism is the product of a Jewish culture that has been transformed by an ongoing engagement with Western civilization over two centuries and more. With that, the vast majority of European Jewry and their brethren in the Americas fully embrace the ideas of an enlightened modernity. Had Jews remained solely within a narrowly defined national religious culture, they would not have embarked upon the enormous enterprise of reconstituting themselves in their ancient homeland. Even if they had sought to settle in the Land of Israel, religious Jews who were given to insularity and distrust of all gentiles could not have developed political cadres capable of negotiating in international corridors. Above all, they could not have considered coming to terms with their Arab neighbors, the other inhabitants of a sacred land claimed by both peoples, for Jewish scripture is clear. The Israelites alone were promised exclusive rights to ancient Canaan.

In contrast, most Israelis have acknowledged and continue to acknowledge the concept of territorial and political compromise with the Arabs of Palestine and the surrounding lands. That need for compromise has been conditioned by objective realities as well as moral considerations. The Zionists always understood that their claims for a national home in Palestine depended on their achieving an absolute majority. Were the Jewish state to absorb Gaza and the West Bank, the fruits of the 1967 war, it would produce a greater Israel that included most of the landscape settled by the ancient Israelites of biblical times. But such an expanded state would include, of necessity, millions of Arabs who, given their extremely high birth rate, represent a demographic time bomb. Within decades, the Palestinian Arabs would become the dominant element of society, thus altering the Jewish character of Israel. There is a fringe group on the Israeli Right, represented largely by followers of the banned Kach party, the political base of the late Meir Kahane. The militant nationalists who fly the banner of a Greater Israel are certainly aware that, given their wishes, there will surely be a demographic crisis in the not-so-distant future. They would solve that inevitable problem by "transfer," that is, expelling the Arabs currently within the borders of the old Palestine mandate. There is, however, no support for this extreme view among the Israeli public. For the vast majority of Israelis, the growing demographic imbalance will be solved by a two-state solution: a Jewish state of Israel living side by side with a Palestinian polity whose character and boundaries are yet to be determined. There is also a substantial number of Israelis, mostly on the left of the political spectrum—but also in the center and even on the right—who regard the establishment of an independent Palestinian state not simply as a practical solution to a long-standing political problem, but also as a matter of justice. No such sentiment toward a Jewish state is widely expressed among the Arabs or in the Islamic world beyond.

Arabs, who have come to accept the reality of a Jewish state, have done so grudgingly and in full recognition of Israel's power and the international approval of Israel's right to exist as a free and sovereign state. There is, however, no recognition among Arabs that the two-state solution, which many of them are now willing to accept, will do justice to their cause or that there is any moral or ethical basis to Zionist pleadings. Forward-looking Arab statesmen understand very well that you cannot make an omelet without cracking eggs. But for them there is always the possibility that the scales of power will shift and a new and more palatable dish can and will be concocted in the future, vindicating thereby the inherent right of the Palestinian position. While Jews seek a decisive end to their conflict with the Arabs, the Arabs regard any political "solution" with the Zionists as a temporary acceptance of an unwanted and unjust reality. The inevitable change of that reality is the declared objective of the Islamists who currently lead the Palestinian Authority.

Should a comprehensive Arab-Israel peace be achieved somehow, the hoped-for borders are not likely to resemble those that divide Canada and the United States, or even Sweden and Denmark, old enemies not that long ago. Nevertheless, the Egyptian-Israel and Jordan-Israel border arrangements, and more generally the relations that now exist between those sovereign states and Israel, are an indication of what is possible, a first step on which to build stronger ties and a better future. That would not satisfy those who can live only in a perfect world, but such a settlement would be no small achievement.

If it is to lead to success, the road to peace will require a new convergence of Muslim and Jewish historical consciousness, not one based on Muslim triumphalism and Jewish compliance as in the past, but on mutual respect. There will have to be recognition on the part of Jews and especially Muslims that history is the sum of discrete parts rather than a seamless web of persons and events conforming to paradigmatic renderings of a received and familiar past. Jewish ideologues will have to forgo employing their religious tradition as a map and imperative for seeking political goals or satisfying religious striving at the expense of their neighbors. The marriage of religious Zionism to an apocalyptical outlook is no less unsettling to Muslims than Islamic revival is to Jews. Such an outlook liberally sprinkled with a Diaspora mentality that is, by its very nature, exceedingly suspicious of all gentiles and their intentions can only work at cross-purposes with the real needs of Israel and the Jewish people.

Any meaningful resolution to the current conflict calls for a better understanding of Arab culture and hence a real rather than stereotypical Arab society. A good place to start would be to reestablish the centrality that Arabic language instruction once held in Israel's secondary schools and that the Islamic religious tradition once played in the training of Israel's Middle East specialists. A generation of Israelis whose only acquaintance with Arabs has been limited to encounters with waiters and low-skilled and low-paid laborers of all sorts will have to consider the complexity and vibrancy of Islamic civilization and the dignity that is demanded by Muslims because of their achievements throughout the long and rich history of the Islamic Near East.

In turn, Muslims will have to examine the culture of their adversaries so that they, the Muslims, will be able to recognize and then understand that the deep and profound roots Israelis have in the ancient land they occupy are no less compelling than Arab feelings for Palestine. Arabs will have to realize that no useful purpose is served in dismissing Israel as the surrogate of the West, in declaring that the Zionist settlers bear no relationship to the ancient inhabitants of the Holy Land but are instead the descendants of the medieval Khazars of Europe, or in declaring that the temple in Jerusalem is a figment of Zionist imaginings. Such ahistorical assertions, which are intended to deprive the Jewish state and its citizens of legitimacy, and Judaism of its religious integrity, pervert reality and hinder real accommodation.

A real litmus test of the prospects for peace in the Middle East will be whether the Arab states will accept a forthright Israel as a truly legitimate player in regional affairs and not as a dangerous implant to be temporarily accepted on the promise of good behavior. The key to reading this test will be the language of negotiations and, more particularly, how the heated discussions between the parties publicly invoke allusions to the past. We refer here not only to the politics of the past century—the politics occasioned by the clash of Jewish and Arab nationalisms—but to the accretion of negative attitudes forged over fourteen Islamic centuries. Much courage, learning, and intelligence, as well as a very subtle analysis of past and present, will be required to sustain the gains that have come with recently broken ground and that are currently in danger of being completely undone. Unfortunately, courage is not the usual strong suit of politicians; learning is rarely applauded or sought by the media who play such a powerful role in shaping events; and the policy analysts who operate behind the scenes are often so subtle in their analysis that they tend to see through walls where none exist in the search for higher truths.

There is, nevertheless, a certain discernible and powerful movement toward change, and with that movement, there still remains the narrowest window of opportunity for real peace and not a temporary cessation of hostilities. How long that window will remain open is not clear, nor is it certain how long peace will last if it is achieved. What is clear is that the current situation of no war/no peace is not likely to go on forever. Either there will be some accommodation to mute the conflict or there will be a serious escalation in fighting in which the destructive power of the Israel Defense Forces will be unleashed to an extent not seen in recent memory. If there is a resumption of sustained hostilities, and if other Arab states feel compelled to join in against their better interests and judgment, the battle-field is not likely to be confined to the West Bank and Gaza, or to the desert wastes of Sinai, or the basalt plain of the Golan. It may well come to the civilian populations of the confrontation states, but with much greater force than ever before. The nature of modern technology makes that kind of doomsday scenario terrifying. Like all historic movements, the movement toward change to which we refer will play itself out, for better or worse.

Those who seek a just solution to the Arab-Israel conflict ought to consider the delicate balance of today's world in assimilating the lessons of history. In a complex political environment of interlocked cultures, each with its own sense of historical consciousness, the first step is to recognize difference without falsely demeaning the other's culture. Failure to account for difference can only lead to self-deception for those who, with the best of intentions, desire a better future for all the peoples of the Near East. Let us hope that the parties to the conflict and those who wish them well will join hands to advance a positive and realistic vision.

MAPS OF THE
CHANGING BOUNDARIES
OF "HISTORIC" PALESTINE

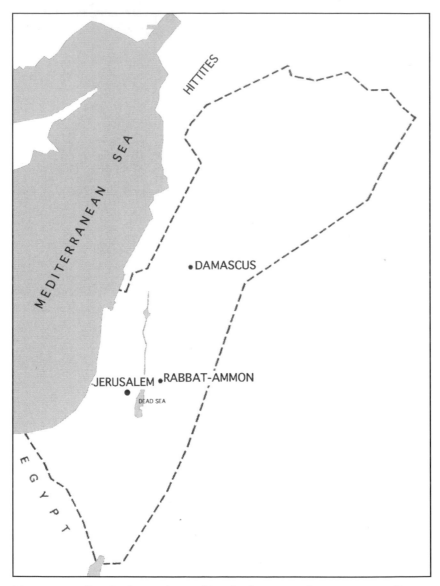

Map 1.   Israelite Kingdom under David and Solomon, Tenth Century B.C.E. All maps created by Mike Berns.

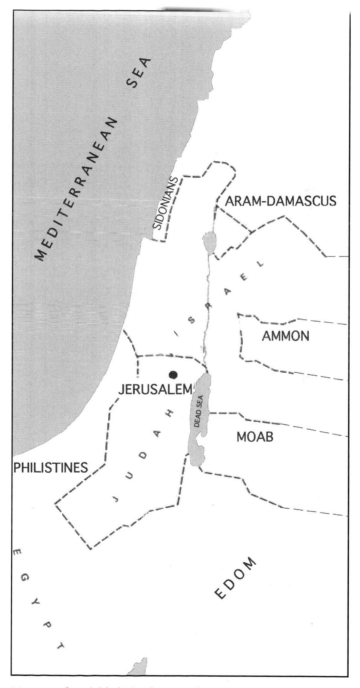

Map 2.   The Divided Kingdom, Tenth Century B.C.E.

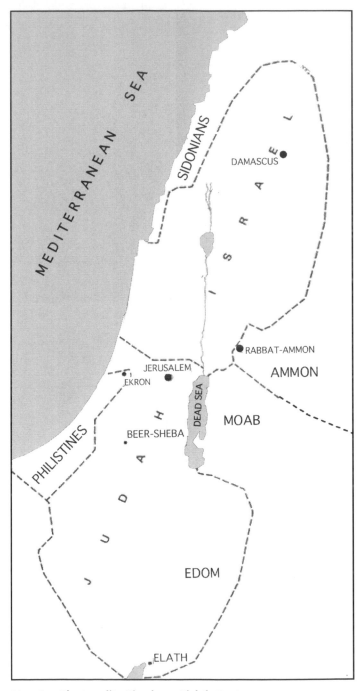

Map 3. The Israelite Kingdoms, Eighth Century B.C.E.

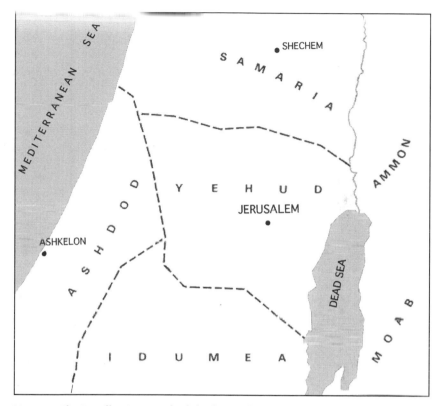

Map 4.   The Israelite State (Yehud) in the Persian Period, Fifth Century B.C.E.

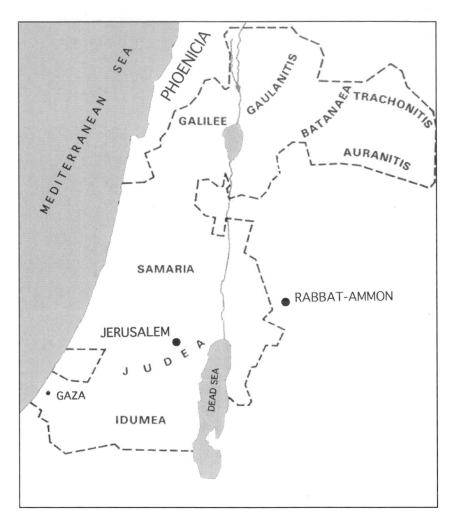

Map 5.   Herod's Kingdom, 37–4 B.C.E.

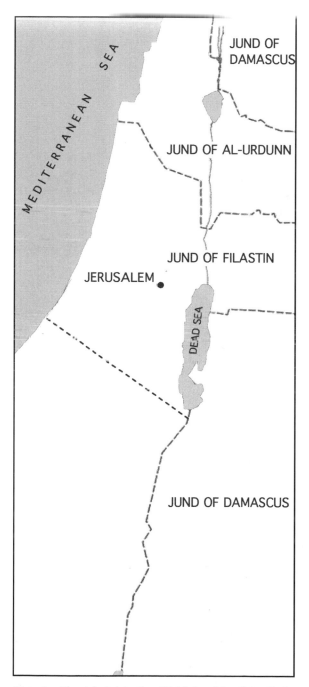

Map 6. The Administrative Districts of Southern Syria
(Al-Sham), Eighth Century C.E.

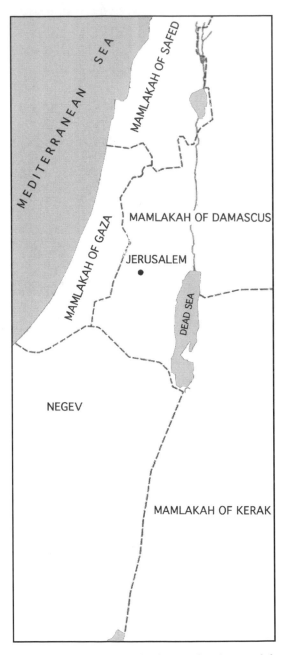

Map 7.   Districts of "Palestine" under the Mamluk
Sultans, Fourteenth Century C.E.

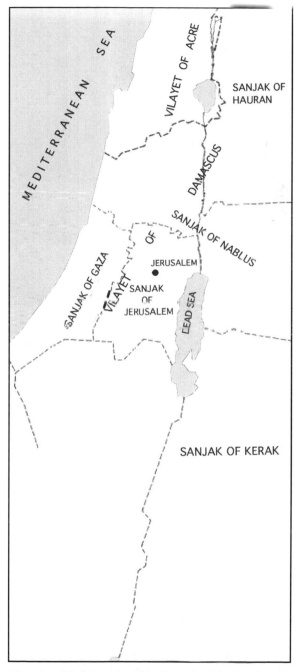

**Map 8.   Administrative Districts of "Palestine" under
Ottoman Rule, Seventeenth Century C.E.**

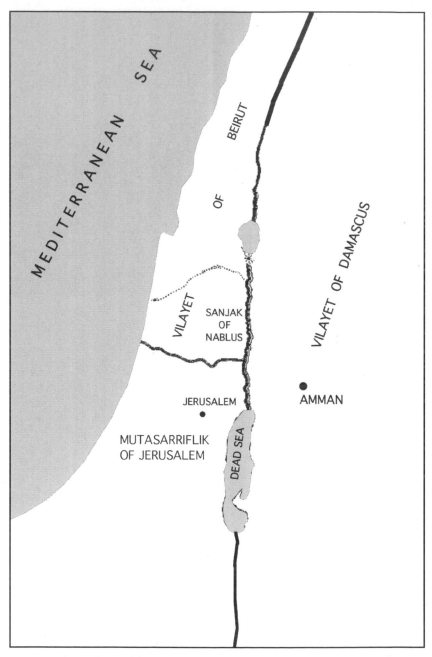

Map 9.   The Holy Land in Late Ottoman Times during Early Zionist Settlement, 1882–1914

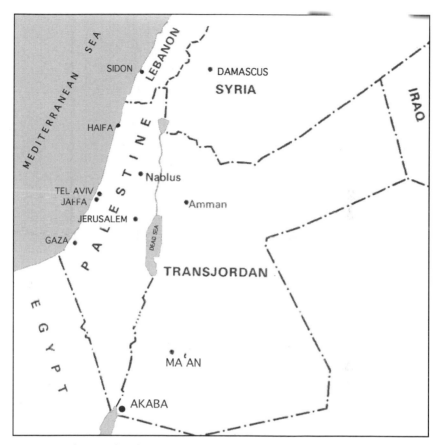

Map 10. The Mandated Territories, Twentieth Century

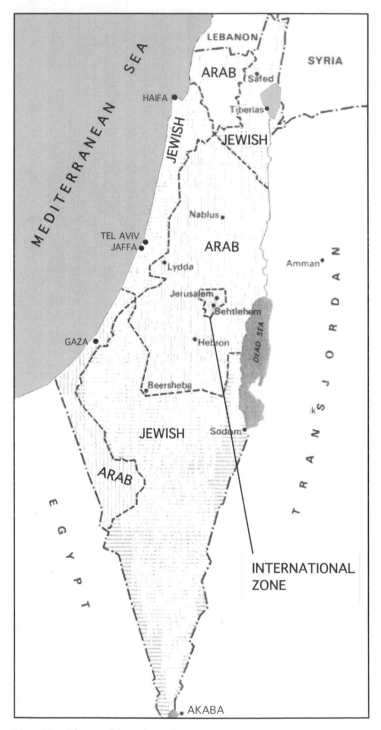

Map 11. The Partition Plan, 1947

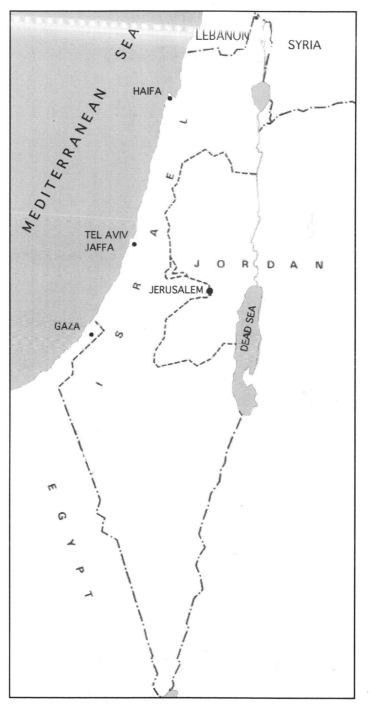

Map 12. Armistice Demarcation Lines, 1949

Map 13.   The Map of Israel's Conquest, 1967

SELECTED BIBLIOGRAPHY

This book is informed by a lifetime of reading and reflection in several languages and discourses. Given the anticipated audience for our extended essay, we have decided, after much thought, to be extremely selective and confine our short bibliography almost entirely to English language works, particularly studies that will be accessible to the general reader. Some choices were obvious, others were arrived at after much reflection. Nevertheless, many of the works listed here contain extensive bibliographies that may guide our target audience to other books and articles, should readers wish to explore more fully the Jewish-Muslim encounter and related subjects. Inquisitive readers will not have far to search. There is by now a voluminous literature in several languages on the long history of Jewish-Muslim/Arab relations. Regarding the modern period, there is a plethora of archival sources and published works. Our hope is that readers digesting our remarks will turn to this literature and interrogate it as they seek further instruction and guidance.

CHAPTER 1

Anderson, B. *Imagined Communities: Reflections on the Rise and Spread of Nationalism.* London, 1991.

Gellner, E. *Nations and Nationalism.* Ithaca, 1983.

Hobsbawm, E. *Nations and Nationalism Since 1780: Programme, Myth, Reality.* Cambridge, UK, 1990.

Lassner, J. *The Middle East Remembered: Forged Identities, Competing Narratives, Contested Spaces.* Ann Arbor, 2000.

Lewis, B. *History Remembered, Recovered, Invented.* Princeton, 1975.

———. *The Jews of Islam.* Princeton, 1984.

———. *The Multiple Identities of the Middle East.* London, 1998.

———. "Rethinking the Middle East." *Foreign Affairs* 71, no. 4 (1992): 99–119.

Mansfield, P. *The Ottoman Empire and Its Successors.* New York, 1973.

Yapp, M. E. *The Making of the Modern Middle East 1792–1923*. London and New York, 1987.

———. *The Near East Since the First World War*. London and New York, 1991.

CHAPTER 2

Dawn, C. E. *From Ottomanism to Arabism: Essays on the Origins of Arab Nationalism*. Urbana, 1973.

Goitein, S. D. *Jews and Arabs*. New York, 1955.

Haim, S. *Arab Nationalism*. London, 1975.

———. "Islam and the Theory of Arab Nationalism." In *The Middle East in Transition*, edited by W. Laqueur. London, 1956.

Humphries, R. S. *Between Memory and Desire. The Middle East in a Troubled Age*. Berkeley and Los Angeles, 1999, pp. 60–82.

Khalidi, R., et al. *The Origins of Arab Nationalism*. New York, 1986.

Lewis, B. *From Babel to Dragomans*. London, 2004, pp. 194–225.

Porath, Y. *In Search of Arab Unity*. London, 1986.

CHAPTER 3

al-Assiouty, S. A. *Recherches comparées sur le Christianisme primitif et l'Islam premier*. 2 vols. Paris, 1987.

Baram, A. *Culture, History, and Ideology in the Formation of Bathist Iraq, 1968–1989*. New York, 1991.

Barton, G. A. *A Sketch of Semitic Origins, Social and Religious*. New York, 1902.

———. *Semitic and Hamitic Origins*. Philadelphia, 1934.

Bernal, M. *Black Athena: The Afroasiatic Roots of Classical Civilization*. 2 vols. New Brunswick, 1987–1991.

Chwolson (Khvol'son), D. A. *The Semitic Nations*. Translated by E. M. Epstein. Cincinnati, 1874.

Dunlop, D. M. *A History of the Khazars*. Princeton, 1954.

Eph'al, I. *The Ancient Arabs*. Jerusalem/Leiden, 1982.

Gobineau, A. (Comte de). *Essai sur l'egalite des races humaines*. Paris, 1853–1855.

Khalidi, R. *Palestinian Identity*. New York, 1997.

Lewis, B. *Semites and Anti-Semites*. New York, 1986.

Macdonald, D. B. *The Hebrew Philosophical Genius*. Princeton, 1934.

Montgomery, J. M. *Arabia and the Bible*. Repr., New York, 1969.

Noeldeke, T. *Sketches from Eastern History*. London, 1982.

Salibi, K. *The Bible Came from Arabia*. Delmar, NJ, 1980.

Soden von, W. *The Ancient Orient*. Grand Rapids, MI, 1974.

CHAPTER 4

Davies, W. D. *The Territorial Dimension of Judaism*. Berkeley and Los Angeles, 1982.
Encyclopedia Judaica, s.v. "Erez Israel." Jerusalem, 1972.
Encyclopedia of Islam, 2nd ed., s.v. "Filastin" and "al-Sham." Leiden, 1953.
Gill, M. *A History of Palestine 634–1099*. Cambridge, UK, 1992.
Lewis, B. "Palestine: On the History and Geography of a name." *International History Review* 11 (1980): 1–12.
Le Strange, G. *Palestine under the Muslims*. London, 1890.
Na'aman, N. "Borders and Districts in Biblical Historiography." *Jerusalem Biblical Studies*, vol. 4, 1986.

CHAPTER 5

Antonius, G. *The Arab Awakening*. London, 1938.
Becker, C. H. "The Expansion of the Saracens: The East." In *The Cambridge Medieval History*. Cambridge, UK, 1967, pp. 329–65.
Busse, H. "The Sanctity of Jerusalem in Islam." *Judaism* 17 (1968): 441–68.
Cohen, A. *Political Parties in the West Bank under the Jordanian Regime 1949–1967*. Ithaca, NY, 1982.
Dixon, A. A. *The Umayyad Caliphate 65–86/684–705*. London, 1971.
Donner, F. *The Early Muslim Conquests*. Princeton, 1980.
Encyclopedia of Islam, 2nd ed., s.v. "al-Haramayn," "al-Kuds," "al-Masdjid al-Aksa," and "al-Masdjid al-Haram." Leiden, 1953.
Galnoor, I. *The Partition of Palestine*. Albany, 1995.
Goitein, S. D. "The Sanctity of Jerusalem and Palestine." In *Studies in Islamic History and Institutions*. Leiden, 1966, pp. 135–348.
Grabar, O. "The Umayyad Dome of the Rock in Jerysalem." *Ars Orientalis* 3 (1959): 33–62.
Kaplony, A. *The Haram of Jeruslaem 324–1099. Temple, Friday Mosque, Area of Spiritual Power*. Stuttgart, 1902.
Kedourie, E. *England and the Middle East*. London, 1956.
———. *The Anglo-Arab Labyrinth*. London, 1977.
Kennedy, H. *The Prophet and the Age of the Caliphates: The Islamic Near East from the Sixth to the Eleventh Centuries*. London, 1968.
Khalidi, R. *British Policy Towards Syria and Palestine 1906–1914*. London, 1980.
———. *Palestinian Identity*. New York, 1997.
Kister, M. J. "Sanctity Joint and Divided: On Holy Places in Islamic Tradition." *Journal of Arabic and Islamic Studies* 20 (1996): 18–65.
———. "'You Shall Set Out Only for Three Mosques'—A Study of an Early Tradition." *Le Museon* 82 (1869): 173–96.

Mandel, N. *The Arabs and Zionism before World War I.* Berkeley and Los Angeles, CA, 1976.

Matthews, C. "A Muslim Iconoclast (Ibn Taymiyyeh) on the 'Merits' of Jerusalem." *Journal of the American Oriental Society* 56 (1936): 1–21.

Muslih, M. *The Origins of Palestinian Nationalism.* New York, 1990.

Porath, Y. *The Emergence of the Palestinian-Arab Nationalist Movement 1919–1929.* London, 1973.

———. *The Palestinian Nationalist Movement 1929–1939.* London, 1977.

Stein, K. *The Land Question in Palestine 1917–1939.* Chapel Hill, NC, 1984.

Tibawi, A. L. *Arab Education in Mandatory Palestine.* London, 1956.

Yaari, E. *Strike Terror.* New York, 1970.

Zurayk, C. *The Meaning of the Disaster.* Translated by R. B. Winder. Beirut, 1956.

CHAPTER 6

Abu-Amr, Z. *Islamic Fundamentalism in the West Bank and Gaza.* Bloomington, IN, 1994.

Abu-Ghazaleh, A. *Palestinian Arab Cultural Nationalism.* Brattleboro, 1981.

Abu-Rabi', I. *Intellectual Origins of Islamic Resurgence in the Modern Arab World.* Albany, NY, 1996.

Ayubi, N. *Political Islam: Religion and Politics in the Arab World.* London and New York, 1991.

Brown, L. C. *Religion and State.* New York, 2000.

Dessouki, A., ed. *Islamic Resurgence in the Arab World.* New York, 1982.

Enayat, H. *Modern Islamic Political Thought.* Austin, 1982.

Harkabi, Y. *Arab Attitudes towards Israel.* Jerusalem, 1971.

———. *Palestinians and Israel.* Jerusalem, 1974.

Hatina, M. *Islam and Salvation in Palestine.* Dayan Center Papers, 127. Tel Aviv, 2001.

Kramer, M., ed. *The Islamism Debate.* Tel Aviv, 1997.

Milton-Edwards, B. *Islamic Politics in Palestine.* London and New York, 1996.

Mishal, S. and A. Sela. *The Palestinian Hamas.* New York, 2000.

Mitchell, R. P. *The Society of Muslim Brothers.* London, 1969.

Oren, M. *Six Days of War: June 1967 and the Making of the Modern Middle East.* New York, 2002.

Peled, A. *Debating Islam in the Jewish State.* Albany, 2001.

Vatikiotis, P. J. *Islam and the State.* London, 1987.

CHAPTER 7

Baer, I. F. *Galut.* New York, 1947.

Chazan, R. *Medieval Stereotypes and Modern Antisemitism.* Berkeley and Los Angeles, 1997.

Cohen, S. J. D. *The Beginnings of Jewishness.* Berkeley and Los Angeles, CA, 1999.

Eisenstadt, S. N. *Jewish Civilization.* Albany, NY, 1992.

Elazar, D. and S. A. Cohen. *The Jewish Polity.* Bloomington, IN, 1985.

Encyclopedia Judaica, s.v. "Demography." Jerusalem, 1972.

Frankel, J., ed. "Jews and Messianism in the Modern Era." In *Studies in Contemporary Jewry,* vol. 7. Oxford and New York, 1991, pp. 3–213.

———. "Reshaping the Past." *Studies in Contemporary Jewry,* vol. 10. New York and Oxford, 1994, pp. 3–16, 66–92, 195–210.

Katz, J. *Tradition and Crisis: Jewish Society at the End of the Middle Ages.* New York, 1961.

Liebman, C. and E. Katz. *The Jewishness of Israelis.* Albany, 1997.

Meyer, M. A. *The Origins of the Modern Jew.* Detroit, 1967.

Saperstein, M. *Essential Papers on Messianic Movements and Personalities in Jewish History.* New York, 1992.

Silberstein, L. and R. L. Cohn, eds. *The Other in Jewish Thought and History.* New York, 1994.

Toynbee, A. *A Study of History.* 12 vols. London, 1934–1961.

Yerushalmi, Y. H. *Zakhor.* Seattle, WA, 1982.

CHAPTER 8

Abu El-Haj, N. *Facts on the Ground.* Chicago, 2001.

Ahituv, S. and E. Oren. *The Origins of Early Israel: Current Debate.* Jerusalem, 1998.

Barr, J. *History and Ideology in the Old Testament.* Oxford, 2000.

Ben Tor, A., ed. *Archeology of Ancient Israel.* New Haven, 1992.

Brettler, M. "The Copenhagen School: The Historiographical Issues." *Association for Jewish Studies Review* 27 (2003): 1–21.

Davies, P. R. *In Search of Ancient "Israel."* Sheffield, 1992.

Dever, W. *What Did the Biblical Writers Know and When Did They Know It?* Grand Rapids, MI, and Cambridge, UK, 2001.

———. *Who Were the Israelites and Where Did They Come From?* Grand Rapids, MI, and Cambridge, UK, 2003.

Finkelstein, I. and N. Silberman. *The Bible Unearthed.* New York, 2001.

Halpern, B. "Eracing History: The Minimalist Assault on Ancient Israel." *Bible Review* 11 (1995): 26–35, 47.

Lemche, N. P. *The Israelites in History and Tradition.* Louisville, KY, 1998.

Moorey, P. R. S. *A Century of Biblical Archeology.* Louisville, KY, 1991.

Prior, M., ed. *Western Scholarship and the History of Palestine.* London, 1998.

Shanks, H. "Face to Face: Biblical Minimalists Meet Their Challengers." *Biblical Archeological Review* 23 (1997): 26–42, 66.

Thompson, T. L. *The Mythic Past: Biblical Archeology and the Myth of Israel.* London, 1999.

Whitelam, K. *The Invention of Ancient Israel: The Silencing of Palestinian History.* New York, 1996.

CHAPTER 9

Ahad Ha'am. *The Transvaluation of Values.* London, 1917.

Almog, O. *The Sabra: The Creation of the New Jew.* Berkeley, 2000

Aranne, Z. *Deepening Jewish Consciousness.* Jerusalem, 1959. [Hebrew]

Avineri, S. *The Making of Modern Zionism.* New York, 1981.

Bar-Zohar, M. *The Armed Prophet: A Biography of Ben-Gurion.* London, 1967.

Ben-Gurion, D. *Rebirth and Destiny of Israel.* New York, 1954.

———. *Israel: A Personal History.* New York, 1972.

Ben-Yehuda, N. *The Masada Myth.* Madison, WI, 1995.

Bialik, H. N. "The City of Slaughter," in *Complete Poetic Works of Hayyim Nahman Bialik,* ed. Israel Efros. New York, 1948, vol. 1, 129-43.

Buber, M. *Paths in Utopia.* London, 1949.

Dowty, A. *The Jewish State: A Century Later.* Berkeley, 1998.

Elon, A. 1971. *The Israelis: Founders and Sons.* New York, 1971.

Friling, T. *Arrows in the Dark.* Madison, WI, 2005.

Hertzberg, A. *The Zionist Idea.* Philadelphia, 1997.

Herzl, T. 1896. *The Jewish State.* New York, 1946.

Katriel, T. *Talking Straight: Dugri Speech in Israeli Sabra Culture.* New York, 1986.

Lamdan, I. "Masada," translated in Leon Yudkin, Isaac Lamdan: *A Study in Twentieth-Century Hebrew Poetry.* Ithaca, NY, 1971.

Laqueur, W. *A History of Zionism.* New York, 1976.

Liebman, C. and D. Don-Yehiya. *Civil Religion in Israel.* Berkeley, 1983.

Ministry of Education, *Curriculum for the Public and Religious Public School: The Oral Law.* Jerusalem, 1968. [Hebrew]

Ministry of Education, *History Curriculum in the Elementary Schools.* Tel Aviv, 1957. [Hebrew]

Pinsker, L. *Auto-Emancipation: An Appeal to His People by a Russian Jew* (1882). In A. Hertzberg, *The Zionist Idea: A Historical Analysis and Reader.* Philadelphia, 1997, 181-98.

Ravitzky, A. *Messianism, Zionism, and Jewish Religious Radicalism.* Chicago, 1996.

Sachar, H. M. *A History of Israel.* New York, 2000.

Segev, T. *The Seventh Million*. New York, 1993.

Shimoni, G. *The Zionist Ideology*. Hanover, NH, 1995.

Sternhell, Z. *The Founding Myths of Israel: Nationalism, Socialism, and the Making of the Jewish State*. Princeton, NJ, 1999.

Troen, S. I. "The Construction of a Secular Jewish Identity: European and American Influences in Israeli Education." In *Divergent Jewish Culures*, edited by D. Moore and S. I. Troen. New Haven, CT, 2001, pp. 1–26.

Zerubavel, Y. *Recovered Roots*. Chicago, 1995.

CHAPTER 10

Ahad Ha'am. "Truth from the Land of Israel." *HaMelitz*, 19-30 June 1891. [Hebrew]

Begin, M. *The Revolt*. New York, 1977.

Ben-Gurion, D. and Yitzhak Ben-Zvi. *Eretz Israel in the Past and in the Present*. New York, 1918.

Benvenisti, M. *Sacred Landscape*. Berkeley, CA, 2000.

Conder, C. R. *The Fertility of Ancient Palestine*. London, 1876.

Gorenberg, G. *The Accidental Empire: Israel and the Birth of the Settlements, 1967–1977*. New York, 2006.

Granvosky, A. "Land Settlement and Development in Palestine," *Palestine and Near East Economic Magazine* 6, nos. 2-3 (1931): 25-62.

Herzl, T. *Old New Land*. Trans. L. Levensohn. Princeton, 2000.

Hobsbawm, E. and T. Ranger, eds. *The Invention of Tradition*. Cambridge, 1992.

Horowitz, D. and M. Lissak. *The Origins of the Israeli Polity*. Chicago, 1978.

The Jewish Agency for Palestine. *The Jewish Case Before the Anglo-American Committee of Inquiry on Palestine*. Jerusalem, 1947.

Locker, B. *The Jews and Palestine: Historical Connection and Historic Right*. London, 1938.

Lustick, I. *For the Land and the Lord: Jewish Fundamentalism in Israel*. New York, 1988.

Luz, E. *Wrestling with an Angel*. New Haven, CT, 2003.

Magnes, J. L., M. Reiner, Lord S. E. Simon, M. Smilonski. *Palestine—Divided or United? The Case for a Bi-National Palestine Before the U.N.* Jerusalem, 1947.

Palestine Royal Commission. *Minutes of Evidence Heard at Public Sessions*, vol. 1 (London: H. M. Stationery Office, 1937).

The Palestinian National Charter: Resolutions of the Palestine National Council, 1-17 July 1968, available at http://www.yale.edu/lawweb/avalon/mideast/plocov.htm.

Rogan, E. and A. Shlaim. *The War for Palestine: Rewriting the History of 1948*. Cambridge, 2001.

Shafir, G. *Land, Labor and the Origins of the Israeli-Palestinian Conflict, 1882–1914*. Cambridge, 1989.

Shapira, A. *Land and Power*. Oxford, 1992.

Sprinzak, E. *Brother Against Brother*. New York, 1999.

Troen, S. *Imagining Zion*. New Haven, CT, 2002.

Warren, C. *The Land of Promise*. London, 1875.

Winthrop, J. *Conclusions for the Plantation in New England*. Cited in Albert Weinberg. *Manifest Destiny: A Study of Nationalist Expansionism in American History*. Baltimore, 1935.

CHAPTER 11

Ajami, F. *The Dream Palace of the Arabs*. New York, 1998.

Antonius, G. *The Arab Awakening*. London, 1938.

Bar-On, M. *In Pursuit of Peace*. Washington, DC, 2005.

Ben-Gurion, D. *My Talks with Arab Leaders*. Jerusalem, 1972.

Dowty, A. "'A Question That Outweighs All Others': Yitzhak Epstein and Zionist Recognition of the Arab Issue." *Israel Studies* 6.2 (2001): 34–54.

Friedman, R. I. *Zealots for Zion*. New Brunswick, 1992.

Harkabi, Y. *The Palestinian Covenant and Its Meaning*. London, 1981.

Jabotinsky, V. "The Iron Wall." In *On the Way to a State*. Jersualem, 1953. [Hebrew]

Netanyahu, B. *A Place among the Nations*. New York, 1993.

Peres, S. *The New Middle East*. New York, 1993.

Rabinovich, I. *The Road Not Taken*. Oxford, 1991.

Ross, D. *The Missing Peace*. New York, 2004.

Rubin, B. *The Tragedy of the Middle East*. Cambridge, MA, 2002.

Tessler, M. *A History of the Israeli-Palestinian Conflict*. Bloomington, IN, 1994.

INDEX

ABOUT THE AUTHORS

Jacob Lassner is Philip M. and Ethel Klutznick Professor of Jewish Civilization in the Departments of History and Religion at Northwestern University. He is the author of numerous articles on Jewish-Muslim relations and Near Eastern history as well as the author of seven books. His most recent book is *The Middle East Remembered: Forged Identities, Competing Narratives, Contested Spaces.*

S. Ilan Troen is the Karl, Harry, and Helen Stoll Chair in Israel Studies at Brandeis University and the Sam and Anna Lopin Professor in Modern History, emeritus, at Ben-Gurion University of the Negev. He is the founding editor of *Israel Studies*, the leading journal in the field, and the author or editor of ten books on American, Jewish, and Israeli history. His most recent book is *Imagining Zion: Dreams, Designs and Realities in a Century of Jewish Settlement.*